The Home Cabinetmaker

Woodworking Techniques, Furniture Building, and Installing Millwork

Monte Burch

Drawings by Dick Meyer

Popular Science Books

Published by
  Popular Science ® Books
  Meredith ® Press
  150 East 52nd Street
  New York, New York 10022

Library of Congress Catalog Card Number: 79-4747
ISBN: 0-696-11104-7
Library of Congress Cataloging in Publication Data

Burch, Monte.
  The home cabinetmaker.

  Includes index.
  1. Cabinet-work. I. Title.
TT197.B94   684′.08   81-11912
                               AACR2

     10
Designed by Harold Stancil

MANUFACTURED IN THE UNITED STATES OF AMERICA

Contents

PART II Basic Cabinetry Techniques

5. Joints

6. Case Construction

7. Cabinet Doors

8. Drawers

9. Shelves

10. Legs and Frames

PART III   Finishing

PART IV Projects

18. Furniture Projects 293

19. Kitchen Cabinets and Vanities 349

PART V The Cabinetmaker's Workshop

20. Planning a Workshop 381

21. Hand Tools 397

22. Power Tools 418

23. Sharpening Tools 450

PART VI Millwork

24. Installing Millwork

PART VII Making a Career of Cabinetmaking or Carpentry

25. Going into Business

PART VIII Reference

Introduction

I grew up on a Missouri farm in a family of woodcraftsmen. They knew wood: they knew what kinds were best for what purposes, and when and how to cut a tree to get the best possible uses from the wood. They knew the shape and feel of wood, the smells and textures. They knew how to make whistles from maple sprouts, and wagon tongues from white oak saplings. And they knew how to make beautiful heirloom furniture from pieces of walnut that had been carefully cured in a barn hay loft for several years.

There was the uncle who made plaited whips out of the inner bark of wild cherry, and the uncles and cousins who were gunsmiths, becoming well known in the trade for producing some of the finest gunstocks around.

Today my father's house abounds in handmade wooden furniture and other items passed down from generation to generation. There is a five-string banjo made from an abandoned oak wagon, with a groundhog-skin head. There are numerous walnut and cherry tables, bedsteads, chairs and small chests, all carefully and beautifully made years before the advent of power tools.

Like many folks, I have spent a great deal of time lately looking back. I only wish I had asked more questions of the patient old gentlemen who watched us play our kids' games from the back steps as they carefully shaped or sanded a chair leg.

Learning woodworking skills is not something that can be accomplished overnight. After many years of working with wood, I still find new ways and better methods. Some of the skills and knowledge came easily. I learned a great deal of woodworking from my father, who was a 4-H instructor to a shop full of neighborhood kids during the summer. The only tools allowed in those 4-H classes were hand tools, and the projects were judged on how straight a board was cut, or how neatly the edges chamfered. After several years of building projects using only hand tools, I had a good background in woodworking craftsmanship when I graduated to power tools. Although power tools will do the job faster and in many cases more accurately, I still love the feel of working with old-fashioned hand tools.

Of course I didn't learn it all easily. There was the winter evening when I had to repair the stallion stall, which was made of native lumber. That was a job that gave a life-long respect for the toughness, tenacity and nail-bending powers of red oak. I will also never forget the chair I built many years ago that collapsed under a guest during a dinner conversation. Or the frustrating times when I mis-measured on a fine piece of wood and cut it too short, or turned the grain the wrong way.

But some of my finer memories of woodworking came later when, fresh out of college, I couldn't get a job in my academic field. So I started to work in my dad's cabinet shop. I remember the long, hot days spent sanding what seemed like 40,000 cabinet doors and drawers, but there was also the fun and profit of building stereo cabinets and gun cases at night after work, then selling them before Christmastime. I remember the sweet, pungent odor of cedar being planed on a surface planer, and the bitter, acrid, lung-biting smell of wild cherry burning every saw blade and tool in the shop.

Later I became Associate Editor of *Workbench Magazine* and found that I wasn't alone in my love for wood. Some of the most enjoyable moments of my time with the magazine were spent chatting with other woodworkers. Some were just beginners and I secretly felt sorry for the frustrations they were just beginning to learn. But I knew the pleasures and satisfactions that were to come if they stayed with the craft long enough to learn it properly. I found that wood craftsmen were all the same, from Mr. Watts, a very dedicated craftsman of fine violins in Kansas City, to the lawyer, doctor or retiring road engineer to whom woodworking was a break from the fast pace of a professional life.

I have made several houses full of furniture, ranging from Mediterranean to Country English to French Provincial. There have been tables, chairs, bedsteads, chests, and each and every piece has been a learning experience. I have learned that woodworking is an ever growing skill. The more you do, the better you become, and you learn to take an unhurried approach. It takes time to insure that you use proper techniques not only for cutting and joinery, but also to make sure the wood grain, colors and surface will match or blend correctly. Choosing the proper wood for the specific project is also a deliberate process.

For the craftsman, cabinet and furniture building is a way of life. Some craftsmen make a very fine living from their hard-won skills; to others woodworking is a form of relaxation. But for any craftsman there is a great deal of satisfaction in creating beautiful pieces of furniture or cabinetry which will, in a way, immortalize the builder as they're handed down from generation to generation.

It's unfortunate that the apprenticeship method of teaching such skills doesn't exist today, because the best way of learning any skill is through actual practice, at the side of a master craftsman. Knowledge, however, can also be passed on through books and articles, and I hope this book will suffice as a source of information to the beginner in woodworking as well as to some of the old-timers.

The skills and knowledge of woodworking are not to be taken lightly. They are too valuable. And in our present world of profligate use of limited resources, the use of materials such as wood that can be replenished will become even more necessary in the future.

PART I

Materials

Learning About Wood and Acquiring a Supply of Native Hardwoods

To be a good craftsman, whether you enjoy making fancy furniture, building kitchen cabinets, or whittling for the fun of it, requires a love of wood and a good working knowledge of the different kinds of wood and how they are best used. Almost any kind of wood can be used to build almost any item, but there are certain woods that do a better job than others. Some woods are stubborn, some are tough and some are yielding. Knowing how to work with each makes the difference between a frustrated craftsman and one whose work complements the various types of wood.

Chapter 2 will describe the structure of wood, and how wood products are graded and sized commercially, but before that a discussion of woods in general and how to find them will help many beginners understand this infinitely valuable material.

Locating Wood

Finding suitable plywoods pretty much depends on what we can get from our local lumber-build-ing supply dealers. Almost all of them, even in tiny towns, will keep on hand the standard-thickness sheets of plywood made from softwoods such as fir. But you will probably have to order hardwood-faced plywood from them or from one of the specialty wood supply people on the source list at the back of this book.

Solid wood, such as white pine and other softwood dimension lumber, is also readily available from most lumberyards. The solid hardwoods, however, such as walnut, oak, and cherry, are rarely stocked by most building-supply or lumber dealers. These may also be acquired quite easily by ordering through your local dealer, or through the specialty wood suppliers in the source list.

There are two basic methods of acquiring wood other than buying it—cutting and curing your own, and "scrounging," or foraging reusable material. There are many advantages to acquiring wood in either of these ways. Most important, you can often find those "one-of-a-kind" woods for a very special project, woods that show a beautiful grain or unusual coloring.

Foraging Reusable Wood

Scrounging for wood can be a very satisfying activity, and often becomes a hobby in itself. There are literally thousands of different places to forage woods, and here is where the fun comes in: the acquiring and recycling of fine old pieces of walnut that have been curing in a barn for 20 years, or of pieces of spalted maple from a slash pile left by today's hurry-up-and-cut loggers. But probably the main advantage to the woodworker is that much of the wood located in this manner is well seasoned; note that I did not say dry. No wood is perfectly dry, and depending on how it has been used in the past, it may or may not be suitable for use at a particular time. It should be given the in-shop treatment described later in the chapter before it is used for constructing anything.

Old buildings that are to be torn down are often an excellent source of fine woods for building furniture and cabinets.

One of the main sources of recyclable woods is in farm or estate auctions, as many of these old farmsteads give way to big agribusinesses or urban development. In many instances farmers or their fathers or grandfathers have had lumber stored in their hay loft or barn for years.

Watch your local paper for ads of such sales. If the auctioneer or family is not familiar with the values of wood, they may not advertise the woods very heavily and may sell them cheaply. I have purchased several truckloads of fine walnut, oak, and even some one-hundred-year-old wild cherry in this manner. The wild cherry cost only a few pennies a foot, and there was enough for a full set of French Provincial bedroom furniture. Of course the wood was in the rough and had to be planed. (I stored it in my shop for four years before working with it.)

Another excellent source of scrounged woods is in old buildings that are being torn down. Quite often a good relationship with a building demolition superintendent can help in finding out about some very good, rare old pieces of wood. Or in some cases you can find them yourself. One friend of mine dismantled an old post-and-beam building that was in the way of a new highway exchange. He slabbed off the axe-hewn beams and sold over half of them, then used the other half to decorate his family room. The centers of the slabs of oak were then used to make baluster

The wild cherry for this French Provincial-style dresser was purchased at an auction. Some of the boards were over 14 inches wide.

turnings for his family room staircase as well as some spindles for a bed headboard.

The cradle shown later in this book was made entirely from foraged walnut materials. The wood came from church pews that were sold when an old church was dismantled. The pews were over 100 years old and covered with layers of paint, but beneath was some of the most beautiful walnut I have ever seen. Yes, it took a great deal of time to dismantle the pews, remove the nails, and then plane the stock. With all my care I still hit a couple of nails, but the cost of regrinding the knives on my surface planer was more than paid for in the resulting beautiful walnut.

A true "wood scrounger" eventually gets a "nose" for woods and can sniff them out even in the most unlikely places. Several years ago my dad and I noticed that backstops were being replaced at a bowling alley. We asked for the pile of stops that had been removed. They were made of solid hard maple that had been covered with heavy plastic. We removed the plastic, sawed the maple into two-inch-wide strips and made about 50 butcher block countertops from the wood.

In any case the scrounger has to be a good "shopper" and know his woods quite well, because woods will often be camouflaged beneath several layers of paint, and usually no one knows what's underneath. The only way to find out is to cut off a piece with a sharp knife.

Finding New Wood

A second method of acquiring fine cabinet and furniture woods is to cut and cure your own. This may seem to be a formidable task, but it is really fairly simple, although it does take some back-breaking work, a lot of patience, and some special tools. "A fine wine takes its own time," and wood, to be properly cut and seasoned, is just as demanding. Wood that is only partially seasoned will cause nothing but frustration and headaches, regardless of how good a craftsman you are.

An important advantage of using this type of wood is that you can end up with some of the more beautiful woods of the tree. For instance, the stump, crotch, and burl figures are found in those sections often discarded by loggers in a hurry.

Of course, the wood that can be acquired in this manner is limited to the domestic hardwoods such as walnut and oak, and fruitwoods such as cherry. Quite obviously you won't be able to find rosewood, zebrawood or other exotics.

Our ancestors made some truly beautiful furniture from wood that had been cut and carefully cured for many years, often in an old shed or hay loft. In fact, my granddad's old barn is still full of assorted pieces of wood. Many have been there for over 20 years, carefully stacked with thin strips of wood between to provide adequate air ventilation.

You may think, "But I don't have any trees to cut woods from." Well, maybe not and maybe so. The next time a neighbor has a wind-blown tree, ask to cut it up for him. Woods such as apple, cherry, and the oaks and other woods attain a large size in urban communities. And there are any number of fine woods destroyed each year by the commercial tree cleaner-uppers who work the cities and towns.

Even if you live in an urban area, there are farmlands and quite often timberlands not too far away. Following a logging crew in timberland, and cutting up the slash, which are the stumps, tree tops and other parts of the tree left behind, can result in some extremely fine cabinet and furniture woods. Of course, they won't be very long pieces, such as the straight 12- or 16-foot log sections that are cut from the main portion of the tree. But they can be used to make almost any type of furniture except those with long tops such as stereo cabinets. What is too small for you to use as lumber can be used as firewood, and lastly the small twigs at the branches can be stacked in neat brush piles to make a welcome home for wildlife.

This method has been quite popular with several woodworking friends of mine for years, but with the sudden rush to wood burning they're finding that many tree farmers and landowners are either cutting up their own tree tops, or selling the slash. But even if you pay a little for the wood, you should come out well ahead of purchasing today's kiln-dried hardwoods.

If you have your own wood lot and if it is managed properly, it can provide you not only with a source of firewood for heating your home,

If you wish to cut and cure your own woods, an excellent source is the slash left by a logging operation.

but good woods for building furniture, cabinets, and even houses and outbuildings. Standing dead timber can also be cut on some state and federal owned land—with the proper permission and permits.

Logs that have been lying on the ground for more than six months from trees that fell naturally are usually full of decay and not worth the bother of cutting. An exception is some timber such as maple which may be "spalted," a form of decay which produces dark, mottled streaks.

If you don't wish to cut wood, you can still purchase it and cure it yourself. Look in the Yellow Pages for sawmills. The lumber sold will naturally be green native lumber, but you can usually have it rough cut to the dimensions you need. (Add ¼ to ½ inch, depending on the wood type, to each side to allow for curing shrinkage and planing to size.)

Cutting and Curing Wood

Cutting and curing your own woods certainly isn't as easy as driving down to the local building supply outlet and purchasing a perfectly sawn, planed, graded and dried piece of stock which can be used immediately and without any waste. But

to many woodworkers, cutting and curing their own woods is not only a way to economical wood supplies but a challenging hobby.

Turning-Block Pieces

There are several methods of cutting wood into usable form. Branches to be used as turning blocks can merely be cut to length. Remember that if you intend to use only heartwood the branch must be quite a bit larger than the intended turning so you can discard the sapwood. This is especially true of woods such as walnut. These turning-block chunks are then treated with a wood preservative such as polyethelyne glycol to aid in curing.

If you prefer to cure such chunks naturally, coat their ends with paraffin and allow them to cure for a couple of years before using. You'll find that some of them will split, but these can often be used for smaller turnings.

If your main hobby is woodturning you won't need anything much more than a small, lightweight chain saw, which most suburban homeowners already have. But if you intend to work up cabinet and furniture woods you will need a larger chain saw. The bar should be at least 16 inches long, and a longer bar is even better.

When felling a tree, first determine the direction of the tree's natural lean. (If it is not convenient for the tree to fall that way, another "lean" can sometimes be created with the use of wedges or pull ropes, or by limbing.) The first two cuts on the side to which you want the tree to fall should penetrate about one-third of the trunk's diameter and make an empty "pie" through which the trunk can fall freely. The third cut is horizontal, and is about 2 inches higher than the intersection of the first two cuts, resulting in a step that keeps the trunk from jumping backward. Note that the third cut penetrates only to within an inch or two of the maximum depth of the pie. This leaves a strip or "hinge" of wood that will stabilize and guide the falling tree.

Here, a support log was placed in the path of the trunk's fall for several reasons: (1) to elevate the trunk for ease of bucking, (2) to keep the bark out of saw-dulling dirt, and (3) to provide a fulcrum that allows a simple overbuck down through the trunk. The sagging sort of stress on the trunk in the crotch area puts the wood under tension, so it is necessary to make a short overbuck on this cut before underbucking. Otherwise, the kerf will close and pinch the saw. Limbs can be used as turning pieces or cut to stovewood length. (When cutting limbs for use as turning wood, save the knots and burls; these provide a good decorative figure.)

18'

Tree's natural lean

Third cut

First cut

45°

Second cut

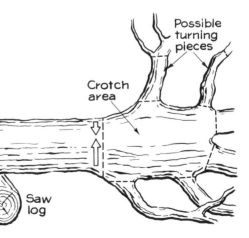

Possible turning pieces

Crotch area

Saw log

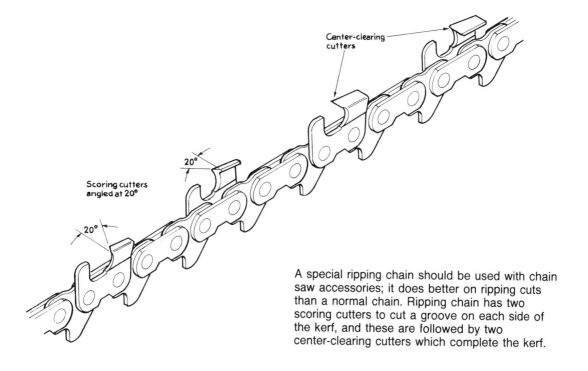

Center-clearing cutters

Scoring cutters angled at 20°

20°

20°

A special ripping chain should be used with chain saw accessories; it does better on ripping cuts than a normal chain. Ripping chain has two scoring cutters to cut a groove on each side of the kerf, and these are followed by two center-clearing cutters which complete the kerf.

Logging and Cutting Planks

When felling a tree, use the proper felling techniques, and wear safety equipment such as face shield, hard hat and leather gloves.

After the tree is felled, it is bucked into convenient lengths with the chain saw. Observe the proper safety rules when bucking the tree. The log may roll when supporting limbs are cut, so stay alert.

Once the tree has been trimmed and bucked and the log cut to a convenient size, the next step is to cut it into slabs or boards. This is done using one of the lumber-cutting attachments for a chain saw. Several of these are listed in the source list at the back of the book. Shown in the accompanying illustrations are two different types and the techniques used with each to make slabs and boards from logs. One suggestion for using either one of the attachments is to purchase a special ripping chain for your saw. Keep the chain well oiled during the cuts.

I cut the slabs on woods such as oak or walnut 1⅛-inch thick to allow for a full ¾-inch board when cured and surface planed on two sides. Of course, with either of the two units shown the planks can be cut almost any thickness desired.

One advantage of using these machines is that you don't waste any lumber. Any slabs cut off can be used as fireplace wood, and the piles of sawdust as mulch or compost.

If you have a fair amount of timber it might be worthwhile to purchase a small one-man sawmill. These are available for less than $2,000 and can even be used for some light commercial cutting. Some of them can handle logs up to 18 inches in diameter.

It is much easier to saw woods soon after they are felled than to allow them to dry or partially cure before cutting. The green wood is much softer.

Curing Methods

Cutting the wood is easy compared to curing it. Curing wood isn't hard, but it does take something many of us are short on these days—patience and time. From start to finish it can require from four to six years to properly air dry wood suitable for furniture or cabinet working, and some woods may require as long as ten years or more. Of course, once you get past that period, if you have been continually putting more wood away for curing, you will have a steady supply.

Cutting Planks and Slabs

Chain saw accessories can be used to cut planks and slabs. Here, guide rail for Granberg's Alaskan MK III is fastened to log. (A thick plank can also be used as a guide rail.)

Alaskan MK III mounts on bar of chain saw with clamping pads and rides along guide rail to slab top of log. Log is then turned to slab two other sides.

An assortment of planks cut with the MK III.

Then the rails are set for desired thickness of planks.

Above: Another chain saw accessory is Granberg's Mini-mill. Guide rail is nailed to a plank and fastened to log.
Right: First slab is cut from side of log, and log is then turned to make two more slabs.
Below: Rip fence of Mini-mill is adjusted to required thickness, and planks sawed.

If you have a fair amount of timber to cut, you can purchase and set up a small one-man mill such as the unit shown. It sells for less than $2,000. *Belsaw.*

I have heard many different artisans argue the difference between kiln-dried and air-dried woods. To me the air-dried woods seem a bit more alive, but they are also a bit more unpredictable. I think this is not because they are air-dried, but because in many cases those doing the job of drying the woods haven't followed the best procedures and in many cases have hurried a job that just can't be rushed.

Moisture Content. In order to properly cure wood you must first understand a little about the structure of living wood. Living wood is composed of cells full of water and nutrients. The type of wood determines the number of cells, the size of the cells and the amount of water and nutrients each cell holds.

The water and nutrients go up through the cells from the roots of the tree to the leaves, where they are transpired or evaporated. When a tree is cut, the amount of this water that is in the cells is called the *moisture content.* Some woods have a greater moisture content than others because of the nature of their cells. For instance, a conifer such as pine typically has a very high moisture content, while a wood such as ash has a low one.

Another important factor is the time of year that the wood is cut. The old-timers knew the importance of cutting woods when the sap was low, and never cut wood when the sap was rising. The reason was that the woods cut then were inevitably hard to properly cure. Usually the best time to cut green woods for use as cabinet and furniture woods is in late winter, in January or February.

The use that a wood is put to determines to a great extent the amount of moisture that is allowed. Shown in the chart is the proper moisture content of wood for various uses. Generally, the allowable moisture content depends on the range of temperature and humidity that the wood will be exposed to. For instance, the lumber used in building a house typically has about 15 percent moisture content, but furniture woods should only have 6 to 10 percent.

About the only way of properly measuring moisture is with the use of an electric moisture meter. However, many old-timers merely air dried lumber for what they guessed was long enough to do the trick and, I might add, they were very successful.

Kiln Drying. The first stage of drying wood is to remove the "free" moisture in the wood; that is, the moisture not contained in the cell cavities or fibers. The lumber is placed on a rack in an oven and the moisture in the air very slowly removed (though in a relatively short period of time as compared to air-dried wood). Shrinkage of the wood will begin after the free moisture has been eliminated, or the moisture content reduced to 25 to 30 percent. If the temperature is too high, premature shrinkage will result (due to the collapse of the cell walls in the wood), greatly reduc-

Correct Moisture Content of Wood According to Use

Use	Moisture Percentage		
	Min.	Max.	Usual
Chairs and chair stock	5%	12%	6%
Flooring	6	10	6
Furniture stock	4	10	6
Sash and doors	4	8	6
Veneers:			
Face	2	7	4
Crossband	2	10	5
Cores	4	6	5
Plywood	2	9	6
Shingles	10	12	10
Lumber:			
Rough construction	10	24	15
Joists, studs, sub-flooring	6	20*	8
Timbers, poles, etc., to be treated with creosote or other preservatives	Free water should be removed and m.c. reduced to about 25% before treatment		

*Many experts consider 20% too high for sub-floors and framing. 15% would be safer.

Courtesy New York State College of Forestry

The first step in air drying is to coat ends of stock with paraffin or linseed oil.

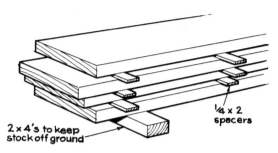

Then stock is separated with ¼-inch spacers and stored in a shed or barn.

ing the stability and strength of the wood. Thus, it takes a great deal of engineering expertise to do the job properly. It's quite a sophisticated process, and results in the relatively stable woods that we purchase. But don't think that kiln-dried wood is always perfect. Even though the wood may have been dried to the exact moisture content necessary, it may have been stored outside in a high moisture area. Since the cells can still pick up moisture, you end up with a wood that will split and pop the first time it is in the dry, hot air of today's heated homes. This is a problem that has frustrated many woodworkers, even the pros. The answer is to store the wood for a month or so in an intermediately dry, heated area; near the furnace in the basement or a similar area.

Air Drying. The same principles involved in oven curing must be used in air drying to achieve satisfactory results. The difference is only in the time required and the patience of the craftsman. The steps in air drying are simple, but they must be carefully and lovingly followed.

The first is to coat all exposed ends of stock with paraffin or boiled linseed oil, preferably paraffin. Then stack the wood outside in a barn, shed, or unheated garage, with ¼-inch "stickers" or thin strips of wood between the pieces. These not only prevent the boards from warping but allow air to circulate around each piece. The stock should also be kept well off the ground.

Softwood, such as cedar or pine, will normally be air-dried enough for the next step in a couple of years, but hardwoods such as walnut, or even cherry, may require up to another two to six years, or a total of six to ten years.

The best way to measure moisture in wood is with an electric moisture meter. After initial stage of air drying, moisture content should be about 22 percent. Then the wood is moved to a warmer, drier spot, the ends recoated with paraffin or linseed oil if necessary, and the stack covered with plastic.

In any event the stock should be air-dried at this point to around 22 percent. Again, as mentioned before, the use of a good electric moisture meter can be a great deal of help here, but if you're cautious as were the old-timers, allow the wood to cure for up to ten years before even thinking about it.

After this initial period of curing, the wood should then be taken down from the stack, and placed in the shop or an area where there is normal room heat. The wood should be spaced with ¾-inch spacer sticks and covered with a sheet of plastic for about six months. Then remove the plastic and allow the wood to air dry for at least six months before using. By this time the wood will probably be as stable as it can be with air drying.

Final Preparation. After the woods have cured, the next step is to make them usable as furniture and cabinet woods, and for this you will need several tools including a surface planer, jointer, and heavy-duty band saw.

If you end up with larger pieces than needed, the band saw can be used as a resawing tool to reduce thicknesses.

Types of Woods

Different craftsmen have different experiences of wood. The makers of fine violins and guitars know the light but tough feel of spruce, and the hard, crisp lines that can be cut with maple. The carver knows the feel of basswood and mahogany. The boat builder is interested in spruce and cedar because of their light weight and strength.

To the cabinet builder the oaks, pecan, birch and ash are the primary woods because of their durability, strength, and relative economy. To the furniture builder, almost anything goes, from fruitwoods such as cherry and pear, to pine, walnut, oak, and mahogany.

Quite often the style of the particular piece of furniture or cabinet dictates the wood that will be used. This is for a very real reason; some woods are particularly suited to certain jobs. For instance, Early American style furniture is often made of hard maple or white pine because of the excellent turning qualities of these woods. The traditional furniture of such famous furniture makers as Duncan Phyfe and of the Hepplewhite and Sheraton Schools was almost always made of fine-grained mahogany, an extremely durable and stable wood that produces clean lines when machined.

Knowing how a wood works is very important to the cabinetmaker. For instance, although white pine is very easy to work with, it is quite soft and will often tear rather than shear off cleanly as will the harder woods such as oak, walnut or mahogany. For this reason white pine is not used when fine detailing or high-gloss surfaces are desired. Some early American and primitive styles will do quite well with the wood,

After wood has cured, it can be surfaced with a planer and cut to desired width with a band saw.

Mahogany has long been a favorite wood for fine furniture because of its unsurpassed machining qualities. The intricate detail and clean lines of this Hepplewhite-style chair are an example of what can be achieved. *The Metropolitan Museum of Art, the Sylmaris Collection, Gift of George Coe Graves, 1931.*

Hard maple is often the wood chosen for Early American-style furniture—both because the wood was traditionally used, and because it is a good turning wood.

Birch is a popular wood both for furniture and kitchen cabinets. It has a warm reddish-tan coloring, and stands up well to years of wear.

though, since dents and other marks of use are desirable in these styles.

There are many different kinds of woods from all over the world, but most furniture and cabinetry items are made from a fairly standard list of a select few woods. One major wood supplier company lists almost 300 different kinds of woods, but many of these woods are available only as veneers or in very limited sizes and quantities.

The principal cabinet and furniture woods are as follows.

Ash *(Fraxinus)*

Characteristics. There are a number of different species of ash, but the white ash is the best known among woodworkers. It is a very hard, dense and strong wood. It can be machined quite well, producing crisp saw cuts and planed surfaces. It is able to resist a great deal of shock, and is well known for its bending abilities.

White ash is light tan in color, sometimes with light brown or red streaks. It is considered a very stable wood, as it is less apt to warp or change dimensionally than almost any of our other native hardwoods.

The ash is a deciduous tree, and the strong contrast between the spring and summer wood produces a very attractive figure in the wood.

Ash and hickory are sometimes mistaken for each other, but on close examination you will see that the large-pore zone is more pronounced in ash than in hickory. Another indication of ash is the visible line of white dots in the summerwood. These are not visible in hickory without a microscope.

Uses. White ash is commonly used for producing baseball bats, and tool handles for shovels, rakes, and hammers, etc. because of its tough qualities. It is also very commonly used in manufacturing furniture, especially pieces that are to be bent.

Ash is fast becoming a very popular kitchen cabinet wood because of its machining qualities as well as the distinctive grain pattern of the wood.

Basswood (*Tilia*)

Characteristics. Basswood is a soft, light-weight hardwood with an even, fine grain. It is light tan in color. The wood is quite stable when properly seasoned, and is easy to work.

Uses. Basswood is rarely used in cabinetmaking because of its softness. It is used as a carving wood, in the manufacture of stamped moldings, and as a plywood core material.

Beech (*Fagus*)

Characteristics. Beech is also a popular wood with furniture manufacturers. Although it is hard to season properly, it is considered quite hard, strong and is fairly dense. It can be bent and machined quite well. It is often used as a substitute for more expensive woods, especially in Provincial-style furnitures. The beech is a deciduous tree, and the wood runs from pale tan to reddish-brown in the heartwood. There isn't much contrast between the summer and spring wood; the wood has a uniform texture and an inconspicuous figure.

Uses. Because of its excellent wearing qualities it is quite often used as a flooring material, but it is also used for millwork, crates, boxes, handles and even containers for food.

Birch (*Betula*)

Characteristics. There are three principal species of lumber birch: yellow; sweet, also called black or cherry; and paper, also called canoe birch.

The wood of the first two species is moderately heavy, quite strong and hard. It machines well and finishes to a fine luster. There is little contrast between the summer and spring wood, but the annual growth rings are usually quite distinguishable. Color is yellow to pinkish-white in the sapwood and tan with a tinge of red in the heartwood.

Uses. Birch is considered one of the major cabinet woods, and I can remember a period when we built kitchen cabinets of nothing but birch. A great deal of birch is used in plywood, which is one of the reasons for its popularity as a cabinet wood.

Other uses of birch are in general millwork,

Aromatic red cedar is used principally as a lining for closets and cedar chests.

Early American cabinetmakers often stained cherry to simulate other woods. Today, a natural finish is almost always preferred. *The Metropolitan Museum of Art, Gift of Mrs. Russell Sage, 1909.*

flooring, doors and interior trim. Birch plywood is usually sold as "selected white," which means all sapwood on one face, or "selected red," which means all heartwood on one face. But a more distinctive plywood is unselected-face plywood, as it usually contains portions of both heartwood and sapwood.

Cedar, Aromatic Red (*Juniperus*)

Characteristics. Actually not a cedar at all, but a juniper, this is the wood that is famous for cedar chests and for lining closets. It is practically all cut from second-growth timber, and the trees rarely attain any size at all. It is a medium-density softwood, but has excellent machining qualities. It has very contrasty red heartwood and white sapwood. It is extremely aromatic. The wood is very knotty and this is also part of its charm.

Uses. Because of its aroma and reputed moth-repelling qualities, it is most commonly used in building cedar chests, for lining drawers in quality bedroom furniture, or for closet lining. It is sometimes used as paneling.

Cherry (*Prunus*)

Characteristics. The species of cherry used for cabinetmaking is the black cherry, or wild cherry. It is one of the top cabinet woods. It is a fruitwood and is fairly heavy, quite strong and

hard. The wood has a fairly uniform texture, and it machines extremely well to produce a fine silky smoothness. The sapwood is yellow to pink; the heartwood reddish-brown, sometimes tinted with a bit of green.

Today most of the larger cherry trees are gone and all that's left are the scrub trees, so most cherry wood is quite narrow in width. It takes a bit of planning to figure out how to cut around the many knots and other defects.

Uses. Cherry was a favorite furniture wood of the early American cabinetmakers, and was often substituted for the harder-to-get mahogany woods. Many of the older pieces were stained a dark reddish-black to simulate mahogany, and as a consequence many folks today think that cherry is a dark black-reddish wood. Quite the contrary; cherry is a most delicately hued, yet beautiful wood, with a light tan to cherry coloring and distinctive grain pattern. It is especially popular for building French Provincial furniture.

Cherry wood is usually quite expensive because the logs are fairly small and there is a great deal of waste in the logging and sawing operation. Many furnitures called "fruitwood" are actually cheaper grades of wood stained to simulate the subtle tans and reds of cherry.

Douglas-Fir (*Pseudotsuga*)

Characteristics. Douglas fir is a moderately heavy and strong softwood. It is easy to work, but does tend to splinter during crosscutting operations—sharp saw blades are a must. Color ranges from yellow-red to yellowish- or reddish-brown, and growth rings show up prominently in the plain-sawn wood.

Uses. It is one of the most commercially valuable North American trees, and is one of the primary woods used for plywood veneers. It is also used for house framing, millwork items, and a variety of other applications.

Elm *(Ulmus)*

Characteristics. Of the elms, the common American elm is the most important lumber species. It is a medium-density, but tough and strong wood. It machines fairly well, but has a somewhat coarse texture. It is prone to warp and shrink. Color runs from light yellow to pinkish-brown in the heartwood. Another species of elm often used in woodworking is the *rock* elm. Rock elm is heavier and stronger than American elm, and somewhat more difficult to work. Its heartwood is darker, ranging from light to dark brown. Like American elm, it has excellent bending qualities.

Uses. Elm is used primarily in the cooperage industry for barrel staves and hoops, and for making baskets and other bent-wood items. It is also sometimes used in furniture because of its distinctive grain, and is quite often used as a veneer for paneling.

Hickory *(Carya)*

Characteristics. A very dense, hard, and shock-resistant wood, hickory can be machined and turned quite well. The sapwood is white, and the heartwood is usually brown or reddish-brown.

Uses. Hickory is primarily used for tool handles, ladder rungs, sporting goods, and lawn furniture.

Holly *(Ilex)*

Characteristics. A fairly dense hardwood from an ornamental evergreen tree. Color is pure white, and there is almost no figure.

Uses. Holly is often used for inlays and borders in fine furniture: it contrasts well with woods of darker hue. It is hardly ever used in construction of furniture.

Mahogany, Genuine *(Swietenia)*

Characteristics. Genuine or New-World mahogany is usually considered the best cabinet and furniture wood in the world, and has been popular with cabinetmakers and furniture builders for many years. It is unsurpassed in machining and finishing qualities. It turns and carves extremely well, with resulting crisp, sharp lines. It has high strength in proportion to weight and it can be polished to an extremely high sheen. The pores of the wood are fairly large and thus the use of a filler is required in most finishing operations. Color is reddish brown. The wood is excellent in both plywood and solid form.

Uses. It is excellent for building furniture as well as for building boats and is used in the pattern-making business because of its excellent carving qualities. It is the only mahogany that can be sold without a prefix before the word *mahogany.*

Mahogany, African *(Khaya)*

Characteristics. There are several species of African mahogany and they are quite similar in working capabilities to Genuine mahogany. African mahogany usually has a slightly coarser texture than does Genuine mahogany, so it takes a bit more application of filler in the finishing process. It is considered an excellent furniture wood by knowledgeable wood workers.

Mahogany, Phillipine *(Shorea* **and** *Parashorea)*

These species are not related to the Genuine or African mahoganies and are called "lauan." The woods have a medium hardness and density. They are usually available in two distinct patterns and colors, dark red and light red. They machine well, and since they are more economical than

Mahogany is considered the finest cabinetmaking wood by craftsmen throughout the world. It is used on many traditional styles of furniture, and produces crisp, clean-cut lines. (Shown is a blockfront chest, a design associated with 18th-century Rhode Island cabinetmakers.)

Genuine mahogany, are used quite often as a substitute.

Maple, Hard *(Acer)*

Characteristics. Hard maple, from the sugar maple tree, is a hard, dense and strong wood. It is very resistant to wear and abrasion. It is tasteless and odorless and has an extremely fine texture and grain. The color is usually creamy-white to light tan. It has excellent machining abilities.

Uses. One of the prime uses of this extremely durable wood is as fine furniture. It is also used for flooring, especially in skating rinks, dance halls and bowling alleys, and for boxes and crates. It is the standard wood used for cutting-boards and "butcher block" table and counter tops.

It sometimes develops figures called "bird's-eye," and "curly" or "fiddleback," which are truly beautiful and distinctive patterns. They are famous for use in violins and other musical instruments, and as veneer facing for furniture drawers and door fronts.

Maple, Soft *(Acer)*

A medium-density and fairly hard and strong wood, it is quite similar to hard maple, but actually includes a different group of trees, such as the silver and red maples, and boxelder.

Sugar maple was a favorite wood of early American furniture builders. Shown is a slat-back maple chair, c. 1700–1725. *The Metropolitan Museum of Art, Gift of Mrs. Russell Sage, 1909.*

Oak has been used as a cabinet wood since Roman times. Like other heavy, dense woods such as mahogany, walnut, cherry, and hard maple, it produces excellent turnings. This Connecticut oak cupboard (c. 1700) has both split turnings and bead-and-ball turnings, a design element borrowed from Jacobean-style furniture of the period. *The Metropolitan Museum of Art, Gift of Mrs. S. Woodhull Overton, 1953.*

The majority of the soft maple woods go to the furniture industry to produce the more economical maple furniture, such as the lower grades of Colonial and Early American styles.

Oak *(Quercus)*

Oak is probably the most famous furniture wood. There is evidence that it was in use during the Greek and Roman ages, but it really became popular during the Middle Ages. In fact the period from the fourteenth to the seventeenth centuries is called the "Golden Age of Oak." Today it is still just as popular as both a furniture and a cabinet wood. There are so many different species of oak used for lumber that it would be difficult to name them according to their characteristics and uses. Because of this, most oak is usually sold as either *white* oak or *red* oak. The differences between them are important in selecting the proper wood for a project. The following information is supplied by the Southern Hardwood Producers.

White Oaks. The color of the heartwood tends to be tan or brownish. The vessels of heartwood have abundant tyloses; and the wood consequently is waterproof. Freshly cut wood has a distinct, but not unpleasant odor. The pores in summerwood are numerous and small, and cannot be counted even with a hand lens. Annual rings are usually compact, resulting in finer textured wood.

Red Oaks. The color of the heartwood is somewhat reddish. The vessels of heartwood have few tyloses; and the wood consequently is not waterproof. Freshly cut wood has a sour, often unpleasant odor. Summerwood has few pores, but they are large enough to be seen under a hand lens. Annual rings are usually widely separated, resulting in coarser textured wood. The heartwood is not particularly durable under conditions favoring decay.

Either type of oak is an excellent wood for furniture and cabinetry. Oak machines and bends quite well and polishes to a silky texture. But

Oak is still a popular furniture and cabinet wood today because of its distinctive grain pattern and fine finishing qualities.

most important, it is quite sturdy and, when properly seasoned, one of the most stable of woods.

Uses. Oak has long been used for flooring, as well as for fine furniture and cabinetry. For a long period it was a popular kitchen cabinet wood, but it is now somewhat expensive for this use.

Pecan *(Carya)*

Characteristics. Pecan is a member of the hickory family, and it has many of the same characteristics. It is a very strong and durable wood. It has a light brown heartwood and white sapwood.

Uses. Pecan has been growing in popularity as a furniture wood and should also become a popular cabinet wood. It can be finished to resem-

Pecan is often used to simulate oak, but it has its own beauty if properly finished.

The knotty species of pine are often utilized for decorative veneers and panels for built-ins such as this one.

ble the coloring of the more expensive oaks or even walnut, yet it has its own beauty if finished properly. It is often finished to produce a distressed effect in Provincial style furnitures.

Pine *(Pinaceae)*

There are 35 species of pine native to North America, and about half of these are used to produce lumber. Because there are notable differences between certain species of pine—in terms of color, texture, knottiness, weather resistance and stability—many lumber dealers offer a selection of imported pines as well as local species.

Characteristics. On the West Coast, four of the principal species used for lumber are the ponderosa, lodgepole, Western white (also known as Idaho white) and sugar pines. The heartwood of these species ranges from light yellow to light brown, and the sapwood is nearly white. The wood is generally straight-grained, light in weight, and easy to work. Of the four, the Western white and sugar pines are the most stable dimensionally and are least apt to shrink or warp.

On the East Coast, the principal species are the Eastern white and red or Norway pine. These species are both marketed as white pine, but there are some differences between them. The Eastern white pine has a light brown heartwood which darkens markedly on exposure to air. It is generally straight-grained, easy to work, and highly stable. The red or Norway pine is somewhat heavier and not as uniform in texture as the white pine. Its heartwood varies from pale red to reddish brown.

In addition, there are the "Southern" pines, which include the shortleaf, loblolly, slash and longleaf species. (Other Southern species are designated as "minor" species to distinguish them from the principal four.) The shortleaf and loblolly pines have relatively coarse-grained wood that is easy to work; the longleaf and slash pines are somewhat heavier and more durable. The four species are very similar in appearance, with reddish-brown heartwood and yellowish-white to light orange sapwood.

Uses. Pine is a favorite furniture wood because of its excellent machining qualities, and it is also used extensively in the manufacture of moldings and other millwork items. The heavier, more durable woods are made into heavy timbers for construction, and the knotty species are used for decorative panelings and interior carpentry.

Redwood *(Sequoia)*

Although redwood is grown only in California, it is sold in all parts of the United States.

Characteristics. The color of the heartwood varies from light to deep reddish-brown, and is generally very uniform in color. The wood is fairly light in weight and easy to work. It is very stable, and is often used in areas that will be subjected to variations in climate.

Uses. Redwood is used extensively in construction of siding and sash because of its durability and stability. It is also a popular material for wall shelves and paneling.

Sweetgum *(Liquidambar)*

Characteristics. Also sometimes called *red gum* because of the color of its autumn leaves. This is now a very important furniture wood, especially in the Southern states, although at one time it was used very rarely for this purpose. Today, more red gum is probably used for building furniture than any one other wood. The main reason for its popularity is that it can blend in with more valuable woods such as walnut. The wood is fairly hard and strong, and machines and finishes quite well. The sapwood is usually a bland white, but the heartwood can be anything from a mild tan or brown to a heavily figured dark-brown.

Uses. Although at one time it was primarily used for building crates and boxes, today it is a very important furniture and millwork wood. It is an excellent wood for wood turning as well as for steam-bending projects.

Sycamore *(Platanus)*

Characteristics. Sycamore trees are one of the largest hardwood species in North America, and are commonly planted in urban areas. The wood is relatively hard and heavy, with fairly good shock-resistance. The heartwood is light brown to reddish-brown in color, and wood rays are visible on both plain- and quarter-sawn lumber.

Uses. Because of its toughness, sycamore is a favorite wood for butcher blocks. It is also used for inexpensive grades of funiture, drawer sides and backs, and for veneer.

Walnut, North American *(Juglans)*

Characteristics. Of the five species of North American walnut, black walnut is the principal lumber species. A dense, hard and strong wood, it is one of our most popular furniture woods. It polishes and finishes excellently. The sapwood is white; the heartwood ranges from light gray-brown to dark purple. For many years walnut was the most popular furniture wood, and today it is in limited supply.

Uses. Walnut is an excellent wood for carving or other machining techniques requiring crisp, good-looking joints and lines. Because of this property, it is quite often chosen for sculptured and contemporary furniture.

Because of its beauty, walnut is also used for other kinds of fine furniture; for cabinets, musical instrument cases, radio, television and stereo cabinets, and gunstocks. Because of the scarcity of walnut, a great deal of it is used as veneer. In addition to plain-sawn lumber, veneers may include the unusual crotch, burl or stump figures. These are highly prized for use in making drawer and door fronts.

Another reason for the popularity of walnut as a furniture and cabinet wood is that it takes al-

Walnut has traditionally been a popular furniture wood, but is now becoming scarce and expensive. It looks extremely well with almost any furniture style, and is used for modern as well as traditional pieces.

most any finish quite easily and is especially compatible with oiled finishes. Therefore, it can be finished very beautifully by even the beginner.

One of the most fascinating things about walnut is that it seems to have an infinitely variable grain pattern, which endears it thoroughly to all woodworkers. It is especially popular as a carving or turning wood.

Walnut, Persian *(Juglans)*

This is the species of walnut that produces English walnuts. It ranges all over Europe and is known by several other names including English walnut, French walnut, Italian walnut, and Circassian walnut. It is quite similar in characteristics to native American walnut, except it has a

tendency to be a bit lighter and with more of a gray tone. One mistake many woodworkers make is in thinking that the Persian walnut is more highly figured. This is probably because most of the imported Persian walnut is from the crotch and burl areas of the tree. But although the wood is a bit lighter in color, the most figured walnut patterns come from American walnut.

Walnut, South American *(Juglans)*

Although very similar to American walnut in characteristics, coloring and uses, it is a tropical wood and does have some differences. The wood is a bit coarser grained with more large open pores. It is also a bit darker in coloring, yet somewhat lighter in weight.

Some machining and related properties of selected domestic hardwoods

Kind of wood	Planing— perfect pieces	Shaping— good to excellent pieces	Turning— fair to excellent pieces	Boring— good to excellent pieces	Mortising— fair to excellent pieces	Sanding— good to excellent pieces	Steam bending— unbroken pieces	Nail splitting— pieces free from complete splits	Screw splitting— pieces free from complete splits
	Pct.	Pct.	Pct.	Pct.	Pct.	Pct.	Pct.	Pct.	Pct.
Alder, red	61	20	88	64	52				
Ash	75	55	79	94	58	75	67	65	71
Aspen	26	7	65	78	60				
Basswood	64	10	68	76	51	17	2	79	68
Beech	83	24	90	99	92	49	75	42	58
Birch	63	57	80	97	97	34	72	32	48
Birch, paper	47	22							
Cherry, black	80	80	88	100	100				
Chestnut	74	28	87	91	70	64	56	66	60
Cottonwood	21	3	70	70	52	19	44	82	78
Elm, soft	33	13	65	94	75	66	74	80	74
Hackberry	74	10	77	99	72		94	63	63
Hickory	76	20	84	100	98	80	76	35	63
Magnolia	65	27	79	71	32	37	85	73	76
Maple, big leaf	52	56	80	100	80				
Maple, hard	54	72	82	99	95	38	57	27	52
Maple, soft	41	25	76	80	34	37	59	58	61
Oak, red	91	28	84	99	95	81	86	66	78
Oak, white	87	35	85	95	99	83	91	69	74
Pecan	88	40	89	100	98		78	47	69
Sweetgum	51	28	86	92	58	23	67	69	69
Sycamore	22	12	85	98	96	21	29	79	74
Tanoak	80	39	81	100	100				
Tupelo, water	55	52	79	62	33	34	46	64	63
Tupelo, black	48	32	75	82	24	21	42	65	63
Walnut, black	62	34	91	100	98		78	50	59
Willow	52	5	58	71	24	24	73	89	62
Yellow-poplar	70	13	81	87	63	19	58	77	67

Courtesy Forest Service, U.S. Dept. of Agriculture

Willow (*Salix*)

Characteristics. Of the many species of willow found in North America, the black willow is the most frequently used for lumber. Although classified as a hardwood, willow is actually quite soft. Because of this softness, it has a tendency to fuzz when machined. One advantage, and one reason for its recent popularity, is that it can be stained to simulate walnut. It ranges in color from a whitish sapwood to a dark brown or dark reddish-brown heartwood.

Uses. Although willow was once used only for boxes and for the production of charcoal, it is now gaining popularity as a furniture wood because of the scarcity of many other hardwoods.

Yellow-Poplar (*Liriodendron*)

Characteristics. Poplar is a close-grained, moderately light and fairly soft wood. Color ranges from yellow to brown, usually with a grayish tinge. The wood is quite stable when properly seasoned.

Uses. This is a popular wood with woodworking classes because it machines quite well with hand tools. In the furniture industry, it is primarily used for the more economical grades of furniture.

The Exotics

The woods classified as exotics include zebrawood, rosewood, tigerwood, and many others. Usually these woods are available in such small quantity and sizes and the cost is so high that they are rarely used for furniture and cabinetry except as accent pieces on door and drawer fronts.

From the Tree to the Lumberyard: Characteristics of Wood and Grading of Lumber Products

verted by photosynthesis into sugar and protein. These elements then travel back to nourish the branches, trunk and roots of the tree.

A living tree trunk contains five major parts. The *bark* acts as an insulator from heat and cold and helps keep out insects and disease. The *phloem,* or inner bark, carries food from the leaves back down through the tree to its roots. As the tree grows, the phloem gradually turns into bark. The *cambium* layer, composed of living cells, creates new bark and new wood annually through cell division. As new wood is created, the bark is pushed outward, often creating the cracks or ridges which characterize the bark of many species. The *sapwood* contains the internal piping that carries water from the roots to the leaves. The *heartwood* is the supporting column of the tree. Although it is actually dead wood, it won't decay or rot as long as the other protective layers of wood surround it.

Composition and Structure of Wood

To work with wood, it is helpful to understand how it is produced. All wood is essentially made up of compounds of carbon, oxygen and hydrogen, and cellulose and lignin are the two basic compounds. Lignin is a binding compound, and contributes to the hardness of the wood. The difference between the wood of different species of trees is largely due to the thickness of the cell walls, as well as the size and density of the cells.

In softwoods, the short fibers of the tree are actually its internal plumbing system, and they act as a sort of wick as they pick up moisture and nutrients from the ground and carry it through the tree trunk and branches to the leaves. In hardwoods, fibers are also present, but the job of conducting water is done by separate vessels or tubes. (The pores sometimes visible in a cross section of hardwood are actually sections of these tubes.) In either case, the water and nutrients are then con-

A tree trunk consists of several different "layers": The outside bark, the inner bark or phloem, the cambium or cell-producing part, the sapwood, and the heartwood. In today's manufacturing, every part of the tree is used.

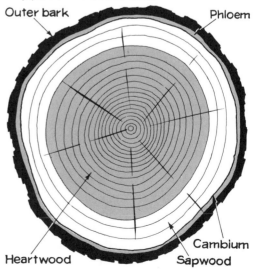

Outer bark

Phloem

Heartwood

Cambium

Sapwood

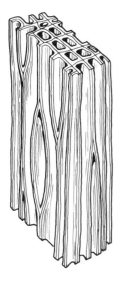

In a living tree, wood fibers serve as conduits to carry water and nutrients from the roots to the leaves and back. The structure of these fibers is what makes wood such an excellent building material.

Softwood and Hardwood

Trees are classified into two groups: hardwood (broad-leaved, with true flowers), and softwood (conifers, or cone-bearing). Hardwoods are deciduous trees such as oak, walnut and maple. Softwoods are the evergreens such as pine and fir. These classifications do not necessarily give a true indication of the hardness of the woods, however. For example, there are many softwoods which have harder woods than such hardwoods as balsa, basswood and aspen. One important difference between the two groups is that softwoods do not contain the pores (actually sections of water-conducting vessels) seen in hardwoods, and are thus referred to as *non-porous.*

What Determines the Appearance and Characteristics of Finished Wood

The grain, texture and color of wood are all important in determining what use it will be put to. These characteristics in finished wood are determined by the type of tree, its age, what part of the tree is used, how it is cut, and growing conditions.

Grain

The growth of the new cells in the cambium layer is what produces the annual rings in a tree, and the resulting grain patterns. In most North American species, there is a burst of growth each spring, and this produces cells of greater size but less strength than those formed later in the season. In some species, there is little difference between the earlywood and latewood portions of the growth ring. When the contrast between them is pronounced, the growth rings will be correspondingly prominent. The growth rings of most softwoods are prominent.

Most of the fibers and vessels of wood are oriented vertically in the tree, thus contributing to its support. (It is this structure that makes wood such a marvelous building material.) Although most cells are oriented lengthwise through the trunk, there are also cells that run across it, and these are called rays or medullary cells. Rays are quite small and unnoticeable on most wood, but they do show up on oak, especially when it is quarter-sawn.

When hardwoods are sawn, their water-conducting vessels or tubes show up as pores. As noted earlier, the difference between the spring- and summerwood cells is more pronounced in some species than in others. When the two portions of the growth ring are markedly different in color (springwood much lighter than the summerwood), the wood is described as *ring-porous.* The light color of the springwood indicates that its cells are relatively large, and with weaker cell walls than the summerwood. A good example of this type of wood is oak. *Semi-ring-porous* wood

Wood rays are cells oriented perpendicular to the grain. They are prominent in oak, especially when the log is quarter-sawn.

has easily-seen growth ring patterns, but they are not as distinctive. An example is hickory. *Diffuse-porous* describes wood that does not have a very distinct growth pattern, such as maple.

The part of the tree that the wood is cut from, and the growing conditions of the tree also make a difference in the grain or figure of the finished wood. The *crotch, burl* and *stump* portions of the tree yield wood with a highly irregular grain pattern. The unusual "bird's eye" figure sometimes found in sugar maples is similar to a burl figure, but appears in the trunk wood. It is thought to be due to stunted growth. Because of the scarcity of these unusual woods, they are almost always made into veneers. (For examples of the use of unusually figured veneers, see pages 42–44.)

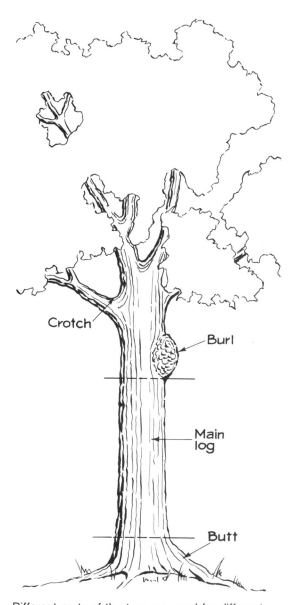

Different parts of the tree are used for different purposes. The main log is normally made into lumber or veneer. The crotch, burl, and butt areas are made into veneer to make best use of the unusual configurations found there.

An example of walnut crotch figure (above) and walnut burl.

A bird's eye figure sometimes appears in maple logs.

The way wood is sawn determines how the grain pattern of the wood will appear in the finished lumber. Basically, there are three different methods of sawing wood.

Plain- or **flat-sawn** lumber is cut tangent to the annual rings. This type of sawing produces the least amount of waste, and results in less costly lumber. It is commonly used to produce construction lumber from such softwoods as pine

Plain-sawn lumber shows a V-shape grain figure. Quarter- and rift-sawn boards have a relatively straight grain figure.

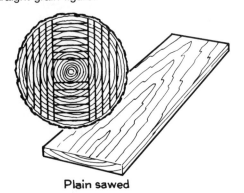

Plain sawed

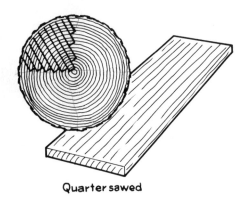

Quarter sawed

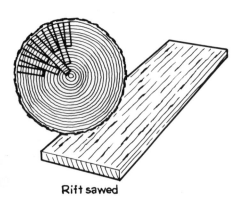

Rift sawed

and fir. Lumber produced this way is easier to kiln-dry, and comes in wider average widths.

Quarter-sawn lumber is made by first cutting a log into quarters, then slabbing the quarters. This produces some of the most beautiful wood figures, especially on oak, where the wood rays will be seen to better advantage. Quarter-sawn material shrinks, twists, checks and splits less frequently. Most wood used for furniture and cabinets is cut this way.

Rift-sawn lumber is also cut from quartered lumber, but the angle of the cut is different from that in the quarter-sawing method, and produces a slightly different grain pattern. It is normally done only for special effects.

Texture

The texture of wood has a great deal to do with its grain, but the word also refers to the basic character of the wood fibers. Softwoods generally have a finer texture than hardwoods because their cells are smaller. Species that show little contrast between the spring- and summerwoods are referred to as *even-textured,* and those with a strong contrast are said to have *uneven* texture. Among the hardwoods, the diffuse-porous (close-grain) woods are known as even-textured, and the ring-porous (open-grain) woods as uneven-textured. *Coarse-textured* hardwoods are those with large pores or prominent rays, or both, such as oak.

Color

The color of the wood is also important. It may range from the bright red of red cedar to the black of ebony, or to the pure white of holly, with hundreds of tones between. There will also be a great variance from tree to tree and even in individual trees. As a result, matching woods as to grain and color for a fine piece of furniture is one of the most difficult but interesting aspects of cabinetmaking.

Grades of Wood

In addition to the grain patterns and color, wood produced commercially is also separated into different grade classifications depending on number of knots, soundness of knots, splitting or cracking along grain lines, etc. Each type of use requires a wood product of a specific grade. For most practical purposes in cabinetmaking, you will be dealing with softwoods for basic construction. The charts on pages 32 and 33 indicate the considerations used in softwood and hardwood grading.

Choosing Lumber

The type of wood to be used in a project will depend largely on the size of the project and how visible the elements will be. For instance, the back, panels, or shelves in a cabinet don't have to be made from clear or select stock. No. 2 Common, or even No. 3 Common could be used. If you're allowed to go into the lumber yard and select the material yourself, you can almost always find a suitable lower-grade piece by digging through the stacks. (This isn't allowed in many larger yards, however, because of the work involved in restacking after a customer is through.) When building several small projects you can often get by with the lower grades by cutting around defects. For larger projects, the lower grades produce so much waste that they aren't economical.

Size. The next important step in purchasing lumber is to determine the correct size. Lumber is sold according to its *nominal* size, which indi-

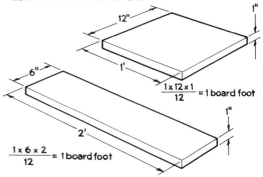

Each board is 1 board foot

$$\frac{1 \times 12 \times 1}{12} = 1 \text{ board foot}$$

$$\frac{1 \times 6 \times 2}{12} = 1 \text{ board foot}$$

Wood is purchased by the *board foot,* a measure of volume. To determine board footage, multiply the nominal dimensions of the board (in inches) by the actual length (in feet), and divide this product by 12.

cates the dimensions of the rough lumber in inches (1×2, 2×4, etc.). The first dimension is the thickness of the board and the second its width. After a board has been surfaced with a planer on all sides and dried, it will then be the *actual* size. For instance, the actual size of a 2×4 is $1\frac{1}{2} \times 3\frac{1}{2}$-inches.

If you have a planer you can purchase unsurfaced hardwood stock and plane it yourself, not only saving money, but in some cases planing stock to a specific size not commonly sold.

Volume. Lumber is commonly sold by the *board foot.* This unit is actually a calculation of volume. To find the number of board feet in a board, multiply the nominal thickness times the nominal width times the actual length in feet. This product is then divided by 12. Thus, a one-foot-long 1×12 and a two-foot-long 1×6 would both be sold as one board foot.

Moisture Content. When wood is sawn at the mill it is still "green," and its cells are saturated with moisture. In order to achieve a stable product, the excess moisture must be removed by drying the wood. Most cabinet and furniture wood is kiln-dried until its moisture content is reduced to 7 to 10 percent. The stability achieved by drying is not permanent, however. The empty cells will quickly pick up moisture if exposed to it for any length of time. For this reason wood that is

Nominal and Actual Sizes of Lumber (In inches)

Nominal Size	Actual Size
1×2	$^{25}\!/_{32} \times 1\frac{5}{8}$
2×2	$1\frac{5}{8} \times 1\frac{5}{8}$
1×3	$^{25}\!/_{32} \times 2\frac{5}{8}$
2×3	$1\frac{5}{8} \times 2\frac{5}{8}$
1×4	$^{25}\!/_{32} \times 3\frac{5}{8}$
2×4	$1\frac{5}{8} \times 3\frac{5}{8}$
1×5	$^{25}\!/_{32} \times 4\frac{5}{8}$
1×6	$^{25}\!/_{32} \times 5\frac{5}{8}$
2×6	$1\frac{5}{8} \times 5\frac{5}{8}$
1×8	$^{25}\!/_{32} \times 7\frac{1}{2}$
2×8	$1\frac{5}{8} \times 7\frac{1}{2}$
1×10	$^{25}\!/_{32} \times 9\frac{1}{2}$
2×10	$1\frac{5}{8} \times 9\frac{1}{2}$
1×12	$^{25}\!/_{32} \times 11\frac{1}{2}$
2×12	$1\frac{5}{8} \times 11\frac{1}{2}$

Grading of Western Pine

Select Grades

B & Better Select (1 & 2 Clear)

B & Better is the highest recognized grade of Pine—a practically perfect grade.

Although graded from the better side, even the backs of pieces in B & Btr. are of extremely high quality. To all practical purposes, the grade is clear.

B & Btr. Ponderosa Pine is used for finishing work of the very highest order, including interior trim, siding, paneling and cabinet work. It is also used for special industrial purposes where practically clear lumber in fairly large pieces is desired.

C Select

C Select is the second grade of Pine finish lumber and is designed to provide a top grade paint finish wood. Many pieces have a B & Btr. face with backs of a slightly lower quality than are permitted in the higher grade. Other pieces have a clear appearance but contain small spots of slightly torn grain, fine checks or possibly light pitch.

C Select is suitable for the very highest uses where entirely clear lumber is not required.

D Select

D Select includes pieces showing a finish appearance on one side only, the back of the board at times containing knots, pitch, wane or a combination thereof. In such cases, the face is correspondingly high. A type often used is a high line piece requiring a cut to eliminate a defect too serious to go into finish work.

It is an especially useful grade for the small planing mill and works up into various articles of woodwork with little waste.

Molding Grade

This is a special grade exhibiting characteristics of both Select and Factory grades. As the name suggests, a high yield in long, clear but *narrow* cuttings suitable for producing moldings is the basis of the grade.

Price of Molding Grade is intermediate between D Select and Third Clear, and the board will normally be found to be too good for Third Clear and not good enough for D Select. It is a sound value for the custom woodworker, because he can produce almost anything he needs from it at relatively reasonable cost.

Common Grades

Number 1 Common

Number 1 is the highest of five grades into which Pine Common is classified and contains pieces of the small knot variety. Knots are always sound, red or intergrown, smooth and are limited in size to slightly more than 2″ in diameter, depending upon the size of the piece. As a rule, the knots average very much smaller and are well distributed along the board.

Only pieces that show smooth dressing around knots are allowed in No. 1 Common. Knots in No. 1 Common are usually round or oval in shape and seldom occur on the edges of the board.

Number 2 Common

Number 2 Common, a very popular grade, represents a large percentage of the total production of Ponderosa Pine lumber. An all-around utility grade, it is suitable for all uses where a good grade of Common is required. It contains the same type of defects as No. 1, but in greater degree.

Generally similar to No. 1 in appearance, No. 2 allows larger and more pronounced characteristics. In narrow widths, knots are usually limited to 2½″ in diameter, and in wider widths to 3½″, but the average is considerably less than the maximum.

Supplied by Western Wood Products Association
Quoted from **Beautiful Wood**, Frank Paxton Lumber Co.

Number 3 Common

Number 3 comprises pieces of less uniform appearance than those in the two higher Common grades, varying from a piece of otherwise No. 1 or No. 2 quality with a single characteristic which causes it to be Grade No. 3, down to pieces showing numerous coarse knots, or boards with loose knots or an occasional knot hole. A piece containing a knot hole is generally of otherwise high quality.

A limited amount of heart shake and pitch may be found in low line pieces of No. 3, provided they do not occur in serious combination with other defects. A type frequently found is a piece with a No. 2 face, but showing several skips in dressing.

Standard Hardwood Grades

Firsts & Seconds (FAS) Grade

Use: For long, generally wide cuttings. As required for fixtures and interior trim.

Board Size: 6″ and wider, 8′ and longer.

Number of Clear Face Cuttings: Determined by Surface Measure (S.M.) of piece.

Size of Clear Face Cuttings: 4″ or wider by 5′ or longer and 3″ or wider by 7′ or longer.

Yield in Board of Clear Face Cuttings: 83⅓% or more.

Selects Grade

Use: For long, medium to narrow width cuttings, where only one good face is required. As required for molding and wall paneling.

Board Size: 4″ and wider, 6′ and longer.

Clear Face Cuttings and Yield: Same as Firsts & Seconds (FAS) on better face. Poorer face to grade not below No. 1 Common.

Number 1 Common Grade

Use: For medium length, narrow to wide cuttings. As required for furniture manufacture.

Board Size: 3″ and wider, 4′ and longer.

Number of Clear Face Cuttings: Determined by Surface Measure (S.M.) of piece.

Size of Clear Face Cuttings: 4″ or wider by 2′ or longer and 3″ or wider by 3′ or longer.

Yield in Board of Clear Face Cuttings: 66⅔% or more.

Important Exceptions

1. Walnut, butternut and all quarter-sawn woods are 5″ and wider in Firsts & Seconds (FAS) grade.
2. Minimum size of clear face cuttings in walnut and butternut are:
   a. FAS: 4″ or wider by 3′ or longer and
       3″ or wider by 6′ or longer.
   b. No. 1 Common: A clear face cutting shall not contain less than 144 sq. inches; minimum width 3″, minimum length 2′. There is no limit to number of cuttings.
3. FAS Poplar 8″ and wider must contain not less than 66⅔% heartwood on one side and not less than 50% on the reverse side. Pieces 7″ wide allow 1″ aggregate sapwood on either or both faces; pieces 6″ wide must be all heartwood. Clear stock with excessive sapwood is usually sold as "SAPS," or sometimes FAS (SND), meaning "sap-no-defect."

Supplied by National Hardwood Lumber Association
Quoted from **Beautiful Wood,** Frank Paxton Lumber Co.

to be used for furniture and cabinet construction must be stored inside for some time before usage. This is especially necessary for woods that have previously been stored outdoors.

Weight. Although the moisture content of green lumber varies considerably according to species, the percentage of weight lost in the drying and planing processes is fairly uniform. However, the *actual* weight of lumber also varies quite a bit according to species. If substantial quantities of lumber are to be ordered by mail, this factor is of some importance.

Plywood

Plywood is one of the most important modern woodworking materials. It is used to build everything from cabinets and furniture to boats and airplanes. It can be manufactured in large, relatively defect-free sheets that can be bent. It is light in weight, yet strong in comparison to solid wood. Expensive woods can be utilized because they cover only the top ply. And plywood doesn't split as easily as solid woods, and is more stable across the grain.

Shipping Weight Averages

	1″ Thick Lumber Per 100 feet, measured after kiln drying to 7% moisture content		
	Rough (Weight in lbs.)	S2S—25/32 (Surfaced on two sides; thickness 25/32″) (Weight in lbs.)	% Weight Reduction
Afrormosia	400	300	25%
Alder (S2S 1/16″)	250	205	18
Ash, Soft White or Brown	330	250	24
Balsa	100	80	20
Basswood	220	165	25
Beech	400	300	25
Birch	370	280	24
Butternut	265	200	25
Cedar, Aromatic Red	310	240	23
Cherry	340	255	25
Chestnut	270	200	26
Cottonwood	250	190	24
Ebony	600	450	25
Elm, Soft	310	235	24
Fir, Douglas (S4S)	260	195	25
Hickory	440	330	25
Holly	330	250	24
Magnolia	300	225	25
Mahogany (Genuine)	270	200	26
Mahogany (Philippine)	320	240	25
Mansonia	300	225	25
Maple, Hard	370	275	26
Maple, Soft	320	240	25
Oak, Red and White	400	300	25
Pecan	420	315	25
Pine, Parana	280	210	25
Pine, White and Ponderosa	220	175	20
Pine, Yellow	320	240	25
Poplar	290	215	26
Redgum	320	240	25
Redwood (S4S)	240	180	25
Rosewood	400	295	26
Sassafras	270	205	24
Spruce	240	180	25
Sycamore	320	240	25
Teak	350	260	26
Walnut	350	260	26
Willow	250	185	26

Delm Horst Instrument Co.

Plywood is one of the most important building materials today. It is shown here as paneling, and was also used to construct the shelves, doors, and table.

Plywood is always constructed with an odd number of plies for structural balance, and the grain direction of each sheet runs at right angles to the next to produce a panel that is dimensionally stable. Lumber core plywood is used when the appearance of the plywood edge is important. (Plywood edges can also be concealed with veneer tape or solid-wood molding.)

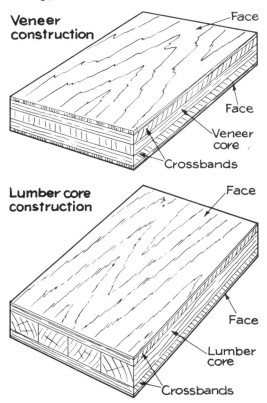

Veneer construction
Face
Face
Veneer core
Crossbands

Lumber core construction
Face
Face
Lumber core
Crossbands

How Plywood Is Made

Logs are peeled in a giant lathe to make the thin sheets of wood or plies that are bonded together to make plywood. Plywood is manufactured in two different ways. *Veneer core* plywood consists of an odd number of sheets, with the grain of each sheet running at right angles to that of the next sheet. This construction eliminates the problem of cross-grain weakness, and results in outer layers with matched grain. The plies with grain running horizontally are called *crossbands. Lumber core* plywood consists of a solid-wood inner core sandwiched between two or more sheets of thin veneer. The edges of lumber core plywood are much smoother than those of veneer core sheets: in many cases the edges can be worked like lumber. Lumber core sheets are primarily manufactured in the better grades of hardwood, and are used for fine cabinet work. These panels are quite a bit heavier than veneer core plywood, but are also more stable.

Plywood face veneers are cut in three different ways to achieve differences in the appearance of the wood. In *rotary cutting,* a large lathe is used to peel the thin veneer sheets from the log. Rotary cutting is commonly used for producing softwood plywood. A second method is *flat slicing.* This provides a more variegated grain pattern, and is

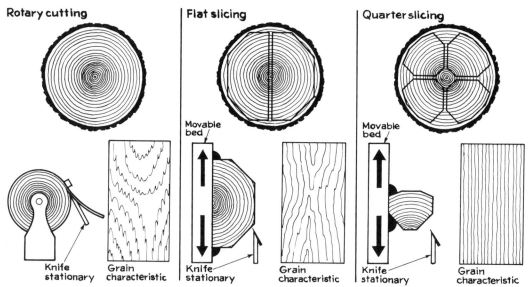

Rotary cutting · **Flat slicing** · **Quarter slicing**

Knife stationary · Grain characteristic · Movable bed · Knife stationary · Grain characteristic · Movable bed · Knife stationary · Grain characteristic

The three principal methods of cutting veneer. *Rotary cutting:* Sheets are cut from whole log after bark is removed. Log is mounted on a lathe, then rotated against knife. Result is a long, continuous sheet of veneer. *Flat slicing:* Log is halved and bolted to a movable bed. Log moves up and down, contacting knife on downstroke. Because veneer is sliced parallel to axis of tree, grain characteristic is like that of plain-sawn lumber. *Quarter slicing:* Log is quartered and veneers sliced at a tangent to axis of tree. Result is relatively narrow, straight-grained veneer pieces.

quite often used on hardwood plywoods. In this method, a half log is placed against a large knife and brought up and down against the knife to slice off slabs. This provides pieces that can be grain-matched. *Quarter slicing* is a third plywood veneer cutting method. The log is first cut into quarters, and these are then sliced at right angles to the growth rings. This produces veneer with quite an unusual appearance, with a good predominance of stripes in the grain. Veneers cut this way are used to produce matching panels of plywood. Because of the waste involved, these veneers are quite a bit more expensive.

The plywood veneers are held together with adhesive, and the type of adhesive used in bonding them together also determines what the plywood can be used for. There are basically three adhesive classifications:

EXTERIOR TYPE I: Fully waterproof, can withstand exposure to water.

EXTERIOR TYPE II: Water resistant, but not waterproof (the most common hardwood bond).

INTERIOR TYPE III: Somewhat water resis-

tant, but not recommended for high-humidity areas.

There are literally hundreds of types of plywood to choose from, including sheathing, or engineered grades; siding; paneling; fine-hardwood

Plywood is graded according to standards set by the American Plywood Association. The first line of this sample stamp (A-D) indicates the grade of the front and back faces. (For some types of plywoods, a general designation such as "Underlayment" is given instead.) Second line (Group 1) indicates the standards group followed in manufacture. (On construction plywoods, a span index may be substituted here.) Third line (Interior) indicates suitable use of the plywood. Last line (PS 4-320) indicates the product standards number and mill number.

A-D
GROUP 1 APA
INTERIOR
PS 4-320

Western Softwood Plywood

Standard Grades—Douglas Fir and Other Species

Interior Type

Grade	Face Veneer	Back Veneer
N-N	N[1]	N[1]
N-A, N-B or N-D	N[1,2]	A[2], B[3], or D[4]
A-A	A[2]	A[2]
A-B	A[2]	B[3]
A-D	A[2]	D[4] (Int. Back)
B-D	B[3]	D[4] (Int. Back)
C-D Underlayment	C[4] (Plugged)	D[4] (Int. Back)
C-D (Sheathing)	C[4,5] (Ext. Back)	D[4,5] (Int. Back)
B-B (Concrete Form)	B[3,6]	B[3,6]

Exterior Type

Grade	Face Veneer	Back Veneer
A-A	A[2]	A[2]
A-B	A[2]	B[3]
A-C	A[2]	C[4] (Ext. Back)
B-C	B[3]	C[4] (Ext. Back)
C (Plugged)-C	C[4] (Plugged)	C[4] (Ext. Back)
C-C (Sheathing)	C[4,5] (Ext. Back)	C[4,5] (Ext. Back)
B-B (Concrete Form)	B[3,6]	B[3,6]

Each type of plywood is graded according to how it is manufactured, what it is made of, what types of glues are used, and, generally, where it should be used. Although the grading system seems quite complicated, most building supply yards will carry only the most commonly used grades of plywood, thereby reducing some of the confusion. Hardwood and softwood plywoods are graded separately, according to rules set by the American Plywood Association.

Notes on Working with Plywood

Plywood is the best material for many projects, but in order to take advantage of its special characteristics, different techniques are needed to work with it. Most importantly, because plywood comes in large sheets it is necessary to lay out your project in advance to avoid wasting mate-

[1] "N" is top grade for natural finishes. Matched color and grain, with smooth surface. Small repairs are permitted, and up to three small mitered patches in 4×8 face. Usually found only in ¾" plywood, and not always available.

[2] "A" is top painting grade. Sound; contains no knots or pitch pockets. Numerous neat, mitered patches are permitted.

[3] "B" is solid grade. Contains no large open defects but allows small tight knots, pitch streaks, discolorations, square-edged patches and synthetic plugs.

[4] "C" and "D" grades permit numerous open defects. Normally used on back of panels with one good face; "C" on exterior type, "D" on interior type. "C-plugged" veneer is patched for use as underlayment.

[5] All fir plywood is sanded on two sides except sheathing, which is normally unsanded. Sheathing is also obtainable with plugged face, in which case it may be touch-sanded. Underlayment and sheathing are the same grade, except that veneer directly under face veneer is "C" in the former, "D" in the latter.

[6] Unless otherwise specified; concrete form fir plywood is oiled on faces and edge-sealed at the factory.

Hardwood Plywood Standard Grades

Grade	Face Veneer	Allowable Defects
1	PREMIUM—Book or slip matched for pleasing effect.	Burls, pin knots, slight color streaks and inconspicuous small patches in limited amounts.
1	GOOD— Unmatched, but sharp contrasts in color, grain and figure not permitted.	Burls, pin knots, slight color streaks and inconspicuous small patches in limited amounts.
2	SOUND—Free from open defects; a painting grade.	All appearance defects permitted so long as smooth and sound. Smooth patches permitted.
3	UTILITY—	All natural defects permitted; including open knots, worm holes and splits, maximum size of which are defined.
4	BACKING—	Defects practically unlimited; only strength and serviceability are considered.

plywood for furniture building; and even resin-coated plywood that can be painted without much surface preparation.

Plywood cuts should be carefully laid out to avoid waste. Be sure to allow for width of saw kerfs when planning cuts.

rial. You must also remember to cut the pieces so that the surface grain runs in the correct direction. It can be disastrous to cut up an entire piece of plywood, then find that one of your cabinet doors or a similar piece has the grain running sideways instead of up and down! It's a good idea to lay the sheet of plywood down on a pair of sawhorses, then draw every piece that is to be cut directly onto the plywood. To save time and prevent marking up a good sheet of plywood, much of this preliminary work can be done by cutting out scale drawings of the pieces and trial-fitting them on a scale drawing of the sheet of plywood. By twisting and turning the pieces different ways, you may find means of getting more material from each sheet. But remember to allow for loss of material at each saw kerf. In the case of cuts that are to be absolutely straight, try to line up all pieces of the same width so that they can be cut in one pass.

The simplest method, particularly for those without a large work area around a table saw, is to cut the sheet into smaller pieces for easy handling with a portable circular saw. A saw guide will help keep the cuts parallel to an edge. Once the sheet has been reduced to a more manageable

The first cuts on a full sheet of plywood will usually be made with a portable circular saw. In this case the plywood sheet is cut with the back side up. Be sure to support the plywood sheet so it won't sag during the cutting operation. This allows for a better cut and prevents saw blade from binding.

When cutting plywood with a handsaw, band saw, table or radial arm saw, face side should be *up*. On a table saw, blade is set so that just the teeth project above the surface as shown at right.

size, it can then be cut on a radial arm saw or table saw. A large table saw fitted with an extension arm and a table, or roller outboard supports can also be used to cut plywood sheets, but even then it is almost a two-man operation. If you have a sheet of plywood with a crooked edge and wish to rip a straight line on a table saw, the best method is to tack a wood guide strip on the back of the plywood. Then run this along the outside edge of the table saw to act as a guide.

Sawing techniques. Plywood should always be face down when cut with a portable circular saw or saber saw to avoid fuzzing on the finished side. When cutting with a handsaw, band saw, table saw, or radial arm saw, the face side should be up.

Use only a sharp plywood blade, or a fine-toothed power saw blade to cut plywood, to prevent splintering along the edges. The saw blade should have very little set. A special hollow-ground plywood blade is the best. Allow the blade to project above (or below) the plywood surface just the height of the teeth.

Make sure you support the panel properly so it won't sag during the cutting operation. The piece to be cut off should also be supported to prevent a fall after the final cut. This type of support also prevents a portable electric saw from

binding and jumping out of the cut at the last moment.

If properly cut with a fine-toothed saw blade, plywood edges won't need to be planed or jointed. In fact, they shouldn't be, as the edges will tear or splinter during this operation. Use of the proper saw blade is the answer.

You can prevent further splintering on extremely fine hardwood sheets by taping alongside the cut with masking tape, or by first scoring the wood with a sharp utility knife.

Techniques for joining plywood pieces are discussed in Chapter 5.

Particleboard

Particleboard was born out of necessity after World War II. Because many of the trees and forests in Europe were destroyed or rendered useless for normal timbering activities, scientists created a man-made product that could be used to rebuild war-torn countries. Even pieces of trees or twisted, useless appearing trees could be utilized in this manner. When the idea was brought to the United States, wood product manufacturers saw a chance to utilize what had before been waste wood. Today particleboard is one of the most important wood products for the wood craftsman.

How Particleboard Is Made

There are basically two kinds of particleboard, *mat-formed* (flat) and *extruded* (shaped). Most of the particleboard used in the furniture and cabinetry industry is mat-formed. In either case the basic raw material is wood particles in the form of flakes, shavings, splinters and "fines," or sifted sawdust. Usually these are residues from planing mills, veneer plants, or pulp mills.

The particles are first screened and classified to size, then dried to a uniform moisture content. They are then sprayed with a resin binder, and the coated particles are deposited in mats. The more resin that is used in proportion to wood particles, the more dense and inflexible the board will be. The mats are compressed under hot presses, sometimes with as much pressure as 1000 pounds per square inch. They are then cut to the proper size, usually 4×8 feet, and sanded smooth.

The particleboard used for most home furniture and cabinet work will be standard *medium density* particleboard. It is available in thick-nesses from ½ to 1 inch and can be found at most local building-supply dealers.

Extruded particleboard is normally ordered by large furniture manufacturers for specific uses, such as bathroom vanity tops. Again, the particles are coated with resin, then pushed through a hot die to form the specific shape. The sheets are then cut to the lengths needed. Some cove-top and rounded-edge pieces for cabinets are manufactured in this manner. An advantage is that plastic laminate can be bonded to the board as it is being formed. Very little extruded particleboard is available for home usage.

One of the advantages of working with particleboard is that there is less chance of warping because it has no grain. This makes particleboard panels a great base for plastic laminates or veneers. Particleboard machines extremely well and can be sawn, routed, or drilled with ordinary shop tools, without splintering of edges. The tools must be sharp, however, and because of the abrasive quality of the binding resins, it's a good idea to use carbide-tipped tools.

The greatest advantage of particleboard, how-

Left: When covered with veneer or plastic laminate, particleboard is an excellent material for kitchen cabinet doors. *Below:* Particleboard can be worked like solid wood in many cases, but because of its abrasive qualities it should be cut with carbide-tipped tools.

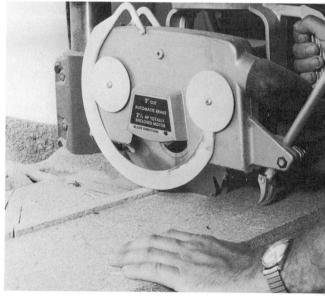

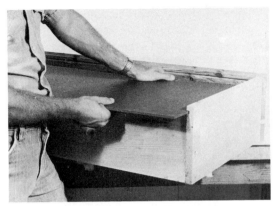

Hardboard is another composition board important to the home cabinetmaker. It is often used for drawer bottoms.

This creates a "plywood" that is very stable and easy to machine. Plastic laminate can also be used as the outside sandwich material. In some cases, the surface of the particleboard itself is printed with wood grains.

Although particleboard can be fastened with nails, it doesn't hold them as well as does solid wood. Small nails no larger than No. 4's should be used, and these should be cement-coated. Pilot holes for screws should be a bit smaller than those for solid wood, and sheet metal pan screws should be used. Almost any joint that is used with plywood or solid wood can be used. However, stronger holding power can be achieved with joints such as dovetail, dado, and rabbet.

ever, is its versatility. There is almost no limit to the variations of this material that can be created, and furniture manufacturers can create a custom style to suit particular needs. For instance, fire retardants, coloring agents, or decay resistant agents can be added to the binders during manufacture. One of the most promising uses is as core material, overlaid with fine hardwood veneers.

Hardboard

Hardboard is also a composition board made up of wood fibers and a binding resin. Because it is a man-made product, it has no grain and it is equally strong in all directions. It is available in standard and tempered sheets. (Tempered hardboard is quite a bit stronger than standard hard-

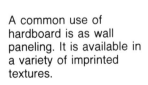

A common use of hardboard is as wall paneling. It is available in a variety of imprinted textures.

board and is also more moisture-resistant.) The hardboard surface is smooth and dense and ready to finish. Hardboard is available with one surface smooth, S1S, and both surfaces smooth, S2S, as well as in a variety of textures such as simulated brick, leather, or stone. It is also available with perforations that enable it to be used as an acoustical material or as a method of hanging items by using special hooks that fit into the holes. Hardboard is available in $1/16$- to $3/4$-inch thicknesses in the standard 4×8 size sheets, and in widths up to five feet and lengths to 16 feet. Most hardboard used in furniture and cabinetry work is utilized for case backs and drawers. However, one of the prime advantages of hardboard is that it can be bent to form in a home workshop. This allows it to be used for covering the fronts of counters or other curved surfaces. Naturally, the thinner the hardboard, the sharper the bend can be made. Wetting the hardboard with warm water will help in making smaller bends.

Hardboard can be machined and worked just like solid wood with ordinary shop tools, but because of the resins the tools will quickly become dull unless you utilize carbide-tipped tools. It can be glued, nailed, stapled, or fastened with screws. Pan head sheet metal screws work best in most cases. When boring holes, bore with the face up and use a backer board to avoid tearing the back.

Veneer

In the earlier civilizations, veneering meant embellishing wooden surfaces with exotic things such as ivory, tortoise shell, metals and even precious stones, but today the word means the use of precious woods to cover more economical woods. There are several advantages to veneers. Probably the most important is that they are available in rare and beautiful woods such as burls, crotches and other grain figures that just aren't available as solid wood. The other main advantage is that face veneers cost a great deal less than solid lumber. What many craftsmen don't know is that veneered panels are actually stronger than solid wood panels and won't warp, shrink, crack or expand as will solid wood panels, especially in

Unusually figured wood is often used in veneer form to provide a decorative accent on door and drawer fronts. Shown is a walnut frame-and-panel bureau with walnut crotch door panels. *Richard Cohen, Warwick, New York.*

Working Characteristics of Composition Boards

	Thick Panels—¼″–1½″	Thin Panels—⅛″–⅜″		
	Particleboard		**Hardboard**	
	40# *cu. ft.*	*Standard*	*Tempered*	*Specialties*
Bending	Fair	Good	Excellent	Good
Drilling	Good	Good	Excellent	Excellent
Hardness	Medium	Medium	High	High
Laminating	Good	Good	Excellent	Excellent
Nailing	Good	Fair	Good	Good
Painting	Unfilled—Fair Filled—Good	Fair	Excellent	Excellent
Punching	Fair	Fair	Excellent	Good
Routing	Good	Fair	Excellent	Good
Sanding	Good	Fair	Excellent	Good
Sawing	Good	Fair	Excellent	Good
Screw Holding	Good	Fair	Good	Good
Shaping	Good	Fair	Excellent	Good
Water Resistance	Interior or Exterior	Interior	Exterior	Interior or Exterior

the larger sizes needed for doors or tabletops.

Veneer is available in large sheets for use in making up plywood slabs; in edge-banding strips to cover the edges of plywood projects; and in small squares that are used to create matched faces as described in Chapter 11. Standard thicknesses of veneer available for home use are ⅟₂₈- and ⅟₆₄-inch.

Veneers are cut from domestic or exotic species of trees with one of the three methods described earlier to produce rotary-, flat-, or quarter-cut grain configurations. In addition, veneers are cut from several other areas of the tree to produce unusual figures that do not appear in the main log. *Butt* or *stump* figures are found in the junction of the larger roots of a few species, notably

Decorative curly or "fiddleback" figure veneer is often used for furniture as well as for musical instruments. On this mahogany tambour desk (c. 1805), curly maple is used to accent the drawer fronts. *Museum of the City of New York.*

walnut. The grain has a distorted, twisted pattern. *Crotch* figures are produced in the fork of a tree where a large branch joins the main trunk. The figure often looks like a feathery plume or a horse's tail. *Burl* figures are produced in a knob on the side of the tree that contains a number of dormant buds. They are characterized by a highly individual pattern of irregular swirls.

Burls from walnut, cherry and redwood trees are among the most beautiful furniture veneers.

Veneers are available in almost every type of wood imaginable. Most veneers are sold by mail order through woodworking supply houses, and in most cases a few dollars will bring a sample box of the veneers in stock. A list of veneer suppliers can be found at the end of this book.

The unusual "bird's eye" figure found in some maple logs is commonly available in veneer form. On this early 19th-century work table, bird's eye maple was used on the top and drawer fronts. *Museum of the City of New York.*

Mahogany is well known for its highly figured wood. Like walnut, it yields highly decorative crotch, burl, and stump figures. This bedroom table by Duncan Phyfe utilizes both solid mahogany and mahogany veneers. *Museum of the City of New York.*

3

Fasteners and Glues

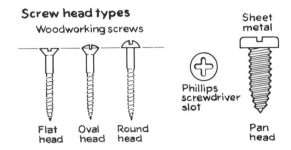

Screw head types
Woodworking screws

Flat head — Oval head — Round head

Phillips screwdriver slot

Sheet metal — Pan head

Other screw head types

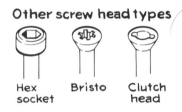

Hex socket — Bristo — Clutch head

Screws

Choosing the proper screw and using the right screwdriver to fasten it in place are important for successful wood joinery. If you use too small a screw, it won't hold; too large a screw may split the wood. Similarly, a screwdriver that is too large or small may slip and mar surrounding wood or tear up the screwdriver head.

Regular woodworking screws have flat, round, or oval heads, and the screw head opening accepts either a regular or Phillips screwdriver. The pan head or sheet-metal screw is also commonly used by woodworkers to fasten plywood, particleboard or hardboard. This is a self-tapping screw designed for fastening metal to wood.

Other screw head openings for special screws include hex socket, bristo and clutch head. Each of these requires a special screwdriver or wrench.

The most common woodworking screw is the flat head, mainly because it can either be set level with the surface of the wood or countersunk and concealed. Where screw head appearance isn't important and the screw doesn't need to be level with the wood, round head screws may be used.

Oval head screws have a low profile so the heads may either be left exposed or counterbored and concealed.

Once the correct type of screw is found, the next decision is the correct size. The screw should not only be large enough in diameter, but long enough to hold properly. Normally, two-thirds of the screw, or the entire thread length, should be in the "bottom" or base piece of wood.

Screw sizes run from No. 0, the smallest, to No. 24. They are available in $3/16$- to 6-inch lengths. In addition to the different sizes and types, screws are available in several different metals including steel, brass, aluminum, stainless steel, and galvanized or plated. When you buy decorative hardware, the package will include screws with decorative heads and finishes to match the hardware.

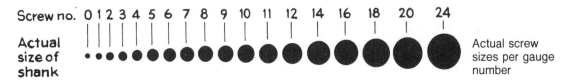

Screw no. 0 1 2 3 4 5 6 7 8 9 10 11 12 14 16 18 20 24

Actual size of shank

Actual screw sizes per gauge number

Driving Screws

Every screw must have a pilot, or starting, hole. Don't drive screws in place or start them with a hammer. This merely dents the wood, and the screw will work loose in a short time.

For small screws a woodworker's awl or an ice pick can be used to punch a small starting hole. For larger screws, however, you should bore a hole. The hole should be sized according to the screw as indicated in the chart on page 49.

For proper holding power and ease of driving, the pilot hole should be drilled first, and then the top of the hole bored larger for the screw's shank. If the screw is to be counterbored and concealed, the top of the hole should be bored with a large

enough bit to recess the head. If the screw is to be flush with the surface—countersunk—use a star-shape countersink bit in a portable electric drill to cut the fan-shaped opening. A better method of countersinking is to use one of the combination bits that bores the pilot hole, shank hole, and either counterbores or countersinks all in one operation.

It's best to clamp, tack nail, or hold parts together in some manner before fastening permanently with screws. Make sure all parts are in correct position and held tightly, then bore the hole. Hold the screw in place in the hole to make sure it is started squarely.

Select the proper screwdriver and drive the screw in place. Hold the screwdriver straight up and down to drive the screw.

Below left: Starter holes for small screws such as those used in fastening cabinet hardware in place can best be made with a woodworker's awl.
Right: Drilling sequence for concealed screw:
A. Drill pilot hole, **B.** Drill shank clearance hole,
C. Counterbore, **D.** Screw driven in place.
Below right: An easier method of boring pilot holes is to use a screwsink. This is a combination bit that can be used to make pilot hole, shank hole and counterbore or countersink all in one operation.

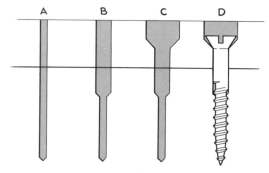

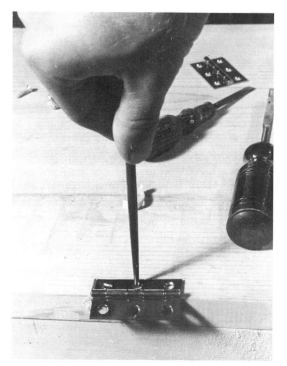

When a long line of screws are to be driven, stagger them along either side of the line for more holding power. A ratchet type screwdriver will speed up the job, or you can use a power screwdriver.

Once the screw has been driven in place you may wish to conceal it. There are three common methods of concealing the screw heads: with Plastic Wood, dowels or wooden plugs, and wood buttons. In rough carpentry, you may wish to cover the screw head holes with Plastic Wood or another similar filler. However, for many pieces you will need a more finished surface. For this, use wooden dowels or plugs cut from wood matching the project. These plugs can easily be cut on a drill press with a special plug cutter that is sized to fit the screw heads. The plugs can be simply tapped in place or glued, then chiseled and sanded level with the surrounding surface.

Another method of covering screws, especially

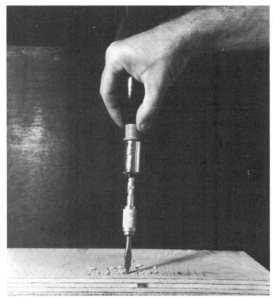

A Yankee ratchet-action screwdriver makes short work of driving screws.

The most efficient way to drive screws is to use a power screwdriver or a power drill. The drill should have an adjustable speed control to allow low speeds needed for driving screws.

In a confined place, you may have to resort to an offset screwdriver.

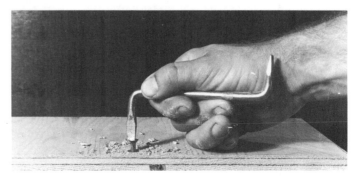

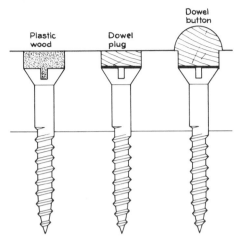

Methods used to conceal screw holes include wood filler compound, wood plugs, and purchased buttons.

Wood plugs can be cut from matching wood with a plug cutter in a drill press. Insert plugs in holes dabbed with glue, then cut off flush with surface.

Wood buttons are a popular method of covering screw holes in furniture. They are merely pushed in place and can be flipped out with a thin-bladed screwdriver.

in fine furniture, is to use wood buttons. These are purchased from woodworking specialty companies, and can merely be pushed in place over the counter-bored screw heads, leaving a rounded surface. To retighten or remove screws, you just pry out the buttons with a screwdriver.

Nails

Using the correct type of nail in the correct size prevents damage to the wood of a project and also provides the necessary holding strength. Basi-

cally, there are two types of nails: *common* nails, those with large flat heads; and *casing* or *finishing* nails. Casing or finishing nails are used for most cabinet and furniture work, and common nails for rough carpentry.

Nails are made in a variety of materials, including brass and aluminum, but the most commonly used nails are made of mild steel. Nails are sized according to the "penny" system, which used to indicate cost but now designates the length of the nail from the point to the head. The length of small nails can be calculated by dividing the penny size by four, then adding ½ inch to this

Most commonly used screw sizes

Shank Number	Length (In inches)
0, 1, 2, 3	¼
2, 3, 4, 5, 6, 7	⅜
2, 3, 4, 5, 6, 7, 8	½
3, 4, 5, 6, 7, 8, 9, 10	⅝
4, 5, 6, 7, 8, 9, 10, 11	¾
6, 7, 8, 9, 10, 11, 12	⅞
6, 7, 8, 9, 10, 11, 12, 14	1
6, 7, 8, 9, 10, 11, 12, 14, 16	1¼
6, 7, 8, 9, 10, 11, 12, 14, 16, 18	1½
7, 8, 9, 10, 11, 12, 14, 16, 18	1¾
8, 9, 10, 11, 12, 14, 16, 18, 20	2
10, 11, 12, 14, 16, 18, 20	2¼
12, 14, 16, 18, 20	2½
14, 16, 18, 20	2¾
16, 18, 20	3
16, 18, 20	3½
18, 20	4

Pilot hole and Clearance hole sizes

Screw Gauge No.	Pilot Hole (In inches)	Clearance Hole (In Inches)
1	¹/₃₂	⁵/₆₄
2	¹/₃₂	³/₃₂
3	¹/₁₆	⁷/₆₄
4	¹/₁₆	⁷/₆₄
5	⁵/₆₄	⅛
6	³/₃₂	⁹/₆₄
7	³/₃₂	⁵/₃₂
8	³/₃₂	¹¹/₆₄
9	⁷/₆₄	³/₁₆
10	⅛	³/₁₆
11	⅛	¹³/₆₄
12	⁵/₃₂	⁷/₃₂
14	³/₁₆	¼
16	³/₁₆	⁵/₁₆
18	¹³/₆₄	⁵/₁₆
20	⁷/₃₂	²¹/₆₄

For driving common nails in rough carpentry jobs, a 16-oz. hammer would be appropriate. For heavier jobs you can use a 22-oz. framing hammer. But for fine finishing work choose the smaller 7- to 13-oz. hammers.

Driving nails for finish work requires more finesse, because you don't want to leave hammer marks around the nail head. To avoid this, drive the nail in the last eighth-inch or so with a nail set. When driving a nail in hardwood, bore a pilot hole before starting the nail. Then drive the nail

When driving nails in hardwoods, predrill nail holes first, using a drill bit that is slightly smaller than the nail. After nail is driven in place, it is set below wood surface with a nail set as shown below. Then nail hole is filled with Plastic Wood or wood putty and sanded smooth when dry.

product. For instance, a 4d, or four-penny nail, is 1½-inches long. This calculation only works for nails up to 10d, however. Nail sizes range from 2d, one inch long, to 60d, which is six inches long. In addition, the diameter of the nail is listed in wire gauge. The chart on page 50 gives the penny number, wire gauge, and number of nails per pound.

The length of a nail should be about three times as long as the thickness of the face piece in order to provide proper holding power.

Just as in fastening with screws, choosing the right driving tool is important when driving nails.

Nail Sizes

Common Nails			
Penny Size	Length (In inches)	Diameter (Wire gauge)	Approximate Number in a Pound
2d	1	15	830
3d	1¼	14	528
4d	1½	12½	316
5d	1¾	12½	271
6d	2	11½	168
7d	2¼	11½	150
8d	2½	10¼	106
9d	2¾	10¼	96
10d	3	9	69
12d	3¼	9	63
16d	3½	8	49
20d	4	6	31
30d	4½	5	24
40d	5	4	18
50d	5½	3	14
60d	6	2	11

Finishing Nails			
Penny Size	Length (In inches)	Diameter (Wire Gauge)	Approximate Number in a Pound
2d	1	16½	1351
3d	1¼	15½	807
4d	1½	15	584
5d	1¾	15	500
6d	2	13	309
8d	2½	12½	189
10d	3	11½	121
16d	3½	11	90
20d	4	10	62

down only until the bottom of the head bulge hits the wood surface, and use a nail set to drive the nail flush or below the surface of the wood. Finally, cover the nail head with Plastic Wood or other filler material.

Driving Screws and Nails in Plywood

The size of the screw to be used is determined by the thickness of the plywood you're using. Below is a screw size chart. In most cases, all screws and

Plywood Thickness (In inches)	Screw Length (In Inches)	Screw Size	Pilot Hole (In inches)	Clearance Hole (In inches)
¾	1½	#8	⅛	11/64
⅝	1¼	#8	⅛	11/64
½	1¼	#6	3/32	9/64
⅜	1	#6	3/32	9/64
¼	1	#4	1/16	7/64

In fastening plywood, the size of screw to be used depends on the thickness of plywood. When nailing a plywood edge (shown below), use a small-diameter nail and take care not to drive it too close to the edge to avoid separating the plies.

nails will be countersunk and the holes filled with wood putty.

When joining plywood edges, it is important to use small-diameter screws or nails to avoid wedging the plies apart.

The old-fashioned "pinch dog" isn't really a fastener at all, but a sort of clamp. It is driven into the back of a project to help hold it together until the glue sets, then removed.

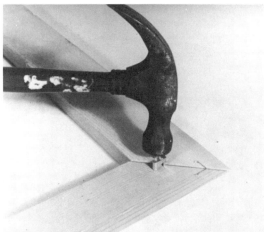

Chevron miter joint fasteners are shaped at 90° angle. They can be driven below the surface of the wood with a nail set and filled over with wood putty compound.

Miscellaneous Fasteners

In addition to nails and screws, there are numerous other metal fasteners for furniture. They range from the "pinch dogs" used by old-time cabinetmakers to help hold together a glued joint, to the newer "clamp nails" engineered to fasten all kinds of wood joints.

Corrugated Fasteners

Corrugated fasteners are ribbed metal pieces with one sharpened end. They are usually used for

Corrugated fasteners are primarily used for rough assemblies.

fastening rough frames in projects where appearance is not important. They can also be used for edge-fastening stock or on wide stock for some rough work. The wood pieces are held tightly together and the fastener started in one piece of wood. Then it is started in the other piece, and tapped on alternate sides until driven home. The fastener should penetrate to about half the wood's thickness.

Corrugated fasteners should not be driven in with the wood grain, as they will split some hard woods. For proper holding power, drive corrugated fasteners in from both sides of the stock, staggering them along the joint line.

Chevrons

Chevrons are used in the same way as the corrugated fastener, except they are made to be recessed below the surface and covered with wood putty. They are also available in an L-shape which gives a bit more holding power on corner joints.

"Skotch" Fasteners

These are another type of steel spline, and are similar to the corrugated fasteners and chevrons except that their edges are wider than the rest of the spline for added strength.

Skotch wood joiners are used primarily for rough assembly, or to repair items such as screen door frames. *Superior Fastener Corp.*

Clamp Nails

These are a special type of steel spline. They are made for both home shop and production use, and are a favorite fastener with many furniture manufacturers. They can also be applied easily by the home craftsman, using nothing more than a special blade in a table saw or radial arm saw. In use, the joint cut is made on both pieces of stock. Then, using a special 22-gauge circular saw blade, a saw kerf is cut to create a spline opening. The metal spline is then positioned and driven in with a few blows of a hammer. A blind spine joint can also be made to conceal the metal fastener. Clamp nails can be used to fasten picture or sash frames, rounded projects, and odd-angled projects.

Teenuts

These are nothing more than a threaded metal nut that can be driven into a piece of wood. A bolt hole is first drilled, then the metal threaded "nut," which has teeth on one side, is driven in place. Turning the bolt from the opposite side pulls the Teenut tightly in place, holding the two wood pieces together. A similar fastening device is the Rosan wood insert, which is threaded to receive a common stove bolt.

Clamp Nails provide somewhat more holding power than other types of steel spline and can be used on odd-angled and round projects. They can be concealed by making a stopped cut in each joining edge as shown. *Clamp Nail Co.*

"Tite-Joint" Fasteners

Similar to the Teenut but a bit more complicated, this fastener also bolts two pieces of wood together. But in this case the bolt is built into the fastener.

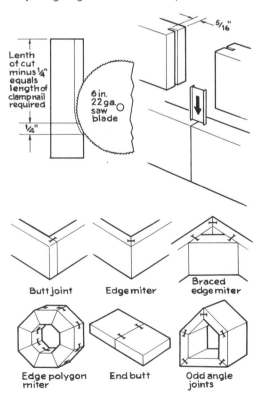

Hanger Bolts

This is a different type of fastener, and it's mostly utilized to hold turned legs in place. A hole is bored in the leg and a somewhat larger hole in the other wood piece. The bolt has a screw thread on one end which is turned in place in the leg. The opposite end has a bolt thread which can be placed through a wooden block and held in place with a washer and nut. Or it can be turned into a threaded metal angle plate specially made for holding wooden legs in place.

Large projects such as picnic tables that should be assembled with bolts can utilize Teenuts. Bore the appropriate size hole and tap "nut" in place. Turn threaded bolt into nut from opposite side.

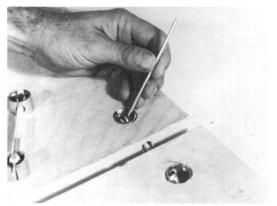

Tite-Joint fasteners are similar to Teenuts, but are more often used for edge joining. To install, bore a ⅞-inch hole in the wood using template supplied. Then bore a ⁷⁄₁₆-inch hole from edge of wood to first hole, tap holding ring in place, and turn in threaded bolt.
Above right: Position the two pieces of wood together, insert the bolt into hole in second piece, and tap second holding ring in place.
Right: Tighten the assembly by turning the small round nut inside first holding ring. *Knape & Vogt Mfg. Co.*

To fasten legs in place on a table you can use hanger bolts. These have a wood-screw thread on one end and a bolt thread on the other so they can be bolted in place or turned into metal leg-holding plates.

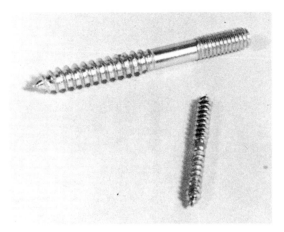

Dowel screws have a wood-screw thread on each end. They are installed by boring a hole in each joining piece, then "screwing" the pieces together by turning them in opposite directions.

Metal mending plates are used primarily for repair. They can also be used to provide more strength on the undersides of chairs and tables and in other places where they won't be visible. They're available in several sizes and shapes.

Dowel Screws

These are like hanger bolts, except they have wood screw threads on each end. They are installed by boring a slightly under-sized hole, then turning the metal screw threads into both pieces.

Metal Mending Plates

These are thin metal plates that come in a variety of sizes and shapes. They are placed in position over a wood joint and wood screws are used to fasten them in place to reinforce the joint. They

are mostly used for bracing, such as on the under side of a table apron, or to brace a thin frame.

Wall and Masonry Fasteners

Other types of fasteners include those that are used to fasten items to a hollow wall or to a masonry wall. Hollow wall anchors or toggle bolts are the typical choice for fastening to a hollow wall, while screw anchors and Rawl plugs are used for anchoring items to masonry. These fasteners are often used to hang cabinets to walls and for fastening built-ins in place.

Corner braces such as the one at left can be used to brace a 90° corner, or as a holding fastener for a leg. Braces with a decorative finish (right) can be used to brace exposed arms of chairs, etc.

Glues

Gluing is one of the most common methods of joining wood. Usually glue is used in conjunction with metal fasteners such as screws or nails, but in some cases glue will still be the primary holding material. Choosing the right glue, and using it properly, can often mean the difference between a successful joint and one that fails.

In days past, the woodworkers didn't have much choice of glues. The old-time cabinet and furniture builders had only one glue—animal glue, also called hide glue. Today we have a wide variety of glues for almost anything from fine furniture to water skis—even airplane parts are glued together.

Hide Glue

The old-fashioned hide or animal glue is still available, but it is not used as much as in the past. It is made from bones, hides, and hoofs of animals. Hide glue comes in two forms, dry and liquid. The powder or flakes of dry hide glue must first be soaked in water for a few hours, then melted in a special melting pot or double boiler. Liquid hide glues available today don't require this treatment, and they're still popular with fine furniture builders, especially those who restore old furniture and antiques. Setting time on liquid hide glue is fairly long, so it gives the operator a bit of time to shift and adjust parts. Hide glue provides a dark glue line and it isn't waterproof. The liquid form is available in a plastic squeeze bottle, and it's one of the stronger glues when applied properly.

Polyvinyl Resin Emulsion (White) Glue

Probably the most popular all-purpose glue used today, common white glue is excellent for the majority of interior woodworking projects. It is a fairly fast setting glue that can be used in a wide range of working temperatures—which is very important. Ordinarily, white glue doesn't stain either wood or tools. However, when it touches metal or oak it will leave a dark purple stain. This type of glue sets as its moisture evaporates, and it is not waterproof. It shouldn't be used for projects exposed to moisture or humidity or for outside projects. The glue is available in squeeze bottles and is easy to apply. Although it cures in a few hours at normal temperatures, it sets sooner. One of its problems is that the thermoplastic material in the glue softens if exposed to heat. This is why large clumps of glue are hard to sand— they actually melt from the heat of a power sander. For the same reason, white glue shouldn't be used for projects that will be exposed to heat.

For many years the only glue available to woodworkers was hide or animal glue. It is still available; in liquid form, or as flakes which must be heated.

The most popular shop glue is polyvinyl, or ordinary white glue. It is ideal for most interior projects because it is easy to use, quick-drying, and cleans up with water.

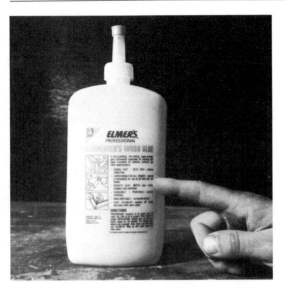

Aliphatic resin glue has quite a bit more holding power than white glue, and sets much faster. It is a favorite with leading furniture manufacturers. Always read instructions for any glue before using.

White glues are odorless, nontoxic, and non-flammable. The glue line is colorless and shelf life is long if it is kept tightly capped. Many craftsmen prefer to buy a few small squeeze bottles, then buy white glue by the gallon, continually filling the smaller bottles as needed.

Aliphatic Resin Glue

This is a cream-colored glue, also called "carpenter's glue," that is available in squeeze bottles. It

Plastic resin glue is used on projects that will be exposed to moisture. It comes as a powder and is mixed with water; mix only as much as needed.

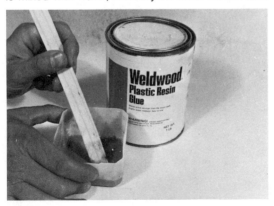

has many of the same properties as white glue, but it is much stronger. In fact, in most cases, the glue line will be quite a bit stronger than the surrounding wood. Aliphatic-resin glues are extremely fast setting glues, and often the project can be worked within a half hour of assembly. Clamping time is 30 minutes. It is a bit more resistant to solvents and heat than white glue, but is not moisture proof. It should only be used on interior projects. One of its advantages is that it can be sanded more easily than white glue. It can also be used in a wider range of temperatures. This glue is especially formulated for use on cabinets and fine furniture, and it's one of the best glues for this purpose. It cleans up with warm water.

Urea Formaldehyde Resin (Plastic Resin) Glue

The most common form of plastic resin glue is a powder. It is mixed with water to a thick creamy paste. Plastic resin is a moisture-resistant glue which has a tan glue line. Only enough should be mixed at one time to do a specific project. Because it is moisture resistant, it is a good glue for salad bowls, cutting boards, and other items that will be subjected to moisture for short periods of time. It is also a common cabinet glue and often is used to laminate woods together. Plastic resin is a long setting glue, and so can be used only where set time poses no problem. One of its disadvantages is that when dry it absorbs water unless the container is kept tightly closed, so shelf life is shorter than for prepared glues. Plastic resin glue requires four to eight hours of clamping time at normal room temperatures; however, heat will shorten the time.

Resorcinol Formaldehyde Glue

A completely waterproof glue that can be used for gluing items such as boats, water skis, and other items that will be continuously in contact with water. It should be used only with exterior plywoods. It has a dark purple glue line. This thermosetting glue is available in two parts: a dark purple resin and a powdered catalyst. Mix only enough needed for the job. It is quite expensive and sets in eight to ten hours at room temperature. Heat will shorten the curing time.

Casein Glue

This glue is made from mild curds and is available in powdered form to which you must add water. It is water resistant and is often used in areas where the moisture content of the wood is fairly high. It is highly abrasive to tools and stains wood. It is not often used except for special jobs.

Contact Cement

This is one of the most important glues for the cabinetmaker because it's used for gluing plastic laminates and veneers to wood surfaces. It is applied by spreading a thin layer of glue with a brush or short nap roller over both of the mating surfaces. After the glue dries, the two pieces are pressed together using a roller or block of wood and hammer. The pieces bond on contact, so a bit of experience is necessary to make sure the pieces are in position before allowing them to touch. (See Chapters 11 and 12 for details on bonding techniques.) The glue cleans up with lacquer thinner. The nonflammable type of contact cement is much safer to use than the flammable type; it is a latex formulation that washes up with water (before it sets up). However, the nonflammable type can't be used on thin veneers because the moisture in the glue causes the wood to curl. When using flammable contact glue, make sure there is adequate ventilation and that there are no flames or pilot lights in the building.

Epoxy

Epoxies and other "wonder glues" are glues that come in two parts that must be mixed. They are used for special purposes, such as gluing metals, plastic, or glass to wood. They are extremely strong but brittle glues.

Glues and Their Applications

Name	Description	Temperature	Preparation	Application	Clamping Time
Hide	An excellent glue for fine furniture building. Good holding power. It is not waterproof. Long clamp up time.	Room temperature (70° or better).	None needed for liquid kind.	Apply thin coat to both surfaces. When tacky, adhere.	2 to 3 hours
Polyvinyl	A good all purpose glue that can be used for most interior cabinet and furniture building.	Room temperature (best at 60° or above).	None needed	Squeeze bottle	1 to 2 hours
Aliphatic Resin	Similar to polyvinyl glue but has stronger holding power. Is more resistant to heat and solvents than polyvinyl.	Above 45°	None needed	Squeeze bottle	1 to 2 hours
Resorcinol Form-aldehyde	Excellent glue for exterior work, or work that will be subjected to water.	70° or warmer. Applying heat helps.	Mix powder and liquid	Spatula or stiff brush to both surfaces.	16 hours
Casein	Mostly used for gluing oily woods such as teak, ebony, lemon, etc.	Above 32°. Works better in warmer temperatures.	Mix with water	Spatula to both surfaces.	2 to 3 hours
Contact Cement	Good for adhering plastic laminate or veneers to wood.	70° or above	None	Spread thin coat on both surfaces; allow to dry.	None, adheres instantly.
Epoxy	Used to bond metal, glass, etc. to wood.	Temperature isn't important	Mix two parts together	Spread thin coat on both surfaces.	None needed

Contact cement is used to bond veneer and plastic laminate to wood surfaces. It available in nonflammable (water base) and standard formulas. (Nonflammable type cannot be used on thin veneers.)

Applying Glues

The first and most important rule in applying glues is to carefully read the instructions on the back of the glue package. Some glues work best at certain temperatures. Try to work at the proper "room temperature." But don't forget the wood. It doesn't do any good to work in a warm room but with woods that have been brought in cold from the outside. Two-part glues, and other glues that must be mixed, should be mixed carefully following directions. Mix only a little more than you estimate is needed for the job. If you mix too little, you will run out of glue before the job is finished and have to stop in the middle and mix up a new batch. Make sure glues are mixed thoroughly with no lumps.

Spread the glue according to directions. In the case of squeeze-bottle glues this is normally no problem, but avoid glue runs and drips on the project and around the shop. They're not only messy, but can be hazardous. Mixed glues are often spread with a small paddle, spatula, or in some cases with a small stiff-bristle brush.

Make sure you have everything on hand before you begin gluing: all parts, all clamps needed, special jigs, a solid flat work space, clamp pads,

etc. Also have on hand several paper towels, three or four inches in size, to wipe excess glue. If gluing a large project, you may wish to cover the work space with a sheet of newspaper for easier clean up. A flat work surface will make it easier to get the work square and true.

Before applying any glue, dry fit the joints together to make sure they fit. If there are a number of pieces to be assembled, number or letter the pieces with mating joints. Then spread the glue evenly and mate the joining pieces together. Many craftsmen apply a little glue on each piece, then spread it with a wooden paddle.

Glue can be applied in two ways. The *single-spread* method is applying glue only to one surface; *double spread* is applying glue to both surfaces. In most cases all surfaces should be well coated, but not with so much glue that you will have excessive glue squeezing out of the joint. A normal good glue film would be about .005 inches thick. But it takes a bit of practice to judge this accurately. For most projects use a double spread. Fit the joints together and, if possible, slide them back and forth a bit to insure that all edges of the surfaces are well coated.

Apply the clamps. Even when nailing or screwing, it is often best to clamp the pieces first to

The result of not wiping away glue squeeze-out. Stain will not take over glue.

Clamp a glued project with enough pressure to hold it securely. Note use of wood block between project and clamp jaws.

prevent their being knocked out of place during the nailing or screwing operation. Use protective wooden or leather strips under the clamps, and if many clamps are used, such as when laminating or edge-gluing, tighten each clamp a bit at a time so the stock doesn't become warped from too much pressure at one point. In most instances, glue manufacturers recommend a clamping pressure of about 100 to 150 pounds per square inch for softwoods. For hardwoods, 150 to 200 pounds is required. A normal bar clamp can be turned with both hands to produce over 1200 pounds *in the immediate area.* The proper spacing and use

of clamps is important. If pieces don't fit together without a lot of pressure, reset them.

As soon as the wood is clamped solidly, wipe away excess glue. In many instances this can be done with a soft cloth dipped in warm water, then rung out. Make sure you get all glue from the surface. On easy-to-get-to joints, such as edge joints, you won't have to worry so much about clean up. The resulting glue joint can be cleaned with a scraper, or belt sander. On mortise-and-tenon joints, where it's almost impossible to get at the corners with sanding equipment, just enough glue should be used for a good bond but

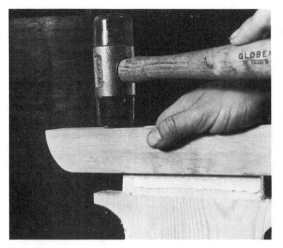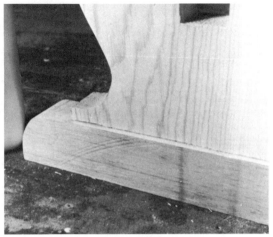

When gluing up inside joints such as this mortise-and-tenon, use only enough glue to hold and not so much that it squeezes out of joint. It is almost impossible to sand glue out of a joint like this.

not enough to allow any to squeeze out around the joint. You can protect areas that are difficult

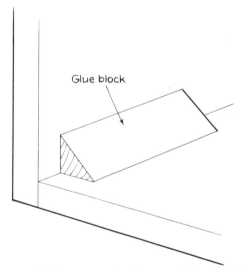

Some projects may require the use of glue blocks to increase the gluing surface. Glue is applied on both surfaces of the block; then it is put in position and moved back and forth to spread the glue and "set" block properly.

to reach and clean with masking tape before gluing. The amount of glue needed can only be learned through experience.

Gluing wood that hasn't been properly cured will present problems. For most moisture-evaporating glues, the moisture content of the wood should not be higher than 10 percent. But if the moisture content is too low it can also cause a problem; in either case, you will have a poor joint. If the wood has too little moisture, it will absorb too much moisture from the glue, and you'll end up with an expanded joint. If the wood has too much moisture, the joint will shrink as it dries, and you'll have a sunken joint. When using polyvinyl glue, don't plane wood that has been edge joined too soon. The moisture in the glue will expand the joint, and the wood needs to lose this moisture and return to normal size *before* the joint is planed.

In some cases you may have to use glue blocks to help provide enough gluing surface. This is a common method of joining furniture parts together without the use of metal fasteners.

4

Clamps

You can usually tell if a cabinet or furniture maker is a professional by the number of clamps he owns. But there are times when the best-equipped shop won't have enough clamps. And if you ever try to reglue and clamp an old platform rocker, you'll realize that clamps are one tool you just can't have too many of. There are hundreds of styles and sizes of clamps, but there are a few basic ones in particular that every woodworking shop should have.

Wooden "Handscrew" Clamps

These are the classic woodworking clamps. If well made, they may be used by several successive generations of woodworkers. They consist of two pieces of a smooth-grained hardwood, such as beech, with two finely-threaded long metal "screws" through each. There is a handle on each screw, on opposite sides of the clamps, and the clamps are loosened or tightened by turning the metal screws.

The easiest way to operate wooden handscrew clamps is to grasp one wooden handle in each hand and rotate your hands to open or close the clamps, keeping the jaws parallel. When setting the jaws, tighten screw on inside of work first, then adjust the outside handle to make the jaws parallel. When they are adjusted, twist both handles as tight as possible.

When clamping two flat surfaces together, the jaws of the clamps should be kept parallel. Otherwise you won't create an even clamping surface, and you run the risk of denting or damaging the wood surfaces. But the capacity of the jaws to accept irregularly shaped surfaces is an advantage of these clamps. For instance, you can clamp tapered objects just by opening and adjusting the jaws to match the angle of the taper, then tightening them in position.

The most common woodworking clamps are wooden handscrews. They can be used to clamp irregular or uneven shapes as well as square shapes.

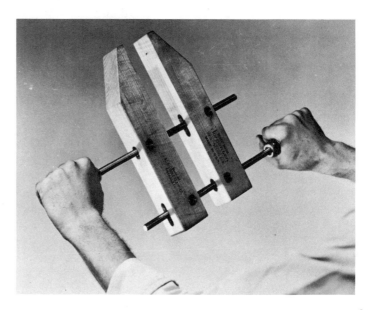

When using handscrews, it is important to keep the surface of the jaws parallel with the clamping surfaces.

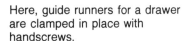

Here, guide runners for a drawer are clamped in place with handscrews.

To maintain wooden screw clamps, occasionally wipe the wooden surfaces with linseed oil and spray the metal screws with WD-40.

Bar and Pipe Clamps

Bar clamps are the "long toms" of the clamping line, and are available in lengths from a couple of feet to over six feet long. They consist of a long hardened steel bar with a sliding "foot" which is used as one of the clamping surfaces and is moved on the bar by squeezing its opening lever and pushing the foot into position. The opposite end of the bar has a screw-foot for final tightening.

Another type of bar clamp consists of two end fixtures shaped to fit over a section of metal pipe. Using these units you can make a bar or pipe clamp of any length you wish—as long as 25 feet or more if you need to. You should always purchase, or make up, bar or pipe clamps in pairs; you use at least two for most clamping situations. These clamps are used on chair bottoms or for edge gluing boards together to make wide stock for table tops or cabinet doors. When doweling and gluing up a wide stock, always place at least two clamps on the bottom and two on the top. On sections longer than four or five feet, it's a good idea to use three clamps on each side. When tight-ening the clamps watch carefully to make sure that all corners of the material ride flat and secure against the clamps. This insures that the glued surface will be flat with no warping or twisting. If the materials to be glued are somewhat warped themselves, you can often remove some of the warp by clamping all four corners of the material tightly against the bar of the clamps with small C-clamps.

Bar clamps are a necessity in a woodworking shop. They are commonly used to glue up wide stock.

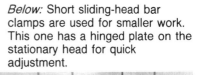

Below: Short sliding-head bar clamps are used for smaller work. This one has a hinged plate on the stationary head for quick adjustment.

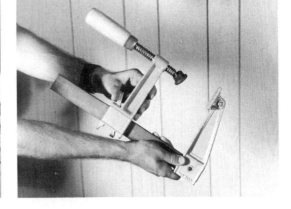

Above: This bar clamp has a ratchet mechanism and operates much like an auto bumper jack.

Right: Pipe clamps are made up with fixture sets that fit on lengths of metal pipe. Here, they are used to hold frame members. There are similar fixtures that can be mounted on lengths of wood.

The carriage clamp, more often called a C-clamp, is available in many different sizes and weights.

C-Clamps

C-Clamps come in all shapes and sizes—from a tiny inch clamp to giant clamps with more than 12 inches between their jaws. They are shaped like the letter **C** from which they get their name. There are all kinds of C-clamps—wide jaw, deep throat, etc.—and each can do a specific job better than others. C-clamps are the simplest clamps to operate. They have only one screw with a clamp-

ing foot on its end. This is turned against a solid "anvil" foot on the opposite end of the C. The turning handle fits loosely in the hole in the screw and can be pushed back and forth, allowing the C-clamps to be used in hard-to-reach spaces.

Heavy-duty C-clamps are excellent for metalworking, such as welding and brazing, while tiny lightweight C-clamps just can't be beat for model work and other delicate jobs.

Edge Clamps

This clamp has a three-point design to allow clamping of tabletop or shelf edges and other similar jobs. A special fixture (shown at top of photo) can be used to convert a regular bar clamp to an edge clamp.

Band Clamps

One of the handiest clamps the woodworker can own is a good band clamp. This clamp is a band

The edge clamp combines features of the bar and C-clamps. It is often used to clamp molding or other edging strips to table or counter tops.

Band clamps are indispensible for irregular and round surfaces. They are tightened by turning a small bolt head with a wrench.

of nylon about 1½ inches wide with a metal gripping piece that the nylon band threads through. A ratchet screw turns the band around a bolt and makes the loop of nylon smaller. This clamp can be used for clamping anything from a round drum table to hexagonal flower boxes, square boxes, and those "hard-to-figure" clamping jobs that are impossible for most other clamps. One problem with band clamps is that glue sticks to them. This can make it hard to remove the bands from the glued material, and dried glue can also scratch the surfaces of later clamping jobs.

Corner Clamps

The corner or "picture-frame" clamp is a specialty clamp. It is made in several styles. One consists of a 45° platform in which two pieces of a frame or box are clamped to be glued or bradded together. Another type, and a much more versatile style, has four 90° braces threaded on a steel cable. The frame is positioned flat on a worktable and the braces placed on each corner.

Picture frame clamp has a 90° platform to accept frame pieces. *Stanley.*

The metal cable is drawn up snugly and then tightened with a turning device to clamp the frame together, all corners at one time. This style of clamp is also available with 45° and 60° corners (see photos on next page).

Another type of corner clamp consists of a steel cable and four 90° corner blocks. When the turnbuckles are tightened, the cable draws the corners in snugly. It can also be used to clamp irregular-shape items such as a chair.

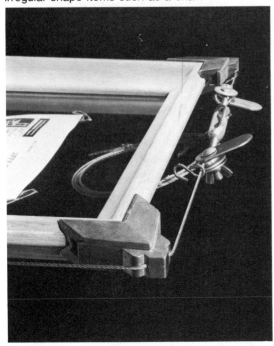

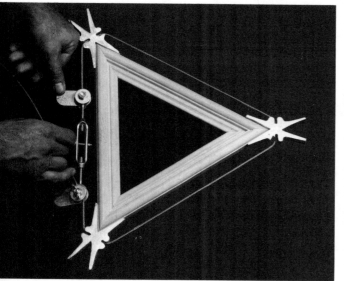

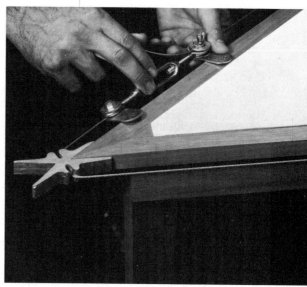

Steel-cable corner clamps also come with 45° and 60° corners.

Above: Hold-down clamps are available in many different styles. Some can be fitted to a workbench top, and others can be used on a drill press table.

Below: Spring clamps are used for many small jobs. They are inexpensive and it pays to have many of them.

Spring and Hold-Down Clamps

A well equipped home shop needs spring clamps and hold-down clamps. Although both of these are a bit specialized, both can really help with a tricky job. Spring clamps can be used to hold down screen-wire molding or to hold a thin flat wood surface to a frame. Hold-down clamps are made with a special bottom foot that is mortised into a workbench, table, or drill-press table. They can be used for holding work down on a surface, as for wood carving.

Specialized Clamps

One type of specialized clamp is the press screw. They are used in veneer presses to hold veneer in place, and can be adapted to other uses.

One of the most unusual and, I might say, one of the highest quality tools I have seen is the frame clamp. It's made of machined aluminum and is great for gluing panel doors or picture frames. It is especially good for larger, ornate picture frames. Pieces of felt in the corners prevent marring of frames.

Then there are the "do anything" clamps. Some of these come with a set of accessories that allow the clamp to be used on picture frames as well as in larger projects as shown.

Press screws are a commercial type of clamp that can be used for special jobs. Here, they are mounted on a table and used to assemble a wall for a mobile home.

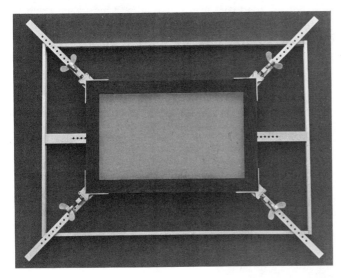

One of the best-made clamps is this Porta-Press "frame-and-door" clamp. With it, all pieces of a frame can be assembled at once. *Universal Clamp.*

The "do-everything" clamp comes with a variety of fixtures and can be used for assembling frames or installing facers as shown. *Universal Clamp.*

There are many more unusual and specialized clamps that can be used in a home workshop, but the ones I've mentioned will handle most projects tackled by the home craftsman.

Notes on Clamping

No matter what type of clamp you're using, there are several tips that make using them easier and more successful. The first is to use leather or hardboard pads under bars and pipes and on the feet of all clamps when clamping soft woods or finished projects. Secondly, wipe up excess glue as soon as the items are clamped securely together. Use a damp cloth to wipe all glue off the clamps and the wood. This makes sanding and smoothing operations easier and prevents clamps from becoming coated with glue and difficult to use.

Removing excess glue is doubly important when working with white oak. The moisture in glue discolors this wood, and there's no way to sand the color out of the wood pores.

Always go slowly when clamping, and make sure you don't break the wood cells or even crack or break the pieces to be joined by applying too much pressure. Clamps are designed to exert tremendous pressure, and it can be extremely frustrating to break a delicate turning while gluing it to a base. When clamping items such as wooden boxes, check to make sure the item is square and that you haven't forced any of the joints open each time you tighten the clamps.

Clamps are fine, quality tools that will last a lifetime if they are treated carefully and hung on racks so they won't rust. An occasional wipe with a good rust-preventive oil will help keep them in shape.

PART II

Basic Cabinetry Techniques

5

Joints

The old adage "A chain is only as good as its weakest link" is also true in woodworking. A wood project is only as good as the joints holding it together. Knowing which joints are best for each wood and project—and how to make them —makes the difference between well-constructed furniture and shoddy work. Poor choice of joints and bad construction not only look bad, but they don't hold well. In this chapter, I'll describe the important wood joints and their proper applications. Illustrations will show the easiest way to make some of them, including those reinforced with dowels.

Corner Butt Joint

The butt joint is the most common joint, and the weakest. It's usually assembled with glue and nails or screws. The end grain of one of the pieces will always show; so it's commonly used with softwoods for rough work.

Butt Joint with Glue Blocks

Adding a glue block to a butt joint strengthens it a great deal. This is a frequent practice on many types of economical furniture.

Miter Joint

Another type of corner joint is the miter joint. This joint is used when both edges of the wood must be concealed, as when constructing hardwood-face, fancy plywood furniture. It is not an especially strong joint, but it does provide more surface area for gluing than a butt joint. Each edge of the material is cut on a 45° angle to make up the 90° corner.

Miter Joint with Spline

Adding a spline to a miter joint strengthens it considerably. After cutting the edges with the

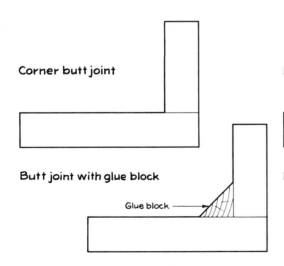

Corner butt joint

Butt joint with glue block

Glue block

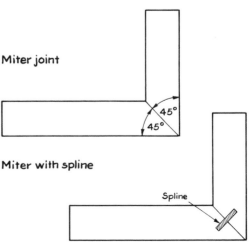

Miter joint

45°
45°

Miter with spline

Spline

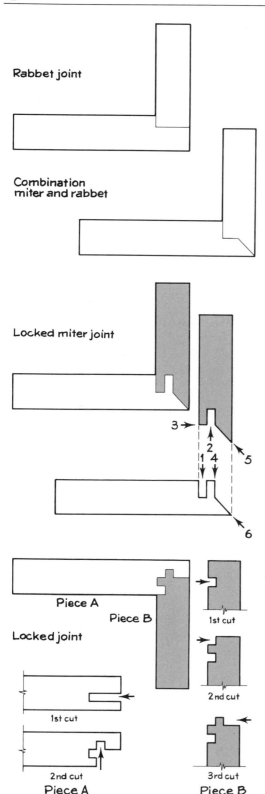

Rabbet joint

Combination
miter and rabbet

Locked miter joint

Piece A

Piece B

Locked joint

1st cut

2nd cut

Piece A

1st cut

2nd cut

3rd cut

Piece B

saw angle set at 45°, turn the stock around and
run it across the saw blade with the blade still set
at 45°. Lower the cutting depth to cut about half
way through the stock. Cut a spline from a thin
piece of hardwood and drive this in place from
the top of the joint after the pieces are clamped
together. Incidentally, old pieces of wood paneling make good splines.

Rabbet Joint

A rabbet joint is similar to a butt joint except that
one piece (and sometimes both) has a groove cut
along its edge to fit over the end grain of the other
piece. Much stronger than a butt joint, the rabbet
joint also provides a better surface for nailing and
screwing. It can be made with two cuts on a radial
arm or table saw, or better yet, in a single pass on
either saw using a dado head. It can also be cut
with a router or hand plane.

Combination Miter and Rabbet Joint

By combining a rabbet and a miter joint, a strong
joint is made that also conceals the edges of both
pieces of stock. Cut the miters first, then follow
with rabbet cuts.

Locked Miter Joint

An even stronger joint is the locked miter. Although this joint can be cut on a radial arm or
table saw by making the dado cuts with a dado
head, then making the miter cuts, it's easier to use
a combination "locked-miter" cutter on a shaper
or router. If made correctly, this is one of the
most attractive and strongest of joints.

Locked Joint

This is one of the strongest joints, and also one of
the most challenging to construct properly. A
dado head is used on a radial arm saw or table
saw to make the cuts. The hard part is to make
the cuts so that the parts will fit together snugly.

Dado Joint

A dado is a simple yet strong joint. It's commonly used on shelves, dividers, and in cabinets and built-ins. It can be cut with a dado head in a radial arm or table saw, a router, a router hand plane, or by making cuts with a saw and removing stock between the cuts with a chisel. For proper fit, make sure the channel, or dado, isn't so wide that the end pieces slip out easily.

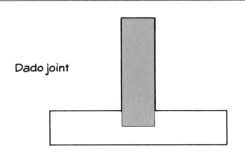

Dado joint

Combined Rabbet and Dado

By cutting a rabbet in one piece and a dado in the other, you produce a combined rabbet-and-dado joint. It is a good joint for joining pieces along their edges, as in drawer construction. It is not a good joint for shelves.

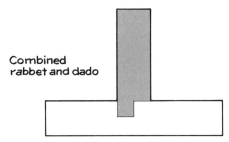

Combined rabbet and dado

Dovetail Dado

One of the strongest of the dado joints is a dovetail dado. It is assembled by sliding the parts together. The tongue of the dado can be made on a radial arm or table saw; and the dado slot with a dovetail bit in a router or with a special attachment for an electric drill.

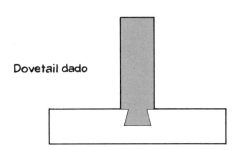

Dovetail dado

Blind Dado

A blind or stopped dado is used when you don't wish to show a notched edge, as on the front side of casework. This joint can be cut with ordinary hand tools.

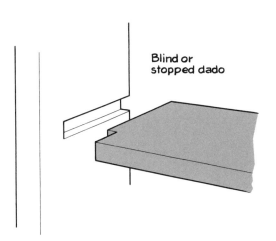

Blind or stopped dado

Edge Joint with Spline

One of the most common joints is the edge joint. It can be as simple as butting edges together and gluing and clamping. But a stronger joint, and one that isn't too hard to make, is an edge joint with a spline. A groove is cut in each edge— usually on a table saw—and a thin section of hardwood or plywood is inserted for the spline.

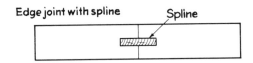

Edge joint with spline   Spline

Edge joint with rabbeted edges

Tongue-and-groove edge joint

Shaped edge joint

Half-lap

Cross lap

Corner bevel lap

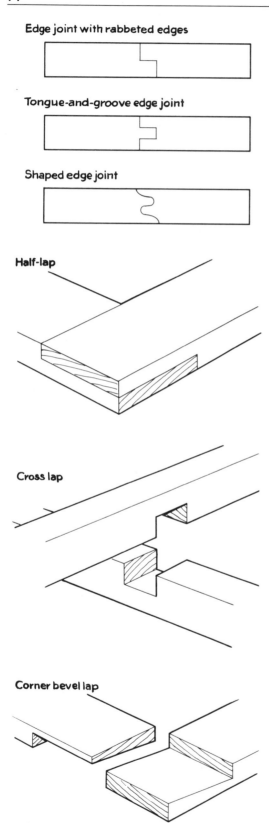

Edge Joint with Rabbeted Edges

Another method of reinforcing an edge joint is to cut rabbets on both edges using a table or radial arm saw with a dado blade. The difficult part is making both rabbets equal so that the stock is flat when joined.

Tongue-and-Groove Edge Joint

An even stronger edge-to-edge joint is the tongue-and-groove. This can be cut with a radial arm or table saw, or by using a combination "tongue-and-groove" cutter in a shaper. Using the cutter is easiest, because you're assured of exact dimensions on both the groove and the tongue. This type of joint is often used without glue on rough projects or exterior house siding. It allows for expansion and contraction with changes in moisture and temperature.

Shaped Edge Joint

This is quite similar to the tongue-and-groove joint, except that the edges are shaped using a special cutter in a shaper. It provides a stronger and smoother joint than the tongue-and-groove.

Half Lap Joint

A half-lap joint is commonly used for joining frame members together. It's also an especially common joint for rough projects. A table or radial arm saw, with or without a dado blade, can be used to cut the joint. Again, the difficulty is making both cuts equal and the surfaces of both pieces flush. If both cuts are not exact, you'll be left with a ridge on each edge and neither surface will be flat and parallel.

Cross Lap

When the half-lap joint joins two pieces in the middle of the stock, it's called a cross lap. It is made the same way as the half lap.

Corner Bevel Lap

When a bevel is cut on a lap joint, it's called a bevel lap. This is one of the strongest joints that can be used on frames, because the pieces wedge together. This is an especially strong joint when used on a frame that will be fitted in a dado; for instance, in constructing dust panels for drawers. It can be cut with hand tools, or with a radial arm saw or table saw.

Dovetail Half Lap

A joint similar to the corner bevel lap is the dovetail half lap. This joint can also be extremely strong, because the wood acts as a wedge, pulling against itself. This one is usually cut with hand tools, although a radial arm saw can be used.

Keyed Dovetail Half Lap

For this joint, the dovetail shape is angled into the edge of the stock, rather than cut straight down as in the dovetail half lap. This joint is stronger along its face than the straight-cut dovetail, and is excellent for the crosspieces on a dust frame or drawer slide. Because of the joint's design, the pieces have to be slid together first in the assembly procedure.

Miter Half Lap

One method of increasing the strength of a half-lap joint is to combine it with a miter. The half-lap sections are cut first, then the miter edges.

45° Miter with Key

A mitered frame joint can often be strengthened by the addition of a thin piece of wood called a key. The key goes in the corner of the joint.

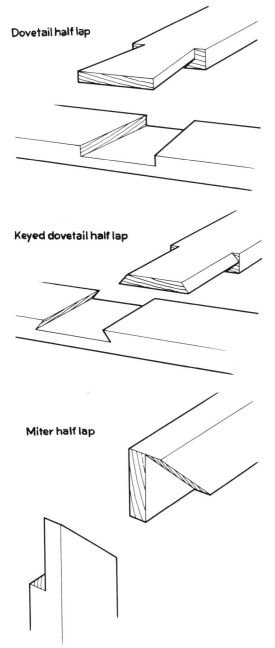

Dovetail half lap

Keyed dovetail half lap

Miter half lap

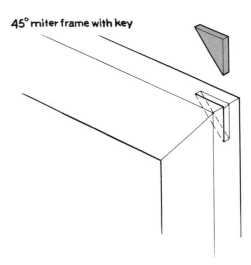

45° miter frame with key

45° Miter Frame with Spline

A thin wooden spline running the entire length of the miter joint provides more strength. It's used when visible spline edges won't matter.

45° Miter Frame with Concealed Spline

By cutting a blind slot, the spline can be concealed in one or both edges of the joint. A small-diameter saw blade is needed to make this cut.

Mortise and Tenon (Open End)

Outside frames, table legs, and chair parts can all be held together with mortise and tenon joints. This is one of the oldest joints and also one of the strongest if constructed properly. The tenon can be cut with hand tools, a radial arm saw or table saw, or with a dado blade in either of the latter. The mortise is cut by first drilling holes at each end of the slot and then in between, and using a chisel to remove material between the holes and to square up the corners. Or you can use a mortising bit in a drill press which cuts "square holes," repeating the cuts along the length of the mortise.

Rounded Mortise and Tenon

This can be cut with a special mortise-and-tenon cutter set from Sears. The tool isn't nearly as expensive as the industrial-type mortise cutters, and can be quickly fitted to most drill presses.

Blind Mortise and Tenon

When a tenon shouldn't be visible, as on the outside frame of a desk, a blind mortise is cut. This is cut like a regular mortise—by boring holes, then using a chisel to clean out the mortise. The mortise doesn't go all the way through the stock, however, and it's quite a bit harder to cut.

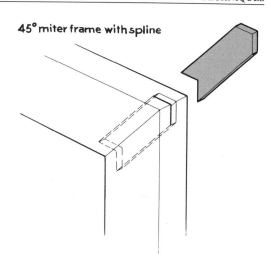

45° miter frame with spline

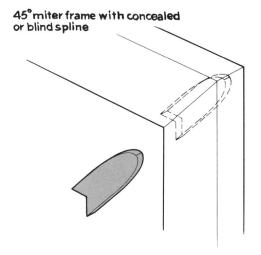

45° miter frame with concealed or blind spline

Mortise and tenon (open end)

Good, strong joints are essential in cabinetmaking. Pinned mortise-and-tenon joints were used on this 17th-century oak chest front. *The Metropolitan Museum of Art, Gift of Mrs. Russell Sage, 1909.*

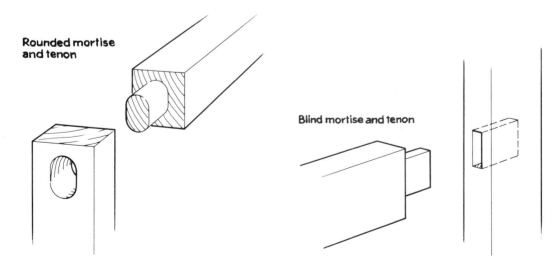

Rounded mortise and tenon

Blind mortise and tenon

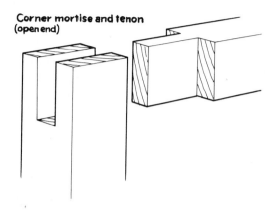

Corner mortise and tenon
(open end)

Corner Mortise and Tenon (Open End)

This is commonly used for frame and panel sections, such as for raised-panel cabinet doors. This type of mortise and tenon can be cut on a radial arm or table saw, or with hand tools. A chisel is used to make the back cut in the mortise.

Pinned Mortise and Tenon

By running the tenon entirely through the stock and then pinning it in place with a small wooden dowel or tapered stick, you can create a sturdy joint which can be made tighter whenever necessary by driving in the stick. The joint disassembles entirely by knocking the pin out and removing the tenon. The hole for the pin should be offset just a bit on the crosspiece to provide a tightening action between the wood pieces. This joint is quite common on Early American and casual styles of furniture.

Pinned mortise and tenon

A pinned mortise-and-tenon joint was used on the cradle shown in Chapter 18. This joint is often used so that an item can be disassembled for storage.

Haunched tenon

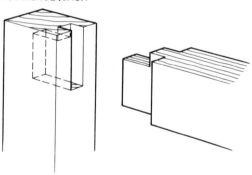

Bare faced tenon

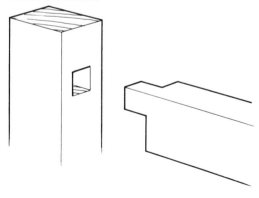

Haunched Tenon

By cutting a step in a tenon you create a haunched tenon. It's used for frame construction and provides a good, strong joint.

Bare Faced Tenon

This joint is usually employed when the mating surfaces are to be flush, such as on leg and rail constructions.

Box or Finger Joint

Sometimes called a drawer joint, the finger joint is most often used to join drawer sides to the front and back. It's also sometimes used on visible joints for decoration. It can be cut in many ways: by hand or by using special jigs on radial arm saws, table saws, routers, or drill presses, or even with an electric drill with proper jigs.

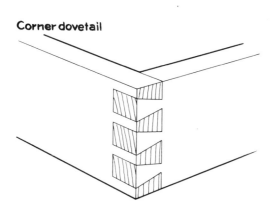

Corner Dovetail

This is the old-style dovetail in which the cuts go entirely through both pieces. It can be cut with hand tools or with a router and special jigs. It can also be cut with a portable electric drill, or even on the drill press with proper accessories. It is one of the most interesting traditional joints, and it is very strong.

Lap Dovetail

This is quite similar to the corner dovetail except that one piece overlaps the other, concealing the dovetail on one edge. It's often used to join drawer fronts to sides.

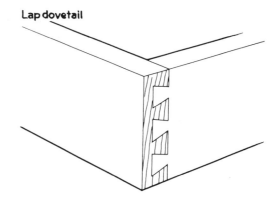

The old-style lap dovetail joint is a good joint for joining drawer fronts to sides as well as for assembling some types of casework.

Making Joint Cuts

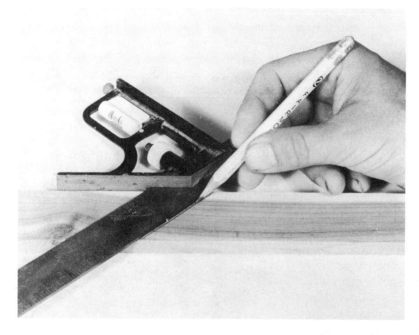

First step in making a joint is to lay it out with a sharp pencil or carpenter's scribe. Here, a 45° cut is being marked with a combination square.

Butt marking gauge is used for marking tenons, half laps, etc. The sliding gauge is set at the required distance from the edge of the stock and secured with the knob on top of the gauge. The sharp point of the gauge scores a fine line in the wood surface to mark the cut.

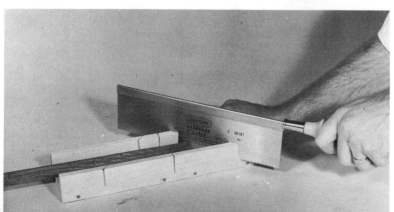

Cutting miter joints is easy if you have a good miter box and a back saw or dovetail saw.

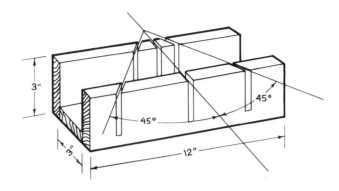

A homemade miter box is easy to construct.

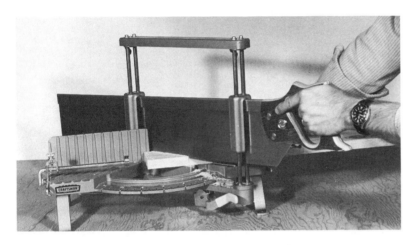

For larger stock or a substantial volume of work, consider one of the larger, adjustable miter sets. This one has a built-in saw and adjusts to cut almost any angle.

Half laps and tenons can be cut with a stiff-back handsaw.

Here, initial side cuts for a dado were made with a saw. A chisel is used to clean out the dado.

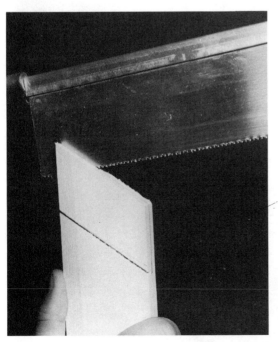

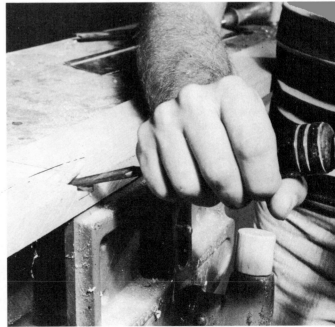

Making Joint Cuts (Cont'd.)

Far left: Mortises can be cut with a chisel and hammer.
Left: A portable drill or drill press can also be used to cut a mortise, followed by a chisel to clean out the edges.

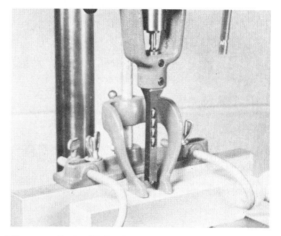

There are also special mortising attachments for a drill press that will do the whole job of cutting and chiseling a round or square mortise, but these require some setting up time. Many cabinet shops have one drill press permanently fitted with this accessory.

Initial cuts for a dovetail can be made with a dovetail saw. Then use a sharp chisel to clean between saw cuts.

Laying out dovetails

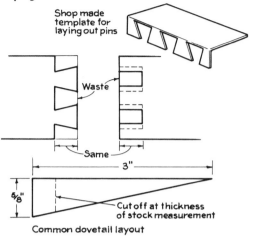

Shop made
template for
laying out pins

Waste

Same

3"

⅝"

Cut off at thickness
of stock measurement

Common dovetail layout

Above: A shop-made template is very useful in laying out matching dovetail cuts.
Right: Dovetail joints can also be cut with a dovetail template accessory and dovetail bit on a portable electric drill.

Special rabbeting plane can be used to cut rabbets on stock.

This rabbeting plane can also cut dadoes, as for tongue-and-groove work.

Router plane cuts dadoes in stock either lengthwise or across the grain. Many of these old hand tools are becoming hard to find.

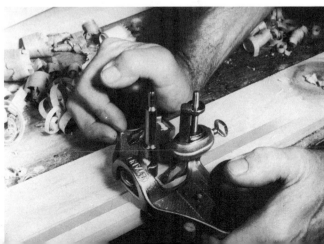
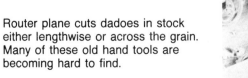

Making Joint Cuts on a Table Saw

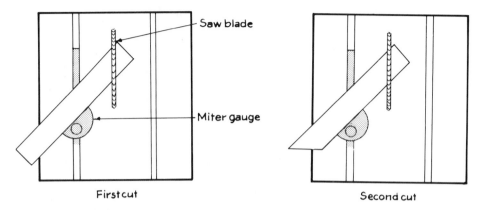

First cut   Second cut

A table saw can be used to cut most joints. To make a miter cut on both ends of a piece of stock, the miter gauge is left as is, and the stock turned over to make the cut.

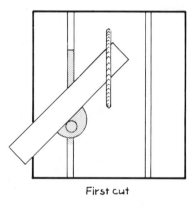
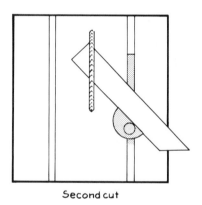

First cut   Second cut

On items such as molding which cannot be turned over for the cut, the miter gauge is adjusted to make the second cut.

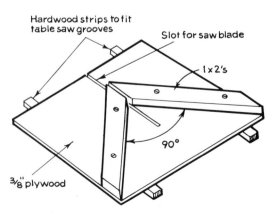

A simple handmade miter jig helps a great deal in cutting miters on a table saw. Jig slides along in miter gauge grooves.

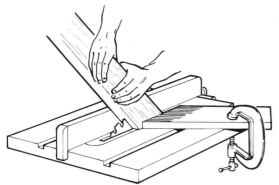

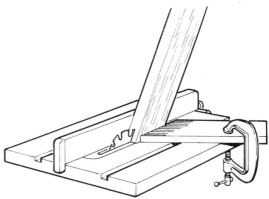

Table saw can also be used to cut spline grooves on end-mitered stock. Saw blade is raised to depth of spline cut, and a featherboard is clamped to table to help brace the stock as the cut is made. To make mating cuts on opposite end of stock, stock is held with the same side facing outward. This assures that the back sides of the pieces will line up, with spline grooves in the proper position.

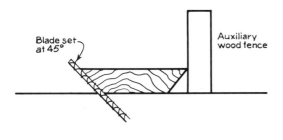

Left: An edge miter cut is made on table saw by tilting saw blade.

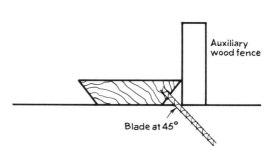

Right: To cut a spline groove, move fence inwards, lower blade, and allow top edge of stock to ride against auxiliary wood fence.

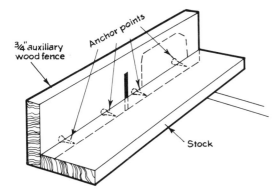

One problem in mitering is that the stock has a tendency to creep away from the cutting blade, producing an open cut or one that won't mate properly. Tacking work to an auxiliary miter gauge fence with small, sharp anchor points helps a great deal.

Making Joint Cuts on a Table Saw (Cont'd.)

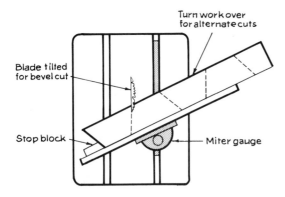

To cut a compound angle on a table saw, set miter gauge at angle needed and tilt blade for bevel angle. Matching cuts can be made by turning stock over.

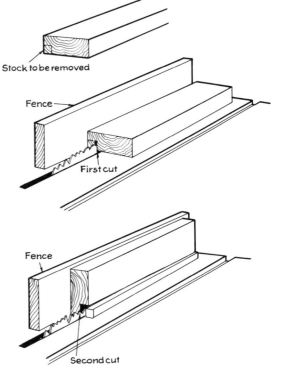

Two cuts are required to make a rabbet with a regular saw blade.

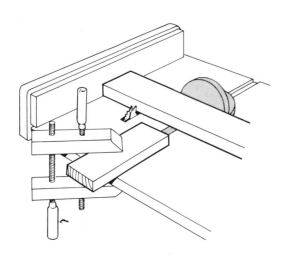

With a dado blade, a rabbet or dado can be cut in one pass.

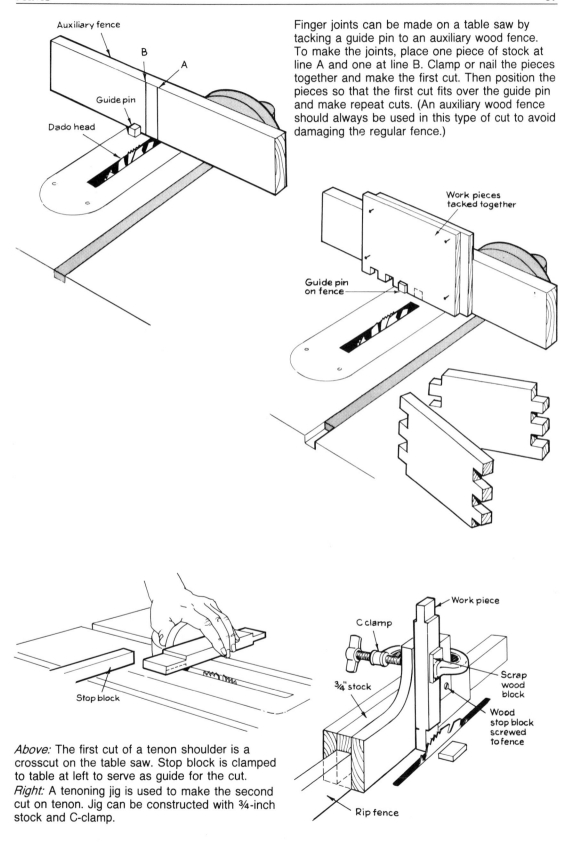

Finger joints can be made on a table saw by tacking a guide pin to an auxiliary wood fence. To make the joints, place one piece of stock at line A and one at line B. Clamp or nail the pieces together and make the first cut. Then position the pieces so that the first cut fits over the guide pin and make repeat cuts. (An auxiliary wood fence should always be used in this type of cut to avoid damaging the regular fence.)

Above: The first cut of a tenon shoulder is a crosscut on the table saw. Stop block is clamped to table at left to serve as guide for the cut.

Right: A tenoning jig is used to make the second cut on tenon. Jig can be constructed with ¾-inch stock and C-clamp.

Making Joint Cuts on a Radial Arm Saw

A radial arm saw can be used to cut most joints. Miter cut is made by setting the movable arm to correct angle.

End miter joints are cut by tilting saw head.

To make a spline groove on mitered stock, the stock is simply turned over and the blade raised.

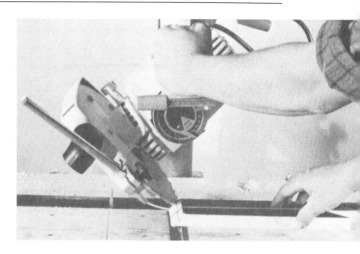

Dadoes, rabbets and tenons can be cut with dado head on radial arm saw.

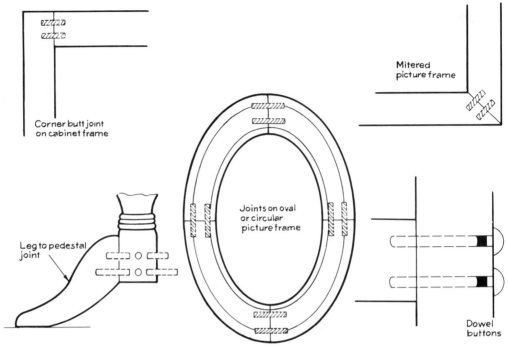

Dowels are used to reinforce many different types of joints.

Dowel Joints

A form of doweling was used long before the invention of nails. Entire houses and barns were secured with nothing more than carefully fitted wooden pegs driven between wood beams and posts. Many of these old joints are still holding today—proof of their quality. Although the methods and tools used long ago are far different from the sophisticated tools and techniques of today, the results are the same: A good, tight joint that won't shift and that provides an easy, accurate way to align mating parts. In most cases, if properly made, a glued dowel joint will withstand more force than the surrounding wood.

The single most important factor in the quality of a dowel joint is the fit of the dowel in the holes. The dowel should fit tightly enough in the hole to hold the wood securely, yet not be so large that it will split the wood when it's tapped home. It's

Dowel pins should be only finger tight in dowel holes. Note spiral grooves cut in pin to enable glue to spread around it.

Three common types of dowels: Spiral pin, fluted pin, and homemade pin with a glue slot on one side.

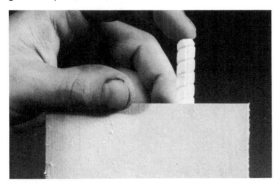

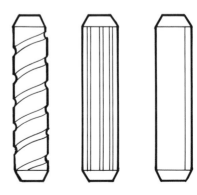

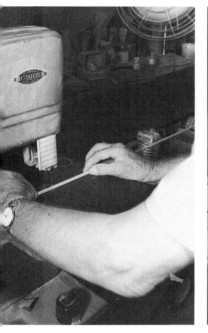 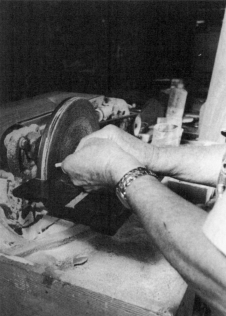 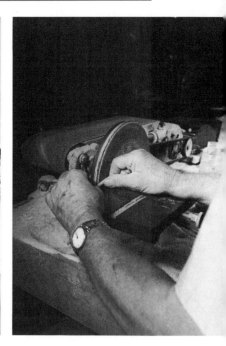

Left: Dowel pins may be cut from ordinary dowel rods of any diameter. Normal length is 1½ inches.

Middle and right: Dowel pin ends can be rounded on a sanding wheel, and the glue slot ground on edge of wheel.

a good idea to drill a test hole and push the dowel in with your finger. If it pushes in tightly by finger strength alone, it's a good fit. To work properly in its hole, the dowel must also be carefully prepared. A piece of dowel rod simply cut to length won't work, because there is no place for the glue to go when both dowel and glue are forced into the hole. A glue channel must be provided.

There are two basic types of dowel pins: manufactured, or ready-made, and homemade. Most ready-made dowels have a spiral glue channel cut in their sides. (One type of ready-made dowel has flutes down the sides, but this type is used primarily by furniture manufacturers. The spirally grooved dowel is the most common for the home shop.) You can also make your own dowels quite easily. Merely cut dowel rods of the proper diameter to the required length—normally 1½ inches. Using a belt grinder or sander, bevel the ends, and then grind a glue slot down one side. Spirally grooved dowels can be cut using a jig. But the cost of the ready-made dowels is so low, it's hardly worth the effort to make them yourself.

For the dowel to fit the dowel hole properly, the hole must be drilled with the right size and

shape bit. A *sharp* twist drill with an angle of 59° is considered best for most woods. Naturally, if the drill bit is too large, the dowel won't have proper holding strength. And if the bit is too small, the dowel will split the wood when it's driven home. As noted before, the dowel should be finger-tight in its hole.

The dowel hole must also be the right depth. Holes should be drilled in each piece no more than ¹⁄₁₆ inch deeper than half the length of the dowel. This leaves some room in the bottom of the hole for a pocket to hold excess glue. If the holes are drilled excessively deep, the dowels can be driven too deep in one piece, and holding strength will be reduced. Another common mistake is to misalign the dowel holes.

Using a Doweling Jig

To make an accurately fitted dowel joint, you must use a doweling jig of some sort. Although there are many on the market, the best I have found is Stanley's. I inherited a very old one from my father, and the only problem with it was that the bushings had worn a little thin. I bought a

A typical doweling jig with various size drill sleeves and a bit depth gauge (left).

new one to use for photographs for this book and, to my surprise, almost nothing had been changed. I guess it's hard to improve on a good design.

Using a doweling jig is quite simple. As you can see in the illustration, there are several different sizes of sleeves, or "bushings," as well as a drill-bit depth gauge. The sleeves are sized for the standard-diameter dowel rods carried by most lumber dealers.

Whether you're doweling a corner joint or edge-joining lumber to make up wide stock, the first step is to position the work together and mark across the face of the work for each dowel. Determine the proper diameter dowel for the stock to be joined, and select the corresponding sleeve. Place the sleeve in the doweling jig with the beveled end up, and clamp it securely in place. The bottom of the sleeve should be practically flush with the underside of the guide.

Place the jig so the centerline stamped on its front aligns with the mark made on the edge of the stock. Clamp the jig securely in place, making sure it is seated squarely. On the side of the doweling jig there is a guide with an index mark for each drill sleeve size and a scale in inches. Move the sleeve-holding piece to index the sleeve at the correct distance (on the scale) from the face side of the stock. Choose the proper size drill bit and place the depth gauge on it. Measure the length of the dowel pin, and position the drill bit gauge to drill the proper depth. Remember to allow for the depth of the drill bit sleeve as well. Keep the cutting edges of the bit from pressing against the top portion of the sleeve; otherwise it will eventually wear out the sleeve and cause uneven drilling.

After your holes are drilled, pour a little glue in each hole and spread glue along the edge of the pieces to be joined. Gently tap the dowel pins in

First step in doweling is to position stock with mating edges aligned and mark across boards at each dowel location. Then turn boards over and continue line on the inside edges.

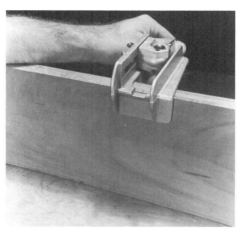
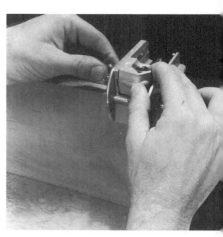

Left: Select the proper sleeve for the drill bit to be used, and clamp it in place in the jig.

Middle: Doweling jig is then positioned so the centerline mark stamped on the front of the jig aligns with the mark on the edge of the stock.

Right: To center sleeve on the stock, loosen the adjustable slide and align sleeve index with the correct point on the inch scale.

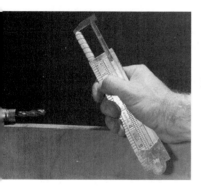

Left: To determine placement of the drill bit gauge, measure the dowel pin and divide its length by 2. Then add 1/16-inch plus the depth of the drill bit sleeve. The drill bit gauge is set at this distance from the tip of the bit.

Middle: Then, position the drill bit in the sleeve and drill the holes.

Right: After the dowel holes have been drilled, apply glue in the holes and along the edge of each piece to be joined.

Below left: Start the dowels in the bottom piece of stock; then put the top piece in place and gently tap it down with a plastic- or rubber-face hammer.

Below right: Clamp the doweled stock securely and wipe away excess glue. When gluing panels, make sure they are square and not pulled out of shape by the clamps.

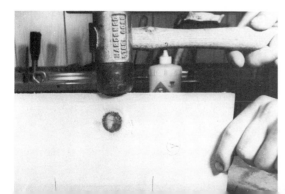
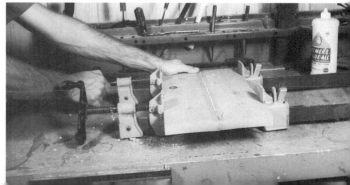

place, just starting them. If you drive them in all the way on one piece, and your holes aren't properly aligned, you'll have trouble getting them to start in the other holes. With all the dowels started in their proper holes, use a rubber or plastic faced hammer to tap the stock together. The moisture from the glue will cause the dowels to swell a little, creating a tighter fit. After driving the pieces together, clamp securely until excess glue is squeezed out, and wipe away the glue with a damp cloth. This is especially important on woods like oak because the chemical properties of glues can turn the wood black. Also, on joints that aren't easily sanded, an excess of glue is almost impossible to remove and will show up when staining.

A jig makes doweling quick and easy, and you don't have to worry about aligning holes perfectly by hand or holding the drill absolutely plumb. The jig can be adjusted to almost any size stock. But there is one very important thing to remember: make sure the bushings fit the drill bits exactly. Some of the cheaper "dime-store" variety bits aren't sized exactly and will dull quite quickly anyway. Select only quality drill bits and make sure they fit the sleeve. Take along the sleeve when buying bits to make sure you get a proper fit.

In addition to the doweling jig, there are other methods of doweling appropriate for specific jobs. For instance, if you wish to dowel the legs of a stool in place and the legs splay out at an angle, a homemade doweling jig would do the job. Also, you can't fit a doweling jig over a 12-inch piece of stock; so to dowel pieces like this you would use dowel points as shown on page 95. Although dowel points aren't as accurate as the doweling jig, they're the only solution in this particular situation. First, drill a shallow hole in the wide stock. Place the dowel point in place, then put the piece to be joined down on top and tap on it. The resulting punch mark made by the steel pin marks the center of the dowel hole.

Making Up Wide Stock

As most craftsmen know, it's almost impossible today to purchase a wide piece of quality hardwood—or even softwood for that matter. Even if

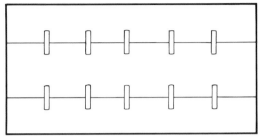

Front view

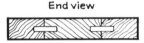

End view

When doweling up wide stock, be sure to alternate the grain direction of each piece as shown to minimize warping.

you do find one, chances are it will warp and twist out of shape once you finish the project. The solution is to use narrow pieces of material and dowel them together. This is quite common even in the manufacture of fine furniture. By carefully selecting the proper pieces for grain and color, the furniture may even be enhanced by this process. The method is quite simple.

The pieces of wood are planed to equal thickness, laid flat on a smooth work surface, and marked A, B, C, etc. All edges must be planed smooth and square so the pieces join without any evidence of an opening in the joints. With the pieces laid together, marks are made across the face of the stock for the dowels, then each piece is in turn drilled for the dowels. By turning pieces over and alternating heartwood up and down, you lessen the chance of the entire piece warping when it is finished. After drilling all holes and applying glue and dowels, the pieces are placed in long bar clamps. The clamps on both top and bottom sides are carefully drawn together, until the glue squeezes out and the wood is secure. Make sure that all pieces lie flat on the clamps and that there is no warping of the wood piece as clamped.

It is extremely important in this type of doweling job that the dowels be placed exactly the same distance near the front edge, so the surface will be

On wider stock, it may not be possible to use a regular doweling jig. In this case, a dowel point can be used to mark the dowel locations.

smooth and none of the pieces lower or higher than others.

Doweling Joints

Almost any type of joint can be doweled, from a 45° angle picture frame to the regular cabinet frames used for raised panel doors. Legs can also be joined quite easily in this manner. Rails of stools and chairs can be placed flush or set in

from the front edge, merely by changing the position of the dowel sleeve guide on the doweling jig. Other unusual joints can be made, including 45° angled flower pots, as well as circular or oval picture frames as shown on page 90.

One unusual use of the doweling jig is as a mortising jig. By marking the outline of the mortise, then using the drill with the gauge set for the proper depth, it's only a matter of moving the doweling jig sideways to drill each new hole, then cleaning out the mortise with a chisel. Fast and simple!

Doweling has been used for some time to hold chairs together. Often the dowel joints on chairs go entirely through one piece, such as the back leg, and into the rails. These dowels are countersunk into the legs and covered by chair buttons or plugs.

The cost of a doweling jig is small compared to most tools in a craftsman's shop, but it's one of the most valuable tools you can own. And once you get the knack of doweling joints, you'll wonder just how you did without this ageless method of joining wood together.

Plywood Joints

Joining pieces of plywood is done in much the same manner as for solid woods. However, there are a few specific joints that work best with plywood. The easiest joint to use on plywood is the

Sometimes a homemade doweling jig is necessary, such as this one for use in fastening splayed legs to a stool. It's made by cutting a compound angle on one end of a wood block, then boring a hole through the center of the block to serve as a guide for the drill bit.

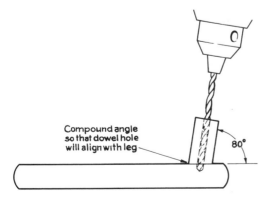

Compound angle so that dowel hole will align with leg

80°

The most common plywood joint is the glued and nailed butt joint. If plywood surfaces are too small to provide sufficient gluing surface, a glue block can be used for reinforcement.

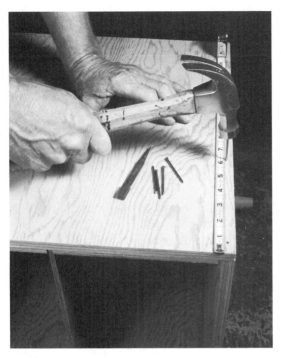

A rabbet joint can also be used to join plywood pieces, but a portion of one unfinished edge will show.

The solution is to cut the lap or rabbet in one piece so only the last (top) veneer is left. The joint is weaker, but the plywood edge doesn't show as badly.

Another method of concealing plywood edges is to utilize a 45° miter joint, but it's hard to construct. A hardwood or metal spline can be added for reinforcement.

common butt joint, but the problem is that one edge of the plywood will then show. The rabbet joint can also be used, but again a portion of one edge will show. One solution is to cut the rabbet deep enough so that only the top thin veneer will show when the two pieces are assembled.

Another method of hiding the plywood edge in a joint is to use a miter joint, although it is a bit harder to construct. A miter joint can be strengthened by the use of a hardwood or metal spline. In many instances a frame construction can be utilized that allows the use of thinner sheets of plywood. Plywood can also be installed in dadoes cut in other plywood pieces.

One method often used, especially with thinner pieces of plywood, is to dado them into a corner post. This is an especially popular method of utilizing plywood in chests, desks and other furniture items.

Both hardwood and softwood plywoods are surface-sanded, and about the only thing needed is to clean up the surface after a project is done. This should be done with fine sandpaper only, using either a sanding block or a power finishing

Thinner sheets of plywood can be utilized in this type of post-and-panel construction.

sander. When gluing up pieces of HDO (hard density overlay) plywood, you should first roughen joints with sandpaper.

Left: Very thin sheets of plywood can be dadoed into a corner post. *Right:* Plywood can also be dadoed to accept shelves, etc.

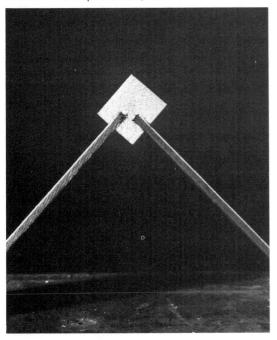

6

Case Construction

The box or basic frame of furniture and some cabinets can be separated into three types of construction: leg-and-rail, frame-and-panel, and box or case. *Leg-and-rail* construction is found on chairs, tables, benches, stools, and on parts of other furniture such as chests. We will go into more detail on this type of construction in Chapter 10. *Frame-and-panel* construction is used to make up component parts of many types of furniture, as for example the cradle shown in Chapter 18. This method is also used to construct the interior web frame with dust panel used on many dressers. *Box* or *case* construction is the basic design of dressers, buffets, desks, chests, and kitchen cabinets.

The material used as well as the type of construction depends to a great extent on the size of the project. Because solid wood shrinks and swells with changes in the climate, plywood is often the best choice for ends, sides, and other large areas of a case. In the dry air of furnace-heated homes, a piece of solid wood may shrink as much as ⅛ inch per foot. For medium-size projects, frame-and-panel construction minimizes the distortion caused by this factor, since only smaller-dimension wood panels are used. The frame can also be fitted to allow for some expansion and contraction of the wood of both panel and frame without damage to the project.

If you must use solid wood for a broad surface, rip it into narrow (4- to 6-inch) strips and reglue, turning every other strip over to alternate grain direction.

If using solid wood for smaller items such as chests, pay attention to the direction of the grain. This is important not only for the strength of the

project, but for the stability of the wood as well. The reason is that wood dimensions are a great deal more stable *with* the grain than across it. If constructed in the correct way, the entire box can expand and contract as needed, rather than pulling the unit apart. Although the back can be plywood, the bottom should be solid wood and should be fastened with screws or a locking joint without glue to allow for expansion and contraction of the wood.

Simple Box Construction

The simplest case construction is a box made of plywood. These boxes can be made of softwood plywood and painted, for more economical projects, or they can be made of hardwood-veneer plywood or of plywood or particleboard which the builder covers with fancy or exotic veneers. The joints used in this type of construction are

Solid wood can be used for smaller case constructions, but the grain direction of the pieces should be alternated as shown so that expansion or contraction of the wood will not pull the construction apart.

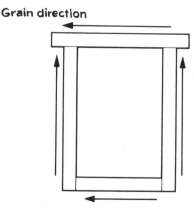

Grain direction

Most built-in cabinets are simple box constructions. At left, economical softwood plywood is used to construct a vanity which will be painted. The plywood panels are fastened together with nails and glue, with the nails indented and later covered with wood putty and sanded. *Right:* The back of a box construction is normally a ¼-inch plywood or hardboard sheet which fits in rabbets cut in the sides and bottom. This provides bracing for the assembly and also squares up cabinet automatically when installed (if back is cut perfectly square).

those best suited to plywood, as shown in Chapter 5. The case may also be of solid wood, but it rarely is.

The front edges of the case are usually covered with a facing which is installed piece by piece with nails or screws. On better-quality furniture, the facing may be assembled and installed with glue and glue blocks. An alternative to solid-wood faces is veneer tape or thin wooden strips which are simply glued over the plywood edges. This is a popular method on furniture with simple, smooth lines.

Left: Facing strips are glued and nailed to the front of a box construction. If the cabinet is constructed with hardwood-veneer plywood, facers of the same type of wood can be installed and later finished to match the veneer. *Right:* Drawer and door hardware are anchored on the facing strips, so facers must be fastened squarely and solidly with glue and nails.

Frame-and-Panel Construction

In this type of construction, the corner posts of the assembly, which may also be the legs, are fitted with panels. The frame may be rabbeted or dadoed to accept the panel, or the panel may be held in place with dowels. This is a popular method of constructing small chests and tables, and it is also a very common method of assembling a kneehole desk. The panels may be either of narrow stock or wider stock that is shaped at the edges. See Chapter 7 for details on cutting and assembling the frames and panels for this type of construction.

Squaring Up a Box or Frame

A case or box, whether it uses solid panels or frame and panels, must be perfectly square. A try square or homemade squareness tester can be used to insure that the box is square. One method often used on casework is to cut a ¼ × ¼-inch rabbet in the back edge of all sides, bottoms, and tops, and then install a ¼-inch plywood back after squaring up the unit. This insures that the piece will stay square.

The panels for this type of construction may be ¼-inch plywood or hardboard. Or solid wood may be used and tapered at the edges to fit in the dadoed frame pieces.

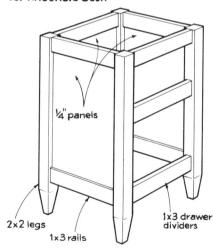

Frame and panel construction for kneehole desk

¼" panels

2x2 legs

1x3 rails

1x3 drawer dividers

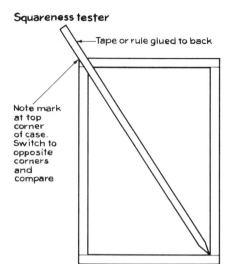

Squareness tester

Tape or rule glued to back

Note mark at top corner of case. Switch to opposite corners and compare

A homemade "squareness tester" can be used to insure that a construction is perfectly square.

Interior Details

The inside framing on simple items such as built-in cabinets or stereo cabinets may consist of nothing more than standards with adjustable wooden shelves, or a metal guide system for drawers. On fine-quality furniture, however, the inside construction is as important as the outside because the inside framing not only provides for drawers or shelves, but also provides support.

Drawers are often supported by inside wooden partitions called *web frames*. (Solid stock or plywood could be used for partitions, but they would weigh a great deal.) If the frames are fitted with thin wood panels, these are called dust panels. A dust panel and web frame are marks of quality furniture. They are always used on desks or bureaus which have locked drawers; otherwise you could remove the upper drawer and get into the contents of the one below. These frames are normally assembled with mortise-and-tenon joints, and with dadoes for the thin wooden dust panels.

Web frames may be held in place in the case by nails and glue or screws and glue. But more often they are fitted into rabbets or dadoes in the sides of the case and glue blocks are used for support under the frame pieces in the back. Although the dadoes in the sides of the case could be the full

A web frame construction provides support for drawers and also adds strength to the cabinet. (In this instance, the web frame pieces also serve as part of the case's front facing.)

Web frames are often assembled with mortise-and-tenon joints. If a dust panel is added, frame pieces are dadoed to accept it.

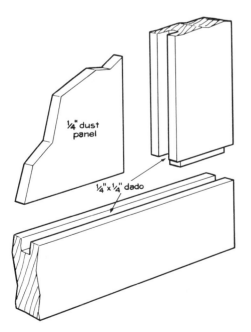

¼" dust panel

¼" x ¼" dado

A dovetail slot provides a very strong joint between a web frame and case sides. The frame must be slid in from the front of the case when this joint is used.

Dovetail slot

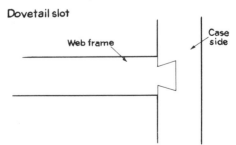

Web frame

Case side

thickness of the frame pieces, it is best to rabbet the frame edges a bit, and cut a narrower dado to provide more gluing surface and a stronger joint. The dovetail joint is the strongest for this type of unit; however, the frames must then be slid in from the front. When a frame-and-panel construction is used for the sides of the case, the web frame may be fitted with stub mortise-and-tenons or dovetail slots.

When putting together a unit with web frames, it's a good idea to glue the frames into one side, and clamp the opposite side dry, then clamp and glue the other side. This prevents the glue from setting before you get all the parts in the right place.

If the front edge of the web frame will also act as the drawer-front facing, it is covered with hardwood to match the exterior of the project. Otherwise, the frame is concealed behind the drawer fronts.

When the drawer support frames are long, as on buffets, they should have a middle supporting rail, or even two if necessary.

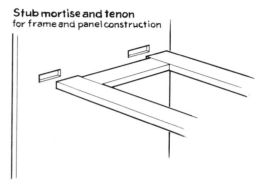

Stub mortise and tenon
for frame and panel construction

Web frames are often joined to cabinet sides with a stub mortise-and-tenon.

In many cases the outside top and bottom edges of the case will be covered by a molding, so plywood edges cannot be seen. You may wish, however, to use the end grain of wood as the decorative feature of the piece. An exposed dovetail joint can even be used as an attractive decorative feature.

7

Cabinet Doors

There are many different types of doors used on furniture and cabinetry, including slab (plywood or solid wood), sliding, tambour, folding, drop, and frame-and-panel. Doors may be merely functional, or they may provide the chief decoration of a piece.

Slab Doors

The slab door is the most common type of door. Plywood is used most often to build this type of door because it's cheaper, easier to work with, and much more stable than solid wood. The only disadvantage of a plywood door is that the edges have to be concealed unless the door will fit flush with the front of the cabinet. One method of treating the edges is to cover them with a band of matching veneer. A lumber-core plywood door can also be edge-banded with solid wood to match the plywood veneer. (An advantage of this method is that the door edge can then be shaped as shown on page 181.)

A solid-wood slab door can be made by gluing up narrow pieces of wood, alternating the grain direction of the pieces to minimize warping. You can strengthen this type of door by joining the pieces with tongue-and-groove joints. Adding cleats across the back of the door also helps to cut down on warping, but won't eliminate it.

On larger projects, it may be feasible to make up a hollow-core door as shown on page 104.

There are three styles of slab doors: *flush, lip,*

Doors are an important design element in many furniture pieces. On this 18th-century walnut corner cabinet, a raised-panel door is used on the lower section, and the Gothic-arch motif is repeated in the frame of the glass-panel door above. *The Metropolitan Museum of Art, Rogers Fund, 1925.*

Gluing up solid wood door

Heartwood   Sapwood

Some small slab doors are made by gluing up solid wood pieces. To decrease the chances of warping, turn the pieces so that the growth rings (as seen in the end grain) point in opposite directions in adjacent pieces. (Grain direction is most easily visible when the lumber contains both heartwood and sapwood as shown here.) This same precaution should be taken when assembling a lumber-core door.

Hollow core door

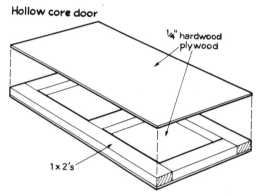

¼" hardwood plywood

1 x 2's

Hollow-core doors can be made up quite easily for larger projects. Use 1×2s or 2×2s for the outside framing, and glue the same type of sheathing (plywood or hardboard) to both front and back.

and *overlay*. These terms refer to the way the door fits in the case.

Flush Doors

These are fitted with their edges *inside* the cabinet framework or front casing. One advantage of this installation is that the edges of the door are concealed, so very little has to be done to them. The exposed edges of plywood in particular aren't very pretty, and flush doors solve this appearance problem. On the other hand, a flush door is much harder to fit because it must be cut to fit exactly; if the cabinet is out of square, or becomes out of square later on, the doors will bind. A flush door must be made about ¹⁄₁₆ inch smaller all around than the case opening to fit properly.

Double Doors. If double doors are to be made flush, there are several ways of concealing the

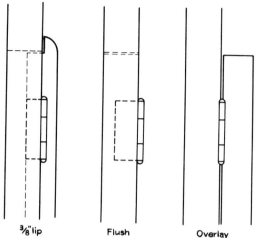

⅜" lip   Flush   Overlay

The three basic types of door installations as seen from the side. *Lip* doors are commonly used on kitchen cabinets and are easiest to fit properly. *Flush* doors are the hardest to fit because the door and opening have to be cut exactly and both have to be perfectly square for the door to work properly. *Overlay* doors that partially overlap cabinet front are easy to fit with spring-loaded hinges.

Double-door edge treatments

The space between double doors can be left open as shown at left, or concealed by use of rabbets or molding. When edges are concealed, the left door has to open first.

Lip doors are usually cut with a ⅜ × ⅜-inch rabbet to accept standard lip door hinges. Large leaf of hinge fits on inside of door: only the pin and a small leaf are visible from front.

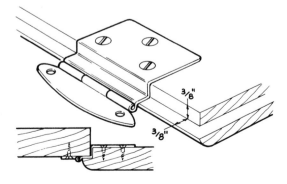

⅜"

⅜"

Here, a table saw is used to make the first cut (left) and second cut for the rabbet on a lip door.

crack between them. One is to cut a rabbet on the front of one door and the back of the other. An alternative method is to install a decorative molding on the front of one door. Of course, you must then open the door with the molding first.

Lip Doors

This style is quite common on kitchen and bathroom cabinets, including those with a frame-and-panel construction. A lip door has a lip, or rabbet, cut all around its edge. This rabbet allows the door to fit in the opening while the lip covers the opening entirely. Stock for a lip door is cut ⅜ inch larger all around than the cabinet opening. An alternate method of making a lip door is to glue two thin slabs together, with the back, or inside, slab smaller so it will fit in the opening. This is one of the easiest doors to fit because even if the door is not exactly the right size, or the cabinet opening is a bit out of square, the door will still work.

Lip doors require special hinges, and most lip doors are made with a ⅜-inch lip (⅜ × ⅜-inch rabbet) to fit the standard hardware. The hinge is fitted on the back of the door, follows the rabbet cut, and is fastened on the cabinet front facing.

Cutting and Shaping a Lip Door. There are basically two methods of cutting the lip. The first and easiest is to use a cutter in a shaper, or you can purchase a special cutter that not only cuts

the ⅜-inch lip, but rounds the edge as well—all in one pass. Another method is to use a table saw. Make the first cut with the door standing on edge, then turn the door down flat and make the second cut. Cut a piece of scrap wood first to check the depth of the rabbet.

On most kitchen cabinet doors, the outer edges of the door are shaped with a quarter-round cutter in a shaper or router to provide a smooth, rounded edge. Naturally, if there are double doors they will fit flush and not have a lip at their mating edges. When measuring, make sure to allow for this. Usually, however, the mating edges of double doors are rounded on the outside to match the rest of the doors' edges.

A quarter-round cutter in a shaper can be used to round the front edge of a lip door.

Sliding doors can be made with plywood, hardboard, glass or plastic—any thin material. Here, patterned Plexiglas is used.

Overlay Doors

The third type of slab door is called an overlay door. This is a solid door that partially or completely overlaps the cabinet framing. When the framing and case sides are not exposed, their edges can be, and usually are, left unfinished. These doors are quite easy to make and install. There are basically two methods of installing them—with pivot hinges or with regular or spring-loaded pin hinges that are almost entirely concealed.

Sliding Doors

Sliding doors are often used on stereo and storage cabinets. Since they don't open out, one of their main advantages is that the cabinet requires no room in front for opening the doors. However, they limit access to 50% of the cabinet at a time. Another advantage is that they don't have hinges and so can be made of thin materials or materials other than wood. Sliding doors can be made of hardboard (perforated or unperforated), thin plywood covered with veneer, glass, or even plastic.

Sliding doors slide in grooves in the inside edge of the casework. These can be dadoes cut in the casework, dadoes cut into trim pieces fitted into the casework, or purchased metal or plastic tracks which are fastened in place. One advantage of dadoes is that they can be run across the entire case front, and into the sides. This is better looking because the door will fit into the dadoes at the

Dadoes are cut in the top and bottom of cabinet to provide the "slides" for sliding doors. Top dadoes are always cut deeper than those at bottom to allow room for lifting the doors in installation or removal.

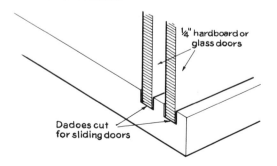

¼" hardboard or glass doors

Dadoes cut for sliding doors

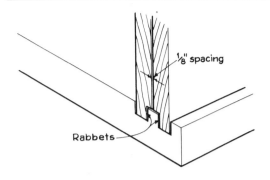

To cut down on the gap between the two sliding doors, rabbets can be cut on the door edges as shown.

sides and not show an ugly crack should the door be carelessly closed or if the case or the door is a bit out of square. The top channels or grooves are normally cut deeper than the bottom grooves so the doors can be installed or removed without dismantling the casework.

Another type of channel for sliding doors can be made by cutting thin wooden strips and gluing and tacking them in place to form the channels. When this is done, a quarter round molding is usually used for the front strip. Ready-made one piece wooden channels are also available for this purpose.

Sliding doors will have a gap between them, but you can conceal this by cutting a rabbet on the front of the inside door and on the back of the outside door. This will bring the doors closer together.

To install the doors, cut to the right size, sand and seal edges, then push them up into the upper tracks and drop them down into the lower tracks. On simple doors a finger hole can be bored to assist opening. These can also be cut and fitted with special metal cups. Or a depression can be cut in the fronts to serve as a finger hold.

Tambour Doors

Tambour doors are specialty doors found on furniture such as roll top desks. They can be made to slide either vertically or horizontally. They provide most of the advantages of the sliding door, and in addition they allow access to all of the cabinet. Factory-made tambour doors are made of thin wood pieces, either interlocked or fitted together with small plastic hinges. A home shop tambour door can readily be made by gluing pieces of thin wood to a piece of canvas or other heavy cloth. For small doors, strips of canvas can be used instead of a solid piece. Like sliding doors, tambour doors fit in grooves cut in the top and bottom of the case.

There are two problems encountered while installing tambour doors. First, the radius of the tracks at the corners where the doors swing around must be large enough to permit the doors to move freely. Naturally, the thinner the wooden slats the smaller the radius can be. About the only way you can make sure the slats will fit the radius is to make a full size drawing of the curved por-

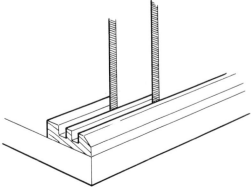

Small wooden cleats or a one-piece ready-made channel can also be used to guide sliding doors.

One typical use of
tambour doors is on the
classic roll-top desk.

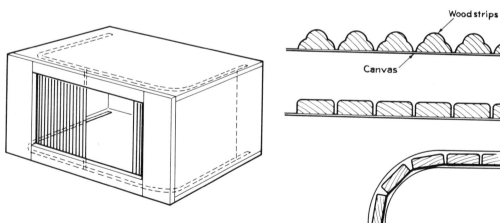

Above: Tambour doors are made by gluing thin wooden strips to
a canvas backing. In most cases the doors are installed before
the back of the case is fastened in. *Top right:* The wood strips
for a tambour door can be of any design as long as they will
slide properly in the grooves. *Right:* The curved portion of the
grooves for a tambour door must have a fairly large radius so
the strips won't jam.

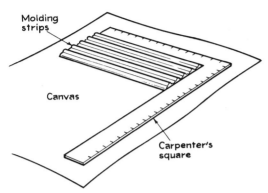

To make up a tambour door, apply contact cement to backs of wood strips and on canvas. Allow to dry and reapply. When second coat is dry, position the strips carefully on canvas, using a square to keep them in line. When all pieces are in place, press them firmly down on canvas.

tion, using the slats as a guide. The other problem is that top and bottom slots must be cut exactly alike (except that the top is cut deeper). Otherwise the doors will bind and be hard to operate. The best method is to make a hardboard template and use this to rout the top and bottom grooves.

The slats can be cut from thin straight pieces of wood, or molding such as screen door molding can be used. The strips are cut to length and glued on the canvas. It's important to keep glue from getting between the slats, as this prevents the door from operating properly. The slats should be spaced just a slight distance apart. Make sure to install the slats squarely as well.

Folding Doors

Folding doors are often used on Early American furniture. They allow more access than do sliding doors, and don't require much swing room in front. Special hardware is available to attach and guide this type of door. The door panels may be joined together with plastic hinges or with standard butt hinges, and the doors are attached to cabinet sides with butt hinges. The doors can be guided by ready-made channels that attach to the bottom of the cabinet, or by a groove dadoed into the case. Larger doors should also have a matching groove in the top of the case, with guide pins at both top and bottom.

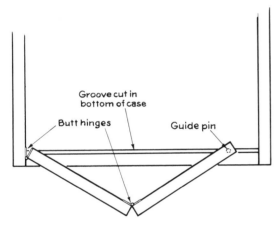

Above: Folding doors are supported mainly by butt hinges that join door to case. Guide pin attached to second door guides it in channel at bottom of case. *Below:* One method of making up folding doors is to insert plastic hinges in saw cuts made in edges of doors.

Drop Doors

A door can also be hinged at the top or bottom, and is then called a drop door. A common appli-

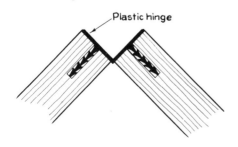

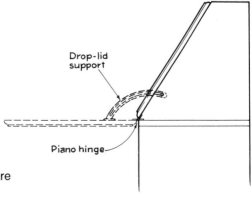

Drop-lids or doors can be supported by special hardware or by a length of metal chain.

Frame-and-panel doors are often used on kitchen cabinets or bathroom vanities as well as on finer furniture. Shown are raised panels and routed flat panels.

Almost any thin, flat material can be used for kitchen cabinet door panels, and the panels can even be changed periodically for variety. Shown are decorated hardboard panels.

cation is to create a drop-lid desk. The problem with this type of door is that there must be support for the lid or door in the down position. This can be done by providing an overhang in front that the door can rest on, or by using special hardware.

Frame-and-Panel Doors

Frame-and-panel doors are used on high-quality furniture and cabinets. They require a great deal more time to make, as well as some special tools and skills. However, the results are well worth it. These doors consist of a wood frame which has an inside panel of wood, glass, metal, hardboard, or plywood. If solid wood is used, the edges are tapered to fit into the grooves of the frame.

Construction of Frames

The frame consists of two upright members, or *stiles,* and two horizontal pieces—the *rails.* Some doors also have a third horizontal piece, or *cross rail,* in the middle. The frame pieces have dadoes cut along their inside edges for panels. Or a rabbet may be cut along the inside edge of the frame,

in which case the panel is held in place by molding. The inside edge of the frame is called the *sticking.* It can be left flat, or shaped, or provided with a decorative molding. A molded sticking or one with molding applied will provide added strength to the structure of the frame.

There are several ways of making frame-and-panel doors. The simplest is to cut the dadoes in the frame pieces, then simply dowel and glue them together, inserting the panel in place as you glue. Or the frame can be assembled with mortise-and-tenon joints. The best method, and the quickest if you have a shaper, is to use shaped stickings as a component of the joints between frame members. This method provides a larger gluing surface at the joints as well as a decorative frame edge.

Square Sticking. A square stuck frame with a flat panel is the easiest type of frame-and-panel door to construct. The stock for the frame is normally ¾ to ⅞ inches thick, and the panels are ¼-inch plywood (or thicker stock tapered at the edges.) The stock is first cut to width and length. For a normal size cabinet door, the top rails and stiles are cut about 2½ inches wide and the bottom rail is cut 3½ inches to make a balanced-

Cutting and Assembling Frames

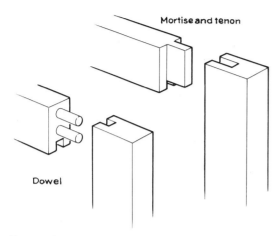

Frame doors may be assembled with dowels or mortise-and-tenon joints.

looking door. The dimensions, of course, will vary according to the size of the door. After cutting the stock to size, the stock pieces are placed in the position they will take when fitted together. Each piece is marked on the face side, and this side should always face up or out during machining. A shaper is used to groove the inside edges of all pieces. Allow the work to ride against the fence, cutting ⅜ inch or more deep. If the work is curved, as for the top of curved door panels, use a collar to control the depth of the cut. Then both ends of each rail are coped to form square-shouldered tenons. In making this cut, a collar is used for spacing as shown.

For light cabinet doors, the tongue-and-groove joint described will normally be sufficient. For larger doors, you may prefer to add dowels. If dowels are to be used, bore the holes before cutting the grooves.

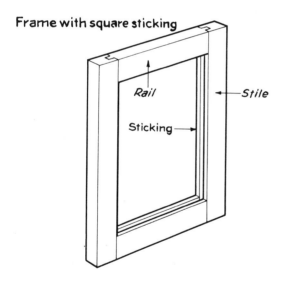

A square-stuck frame is easy to cut on a shaper.

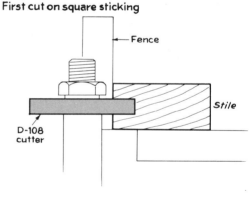

Above: Stiles are cut with Rockwell No. D-108 shaper knife. (Other manufacturers also supply matching cutters for this type of cut.) *Below:* Mating cuts are made on frame rail pieces as shown.

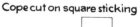

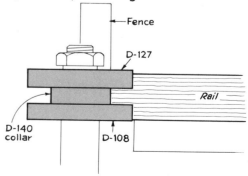

Bead and ogee sticking

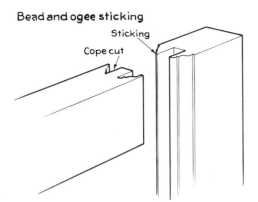

Sticking

Cope cut

A variety of different designs can be cut with matching cutters on a shaper. Shown is bead and ogee design.

Dimensions for bead and ogee sticking

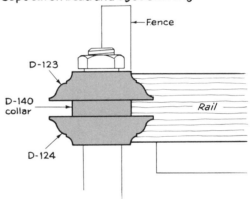

$1\frac{1}{8}$" to $1\frac{3}{8}$"

$\frac{3}{8}$"

Equal

$\frac{1}{4}$"

Stile

First cut on bead and ogee sticking

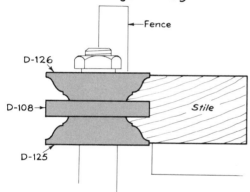

Fence

D-126

D-108

Stile

D-125

Cope cut on bead and ogee sticking

Fence

D-123

D-140 collar

Rail

D-124

Bead and Ogee Sticking. To create a more decorative frame, different combinations of knives can be used on the shaper as illustrated. These joints can be additionally reinforced with dowels. In making the cope cut, the depth of the cut must be set from the fence, and not from the collar, which only serves as a spacer. Again, the panels are ¼-inch thick, or are made of wider stock tapered to this thickness at the edges.

Whatever method is used, the cope cut or end cuts should be made with the shaper sliding jig. Or back up the work with a suitable piece of heavy wood to insure a square cut on the ends.

Applied Molding. Using applied moldings is another way of installing panels in a frame. The frame is cut square or *square stuck,* then the panels and molding are fitted in place. This type of construction is especially good for heavy doors with tenoned joints.

Here, a stile is being cut on shaper. On this frame, a collar was used instead of a cutter at the bottom to leave the sticking square.

When doing cross-grain cutting on shaper, use miter gauge or a heavy backer block to push the work through. Here, backer block is used in making cope cut on rail.

If removable door panels are desired, back of frame is simply rabbeted to receive them. Panels can be held in place with tacked-on molding or other fasteners.

In most cases, panel is inserted when frame is glued. In any case, it is important to make sure frame is square before allowing glue to set.

The use of applied moldings on the inside edges of the frame and panel provides further decoration as well as added strength.

Applied moldings

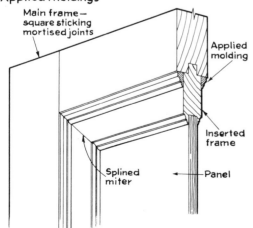

Main frame—
square sticking
mortised joints

Applied molding

Inserted frame

Splined miter

Panel

Opposite: Many different decorating techniques can be applied to frame-and-panel constructions. Shown at top left is a shaped wood frame covered with fancy veneer. The ¼-inch plywood panel is surfaced with diamond-matched veneer.

The cabinet at top right has both carved and veneered panels. The face of the frame is shaped, and molding is added for further decoration.

Curved rails of the French Provincial door can be cut on a band saw. The edges of the irregularly shaped panels can be tapered with a panel-raising cutter on a shaper.

Door at lower left has a typical Gothic arch design with raised panel.

Frame-and-panel door at lower right can also be decorated with ready-made hardwood moldings. Moldings are glued and tack-nailed in place and the brads concealed with Plastic Wood.

Decorating Frame-and-Panel Doors

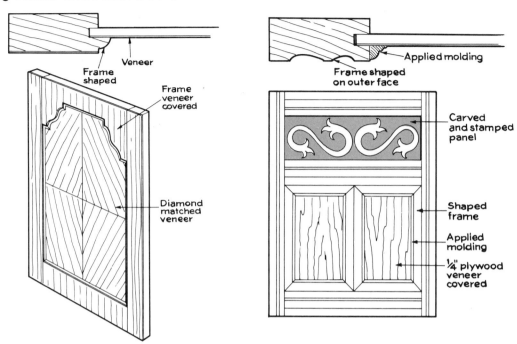

Veneer

Frame shaped

Frame veneer covered

Diamond matched veneer

Applied molding

Frame shaped on outer face

Carved and stamped panel

Shaped frame

Applied molding

¼" plywood veneer covered

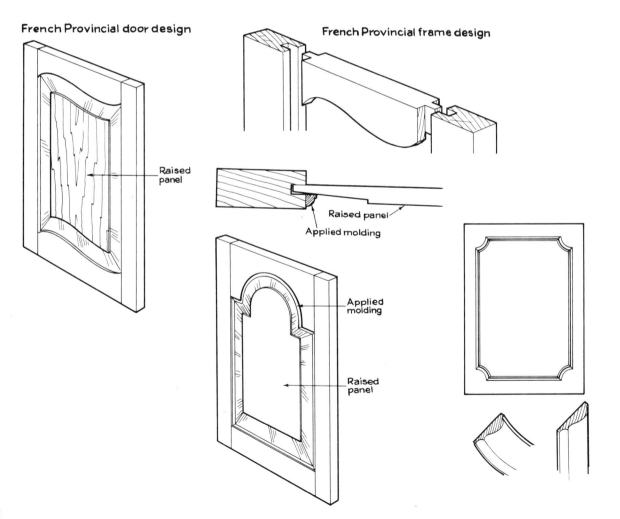

French Provincial door design

Raised panel

French Provincial frame design

Raised panel

Applied molding

Applied molding

Raised panel

Making Panels

The most common panel, and the easiest to make, is simply plywood with a fine veneer on the face. (Cover the back with veneer too if you are applying the veneer yourself.)

A panel can be cut to fit flush with the frame front, or it can be raised out in front, or shouldered (if solid wood), or beveled. On furniture of elaborate design, the frame-and-panel door may consist of an outside frame, a thin wood panel with a thicker plywood panel fitted in place behind, all surrounded by a molding. The frame doesn't have to have only straight lines on the inside. It can have a curved design as characteristic of French Provincial, or a Gothic arch.

One common method used in kitchen cabinets is to provide a beveled, raised-panel front. This method can only be used on smaller doors, however, since the doors must be solid-panel. A shaper cutter can be used to make these panels, or the bevels can be cut on a radial arm saw, drill press, or table saw.

Cutting a raised panel. To cut a raised panel on a circular table saw, tilt the blade up to about 10° to 15° from vertical and away from the fence. Set the fence for ³⁄₁₆ inch width of cut and make the cut with the panel up and against the fence. A tall auxiliary fence clamped or bolted to the saw's fence will help steady the wide stock.

To cut a raised panel on a radial arm saw, set the saw for bevel rabbeting and edge the panel to the desired depth on all four sides. The angle of the bevel determines the effect of the raised panel. Incidentally, the cross cuts should be made first, then the with-the-grain cuts. A rotary planer attachment will make the job easier.

A raised panel can also be cut with a special panel-raising, two-wing shaper cutter. The work is held flat against the fence, or the cutter can be used with a collar. This is the only way to raise panels on odd-shaped pieces such as circular tops for French Provincial furniture.

Assembly

In assembling a frame and panel, the panel is inserted as the frame pieces are glued. Never apply glue to the panel or to the dadoes in which it fits. The panel should fit snugly, but not fastened solidly in place because differences in moisture content between the frame and panel may cause the wood to split. Because it's almost impossible to sand dry glue out of the corners of a frame-and-panel construction, any glue runs must be wiped up before they dry.

Decoration of Door Fronts

Door decoration can be a part of the door assembly, as in the frame-and-panel constructions described, or it can be carvings and moldings glued

Raised panels can be cut many different ways. Straight-line panels can be cut with a regular saw blade in a table saw or radial arm saw, or with a panel-raising cutter in radial arm saw.

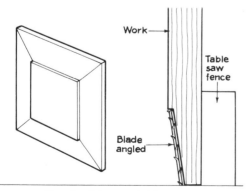

Panel raising on a table saw

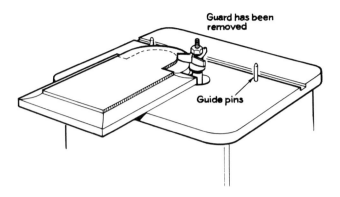

Curved or free-form panels are cut with a panel-raising blade on a shaper.

in place, or the wood frame itself can be routed or carved with patterns. Another method of embellishing a door is to rout a design on the front.

Routing a Design with Templates

An unlimited variety of designs can be routed on a door front with templates or patterns. You can make your own patterns, or use purchased templates. Hardwood-faced plywood or coreboard produces the best-looking door when routed and finished with a stain. Softwoods are second best, then softwood plywood. Solid hardwood doors finish quite well, but you must have a heavy-duty

router and carbide-tipped bits to prevent burning the wood as well as destroying the bit. A router of at least ⅞ hp and carbide-tipped bits make the job easier with any type of wood.

To use a template, you must have a template collar that fits your particular router. There are many different terms for this attachment, depending on the router manufacturer. Without a collar, the router bits will tear the template corners and even roughen the steel side and ends.

The template shown on page 118 is extremely versatile and can make many different designs. It has adjustable "corners" which are held to the main template with screws. By changing the cor-

Hardwood-veneer and solid-wood slab doors can be decorated with routed designs.

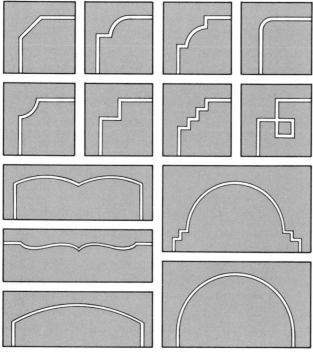

Corner, side and arc designs

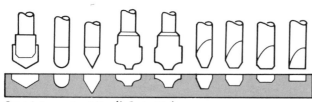

Carbide router bits (¼" shafts)

Shown are some of the designs that can be routed with templates and accessories.

Template shown clamps to door. It can be fitted with different corners and arcs to rout different designs.

ner pieces of the template, you change the corners of the door design. With this setup, you don't have to have a fortune tied up in individual templates. The basic template consists of steel tubing and cast aluminum fittings. There are 14 corners, a side pattern (in addition to the straight side of the basic template), and an arc template. The basic template comes with four sets of corners. The other corners, side, and arc attachments are sold separately.

A router glide comes with the template and is installed on the base of the router as an outboard support. Without it, the router may tip, especially on the long side runs, making the pattern uneven. The outboard glide can be fastened through one of the screw holes on the router base. Position the cutter in place and adjust depth to suit. Then adjust the glide so the router is level on the template.

Before routing a design on a door front, it is a good idea to make a test on a piece of scrap wood of the same dimension and type of wood. Position the decorative template on the wood and loosen the wing nuts on the corners. Push the template in place so that all corner stops fit the corners of the wood piece. Then measure from the edge of the piece to the inside edge of the template side bars. This measurement will be the distance from the routed design to the edge. If you wish to change it, turn the template over and move the corner stops. Make sure they are in the same holes for each corner. Then reposition the template on the door and again make sure the corner stops are up against the corners correctly.

As you rout the design, the door and template will have a tendency to move. To hold the door and template securely, make a wedge vise. By tapping in the wedge you can secure the door to the table. The hardest part is starting the router. Set the router in one corner and hold it firmly in place against the inside of the template, then turn it on. Move in a *clockwise direction*. When you approach the corner design, slow down and feel your way around the corner. You may also wish to position a strong light fairly low so you can see the corners as you come to them. Then proceed around the template to the next corner. Never back up the router—it will only chatter against the sides, enlarging the router groove in that area. If the cutter fails to cut a proper depth in some

When using templates, router must be fitted with special collar to prevent bit from cutting into template.

spots, proceed around the template clockwise and rework those areas. Try to hold the router base flat and secure against the template. After a test or two on scrap wood, you're ready for the good material. Make sure you turn the router off and allow the cutter to stop spinning before you attempt to remove it from the template or you may damage the routed groove or even the template.

There are many router bits that can be used for routing a pattern. With a little practice and care

A shop-made template can also be used to guide the router.

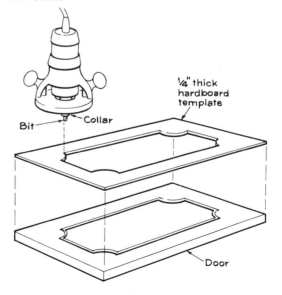

you'll soon be able to rout perfect patterns in cabinet doors, but the first time you'll probably be a bit shaky. It will take some practice to hold the router correctly.

The main points to remember in using the template are to take your time, make sure the template is set properly, position the router properly, and hold it securely. Always wear safety glasses when using a router.

Using the Arc Attachment

By adding the arc attachment to the basic template, you add versatility to the designs you can do. You can do arched design cabinet doors, or even circles if you want. You will have to modify your router somewhat to make the attachment fit. However, it only requires a ³⁄₁₆-inch hole bored in the router base to insert a holding pin for the pivot bar. Make sure the end of the pivot bar assembly which fits against the collar on your router is snugly in place before marking the hole in the router base. Then bore the hole, assemble the unit, and fasten the router to the pivot bar assembly with the pin as well as the outside "edge clamp." Make sure the nut on the pivot bar assembly is tight enough to hold it securely on the router.

To operate the unit fasten the template in place on the door front as before. Then select the proper lock bars and stop bars. These are determined by the width of the panel. Place these bars in the tracks provided in the base assembly of the unit and place the entire assembly in the middle of the template. Make sure the base assembly is centered horizontally, and then tighten the thumb screws on the sides of it. Select the pivot bar that corresponds to the radius of the arc you wish to rout and slide it into the base assembly. Adjust the bar for the length of radius desired. Then position the base assembly vertically for the desired position and tighten the bar clamps. Attach the router to the pivot arm assembly. Test the arc by swinging the router without it running. If it is in the correct position, move the router to the left side, move the stop bar all the way to the left side, and then start the router. Move clockwise. As soon as you leave the left stop, slide the stop bar all the way to the right side. This prevents overrunning the mark. Now just rout the rest of the pattern.

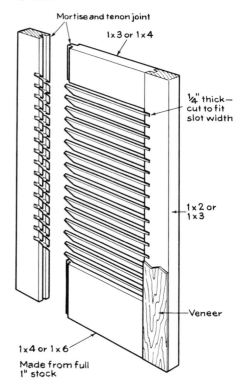

Louver door

Mortise and tenon joint

1 x 3 or 1 x 4

¼" thick— cut to fit slot width

1 x 2 or 1 x 3

Veneer

1 x 4 or 1 x 6

Made from full 1" stock

Louver Doors

Ready-made louver doors are available to fit almost any size opening. However, in some instances, as when a louver door of a special type of hardwood is required, you may have to make them in the shop. Louver doors can be made quite easily, but they won't have the perfectly uniform blind mortises of factory-made doors.

You can cut blind mortises with a router and guide strips. However, the easiest method is to use the same technique used for cutting cross molding on the table saw (see Chapter 14, page 227). After the stiles of the frame have been mortised and the tenons cut in the rails, the angled cuts for the slats are made on the stiles. The table saw guide is angled to provide the angle desired, and pins are used to space the cuts (see page 227). The cuts are made with a ¼-inch dado blade. Then one of the stiles and the two rails are assembled, glued, and clamped solidly until the glue dries. The angled slats are then glued in, and finally the opposite stile. The exposed ends of the slats can be left as is, or you can cover the frame with veneer to conceal them.

8

Drawers

The quality of drawer construction is the measure of a craftsman. A drawer can be anything from a box nailed together and slid into a cabinet case, to a structure approaching fine craft, with raised front panels and dovetail joints. A properly constructed and fitted drawer pulls out easily, yet stops before it tilts out completely, spilling its contents on the floor. In addition, it should pull out squarely.

Materials

Drawer fronts can be made of plywood—preferably lumber core, because this type provides a bet-

ter edge for shaping. But some smaller drawers, particularly the frame-and-panel type, are made of solid woods. Most drawer fronts are made of ¾- to ⅞-inch-thick material, except for some that also have decorative molding. The back and sides are normally of ½-inch material. Most large building-supply dealers carry fairly inexpensive stock that is specially milled to ½-inch thickness for cabinetmakers. The wood is often gum, willow, poplar, or other economical types. Better-quality drawers, however, have sides of oak, maple, or other hardwoods. Also, on better drawers, the top edges of the sides are usually shaped or rounded.

Types of Drawer Fronts

Basically, there are three types of drawer fronts: *lip, flush,* and *overlay* (the same terms used to

Drawers may be plain, such as the simple lip drawers on this Queen Anne-style lowboy.

On this ripple-front chest, drawers are the main design element.

describe cabinet doors). In cabinets that also have doors, the drawer fronts should match the doors, or at least have a design that is compatible with them. However, drawers often can't be made to match the doors exactly, because the drawers are smaller and so can't contain larger design elements such as massive moldings.

Drawer Construction

To ensure that the drawer will be well-fitted and fully operational, the drawers are generally constructed *after* it has been determined what type

of slides or guide system will be used to keep the drawers on track. Once these clearances have been determined and the cabinet framework constructed, the drawer dimensions are figured by measuring the actual opening in the cabinet framework. The drawers are then constructed, trial-fitted and adjusted. Finally, the sanding, staining and finishing operations take place.

Lip Drawers

Of the three basic types of drawer, the lip drawer is the most "forgiving" of small errors. For this reason it is commonly seen in kitchen cabinets as

Lip drawers are the easiest to construct and fit, and are quite often used on kitchen cabinets.

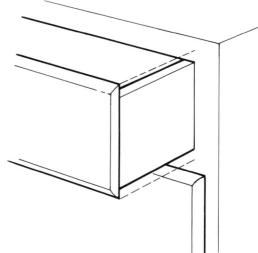

Below: Drawer parts of a common lip drawer include ⅜-inch lipped front of ¾-inch material, ½-inch sides and back, and ¼-inch hardboard bottom which fits in the dadoes and extends under bottom edge of back.

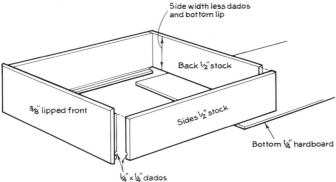

Side width less dados and bottom lip

Back ½" stock

⅜" lipped front

Sides ½" stock

Bottom ¼" hardboard

¼" x ¼" dados

well as in custom-made furniture. The normal lip drawer has a ⅜ × ⅜-inch lip which matches the standard ⅜-inch lip door.

Let's start with a simple routed or shaped one-piece drawer front with a ⅜-inch lip and rabbet joints between front and sides. The technique I'll describe is quick and easy, but it results in a good drawer. (The same technique also serves for frame-and-panel drawers, except that in most instances the frame pieces are lipped before they're assembled.)

Cutting and Shaping the Drawer Fronts. In almost all instances, you'll probably cut the ⅜-inch lip around the edges first, then make additional rabbets for the sides, and then shape the edges. In any case, first cut the drawer front to size, ⅜-inch larger all around (a total of ¾ inch larger in each dimension) than the finished opening. Incidentally, measure the opening in several

Construction of a simple ⅜-inch lip drawer begins with cutting ⅜-inch rabbets around outside edge of the drawer front.

Rabbets on the sides of the drawer front are cut ½ inch more to accommodate the sides.

places and take the smallest measurement so you won't have a drawer that is too small for the opening. You may find as much as a ¹⁄₁₆- to ¹⁄₃₂-inch difference in measurements.

Use a regular saw blade or dado blade in a radial arm saw or table saw to cut the ⅜ × ⅜-inch rabbets along the edges. Then widen the rabbets on the left and right sides an additional ½ inch (or the thickness of the drawer-side stock) to allow for the drawer sides.

As with the doors shown in Chapter 7, you can rout or shape almost any design onto the drawer fronts. When shaping the edges, make the cross-cuts first, then the with-the-grain cuts: The shaper has a tendency to leave splinters at the end of the crosscuts, and the grain cuts will normally remove these.

Next, make a ¼ × ¼-inch dado on the bottom edge, ¼ inch up from the edge of the lip. This dado is to accommodate the drawer bottom. (Note: When using certain drawer slides, this measurement may have to be ⅜ inch.)

Front outside edges of the drawer front are run over a shaper to round them slightly. Make cross-grain cuts first so any splintering will be removed by the long cuts.

Cutting and Assembling the Sides and Back. Cut the drawer sides to the proper dimensions, and make a ¼ × ¼-inch dado ¼ inch up from the bottom edges to accept the drawer bottom. Make sure you cut both a left-hand and a right-hand side for each drawer.

Cut the drawer back ½ or ⅝ inch narrower than the sides so that the bottom edge of the back will meet the top edge of the dadoes in the side pieces. Assemble the pieces, and make sure that the top edges of all surfaces are flush. (The "top edge" of the front piece is the inside edge of its top rabbet.) At the same time, make sure the bottom dadoes in the sides and front mate properly. Glue and nail the drawer sides, back and front together, using cement-coated nails.

Place the drawer upside down on a flat surface, cut a ¼-inch plywood or hardboard bottom to fit in place in the dadoes, and slide it in place. Place a small square on the drawer and square it up, then nail the bottom in place on the back edge. This will hold the entire drawer square.

Above: Dadoes for ¼-inch-thick bottoms are cut in the drawer sides and front.
Right: Sides are fastened to the front with glue and small nails.

Below: Then the back is glued and nailed to the sides.
Right: The bottom is slid in place in the side dadoes and fastened in place with nails. A small shop square is used to assure that the assembly is straight.

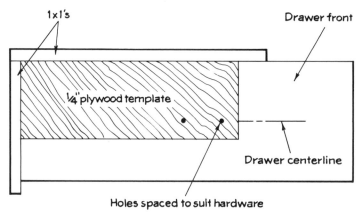

1x1's

Drawer front

¼" plywood template

Drawer centerline

Holes spaced to suit hardware

Jig simplifies placement of holes for drawer pulls if you have a number of drawer fronts of the same size. Two 1 × 1's are tacked to workbench top to hold pieces in place.

Assembly-line production. You can speed up the whole operation by doing it in assembly-line fashion. That is, first cut all drawer fronts to size. Then shape the outside edges of all fronts, cut all backs, and cut all sides at the same time. Then sand all pieces and stack them in order around you on a large table. Have glue, nails and fasteners ready before you begin assembly. Mark the holes for the drawer-pull hardware and bore them. A jig such as shown is a great help in boring the holes in a number of drawers.

Overlay Drawers

An overlay drawer is constructed much like a lip. The difference is that the front piece overlaps the cabinet frame partially or completely, so the edge rabbets or dadoes are cut farther in. When the drawer front overlaps completely, the cabinet frame is left unfinished, since the drawer fronts are actually the facing of the cabinet. The frame is exposed only when the drawers are pulled out.

The entire drawer must fit the opening exactly and not be twisted or warped. Otherwise, it will throw the edges of the flush front out of line with the sides of the case. The precision required makes an overlay drawer harder to construct and fit in place.

Flush Drawers

This type of drawer is fitted back inside the casework so that its front is flush with the front of the cabinet or furniture case. Because of the precise

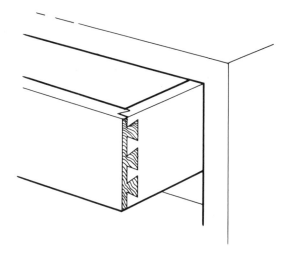

Above: Flush drawer fronts are even with the front of the cabinet. This is the hardest style to fit properly.
Below: Overlay drawers can entirely overlap the front facing of the cabinet.

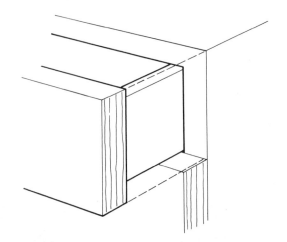

fits required, flush drawers are the hardest to build and install. There should be no more than a 1/16-inch clearance all around the drawer. In addition, a flush drawer that is slightly cockeyed or that warps after construction will cause troubles, as will a drawer that swells from excessive humidity.

High-Quality Drawers

Now, let's construct a high-quality drawer, taking the time with it that we'd take for a fine, handmade piece of furniture. The drawer front can be flush, lip or overlay, depending on the design of the furniture. The most important thing is the joinery used.

Joints. One typical joint, actually a double dado, is called a "drawer corner." Multiple dovetails are also often used on high-quality drawers. When the front extends out past the sides, as in

lip or overlay drawers, the joinery is often a dado or dovetail slot. A milled shaper joint is another type of drawer front joint that is often used by furniture manufacturers. It is made with a special cutter set in a shaper, table saw, or radial arm saw.

On fine drawers the back is the same width as the sides, and it has a groove in the bottom edge to accept the bottom. (In production-line drawers, the bottom is instead tacked or stapled in place from underneath.) The backs of fine drawers will usually be fitted in place with a strong joint such as a dovetail.

When the sides extend farther than the back, as in an extremely deep cabinet, the back is fitted in dadoes in the sides. The bottom is fitted in place at the same time the back is fitted in the sides. When cutting drawer bottoms, make sure you make them absolutely square, and allow 1/16-inch clearance on the sides and the back or front.

Front-to-Side Joints

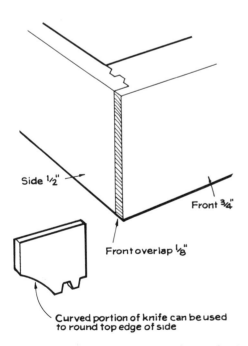

One of the best joints between drawer front and sides is a milled shaper joint. It can be made with a three-wing cutter in a shaper or with a molding cutter in a table saw or radial arm saw.

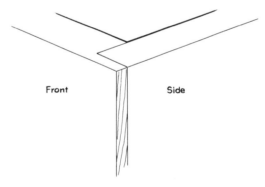

Above: A simple rabbet joint can be used on flush drawers. *Below:* In a typical lip door, the front is rabbeted an additional ½ inch for the sides.

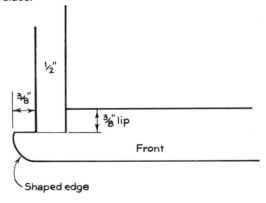

Front-to-Side Joints (Cont'd.)

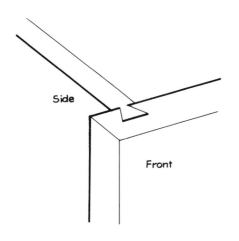

A dovetail dado slot can also be used on lip drawers.

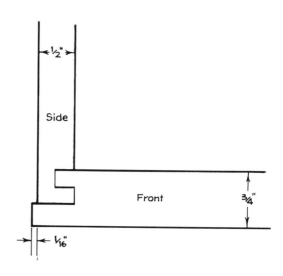

A locked joint is often used in fine cabinetry.

The first step in making locked joint is to cut dadoes in side pieces. A ¼ × ¼-inch dado is cut ¼-inch from end of stock.

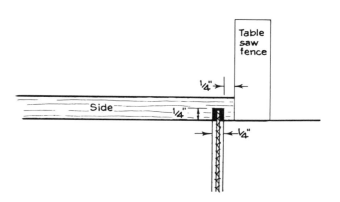

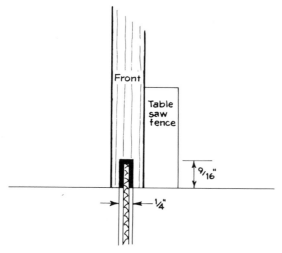

Next, ¼-inch dadoes are cut in the ends of the drawer front.

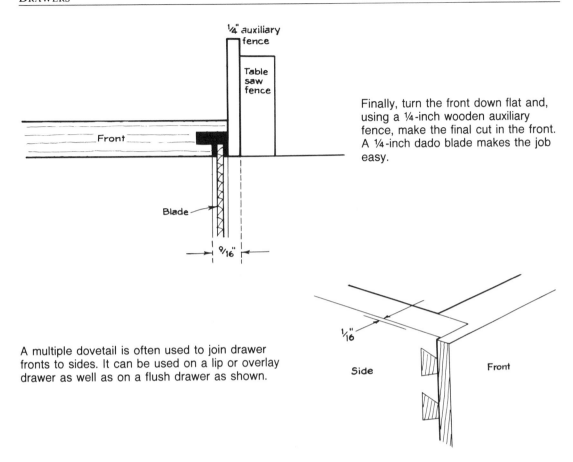

Finally, turn the front down flat and, using a ¼-inch wooden auxiliary fence, make the final cut in the front. A ¼-inch dado blade makes the job easy.

A multiple dovetail is often used to join drawer fronts to sides. It can be used on a lip or overlay drawer as well as on a flush drawer as shown.

A multiple dovetail can be cut with an accessory template and dovetail bit in a router. The dovetail cuts on the drawer front are usually stopped to create a *lap* dovetail.

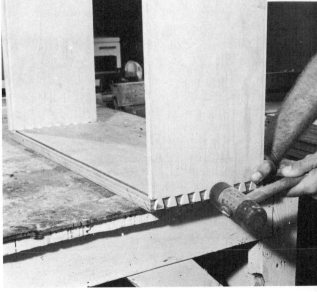

Back-to-Side Joints

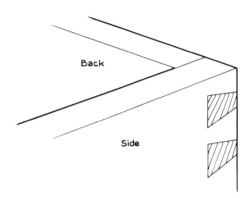

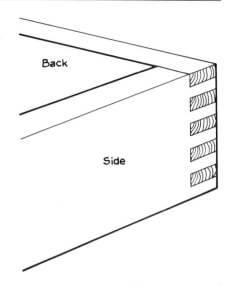

A traditional joint between the back and sides of a drawer is the multiple dovetail.

A box or finger joint is also frequently used. (See Chapter 5 for details on cutting this joint.)

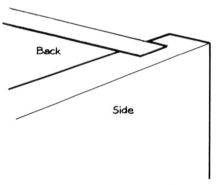

Dado or dovetail slots are good joints for drawer sides and back.

In fine cabinetry, drawer backs are dadoed to accept the bottom. The sides can also extend past the back as shown to create a drawer stop for flush-mounted drawers.

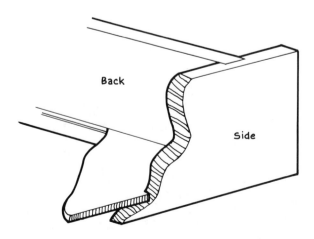

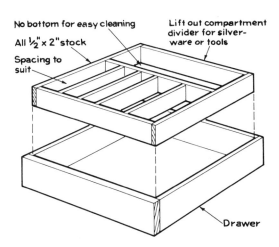

No bottom for easy cleaning

All ½" x 2" stock

Spacing to suit

Lift out compartment divider for silverware or tools

Drawer

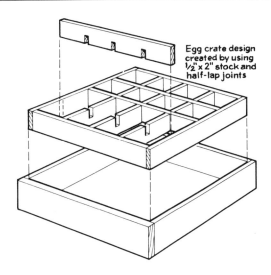

Egg crate design created by using ½" x 2" stock and half-lap joints

Drawer Dividers

A drawer is a plain drawer, unless it is fitted with interior dividers. Then it becomes almost anything from a jewelry tray to a shoe rack. There are hundreds of different divider configurations that can be used to make a drawer more practical. (Shown above are two examples.) A simple lift-out tray in a deep drawer can make the drawer doubly practical. With it you can keep many small items from shifting around. The tray can cover flat items, or it can lie under them, letting you utilize the full depth of the drawer. Or you can install slides on the drawer back and front so that you can slide the tray to either side as needed. One of the most common drawer dividers is that used for silverware.

Drawer Installation

To be fully serviceable, a drawer must be precisely fitted in place as well as properly constructed. This is one of the jobs that is often slighted, because it sometimes takes a great deal of patience and a lot of fitting. In economical furniture, the drawers may be simply slid in place on a shelf. In kitchen cabinets where a large number of drawers are installed, they are often installed on metal rollers and tracks which require only a front facing strip to ride on and a back vertical bar to secure the tracks. Good furniture, on the other hand, will usually have wooden drawer glides or slides, and a dust panel and web

or skeleton frame to hold the drawer securely in place and to guide it.

There are three types of guides that can be used to hold a drawer squarely in place and keep it on track as it is moved in and out. A *center guide* is a channel centered in the cabinet and fastened to the front and back pieces of the cabinet framework. If metal or plastic channels are used, a roller attached to the back of the drawer serves to guide the drawer in the channel. If a wood runner is used, there are several methods of keeping the drawer on track as shown in the illustrations. For wider drawers, two channels can be used to improve stability. *Side guides* consist of rails attached to the sides of the cabinet on which the drawer rides by means of matching rails attached to its sides. Factory-made side guides have rollers mounted on the fixed portion of the rails to help the drawer slide smoothly. Shop-made side guides are made by matching wood runner strips on the sides of the drawers to dadoes cut in the cabinet sides, or vice versa. *Corner guides* are the easiest to install. They are simply blocks of wood that are fastened to the framework to keep the drawers from wobbling to the left or right.

Installing Metal or Plastic Slides

These slides have to be purchased before the dimensions of the cabinet framework and drawers are calculated, because the clearances required depend on the dimensions of the track and rollers. If a horizontal cross rail is used at the back of the cabinet, it should be at the same level as the front lower frame rail. If the cabinet depth is less than the length of the channels you purchase, the channels can be cut to length with a hacksaw. Be sure to follow manufacturer's instructions in all aspects of installation.

Monorail unit. For the unit shown in the illustrations, the clearances required are ¼ inch between the height of the opening and the height of the drawer sides, and ⅛ inch between the sides of the drawer and the vertical frame pieces of the case. The rail brackets are fastened to the front and back of the cabinet framework, and the side rollers to the corners of the frame. The roller bracket is fastened to the back of the drawer as shown.

In some cases you may not be able to mount the channel below the drawer. Here you must use an overhead mounting. The drawer channel is turned upside down, and its brackets are attached to the top pieces of the frame. The roller is installed on top of the drawer back and rides on the overhead channel.

If a drawer is extra wide, you can use two tracks to help stabilize it.

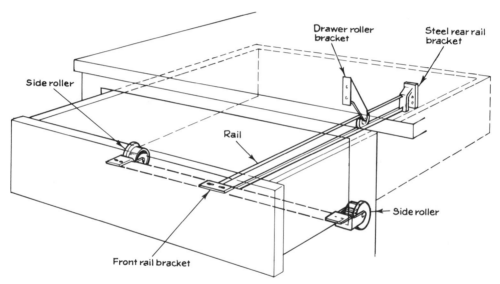

Metal drawer slides make drawer installation quite easy. This is a monorail assembly.

The roller guide that rides in the monorail channel is fastened to the back of the drawer.

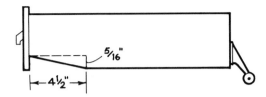

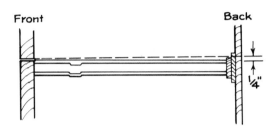

You can make a drawer self-closing by cutting a taper on the front as shown and lowering the back of the runner about ¼ inch.

You can also make the drawer self-closing. For this operation, the cabinet opening must be ½ inch greater than the height of the drawer sides. Also, the drawer front must be high enough to cover the opening when the drawer drops down and is closed. A taper is first cut on the drawer sides as shown. The front rail bracket is mounted as before, but the rear bracket is mounted ¼ inch below this level. Once the drawer gets within 4 inches of the frame it will close automatically.

Side-mounted slides. This type of assembly can be used for drawers that hold a heavy weight, such as a stereo turntable. The main thing in the installation of these slides is to make sure that both are located properly so the drawer doesn't slant or tilt to one side. Any unevenness can make operation quite difficult. In most instances, the clearance between the drawer sides and the cabinet opening will be ½ inch on either side, and total top and bottom clearance ⅛ inch.

The assembly for each drawer consists of two U-channels, two rails, and two rollers with brackets. The smaller rail pieces are attached to each side of the drawer bottom, and ride in the U-channels attached to the cabinet sides. The rollers are attached to the U-channel pieces to help guide the rails. Some side-mounted slides have nylon ball bearing wheels for exceptionally smooth operation.

Shop-made Wooden Slides

The same principles used in metal slides are applied in making wooden ones. As described in Chapter 6, fine furniture typically has a web frame between each drawer, with a dust panel dadoed into it to prevent items from dropping between drawers or getting hung up. Wood runners and other devices can be fastened to this web framing to help guide the drawers and prevent them from tipping out. If web framing is not present, side guides can be used.

Center runner. The simplest type of shop-made guide is a single center runner fastened to the front and back pieces of the web frame, with the drawer back simply notched to allow it to slide on the runner. The front end of the runner should be rounded as shown. This drawer will,

Side-mounted rail slides are used on heavy-duty drawers. Some models have nylon ball bearings for unusually quiet and effortless operation.

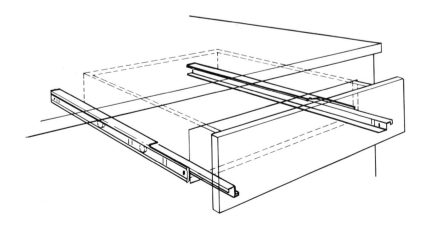

**Web frame and
dust panel**

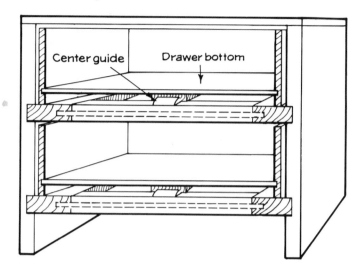

Center guide   Drawer bottom

In cabinets with a web frame
construction, drawer runners can
simply be attached to the front and
back of the web frame.

Runner should be set back about ¾
inch from the edge of the cabinet
front, and its front edge should be
rounded.

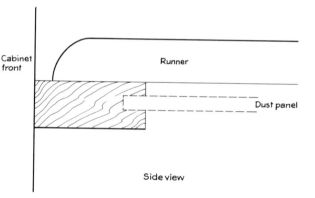

Cabinet
front

Runner

Dust panel

Side view

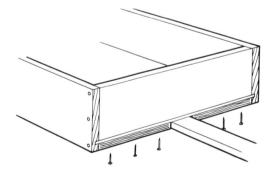

There are several methods of keeping a drawer on
track on a center runner. One is to tack wood strips
on the drawer bottom as shown. U-shape channels
or strips of wood that fit on either side of the center
runner may also be used. (The drawer sides should
support the weight of the drawer, not the guides.)

A simple way to prevent drawers from tipping out is
to install a plastic clip on the drawer back. The clip
fits over the runner and strikes the frame at the end
of the run.

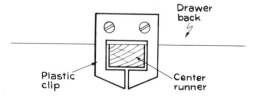

Drawer
back

Plastic
clip

Center
runner

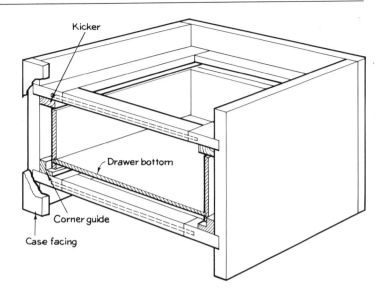

Corner guides are often used on cabinets with front facings. Kickers are fastened to web frame to prevent drawer beneath from tipping down.

however, tip down when pulled out. One means to prevent tipping is to use ready-made plastic clips which fasten to the back of the drawer and fit down over the wood runner. Or you can make your own clips from thin pieces of ⅛-inch plywood. A better method, however, is to install a *kicker,* which is a wood strip fastened to the web frame above the drawer. The back top edge of the drawer rides against the kicker, preventing the drawer from tipping when pulled out.

Corner guides. These are usually formed as part of the web frame construction. A side block or L-shaped block is used to keep the drawer aligned and prevent it from wobbling sideways. A kicker is usually installed over the top to prevent the drawer from tipping down.

Side guides. These guides are quite different from center runner or corner guides, and they actually resemble metal slides. They are usually used in cabinets without web frames. If the cabi-

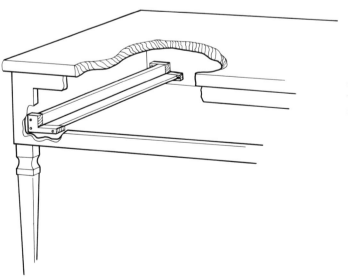

Corner guides are sometimes used as the entire support for the drawer in small tables such as this one.

net sides are solid-panel, a groove or dado can be cut in them to serve as a channel, and a wood strip that fits the groove is fastened to the drawer. In frame-and-panel constructions, the drawer sides can be grooved and a wooden strip fastened to the cabinet sides. When a groove is cut in the drawers, the drawer sides should be of at least ¾-inch stock.

A drawer can also be hung under a top by placing an L-shaped guide over a lip in the top sides of the drawers. Naturally, the grooves must be cut before the drawer is assembled. Applying a bit of beeswax to the drawer slides and cabinet mating edges will help them slide better and prevent sticking. Drawer stops can be installed to prevent the drawer from accidentally being pulled all the way out.

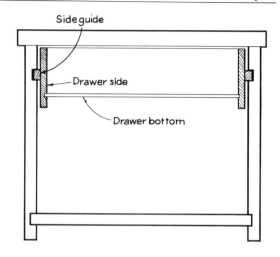

Side guides can be dadoed in solid-wood or lumber-core-plywood cabinet sides. In this case, guides are the sole support of drawer.

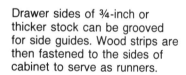

Drawer sides of ¾-inch or thicker stock can be grooved for side guides. Wood strips are then fastened to the sides of cabinet to serve as runners.

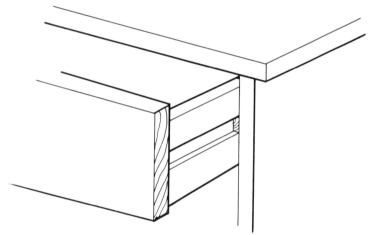

9

Shelves

All cabinets and many types of furniture have some form of drawers, shelves, trays, or vertical dividers. As we discussed in the previous chapter, well-designed, properly constructed drawers are an example of fine workmanship. Shelves and dividers are just as important. The design of the interior arrangement of furniture, cabinets, or built-ins is just as important as the exterior. A poorly designed interior wastes space and in some cases can be totally useless for the job intended. A prime example is overhead kitchen wall cabinets with shelves so deep you can't reach the back, or a china hutch with shelves spaced too closely to allow storage of the items they were intended for.

Cabinet and Furniture Shelves

Cabinet and furniture shelving can be made from a number of materials, including solid wood, plywood, particleboard, hardboard, and glass. When using hardwood plywood, or plywood or particleboard covered with veneer, the exposed edges of the shelves are usually covered with a band of matching veneer or a strip of solid wood.

There are two basic types of shelves: fixed and adjustable.

Fixed Shelving

When building fixed shelving you must carefully plan the shelf spacing. There are some pretty standard rules, but of course they can be broken or "bent" to suit special situations. The standard measurements should give you a starting place:

Book shelves
  Shelf width—8 inches for average books
    12 inches for large books
  Distance between shelves—10 inches on upper shelves for novels, 13 inches on lower shelves for display type books

China cabinets
  Shelf width—8 inches on upper shelves
  Distance between shelves—9 to 10 inches

Vanity bottoms
  Shelf width—24 inches

Kitchen wall cabinets
  Shelf width—12 to 14 inches

Kitchen counter cabinets
  Shelf width—24 inches

In many cases fixed shelving is a structural part of the cabinet or furniture, and is used to brace and strengthen the casework. A common example is a night stand where the bottom shelf acts as a rail. Shelves also are strengthening members for some china cabinets and buffets, as well as some built-ins.

There are several different methods of joining fixed shelving in place. The most common joint used is the butt joint. This is used when the cabinet sides won't be exposed. The shelf is normally butted against the cabinet or furniture sides and

Plywood or veneer-covered particleboard are excellent shelving materials, but their edges are somewhat unsightly. Veneer tape (left) and solid-wood molding are often used to cover plywood edges.

Veneer tape

Solid wood molding

In some types of furniture, such as this open-front stand, a fixed shelf also acts as a rail and serves to brace the construction.

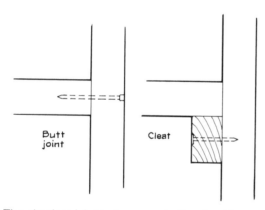

The simplest joint between a shelf and cabinet side is a butt joint fastened with glue and nails or screws. A cleat under the shelf makes the joint much stronger. If a cleat is used, the shelf does not have to be fastened in place, but the cabinet will be strengthened if it is.

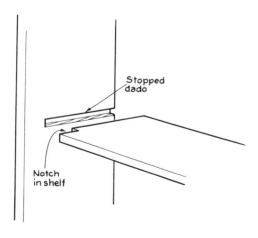

nailed or screwed in place. To strengthen this joint, a quarter-round or flat wood cleat can be placed under the edges of the shelf and fastened to the cabinet sides. The shelf can be fastened to the cleat for additional security.

If the shelf is a long one, it's a good idea to run a cleat along its back edge as well. Or you can use a middle shelf standard to help provide support in the center of the shelf. Most wooden shelves are made of ¾-inch stock, and for most uses they should not be longer than four feet without some sort of center bracing.

A better method of installing fixed shelving, and one that is used quite often, is to fit the shelves into dadoes cut in the cabinet or furniture sides. A stopped dado can be used, or facers installed to make the joint invisible from the front. Still better is a joint such as a dovetail which locks the shelves into the cabinet sides and provides even more strengthening of the cabinet or furniture case.

Adjustable Shelving

There are many obvious advantages to adjustable shelving, if the shelves are not needed as a structural member. Fasteners and standards for adjustable shelves can be shop-made or purchased.

The following methods are usually used on cabinets that have doors or front facers to conceal the interior of the cabinet. It is a little trickier to adjust shelves in a cabinet with front facers, since the shelves cannot be pulled out of the case. However, there's no great difficulty as long as the cleats or brackets are removable.

One way to make adjustable shelving is to bore two lines of stopped holes on each side of the cabinet. (To bore stopped holes, use a drill bit depth gauge, or wrap masking tape around the bit to mark the depth of the hole.) The holes don't have to run the entire length of the sides, but should cover an area of about six inches in the general vicinity of the shelf location. They should

Left: A stopped dado or dovetail slot makes the joint between a shelf and cabinet side invisible from the front. This method is often used on cabinets or bookcases without front facings.

On a cabinet with front facings like this one, either fixed or adjustable shelving can be used. However, the cleats for adjustable shelves would have to be removable.

One of the simplest methods of making shelving adjustable is to bore two lines of ⅜-inch stopped holes a short distance from the front and back of the cabinet or case. Four short lengths of ⅜-inch dowel are then inserted to hold each shelf. Purchased metal or plastic support clips can also be used, and these provide stronger shelf supports than the dowels. (Check the diameter of clips before drilling holes.)

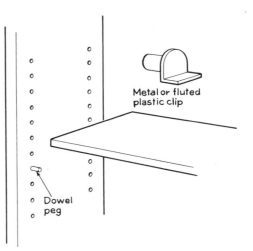

Metal or fluted
plastic clip

Dowel
peg

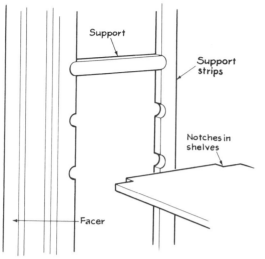

Among the strongest shop-made supports for adjustable shelving are crosspieces fitted into notched support strips. The shelves are notched at the corners to allow their ends to fit over the support bars.

Right: Adjustable shelves are easy to install with metal standards and clips. The standards are simply screwed in place on the case or cabinet sides, and the clips snapped into them. If the standards are not recessed, as shown in left drawing, you will have to allow for their depth at each end of the shelves.

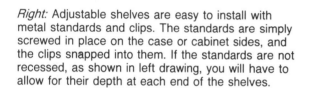

In this built-in installation, metal standards are recessed into the case sides to allow the shelves to run full-length.

be spaced about an inch apart, and bored fairly close to the shelf corners so the shelves won't wobble or tilt. Short lengths of wood dowel, or L-shape plastic or metal pegs, are inserted to serve as removable brackets.

A second shop-made arrangement consists of wooden strips that are cut to receive support bars. A 1×2 board is drilled down the center with 1½-inch holes. Then the board is ripped into two pieces, and the pieces glued to the front and back of the cabinet sides. Strips of wood with 1½-inch rounded ends fit in between the guides to provide a locking, movable support for the shelves. The corners of the shelves are notched to fit around the guides.

Probably the easiest method of installing shelves is to use metal shelf standards and shelf clips. The standards come in a number of different finishes, including wood grain, and can be cut to length with a hacksaw. They can either be surface-mounted on the sides of the cabinet or recessed into dadoes. If the standards are flush mounted, the shelves must be cut short enough to slip down between the metal standards, and there will be a gap between the shelves and the cabinet sides. (For glass shelves, it's a good idea to use rubber tip shelf clips.)

On cabinets without front facers, you can simply cut slightly oversize dadoes spaced about two

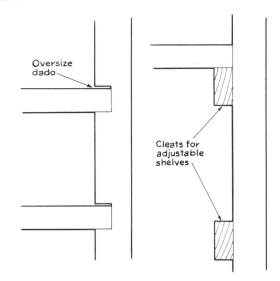

On cabinets or cases without front facings, adjustable shelves can be installed in much the same way as fixed shelves. A series of slightly oversize dadoes or cleats along the cabinet sides will allow shelves to be slid in at the desired level. (On a built-in type of installation, drawers can be fitted with wood strips to fit in the dadoes or over the cleats, and drawers and shelves alternated for more versatility.)

inches apart. By the same token, a line of cleats fastened to the cabinet sides will suffice.

Lining case sides with redwood siding material is another means to provide for adjustable shelving. In this installation, pigeonhole dividers, drawers, and other storage devices were fitted with side guides and integrated with the shelves.

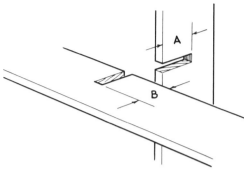

Pigeonhole dividers are made by crosslapping the horizontal pieces with vertical ones. The distances A and B must be equal, and all stock should be the same width.

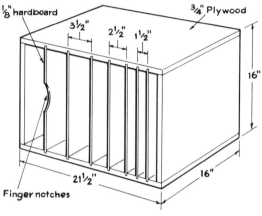

Vertical dividers are useful in many types of cabinets. The example shown is a "pan-rack" cabinet designed to organize the space above a refrigerator. The top and bottom of the case are cut with ¼-inch-deep dadoes to accept the hardboard dividers.

Adjustable wall shelves are easy to install with preslotted metal standards and matching brackets. Any type and size of shelf may be used—including glass, as shown at right.

Adjusting Shelves. To rearrange shelves in a cabinet with front facers, the trick is to place the bottom shelf in place on its brackets, then stack all the rest of the shelves on it. Start installation with the top shelf and work down—slide each shelf up, snap in the metal clips, and then let the shelf drop down on them.

Dividers

A common interior divider system is the pigeon-hole system often seen in roll-top desks. These are made egg-crate fashion by cutting half-way into each divider, then crosslapping the pieces. The system is then fitted in place in the casework.

Vertical partitions are also useful on many types of furniture. These are usually stationary and are fit in dadoes cut in the top and bottom of the case. Usually their exposed edges are covered with a facer strip.

Wall Shelving

Slotted metal standards, brackets, and shelves for adjustable wall shelves are available in hardware stores in a variety of colors and sizes. The standards can be anchored to a hollow wall with toggle bolts or expansion anchors (molly bolts), and the brackets are simply inserted at any point along the standards. Standards, brackets and shelves for wall shelving can also be shop-made, The shelf system shown in the photo is constructed with 1¼-inch pine stock and matching pine brackets. The bolts used to hold unit to wall are concealed with metal rosettes.

The brackets, shelves, and standards for this shop-made wall system are constructed with 1 ¼-inch pine stock. As with the metal standard and bracket systems, the shelves can be arranged in any manner. The shelves and brackets are fastened to the standards with countersunk screws driven through the backs of the standards. The edges of all components can be shaped with a router or shaper.

10

Legs and Frames

There are countless types, sizes, and shapes of furniture and cabinet legs. They can be merely added on, as the tapered ready-made legs on modern furniture, or they can be an integral part of a project, as in a knee-hole desk or other type of frame-and-panel construction. (When a leg runs up through the construction of a project, it is called a post.)

In many cases the legs are the distinctive design element of the furniture, as the cabriole legs on Queen Anne-style furniture, or the heavy turned legs of Spanish styling. Today's craftsman can purchase ready-made legs that enable him to make almost any style of furniture. There are kits for Early American, French Provincial, Mediterranean, modern, and other styles. In some cases they are fitted with built-in screws or metal mounting plates for fastening directly to a top; in other cases they are to be used with rails or aprons.

There are only seven basic leg styles although there are a great many variations and combinations of types. They are: square straight, square tapered, turned, cabriole, compound sawn, rectangular, and pedestal.

Legs are the chief design element in many styles of furniture. This early 18th-century dressing table has the characteristic cabriole legs of Queen Anne-period furniture. *The Metropolitan Museum of Art, Gift of Mrs. Russell Sage, 1910.*

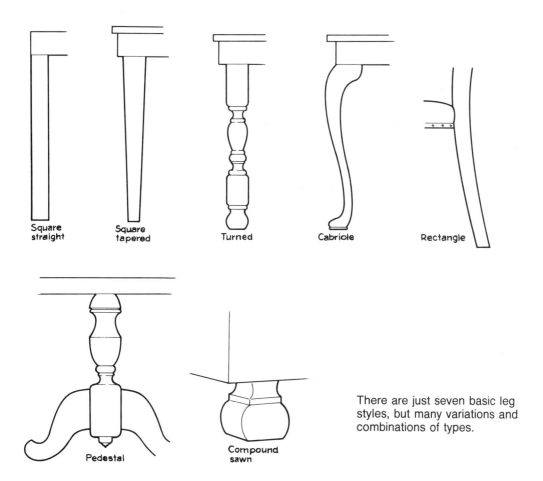

Square straight Square tapered Turned Cabriole Rectangle

Pedestal Compound sawn

There are just seven basic leg styles, but many variations and combinations of types.

Square Straight

This, of course, is the simplest type of leg to make. It is often seen on ultra-modern style furniture such as parson's tables. It is almost always used in conjunction with a rail or apron and provides a sturdy yet effective leg if it is not too thin in cross section. One method of making a more interesting square leg is to laminate it. This provides a contemporary styling that shows off the grain of fine wood, yet the leg is simple and attractive.

Square Tapered

Tapering square legs on just two sides results in an Oriental style leg, but all four sides can be tapered, too. This latter style is used on a great deal of furniture and provides a pleasing, sturdy leg. There are a number of ways to taper legs, depending on the tool that is used. You can taper legs on a table saw, radial arm saw, or jointer. Or you can do it with a hand plane or handsaw. Tapered legs provide a simple elegance that is appealing on many projects. It is the typical type of leg found on Italian Provincial or Mediterranean style furniture. Usually only a portion of the leg is tapered, and the rest of the leg is left square to serve as a post or part of a leg-and-rail construction.

To cut the taper, first run the stock over a jointer to square it and smooth all four sides. It can also be smoothed with a belt or disc sander. Mark where the taper will start at the top of the leg. Then continue the mark all around the leg using a combination or other small square. Mark the amount of taper that must be cut off on the bottom of the leg.

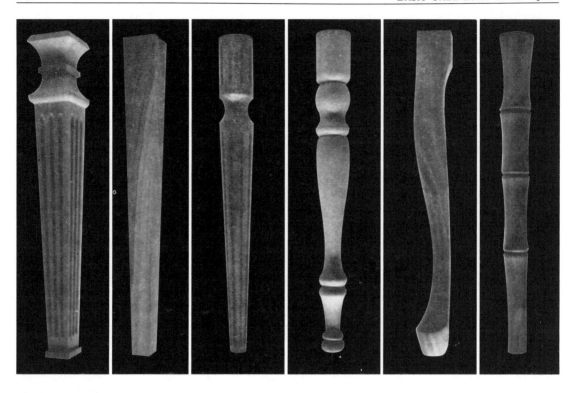

Ready-made legs in wood or metal are available in almost any style. Shown are some of the styles available in woods such as ash, gum, walnut and beech. Most come in several sizes. *M. Wolchonok & Sons, Inc.*

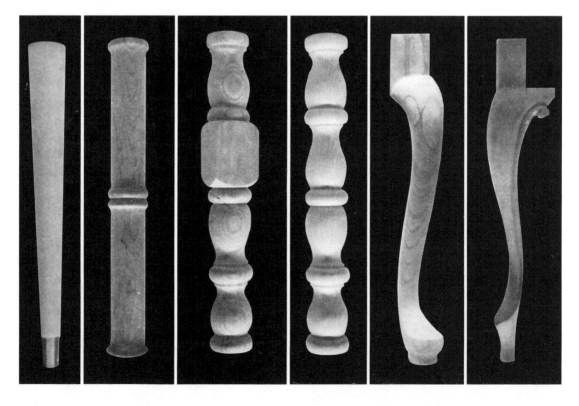

The square legs of a parson's table are the simplest leg design.

Laminated square leg for chair

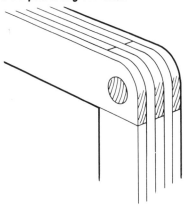

A laminated square leg can be made to match the arms of a chair.

Tapered legs

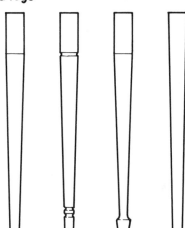

A square leg can be formed into a tapered leg. There are many different types of tapered legs.

Taper Jigs for Radial Arm Saw or Table Saw

A good craftsman can cut a taper on a table saw without any type of guide. However, a taper guide jig, such as the one shown, will greatly simplify the job and assure that all tapers on all legs are exactly the same. The jig can be a simple one that is used for only one taper and leg length, or an adjustable jig can be made. If using a simple jig, make the first two adjacent side cuts with the leg in the first notch, then set the leg in the second notch for the other two cuts. Note that the second notch is twice the width of the taper. The length of the taper is determined by the distance between the end of the guide board and the notch on the step block. For instance, if you want a 12-inch taper on a 16-inch block, you would fasten the step block so that the distance from its first notch to the end of the guide board is 12 inches. To taper the 16-inch block its full length, you would set the taper length at 16 inches. Place the jig and

Simple jig for cutting tapered legs

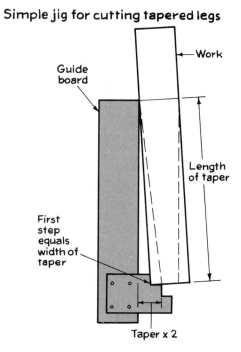

Work

Guide board

Length of taper

First step equals width of taper

Taper x 2

The first notch of leg-tapering jig is used to make the first cuts on two adjacent sides; then the leg is moved into the second notch to taper the next two sides. A fine-tooth saw blade set 1/8-inch above the top of the leg is used to make the cuts.

An adjustable tapering jig is useful if a number of different taper angles and lengths are to be cut.

Adjustable tapering jig

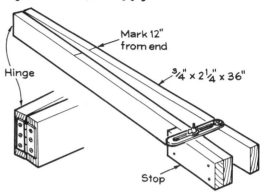

Mark 12" from end

Hinge

$\frac{3}{4}$" × 2$\frac{1}{4}$" × 36"

Stop

Determining taper

Overall taper each side

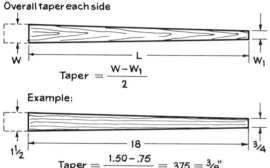

W   L W_1

$$\text{Taper} = \frac{W - W_1}{2}$$

Example:

18    $\frac{3}{4}$

$1\frac{1}{2}$

$$\text{Taper} = \frac{1.50 - .75}{2} = .375 = \frac{3}{8}"$$

Taper per foot each side

$$\text{Taper} = \frac{W - W_1}{L} \times 6$$

$$\text{Taper} = \frac{1.50 - .75}{18} \times 6 = .25 = \frac{1}{4}"$$

Taper per foot (one side only)

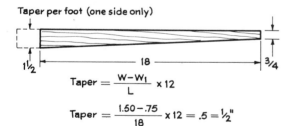

18    $\frac{3}{4}$

$1\frac{1}{2}$

$$\text{Taper} = \frac{W - W_1}{L} \times 12$$

$$\text{Taper} = \frac{1.50 - .75}{18} \times 12 = .5 = \frac{1}{2}"$$

How to set adjustable tapering jig

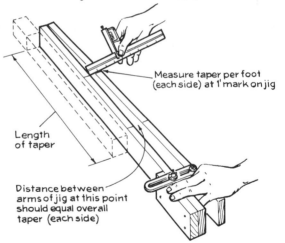

Measure taper per foot (each side) at 1' mark on jig

Length of taper

Distance between arms of jig at this point should equal overall taper (each side)

block on a table saw with a fine-tooth blade set about ⅛ inch above the wood surface, and start at the point shown in the drawing.

You can also make an adjustable jig that can be used for cutting almost any degree of taper. This jig is nothing more than two pieces of 36-inch-long 1 × 2s with a stop on one end and hinge on the other. A small metal sliding clamp is fastened on one end. Make a mark across both pieces of wood 12 inches from the hinged end. To use this jig, spread the two arms so that the distance

between them at this one-foot mark equals the amount of taper per foot on the leg. For instance, if you have a foot-long leg that is to be tapered the full length from three inches at the top to two inches at the bottom, the taper would be one inch. So you would divide by two to find the overall taper on each side of the leg (which in this example is the same as the amount of taper per foot). The arms of the jig would then be set so that the marks are one-half inch apart.

To use the jig, set the saw fence at the com-

Using adjustable taper jig on table saw

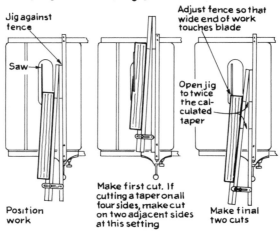

Jig against fence

Saw

Position work

Make first cut. If cutting a taper on all four sides, make cut on two adjacent sides at this setting

Adjust fence so that wide end of work touches blade

Open jig to twice the cal- culated taper

Make final two cuts

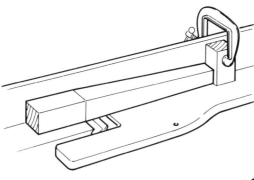

To cut stopped tapers on a jointer, a stop block is clamped to the fence at the infeed end of the table as shown at left. If the taper is to be cut in the middle of the leg, a second stop block is positioned at the outfeed end (as shown below) to stop the cut. All four sides are cut, then the infeed table is lowered just a bit more and the four sides cut again until correct taper is reached. A push stick should be used to hold the stock against the cutter.

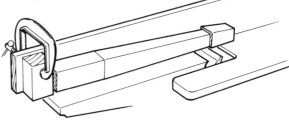

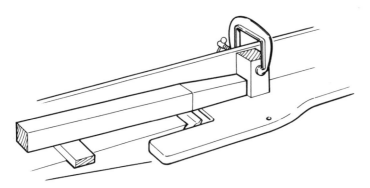

When tapering on the jointer, a small block can be tack-nailed to the leg to support it at correct angle. Front end of leg rests on table, and cutter just contacts work at start of cut. The same block is used on other three sides.

bined widths of the work and the jig. Make the first two adjacent cuts, then reset the jig to double the per-foot measurement and cut the other two adjacent sides. You can also cut a tapered leg on a radial arm saw with the same jigs by running the work through the saw at the rip setting.

Cutting Tapers on a Jointer

You can make tapered square legs with a jointer by tack-nailing a small block as thick as the amount of taper on the end of the stock. Pull the stock toward you in this operation. Another method is to clamp a block to the fence to support the stock at the point where the cut will start and set the jointer depth for the amount of taper. For instance, for a 12-inch tapered leg, you would clamp the block in place 12 inches in front of the cutter. With some softwoods you can set the depth as much as a half inch to cut the taper. However, it's best to make successive light cuts. A protective block should be used to hold the stock against the action of the cutter in this oper-

ation. If you wish to make a stopped taper in the middle of a leg, use a stop block at each end of the cut.

Turned Legs

Turned legs, posts, and spindles—which are all really the same—are traditional on Early American and Colonial furniture styles, and on such classic examples of fine furniture as the Sheraton pedestal table and the Windsor chair. The round tapered leg, mostly used on modern furniture, is also a turned leg. It can easily be made on the home lathe, and a brass end cap can be fitted to it just as on factory-made legs. However, purchased legs of all types are so economical that it's really not worth the trouble to make them yourself unless you need legs of a special wood. Many manufacturers specialize in making legs, and they use large automatic lathes that turn them out every few seconds. In fact, you probably can't purchase the material to turn your own as cheaply as you can buy the ready-made leg.

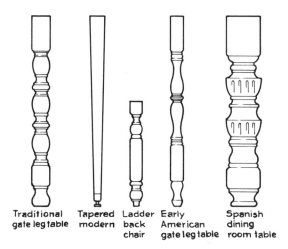

Traditional gate leg table | Tapered modern | Ladder back chair | Early American gate leg table | Spanish dining room table

Turned legs are used on many styles of furniture, and there are hundreds of different designs. Shown are just a few.

Right: This 18th-century settee has the characteristic splayed turned legs and delicate spindles of Windsor chairs. (As is traditional in this style, the seat is molded, and legs are fastened directly to the seat rather than to an apron or rail.) *The Metropolitan Museum of Art, Gift of Mr. & Mrs. Paul Moore, 1946.*

First step in turning leg is to square up turning block and locate the centers of both ends. Make crossing saw cuts on one end and tap spur center in place.

Then match up cup center with center point of stock and turn tailstock snugly in place. Lubricate with light oil.

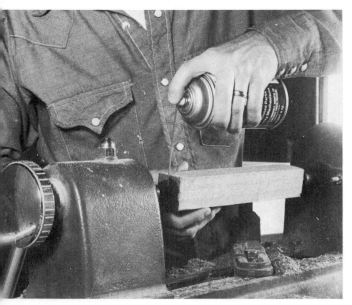

Leg turning is called "spindle turning" because the stock is mounted between the lathe centers. There are just three basic shapes on any turned leg: the convex, which is called the *bead;* the concave, called a *cove;* and the *fillet,* which is the straight portion between. Learning to create each of these is essential. You can then easily make any combination you wish on the lathe. There have been entire books written on the lathe, and we can't cover the entire subject here. However, we can discuss a few basic techniques.

Turning Legs on a Lathe

First, make sure the stock you select is sound and doesn't have any knots or splits running through it. Next, locate the center of each end of the stock. Bore a small hole at the center of one end to fit the pin on the spur center (this step isn't necessary for softwoods). Using a fine-tooth backsaw, make two diagonal cuts on this same end. Tap the spur in place so the tip goes in the tiny hole and the spurs fit down in the saw slots. It's a good idea to place the stock in a vise for these operations. On larger pieces and extremely hard wood, it's a good idea to bevel the edges or rough-cut the stock down before proceeding, with a radial arm saw, table saw, or jointer.

With the spur center driven in place, position it in the headstock spindle. Then move the tailstock until the cup center meets the center point marked on the turning block. Lock the tailstock in place, then move it into the end of the stock by turning the hand wheel. The center point of the cup should be forced into the wood. Turn the lathe on at its slowest speed and continue tightening a bit. You may prefer to do this step by hand. Squirt a small amount of oil around the point of the pin in the cup center. This is actually a bearing provided by the wood and pin.

Place the tool rest about a quarter inch from the extreme edges of the work and about an eighth of an inch above the centerline. Turn the stock by hand to make sure everything clears the tool rest. Turn on the power, and with a large gouge make initial rough "nicks" the entire length of the piece. Then use the gouge to remove the remainder of the wood between to produce a rough cylinder. The reason for the first cuts is to prevent the gouge from tearing long splinters

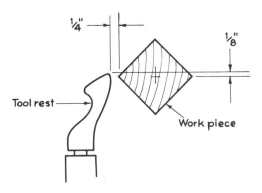

Tool rest

Work piece

Position tool rest about ¼ inch from the outer edges of the stock and about ⅛ inch above the centerline.

With the lathe on, make initial rough cuts along the length of the piece to prevent it from splintering when the cylinder is formed. This is especially important at shoulders.

from the wood. The cylinder can then be trued up and smoothed down with a skew chisel.

Place the leg profile template alongside the work (with the motor off) and mark the profile on the stock. A soft, dark lead pencil or even a crayon will work well. Use the parting tool as shown to make the sizing cuts. This determines the diameter of the leg at each location. For instance, when making tapers, mark both the largest and smallest end using the parting tool. Use calipers to make sure you have the right diameter at each location. You can then use the gouge to rough out the areas between. Finally, hold the skew in scraping position (flat on the tool rest) to finish the cuts.

After the rough cylinder has been shaped, use a profile template to mark the locations of the parting cuts.

A parting tool is then used to make sizing cuts at key points along the profile.

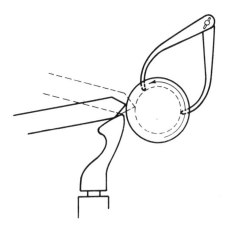

You can use a pair of calipers while making the parting cuts to insure reaching the right diameter.

Then the appropriate chisels are used to complete the turning. Here, a round-nose chisel is used to cut a cove. (Surface was first prepared with gouge held in scraping position.)

The spear point is used to cut beads and V-shapes. (A gouge can be used to rough-cut some of these areas.) A skew can also be used to make the beads and V-cuts, but it takes a lot of practice to do this correctly. Cove cuts can be rough-cut with a small gouge, and the round-nose scraping tool can be used for the final finish cuts. A large gouge can also be used to cut a cove by turning it on edge, then with a curving motion bringing it into the cove to meet the center parting cut. Bring the handle down while making the rolling motion.

In any cut, the most important thing is to keep the entire edge of the tool in contact with the wood surface. With most hardwoods, if you use sharp skew tools and a shearing motion, you will have very little sanding to do. But what sanding is done should be done while the leg is still in the lathe. Sand the work with a small strip of sandpaper. Because the sandpaper is actually being used across the grain of the wood, you must use fine grit paper to avoid leaving sandpaper marks in the wood.

Turning a number of legs the same size and shape is a problem. There are several methods of duplication, ranging from simple cardboard or wooden templates to complicated duplicating machines.

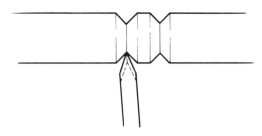

The spear point is used for V-shape and cove cuts.

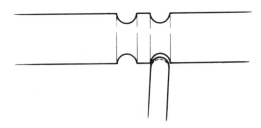

A small gouge is used to make cove cuts, often followed by a round-nose scraper for final shaping.

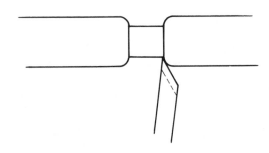

A skew can be used for almost any cut—straight rounds and tapers or V's and beads.

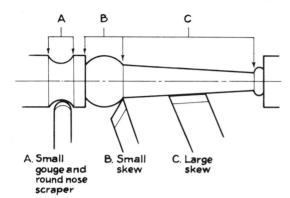

A typical turning and the tools used to make it.

A. Small gouge and round nose scraper
B. Small skew
C. Large skew

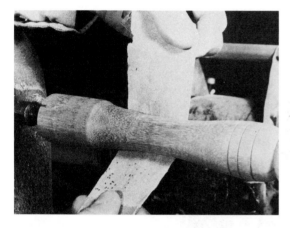
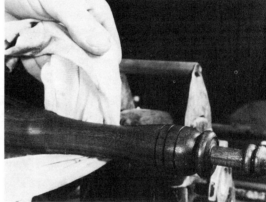

If sanding is required, the leg should be sanded with a fine open-coat paper while still in the lathe. If possible, apply finish at this time as well.

Multiple identical turnings can be produced with a duplicating lathe.

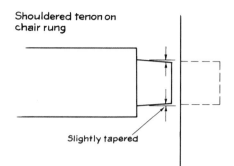

Shouldered tenon on
chair rung

Slightly tapered

The shoulder of a chair rung or leg is often turned slightly oversize and tapered so that it will make a compression fit when glued and clamped into a mortised rail.

One of the most beautiful and classic furniture legs is the cabriole. Cabriole legs can be cut quite easily on a band saw.

In many cases a turned leg will have a square section at the top, or even in the middle, for a stretcher or rail. In this case, the stock should first be squared, then surface-planed on all four sides before the turning is done. In this type of operation the first step is to make a small nick at the corner of the shoulder with a skew. Then use a parting tool to rough-cut the shoulder. After this has been done, rough the spindle to the correct shape and use a skew to finish the shoulder.

Many legs and chair rungs require a turned shoulder to fit into a hole. These should be turned with a slight taper. Furniture manufacturers turn these a bit oversize, then run them through a special machine that squeezes them tightly to compress the wood fibers. When the legs are glued in place the moisture in the glue causes the wood to swell and creates a tighter joint.

Legs which are to have a hole down the center can be drilled after turning, or a couple of pieces of stock with a dado down their centers can be glued together to make the turning block. Use small plugs in the holes to hold the block in the lathe center.

Split turnings are often used for decoration on chair backs and other pieces. To make them, you can glue two pieces of wood together with paper between them, make the turning, then split them apart with a wide, sharp chisel.

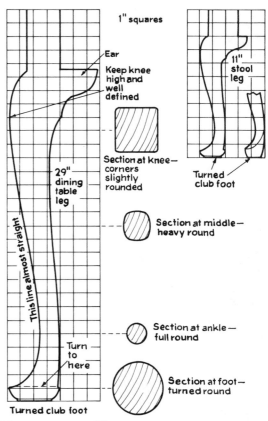

There are many different types of cabriole leg. Patterns for the styles shown here can be made by enlarging the drawings on 1-inch-square paper.

Cabriole Legs

A cabriole leg is one of the most fascinating objects you can create with wood. It can also be one of the most beautiful. There are, of course, many different varieties of cabriole legs, and they are traditional on Italian and French, as well as traditional furniture from the eighteenth century. Cabriole legs look extremely hard to make but are actually quite simple. You'll have so much fun making them that you will start looking for something to put them on. You can make them with a coping saw, which is what the first ones were made with. However, a band saw will speed up the job a great deal.

In most instances the leg will have a square top or a tenon to fit against a rail or to be mortised for rails. The bottom of the foot can be one of many designs, including the simple flat foot, or even a carved one such as the ball-and-claw foot. The stock for the leg must be made perfectly square. This is best done by running it over a jointer. It's a good idea to make a cardboard pattern of the leg, then mark this pattern on two adjoining sides of the leg as shown. Position the pattern against one side with the waste on the opposite, and mark it, then position the pattern on the adjacent side up against the same edge and mark it. Incidentally, if you wish to save on material you can block the stock at the large end of the leg by gluing blocks in place there. Make sure when doing any blocking that the joints are tight and well clamped.

Make the front and back cuts for the first profile on one side of the stock. Nail or tape the waste pieces back in place. If you use nails, make sure you don't nail in places that will mar the appearance of the leg. Turn the stock over, and make the

Marking stock with paper pattern

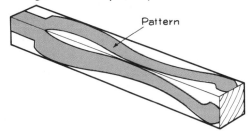

First step in making a cabriole leg is to trace the pattern on two adjacent sides of stock.

After the first profile of the cabriole leg has been cut, the waste stock is taped or nailed back on the block and the block turned over to cut the second side.

Compound-cut leg

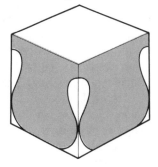

The compound-cut technique can also be used for other types of legs.

two cuts on the adjacent side to complete the leg. The leg will usually be further shaped with a chisel, rasp, or sanding tools. In many cases, such as on French Provincial legs, the legs will have ears on them. In this case make a pattern for the ears and rough-cut them to the right shape on the band saw, then glue them in place on the leg and use a rasp to complete matching of the bottoms of the ears to the inside edges of the legs. Often the foot of the leg is turned on a lathe as a club foot. In this case the center of both ends must first be marked before the leg is cut. After the leg is cut out it is placed in a lathe and the bottom turned.

Other Compound-Sawn Legs

The band saw can also be used to cut other types of legs totally different in appearance from the cabriole. These can be anything from an Italian Provincial-style leg to a tapered leg with a curved portion at the top. The same technique is used as for cabriole legs. Make the cuts on one side of the block, then tack nail or, better yet, tape the waste pieces back in place with masking tape and make the cuts on the adjacent face of the stock.

You can cut down on turning work on some types of legs by making compound cuts on the stock beforehand. The two techniques can also be combined for a really unusual Victorian-style leg.

Rectangle Legs and Trestles

Simple rectangle legs are often seen on chair backs, and trestles on larger pieces. Both types of leg can be cut to shape with a band saw. Then a shaper cutter with a collar can be used to smooth down or round their edges.

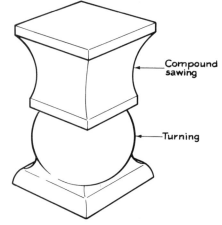

Turning and compound-sawing techniques can be combined to create a Victorian-style leg.

Band-sawn rectangle legs commonly extend up to form the back of a chair.

Band-sawn legs are not limited to the rectangle type. This "Savanarola"-type chair is one of a variety of design possibilities.

This mahogany side chair (c. 1800) has turned front legs and rectangle back legs, still a very typical combination on chairs being made today. *The Metropolitan Museum of Art, Gift of Mrs. Russell Sage, 1909.*

Trestles are another type of band-sawn leg. They are often joined with a stretcher and held with pins.

A typical pedestal leg consists of a turning with three splayed legs attached, as on this walnut tilt-top table (c. 1750). *The Metropolitan Museum of Art, Rogers Fund, 1925.*

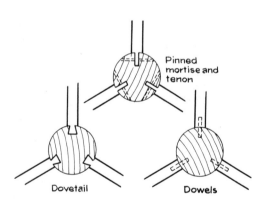

Pinned mortise and tenon

Dovetail

Dowels

There are several different joints that can be used to join splayed legs to a pedestal.

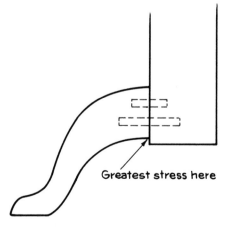

Greatest stress here

If a dowel joint is used, the lowest dowel should be as long as possible—most of the stress is at this point.

Pedestal Legs

A turned pedestal leg is a combination of a turned leg and compound-sawn legs glued in place tripod fashion. The main thing is to make sure you get the wings glued solidly in place. They can be joined with dowels or mortise and tenons. Or the pedestal may sit on a flat platform with three or four wings that is supported by turned feet or knobs.

Decoration

As you can see, each individual type of leg is a direct influence on the styling of furniture. In fact, you can take a table top and rails and by substituting different legs end up with French Provincial, Italian, Early American, Traditional, Modern, or Rustic furniture.

The decoration of the leg as well as its design is important in the styling of furniture. Decoration can be a simple routed design let into a part of the top of the leg, or it can be reeding or fluting running the full length of the leg. For the really ambitious, leg decoration can be relief carving or full round carving such as a ball-and-claw foot.

Routed Designs

Italian-style furniture utilizes a lot of routed designs in the legs. This can be done freehand with a ¼- or ⅛-inch dado router bit, although it's a better idea to use a pattern to make sure the routed lines are neat and square. When using a pattern, make sure you use a collar over the router bit as a guide; otherwise you will cut the pattern.

Another type of routing can be done with the Sears Craftsman Router Crafter, and in my estimation, this is one of the most satisfying tools the home craftsman can own. I know several custom furniture and cabinet shops that utilize the machine to its fullest. With this type of machine you can do reeding, fluting, roping, spirals, or even cut entirely through a piece to make open spirals.

Cutting Reeds and Flutes

Simple reeding and fluting on round legs can also be done with a router on a homemade stock-holding device. If you have a lathe with an indexing head, all that is needed is a simple jig with parallel top rails to guide the router. You can also reed or flute square or tapered legs with a jig that has a movable guide frame. Each of these devices must have stops to prevent overrunning the ends

Another type of pedestal leg consists of a heavy turned pedestal which rests on a platform supported by turned feet.

Routed Decorations, Reeds and Flutes

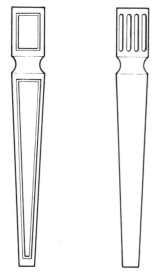

Routed designs and broad flutes are often seen on Provincial Italian-style legs.

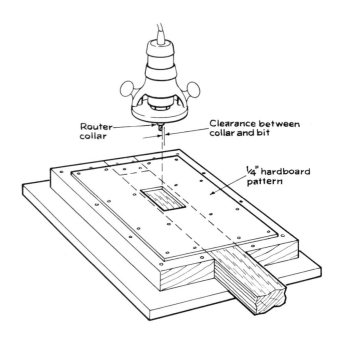

A hardboard template can be used to make routed designs on square portions of legs. Router bit is fitted with a collar.

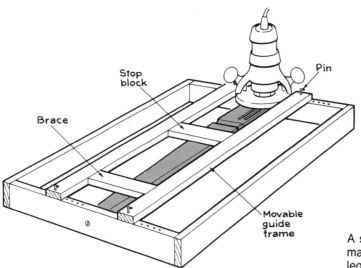

A simple jig can be constructed to make stopped flutes on square legs.

Flutes may also be very closely spaced, as on these Empire-style mahogany side chairs. *The Metropolitan Museum of Art, Sylmaris Collection, 1931.*

Reeds are very similar to flutes, but are made with a different cutter to produce a slightly turned out groove.

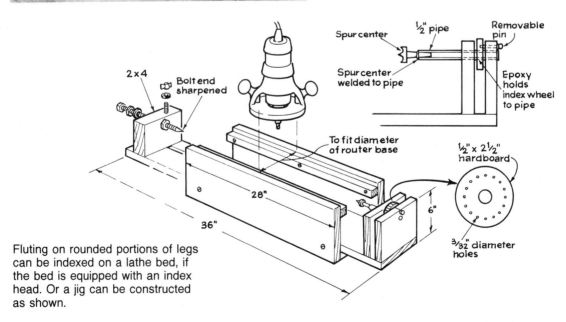

Fluting on rounded portions of legs can be indexed on a lathe bed, if the bed is equipped with an index head. Or a jig can be constructed as shown.

of the areas to be fluted, and should be indexed to provide a method of positioning the router exactly each time around the stock.

A shaper, radial arm saw or table saw can be used to cut reeds and flutes on square legs, or on square portions of round or tapered legs. When using a molding head on a table saw or radial arm saw, an auxiliary fence and table as well as hold-down devices will be needed, as described in Chapter 14. In addition, stop blocks should be clamped to the fence to control the start and end of the cuts.

Routed Decorations, Reeds and Flutes (Cont'd.)

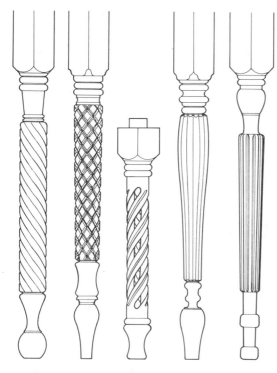

The Sears Craftsman Router Crafter performs a variety of decorative cuts on turned legs. A few of the possibilities are (from left to right): left-hand spirals, left-and-right-hand spirals combined, open spirals, flutes, and reeds.

Below left: The Router Crafter can also be used to make roping cuts.

Below right: On this bedstead post, rope cuts are combined with cove-and-bead turnings at the middle and ends.

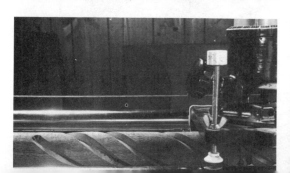

Leg-to-Rail and Leg-to-Slab Joints

As shown in the illustrations, a rail can be shaped in various ways to complement the style of leg used, and a shaped apron can also be attached to a straight rail for decorative purposes. Details on mortise-and-tenon and dowel joints suitable for leg-and-rail assemblies can be found in Chapter 5. For weaker joints, reinforcement with glue blocks, nails, screws, or metal braces is often advisable.

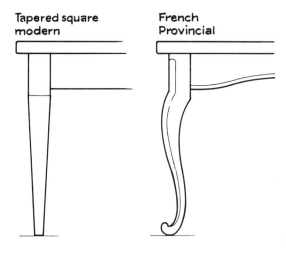

The design of rails or aprons is also important in the styling of furniture.

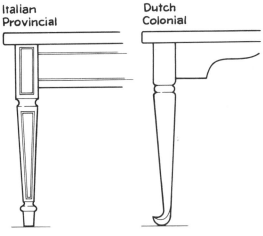

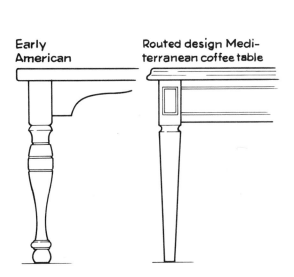

Leg-and-rail assemblies are most often fastened to a slab surface with screws through the rails and dowels from the leg, or with metal hardware such as bolts or mounting brackets secured by screws. In some constructions a leg-and-rail assembly may simply be glued to a table top if the gluing surface is large enough. Again, the considerations in selecting a fastener are the style of furniture and the amount of stress that will be put on the joint.

Leg-to-Rail and Leg-to-Slab Joints (Cont'd.)

Leg to apron joints

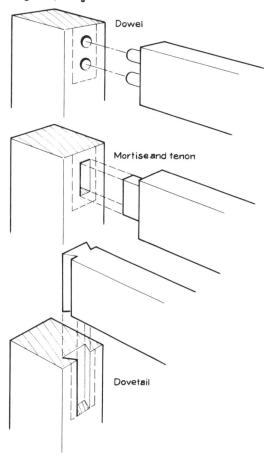

Dowel

Mortise and tenon

Dovetail

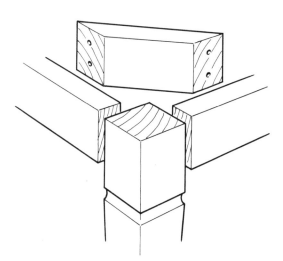

These are three of the joints most commonly used to join legs to rails or aprons.

A leg-to-rail joint may be strengthened by the addition of a corner block.

There are many ways to fasten legs to slabs. The simplest is with a purchased mounting bracket which comes with with threaded lag screws to match the holes in the bracket. The bottom of the leg may also be fitted with a leg leveler— these are available from woodworking supply houses.

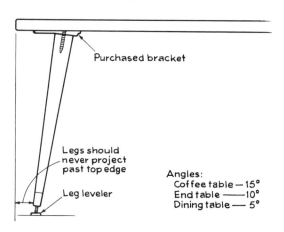

Purchased bracket

Legs should never project past top edge

Leg leveler

Angles:
Coffee table — 15°
End table ——— 10°
Dining table — 5°

Some types of legs may be fastened in place with a wooden dowel or heavy bolt driven through the top.

Heavy trestle legs may be fastened with countersunk wood screws.

If a leg assembly presents sufficient gluing surface, it may be simply glued to a top. Usually, however, additional fasteners and glue blocks would be used to strengthen the joint.

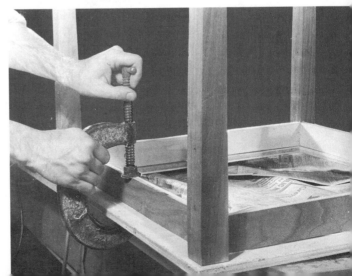

11

Veneering

Veneering can be one of the most challenging woodworking techniques, as well as a lot of fun, and a delightful hobby in itself. In fact, every woodworker deserves to have a go at it at least once. For the furniture and cabinet manufacturer, veneering is the only method of producing furniture from exotic and hard-to-get woods. This is equally true for the home cabinet and furniture builder. In most cases it isn't possible to acquire solid stock in the exotic and beautiful grain patterns found in veneers. And in the case of burls and crotch figures, the wood is structurally too weak to be used solid.

Unfortunately, veneers still have a poor reputation in many quarters, due to a long period when furniture was cheaply mass-produced, and veneers used to cover shoddy workmanship or cheap core materials. In the hands of good craftsmen, however, veneers have been used to produce some of the most beautiful and lasting furniture in the world.

Applying veneer is an art, and if done properly it can result in a piece of furniture or cabinet that is a work of art. Done shoddily, it looks just that, no matter how expensive the veneers are. Veneering is not, however, a skill that can be acquired only through many years of apprenticeship, nor does it require a great outlay for tools. In fact, with a little practice and just a few hand tools, you can do some amazing things with veneer. It's a good idea, as with most other crafts, to practice on small items. Tackling a huge dresser can be a frustrating project for the beginner.

For years, veneering meant a messy job requiring many clamps, and a lot of skill. This was because the only glues available at that time were the animal hide or polyvinyls, or resin glues. With the old-fashioned glues you had to have

Some of the most beautiful furniture in the world has been created with the use of veneers. Applications can range from the simple covering of a small table top with a single sheet of veneer, to the elaborate design of inlaid oak and tulipwood seen in this 18th-century French writing table. *The Metropolitan Museum of Art, Gift of Mr. and Mrs. Charles Writhtsman, 1917.*

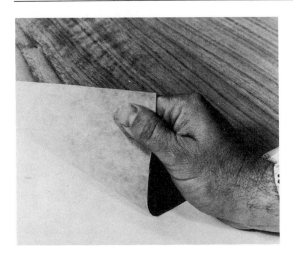

Today's contact cement and paper-backed veneer sheets make veneering a much easier job than it used to be.

As mentioned in Chapter 2, there are many different kinds of veneers. Most veneers are a standard $\frac{1}{16}$ inch in thickness; however, some imported veneers may be as thin as $\frac{1}{60}$ of an inch. These are paper thin and can be sanded through quite easily. They also require a much smoother core surface because they reveal any grain patterns or imperfections from the surface beneath.

Selecting and Matching Veneers

Veneer for small surfaces may be applied in one solid piece, usually with the grain running in the direction it would normally run if solid wood were used. For instance, the top on a small rectangular table would have the veneer running lengthwise. Probably the biggest advantage of veneer, however, is that it can be installed in smaller pieces to make a decorative grain pattern. This is called *matching,* and there are many ways of matching up the grain patterns to produce different effects. Keep in mind that veneer sheets cut from different logs, or even different parts of the same log, will not have the same grain figures. When producing matched surfaces you must either have a batch of small sheets of veneer from the same flitch of wood, or a large enough sheet to cut all the pieces.

Here are some standard matching patterns that will give you an idea of where to start.

special veneering frames in order to successfully veneer a surface. If the surface was curved, such as on a drawer front, you had to have a matching "mold" to clamp the veneer solidly in place until the glue set. With the introduction of contact type cements and paper-backed veneers, that has all changed and the job of veneering is no longer as difficult as it used to be. In fact, with the new materials it is often feasible to renovate an old table or chest with veneer rather than replacing the item.

A sheet of veneer will seldom be large enough to cover most table tops or doors. Pieces are usually joined together to make up a larger sheet, and the manner in which they are arranged is called the *match. Ethan Allen.*

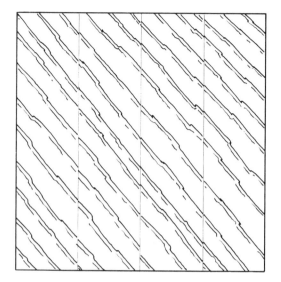

In slip matching, the pieces are laid out in the same order they were cut from the log flitch.

In book matched veneer, every other sheet is turned over.

Slip Matching

This is the most common method of veneer matching and is most often used on wide expanses such as wall paneling, the ends of large pieces of furniture, and sometimes the tops. It is normally used with quarter-sliced veneers.

Book Matching

This is also sometimes called side-to-side matching. In this type of match, the veneer face sheets are positioned so that every other sheet is turned over. Since the veneer sheets are batched and sold in the same order they were cut from the log, this places the two edges from the same side of the log together and produces a beautiful match. Book matching is often used on paneling, as well as for furniture fronts, doors, and large drawers.

End to End Matching

This is a form of book match, with an end-to-end match of the two pieces. It is used when vertical rather than horizontal continuity is desired.

Diamond Match

One very impressive method of matching veneers with a pronounced striped grain is to use the diamond match. Four pieces are cut on the diagonal to produce this pattern. If you wish to get an idea as to how a particular piece of veneer will look in a diamond match, use two pieces of mirror as shown.

There are several variations of the basic diamond match, such as the triangular, and the X or reverse diamond. A diamond pattern can be util-

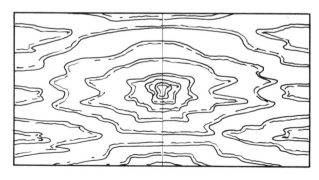

Pieces may also be book matched end-to-end.

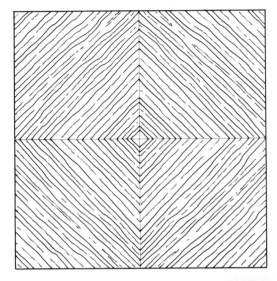

A diamond match is one of the most impressive. It should be used with veneers having a striated grain pattern.

A couple of mirrors can be used to check the appearance of a diamond match before the veneer is cut.

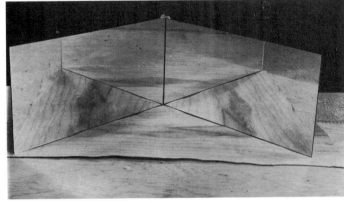

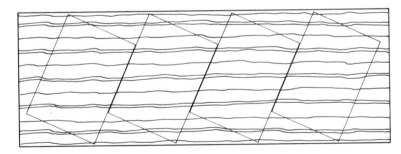

Sheets for a rectangular diamond match are cut at an angle.

This is a reverse rectangular diamond match.

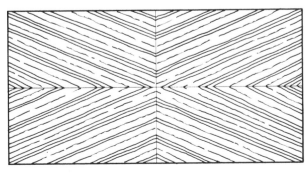

Another type of diamond match is the triangular. An inlaid center section is often added with this type of match.

The herringbone is a form of diamond match.

Four pieces may be book matched to make up a four-piece match. This is quite commonly done with burl veneers to make up a table top.

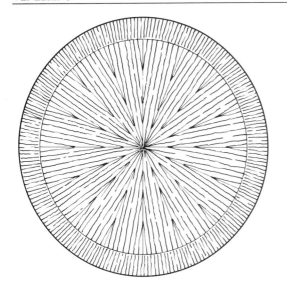

Wedge-shaped pieces may be matched on a circular surface. This is called a segmented match.

ized quite readily on a square, rectangular or circular surface.

A diamond match will often have an inlaid center section for contrast.

One of the most important things to remember in making diamond matched faces is that the exact center of the diamond must fall in the center of the wood surface.

Herringbone

Herringbone match is a form of diamond match utilizing sheets of veneer cut at acute angles to provide a herringbone line effect. This also is best done with highly striped figures.

Checkerboard

This is a quite simple match utilizing four square pieces, merely turning each one a quarter turn to simulate a checkered or parquet effect. This provides a truly interesting front panel for a chest if the squares are kept small.

Four Piece Match

This match is usually used for butt, burl, crotch or other highly figured faces. It consists of side-to-side and end-to-end book matched pieces.

Segmented Match

The segmented match is usually used on round tables. Triangular pieces of veneer are cut to meet at a center point, and the match of the veneer sheets is very important. A second veneer can also be used in this match. For instance, cherry and Carpathian elm produce an effect that is really stunning. Early furniture builders often combined satinwood and mahogany.

A banding of a different wood—or of the same wood but with a straight grain—is often used around a center pattern. Banding corners are usually cut at a 45° angle.

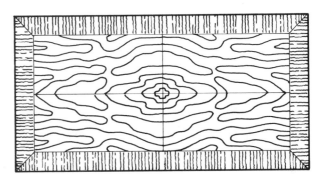

On this Pembroke table, a banding of striped satinwood is used to embellish the diamond-matched mahogany top. *Dard Hunter, Jr., Chillicothe, Ohio.*

Banding

In many cases a veneer banding material is used around the outside edge of a piece to provide contrast and design. This is usually a fairly dramatically striped veneer and is applied in a solid band around the object. It is usually mitered at the corners and installed in the same way as other matched faces. A typical application is the use of plain striped walnut banding to complement a burl walnut center.

Prematched Faces

There are a number of prematched faces available for use on table tops, drawer fronts, etc., and these can take a great deal of work out of a project. They can be ordered by mail from woodworker's supply companies, and include inlaid banding pieces; large faces of diamond- or book-matched veneers; backgammon, checkerboard, and pictorial faces; and decorative inlays. These are already assembled, and merely need to be glued in place.

Core Stock

Core stock for veneer may be plywood, particleboard, solid lumber, or hardboard. Solid lumber cores are usually made up with narrow strips of economical softwood such as pine or poplar. The main thing is that the surface be absolutely smooth and free of defects, grease, grit, or sanding dust before the veneer is applied.

Crossbanding

If you are making up your own lumber-core base, or if the surface to be veneered is uneven or blemished, crossbanding should be applied. This is an economical grade of veneer that is glued to the corestock at right angles to the direction the face veneer will be applied. It also provides added strength and stability to a lumber core.

If veneer crossbanding is used, it should be applied to the back of the corestock as well to prevent warping. Warping usually isn't as much of a problem with plywood-core stock as it is with lumber-core. In fact, with the use of contact

A small game table is a good
project for veneering. A
prematched checkerboard or
backgammon face can be
purchased to simplify the project.

Purchased prematched faces come
completely assembled, ready to glue
down on project. Veneer tape on face
is removed after installation.

When making up veneered
panels, most furniture
manufacturers apply
crossbanding. Shown is a lumber
core with crossbanding applied
on both sides. Veneer is then
applied over the crossbanding,
again on both sides.

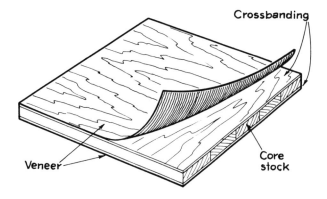

The tools needed for veneering are—a sharp knife or veneer saw, brush, sponge, tape, veneer glue or contact cement, straightedge, a roller or hammer, a block of wood, and push pins.

adhesives it is rarely a problem at all, but the "backer" sheets are the mark of a good craftsman.

Installing Veneer

The only tools required for veneering when using contact type adhesive are: a veneer saw, or fine-tooth backsaw such as a dovetail; a good sharp knife; veneer pins or regular push pins; glue and

There is a front and back side to veneer. Sometimes you can feel the smoothest side with your hands. If not, look for minute sanding marks.

brushes; a roll of gummed paper tape; and a sponge.

There are two basic methods of installing matched faces. In the second method, described on page 180, the matched pieces are trimmed and jointed *after* the veneer has been installed on the core stock. In either case, the pieces are cut so that they will overlap the outside edges of the project by about ½ inch. This overlap is then trimmed after the pieces are solidly adhered to the core stock.

Occasionally you may come across an extremely buckled piece of veneer. To flatten it, use a broom to sprinkle it lightly with water on the top surface; then place it between two boards, weigh it down solidly, and leave it to dry. The use of paper-backed veneers, of course, eliminates this problem.

Cutting and Jointing Matched Faces

If two pieces are to be joined, they are first laid on top of each other, with the two edges that are to be joined flush. Then cut the veneer along a straightedge. A saw or knife has a tendency to follow the grain pattern so it's a good idea to position the pieces so the grain runs out away from the straightedge rather than under it. You should also make the cut on the back side. After the veneers are cut, their edges must be jointed perfectly straight and true. The pieces are held

Veneer sheets to be joined can be cut with a veneer saw or with a razor, using a steel straightedge as a guide.

together with a shop-made clamp such as the one shown below. Their edges can be jointed by running them over a jointer set with a fine cut, or you can joint them with a hand plane. Small pieces can be jointed in the same manner by clamping them between two boards placed in a vise and using a small hand plane.

Another method of cutting the veneer sheets, and one that I personally prefer, is to lay them out with one sheet just overlapping the other by about ¼ inch. Then lay a heavy steel straightedge along the cut line and cut through both pieces at once. You have to make this cut with only one stroke for it to work properly. But it will provide a joint that matches perfectly without further planing or cutting.

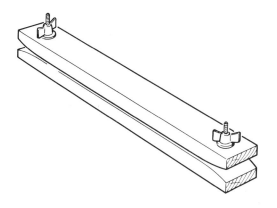

Then the sheets are clamped in a shop-made veneer clamp and their edges jointed with a hand plane or power jointer.

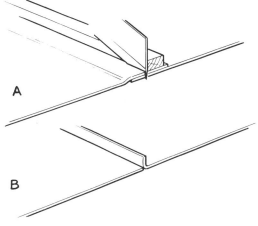

Alternate methods of jointing veneer sheets are: A. Overlap the sheets about ¼-inch; then cut through both sheets at once with a sharp knife or razor blade. B. Leave a ½-inch overlap at the joint, and roll the veneer down into the crack. The top protruding piece can be sanded away after the veneer is installed. (See page 180 for details.)

A

B

Positioning Matched Faces

Make sure you have a smooth, flat, working surface, then position the two veneer pieces together with the jointed edges together. Use push pins placed about an inch away from the joint to hold the pieces securely in place. Using brown paper tape, or veneer tape, a special pregummed type of paper tape, tape the pieces together *on the front or face side*. A small flat stick with one end rounded can be used to press the tape firmly in place. Then a small flat iron bar can be placed over the joint to hold the pieces together until the tape dries. (Although masking tape can also be used for this job it won't hold the joint together as tightly.)

It is a good idea at this point to turn the sheet over, fold back the edges of the veneer and apply a very thin line of white glue to the edges. Then flatten the seam back out, wipe away excess glue and apply masking tape over the joint to hold it until the glue dries.

Matched faces are then joined together with gummed veneer tape. The joints should be weighed down on a flat surface while the tape dries.

After the front face has been taped, some craftsmen like to bend back the veneer edges on the back side and apply a bit of white glue along the seam. Masking tape is then applied over the joint.

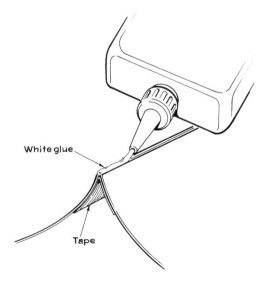

White glue

Tape

Veneer cement is applied to the back side of the veneer face, and to the core stock surface. Allow both to dry until all tack is gone, usually about an hour.

Applying Veneer to Core Stock

After the glue has dried you're ready to apply the face sheet to the core stock. As mentioned earlier, the core stock must be sanded smooth and free of dust, grease, and other defects. Remove the masking tape from the back of the face sheet; then position the sheet in place on the core stock and determine the exact location. When applying a matched face, the positioning must be very exact. Once you have located the right position, punch veneer pins through the veneer on two sides and up against the sides of the core stock.

Remove the veneer sheet and the pins, mark the locations of the pins, and using a brush or roller apply the contact veneer adhesive. Both surfaces, the bottom of the veneer face and the top side of the core stock, are coated thoroughly with the adhesive. This should be applied quite rapidly, and well brushed out while applying. Once it starts to become tacky, don't brush on it any longer; this only creates bumps and irregular spots that will show up under the veneer. Allow both pieces to dry according to the directions on the adhesive can. This will usually be about an hour. The best test for dryness is to take a piece of kraft paper and touch it to the cemented area. If it does not stick, the cement is dry enough to assemble the pieces. However, the entire surface must be dry, not just spots. That's why it's so important to get a good even coat over the entire surface. If the cement is not dry the bond won't develop full strength and you'll end up with bubbles in the veneer face.

In the case of some porous woods you may need to apply two coats of adhesive. If the surface of the dried adhesive is dull, don't take a chance; apply another coat of adhesive. Many craftsmen like to apply a third coat around the outside edges as well.

The face must be positioned exactly where you want it before allowing any part of the adhesives to touch. Contact adhesive bonds instantly on contact, and once it does you can't get the materials apart without tearing up the veneer face. The

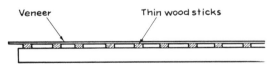

Veneer   Thin wood sticks

Since the two cement-coated surfaces will bond on contact, you must prevent them from touching until you have located the sheet in the proper position. Sheets of waxed paper or kraft paper can be used. However, ¾-inch wood strips or dowels work best for many people. Once the sheet has been positioned properly, pull out the center stick and press the veneer in place. Continue outward toward the corners, pulling out sticks as you go.

Once the sheet has been bonded to the core, a roller or hammer and smooth wood block can be used to smooth it down and bond it securely.

best method of positioning is to place a couple of sheets of waxed paper, newspaper, or kraft paper over the adhesive on the core stock, overlapping them about an inch in the center. Then replace the veneer pins in the locating holes in the veneer face, lay the face down on the paper, and locate it properly. Hold the veneer in place on one end, and with the other hand pull the paper out from the other end. As soon as the center touches, the veneer must be gently pressed in contact with the core adhesive in the spot near the center where the paper has been pulled out. Work towards one end and the two corners in this manner, pulling out the slipsheet and smoothing out any bubbles and wrinkles as you go. Then remove the second piece of paper in the same manner. Using a rubber roller or a block of wood with a rounded edge, roll or burnish the entire veneer face solidly in place on the core stock. Make sure you push down each and every bubble and crack. These won't be as much of a problem with straight veneers, but burl and crotch veneers will be somewhat wrinkled and are a lot harder to apply. (It's a good idea for the beginner to install paper-backed veneer, or straight-grained veneers for the first few practice runs.)

Once the veneer face has been solidly adhered, turn the work upside down on a smooth flat surface and use a very sharp knife or veneer saw to trim away the excess. When you get near the corners, stop and cut in from the corners so you don't push splinters of veneer away from them.

Alternate Method That Can Be Used To Install Matched Faces

Another method of installing veneer is even simpler, and will produce equally satisfactory results in many cases. Select and match the veneers, allowing about ½-inch extra all around for trimming. Position the sheets as described earlier, but overlap each joint ½ inch. During the adhesive spreading operation, brush the edges of the bottom sheets with adhesive as well. Then with a heavy roller, roll the top sheet as hard as you can down into the joint between. This will force the top sheet down in the cavity at the joint. If this is done properly the edge of the top portion will be raised above the surface. This can be sanded off to make a smooth joint during the finishing operation.

Veneering curved pieces is quite easy with this method. However, make sure to dry-fit the pieces to the curve before installing to make sure you have enough material.

Edge Treatments

Plywood edges can be covered with veneer, inlaid strips, or solid wood. If veneer is used, it is applied in the same manner as the face veneer. Usually, the same veneer is used for edges as for the top veneer or banding, but there are several ways to orient the edge pieces, as shown. If the grain is to run up and down in a waterfall style, the pieces must be matched and taped together, just as done for other matched faces.

A solid wood edge can also be made by gluing hardwood strips to plywood stock before the veneer is applied. The hardwood strips should be carefully selected to match the top veneer. After the veneer is solidly adhered to the surface, the edge can be molded. The cutter knife used has to be one that will end the cut just below the veneer edge to avoid splintering the veneer.

Banding pieces are cut and matched in the same way as larger faces. Here, overlapped edges of banding are being cut at a 45° angle.

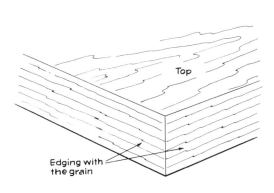 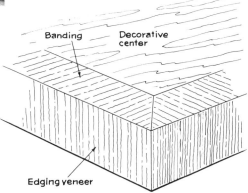

Edging veneer may be applied lengthwise as shown at left, or it may be matched and applied "waterfall" fashion as shown at right.

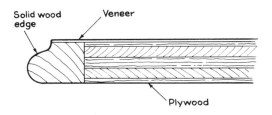

Another way to treat the edge is to fasten a hardwood strip to the core stock before veneer is applied. Then the edge can be shaped with a cutter that contacts the wood strip just below the veneer edge.

Marquetry

Marquetry is a method of creating designs or pictures by cutting and fitting pieces of different kinds of veneer together to form a pattern. This is usually done by making a pattern of the whole design, and templates of the various pieces to be cut. The pattern is laid on the background sheet and the design cut out. Then the templates are laid on veneers of contrasting color, or pattern veneer sheets, and the designs cut out. The pieces are then fitted in the hole left in the ground sheet. This craft takes a lot of patience, but can be used to produce some extremely beautiful designs.

Inlaying

Inlaying is another fascinating aspect of veneering. There is a great variety of ready-made decorative inlays and inlaid borders available, in both modern and traditional designs. Although most of these are quite inexpensive, they are not commonly used by commercial furniture manufacturers because it takes a lot of time to install them.

Line and Border Inlays

Inlaid strips can sometimes be taped together and applied with the veneer face sheet. However, most inlays are applied after the face has been installed. One reason is that the inlays are usually just a fraction thicker than the standard veneer sheets. The recesses for inlays are cut with a router and ¼-inch dado bit, with small, very sharp hand chisels, or with a homemade scratch block tool.

The main thing is to cut a groove of perfectly even width and depth so that the inlay will fit tightly in the recess and the joints will be flush.

Inlaying is one of the most ancient woodworking arts. Shown is a Hepplewhite-style card table, c. 1794, of mahogany inlaid with holly. *Atkins Museum of Fine Arts, Kansas City, Missouri.*

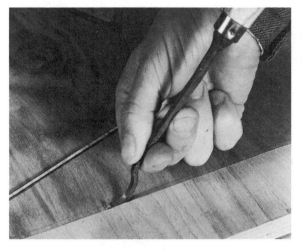

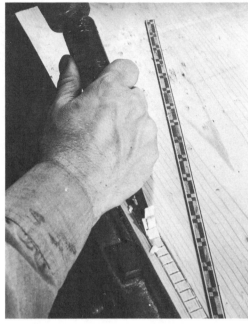

Groove for inlaid border can be cut in veneered surface with a router or with small chisels. (Either tool can also be used to cut grooves in solid wood, as shown at right.)

Border or line inlays are normally mitered at the corners. After cutting the recess, dry-fit the material in place. Then apply white glue in the groove, insert the inlay, and rub back and forth with the head of a hammer to force the inlay in place. If the inlay is a large one, clamp it or weight it down

securely until it dries thoroughly. This should be at least 12 hours. The moisture from the glue will cause the inlays to swell, so they should be allowed to dry thoroughly before you sand them down to avoid creating an open joint.

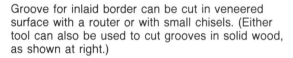

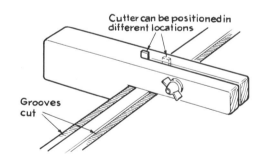

A shop-made "scratch block" tool can also be used to cut grooves for inlaid strips. The hardened steel blades can be obtained from a machine shop, or a rabbet plane blade might be used for the purpose. To operate, set the blade the desired distance from the edge, and draw the tool across the surface. Make several light cuts until the correct depth is achieved. When cutting across the grain of veneer, score the outline of the border first with a razor.

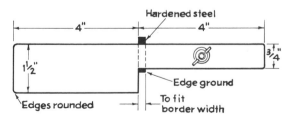

A fine line of white glue is then applied in the groove.

Inlay can be worked into the groove with a hammer.

Be sure to remove excess glue with a damp cloth to avoid staining the surrounding veneer. Then the inlay can be clamped or pressed securely in place with a weight until the glue dries.

Larger Inlays or "Inserts"

Decorative inlays of many different types are also available, and are usually used in the center of a table or chest top. These come glued to a piece of paper and inset in a border of veneer to help protect the edges.

If the inset is to be located in the center of an object, locate the center using crossing lines.

Then make crossing lines on the back or paper side of the inset to locate its center. Cut away the veneer. Position the inset so that the intersecting lines match up, and mark around it with a sharp pencil. Then cut out the recess.

With paper side up, glue the inlay in the recess using a heavy board and weights to hold it securely in place until the glue dries.

First step in installing an inlay is to cut away the protective veneer which surrounds it.

Center the inlay, and use a sharp pencil to mark its outline. The front side of the inlay has a protective paper covering which should be left on during installation.

If the inlay is to be installed on a veneered surface, cut the veneer away with a razor blade and remove the patch. On a solid wood surface, use a chisel or router to cut away the material. Apply adhesive.

Left: Install the inlay paper side up, rolling it down securely. *Below:* A smooth board with a heavy weight on top can be used to hold inlays or borders in place while glue dries.

Cleaning away Paper Tape

Paper on the surface of the veneered face must be removed with a tiny bit of water. It should not be sanded off as you will only drive the glue into the surface of the wood, where it will cause problems.

Dip a sponge in water and wring out most of the water, then dampen the paper tape thoroughly. It is important to use just enough water to do the job. Too much water will make the cells in the wood veneer swell, causing blisters or cracks. If you don't get it wet enough, however, you will leave tiny bits of tape that are extremely hard to get off, as well as a glue film that is hard to sand off.

Then use a wide chisel to scrape away the loosened tape. This takes a bit of time, but if the tape has been properly dampened it will roll right off. Once you have removed all tape, sand the surface using a flat sanding pad and fine sandpaper.

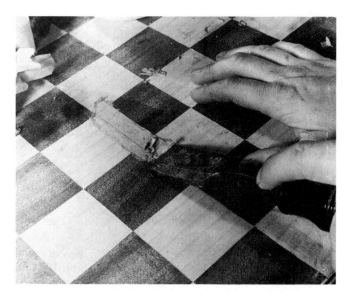

To remove gummed veneer tape or paper covering on inlays, rub it with a damp sponge, then use a wide chisel to scrape it off. Apply a minimum of water to avoid damaging the veneer.

12

Installing Plastic Laminate

One of the most useful materials for cabinetmakers and furniture builders is plastic laminate. It provides a durable and attractive surface for kitchen and vanity countertops, or the tops of modern-style tables. It is easy to work with, but applying it does require special handling techniques and some practice.

Plastic laminate is made by impregnating layers of kraft paper with plastic resins. There are usually several regular layers, with a pattern sheet on top which is also saturated with resin. A protective coating of plastic is applied over the pattern or top sheet; then the material is pressed under high pressure and heat to form a durable, hard-surfaced sheet. Plastic laminate is available in an entire spectrum of colors and patterns, and in several textures.

The most commonly available sheets are 24, 30, 36, 48, or 60 inches wide; and lengths range from 60 to 144 inches. Most sheets are actually

Plastic laminate is the material most commonly used to cover kitchen countertops. It is extremely hard and durable and cleans up easily. Shown is a one-piece preformed top with coved backsplash and front edge.

Plastic laminate is available in many different colors and textures, including wood grain, marble, leather, and slate. It can be used as a cabinet facing material, or as a practical tabletop covering, as shown here.

a bit oversize to allow for trimming, so you can often cut, for example, two 12-inch pieces from a 24-inch piece. The thickness of laminates ranges from $\frac{1}{16}$ to $\frac{1}{32}$ inch. One-sixteenth-inch is the thickness most commonly used in home shops. Backer sheets, a more economical grade of laminate, are often used on manufactured furniture. But they're rarely used on custom, small shop, or home projects. They aren't required unless the top surface exceeds 4 square feet without some sort of under support.

The construction material used as a base for plastic laminate projects is normally plywood or particleboard. Horizontal surfaces should be $\frac{3}{4}$ inch thick, while vertical surfaces can be as thin as $\frac{1}{2}$ inch. Normally, interior grade plywoods are used. However, in humid areas of the house, it's best to use an exterior grade of plywood. Almost all homeshop plastic laminate installation is done

with contact cement or another adhesive that bonds on contact, rather than the slower setting adhesives which require clamping.

The base for a kitchen or bathroom plastic laminate countertop can be shop-made with $\frac{3}{4}$-inch plywood or particleboard stock, or it can be purchased ready-made. Ready-made countertops are available in one-piece units with preformed coves at the backsplash and front edge, and in assemblies with a separate backsplash that is fastened in when the unit is installed. Ready-made units can be purchased with the laminate already bonded to the base and with the sink cutouts already made; the unit is then simply cut to size to fit over the cabinets.

Plastic laminate can be installed with hand tools or with power tools. Power tools will make the job much easier, but the job can also be done with just a few hand tools.

Here, a walnut pattern laminate was used as a facing for cabinets, and a burl design for the shop-made countertop.

This preformed countertop was assembled at the factory, and simply cut to fit the cabinet by the installer. Because of its rounded edges, this type of top will last longer than a shop-made top.

Cutting and Installing Plastic Laminate with Hand Tools

Surface Preparation

The surface to be covered should be flat, and without bumps or depressions. If the surface is new, it should be of at least ¾-inch-thick quality particleboard or plywood, clean and free of dirt, grease, or moisture. Edges should be smooth. Fill voids with a wood patching filler, then sand flat and square.

If you are re-covering a laminate surface, make sure the old laminate is well bonded to the base. If the laminate is loose, remove it and sand the wood underneath until it's flat. If the bond is sound, rough-sand the old surface with garnet or similar coarse abrasive paper (50 to 80 grit, 1 to 0 grade). If covering a painted surface, remove the paint to assure proper bonding.

Cutting the Laminate

Use a soft lead pencil or sharp grease pencil to mark dimensions on the laminate sheet—with decorative face *up.* Allow at least ⅛ inch "over-hang" or clearance on all edges, allowing for the saw kerf (¼ inch is better). The laminate will be trimmed to size after it is bonded to the surface. Double check all your measurements before cutting. If using patterns or woodgrain designs, make sure the "grain" or pattern runs in the right direction for all matching end, butt, or miter cuts.

Plastic laminate can be cut with a finish hand-saw (10 to 12 points per inch), or a hacksaw. Before sawing, be sure the panel is well-supported on each side of the saw cut; not hanging over a table. The decorative face should be *up.* Weigh down, clamp, or hold the work firmly while cutting. Apply pressure only on the down stroke of the saw to reduce "chipping" of the decorative face. Keep the blade at a comfortably low angle for better tracking on a straight marked line. Raise the saw to vertical and take shorter strokes when cutting curves. (If you use a portable electric saber saw, mark and saw the panel with the decorative face *down,* since this blade cuts on the

up stroke.) After sawing, lightly smooth off any burrs with a file angled down and across the face to avoid chipping or flaking while handling.

Spreading Adhesive

There are several types of adhesives suitable for bonding laminates. Choose the one best suited to your particular working conditions. Some types do not bond (set) quickly, thus allowing the laminate to be positioned on any register marks. However, these slower-setting adhesives require prolonged, evenly distributed pressure (for several hours). The pressure can be applied with clamps or, for large areas, with heavy weights such as sandbags or water-filled containers. It's difficult to devise a uniformly loaded press such as used in factory operations. A "contact" adhesive, which bonds instantly (and permanently) on even slightest contact of coated surfaces, is preferred by most do-it-yourselfers. Contact adhesives require only momentary hard pressure—produced by rolling or pounding—to create a satisfactory bond. When using a contact adhesive, you must keep adhesive-coated surfaces apart until they are accurately aligned, since they will bond immediately on contact.

Many contact adhesives are highly flammable, so work in a well-ventilated room, free from an open flame or pilot light, electric heaters, or any other source of ignition. Follow label instructions carefully.

A thick coating of adhesive does not necessarily produce a better bond. But don't skimp—use enough. For coating large areas such as a countertop, a comb-notched spreader or a short-nap paint roller will assure uniform application. For small areas or edge strips, use a ¾-inch animal hair (natural bristle) paintbrush.

Applying Edge Strips

If the countertop you are covering is to have a laminate-finish edge, then the edge strips (cut slightly longer and wider than the edge) should be applied first. Coat the laminate strip first, then the wood or particleboard. Let the glue set as long as required. To attach the edge strip, position it carefully with both hands even with the lower edge, and don't let the strip make contact until it is in position. The top edge and ends should overlap; these will be trimmed later. Then allow the strip to make contact for the full length. Press firmly in place, and immediately pound down the surface with a hammer, using a hardwood block to distribute pressure and protect the face of the laminate.

Trim the overhang along its length, holding a block plane at a slight angle to avoid nicking the countertop base, until it is nearly flush and flat. Dress with a fine file. This edge will be overlapped by the top laminate to minimize the visible joint. (The same method used to make the countertop and edge joint can also be used for table legs or the front edge of bookcase sides and shelves.)

Applying Large Sheets of Laminate

You are now ready for the larger surface application. Again, be sure the base surface is free from dust. Apply the adhesive to the laminate panel first with a notched spreader, roller, or brush. Then coat the base. When the cement is ready to bond, prevent premature contact by laying several ¾-inch sticks or dowels on the coated top at 8- to 10-inch intervals, removing them only when you have aligned the entire laminate sheet.

When the laminate is in position, carefully pull away successive "separator" sticks, beginning at the center, and press down on the laminate with a sweeping or "ironing" motion to prevent air traps. Immediately pound down the center area, then roll out the entire surface. Lastly, pound with a hammer and wood block, especially near the edges, to make sure all areas are securely bonded.

Trimming

To trim off the top laminate overhang, use a block plane held at a slight angle to avoid cutting into the edge strip. Complete the joint finishing operation with a fine mill file, holding it at a 60° angle to the top. Apply pressure from above and only on the down stroke and against the edge to avoid chipping and scuffing.

Clean-Up

After each bonding step, remove the excess adhesive at the edges by scraping with laminate scrap. When all joints are complete, scrape again; then carefully wipe them and all faces with a soft rag slightly dampened with contact adhesive solvent or lacquer thinner. These solvents are highly flammable; use caution. Use thinner sparingly at edges and joints to avoid penetration and possible delamination.

Cutting and Installing Plastic Laminate with Power Tools

Naturally, power tools make the installation job much easier and faster.

Cutting

Plastic laminate can be cut with a circular saw, saber saw, table or radial arm saw, or with a special plastic-laminate cutting bit in a router. The material dulls a saw blade quite rapidly, so it's a good idea to use carbide-tip blades. To prevent chipping, which is sometimes a major problem with plastic laminate, the blade should have very little set. When using a portable circular saw or saber saw to cut laminate, the sheet should be positioned face *down*. When cutting with a table saw, radial arm saw or router, the sheet should be face *up*. When using power tools, especially if a router is used for the final trimming, it's a good idea to cut the material from ⅜- to ½-inch oversize all around.

Handling Laminate Sheets

Large sheets of laminate usually come rolled up in a cardboard wrapper and tied with heavy string. Take precautions when you cut the string; the laminate roll can snap open with enough force to knock you down. Cut edges of plastic laminate can also be dangerous.

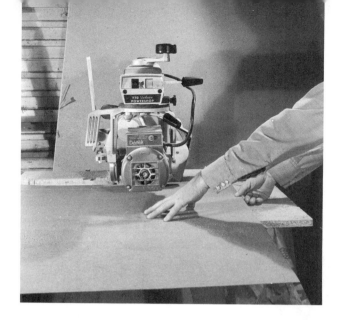

Cutting and Installing Plastic Laminate

Plastic laminate can be cut with a fine-tooth handsaw, or with a stationary or portable power saw. A radial arm saw is the best choice for making long ripping cuts, as for front edging pieces.

On most kitchen cabinets, the counter edge is built up to provide a thicker appearing top. In this case, a ¾ × 1¾-inch wood strip is glued and nailed to the plywood edge.

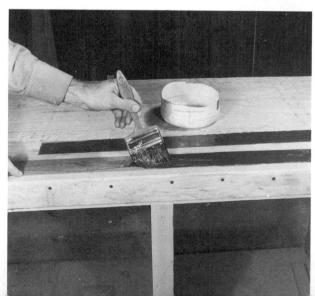

If edge strips are to be applied, they are applied before the large sheets for the countertop. Coat the countertop edge and the back of the laminate strips with adhesive and allow to dry. Bottom edge of the strips is installed flush with countertop edge, and the top and sides are overlapped about 1/16-inch.

As soon as the laminate has been applied, go over the surface with a roller or hammer and wood block to bond it securely to the core.

The protruding laminate edge can be trimmed with a block plane and fine file, or with a belt sander as shown. Move the sander from back to front of the countertop to avoid tearing the laminate edge. Use a vacuum cleaner to remove all sanding dust.

Make sure that the countertop core surface is perfectly flat and free of dust before applying laminate. Spread cement evenly on the back of laminate sheet and on the core with a notched spreader, short-nap paint roller, or brush.

When the cement is dry, place several lengths of ¾-inch wood strips or dowels on the countertop, and position the laminate sheet on top. Starting from the center, pull out successive strips and smooth the laminate down with an "ironing" motion.

Go over the entire surface with a hammer and smooth wood block and a roller to make sure the laminate is bonded securely at all points.

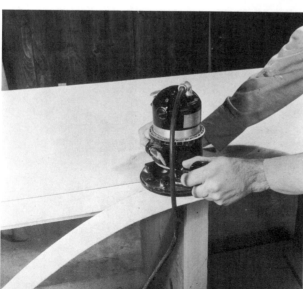

A router is used to trim the countertop laminate flush with the edge.

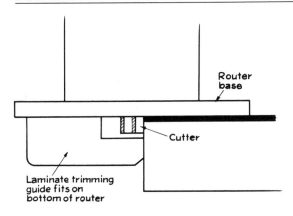

An accessory laminate trimming guide comes with many routers and can also be purchased separately. An alternate method of guiding the router is with a laminate trimming bit, which is fitted with a small pilot wheel.

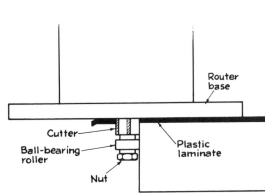

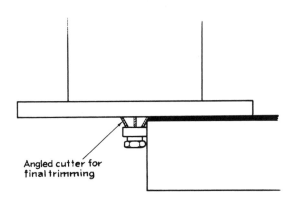

After the laminate has been trimmed flush, an angled cutter can be used to provide the final trimmed edge.

When handling large sheets, be careful not to allow them to bend too much—they can crack or chip. The sheet should be supported on both sides of the cutline when a portable power saw is used.

Joints

If you must join two pieces on a countertop surface, join them at the middle junction of the sink or other cutout, or at a 45° corner. One way to get a smooth joint is to position the sheets in place on the core material and mark across both faces. Then with a jointer or a hand block plane, joint the edges, lay them back in position with the

marks matching, and examine. If there are any gaps in the joint, recut.

Edge strips should protrude about ¹⁄₁₆ inch above the countertop. When the strip has been applied, use a belt sander to sand down the top edge of the laminate as well as to smooth up the plywood counter base surface. This should be done with the sander body on the counter in such a way that the belt will not pull out on the edge strip, forcing it away from the edge. Once the edge strip has been sanded flush and the plywood base smoothed, the countertop laminate can be applied. This is overlapped on all sides so that the edges can later be trimmed flush with a router.

The router is the primary tool for cutting

professional-looking plastic laminate joints and edges. When fitted with a plastic-laminate cutting bit, a router provides a smooth edge that just can't be achieved any other way.

Most routers come with an accessory trimming guide. You can also purchase bits that have a small pilot wheel fitted to them which will guide the router. I prefer the latter arrangement because it can be used in tighter corners than the guide fitted to the router base. However, the cutter with a pilot is a bit harder to learn to use.

Router bits for trimming laminates are either straight-sided or angled. The angled cutter provides a smooth, beveled edge, and it's usually used after the straight-sided cutter does the initial trimming. The angled cutter can make the cut in one pass, but this doesn't provide as fine an edge as the combination of straight and angled cuts. Even if an angled cutter is used, a good, fine-cut mill file can follow to provide an even smoother edge. Allow the file to cut only on the downward stroke. The inside corners of a top will have to be finished with a fine file alone since the router bit won't go into that tight space.

One of the main rules when using a router to trim plastic laminate is to first position the router base flat on the surface but so that the cutter does not contact the material to be trimmed. Turn on the router before moving the cutter into the material; otherwise, the router will grab and tear out or chip the material. When using an angled cutter, the depth of the bit must be set exactly, or you may cut too much away from an edge.

Safety

Eye protection is a must when using a router because a router throws out a fine spray of chips as it cuts. A face shield is better than goggles, in my opinion, because it prevents you from blinking as the sharp pieces hit your face.

Additional Notes

To install plastic laminate on a curved edge, the material can be made pliable by heating it with a heat lamp. Heat-resistant gloves should always be used to handle laminate that has been heated.

Plastic laminate can also be used to give a face lift to an old kitchen cabinet. The stiles, rails, panels, doors and other elements to be laminated should be sanded smooth and cleaned before the laminate is applied. If laminate is applied to a door, it should be applied to the back side of the door as well to prevent warping. If using a wood grain pattern, the most important consideration is to make sure that the grain runs in the same direction as the grain of the wood members underneath: up and down for vertical stiles, and across for horizontal dividers, etc.

13

Selection and Installation of Hardware

There are literally tens of thousands of different kinds, shapes, sizes, and colors of hardware. Choosing the correct hardware for a cabinet or furniture piece is very important. You can change the style of a piece of furniture quite easily merely by switching hardware. For instance, there is hardware specially designed for French Provincial, Early American, Traditional, Mediterranean, Spanish, Dutch Colonial, Italian Provincial, and Country English furniture to name just a few of the more common styles.

In addition to choosing the correct style, the correct size of hardware is also important. If the hardware is too large for a piece of furniture, it will overpower it and make the furniture appear too small. On the other hand, tiny hardware on a massive piece of furniture looks just as ridiculous.

The third important criteria in selecting hardware is to choose hardware to match the use. Some hardware is made for specific problems. For instance, heavy drop lids on desks must be anchored solidly with special drop-lid hinges; butt hinges would simply bend or pull the screws out of the wood. There are also other specialty hardware items such as cedar-chest hinges that enable the lid to stay in an upright position when lifted. One of the problems in the past has been nonavailability of the specialty hardware to the home craftsman, but there are now a number of woodworking supply mail order houses that spe-

cialize in furniture and cabinet hardware. In addition, the "home builder" or hardware supermarkets in the larger cities carry an extensive line these days to cater to the growing numbers of do-it-yourselfers.

Just as in purchasing any other item, you usually get what you pay for. Cheap hardware will

Choosing hardware of an appropriate size and style is an important aspect of furniture and cabinet craftsmanship. This drop-lid secretary (c. 1800) has the small, delicate hardware typical of Sheraton-style furniture. *The Metropolitan Museum of Art, Kennedy Fund, 1918.*

Some hardware styles are traditionally used for certain types of furniture. An example is the porcelain knob (photo inset) used on this Early American-style cabinet. The smaller knob with wood screw is used for light duty; the bolt-head knob serves for heavier pulls.

only cause trouble, so buy good name-brand, quality hardware, especially in hinges and other items that must carry structural weight.

It's a good idea to purchase hardware before constructing the furniture or cabinet. Then you can make sure that the hardware will fit the furniture. For instance, door locks on chests require special mortising, in addition to room for the escutcheon. If you haven't made the door stile wide enough, you may run into problems. By the same token, drawer slides (shown in Chapter 8) and other kitchen hardware are made to fit a specific kind of construction, and the cabinet must be constructed to allow the hardware to work properly.

Hinges

Hinges are used on doors and such items as drop lids, swing legs, chests, and table leaves. In most cases, the hinge used will depend on the style of

The plain butt hinge is the most commonly used.

furniture. The most common type of hinge is the plain butt hinge. It is available in several different styles and sizes, ranging from those used to hang heavy entrance doors for houses to tiny jewelry box hinges about ½-inch long. It is often installed so that the hinge pin is the only element visible when the door or leaf is in the closed or down position. Spring-loaded butt hinges are also available to make doors self-closing. Surface-mounted hinges are a second category. These are usually more decorative than plain butt hinges, and are installed so that both leaves of the hinge are visible. Semi-concealed or cabinet hinges constitute a third category. These are installed so that one part of the hinge is visible on the front of the cabinet, while a second leaf is surface-mounted or mortised into the back of the door. Finally, there are several specialty hinges such as the Soss invis-

ible hinge and the pivot hinge which can be almost entirely concealed.

Plain Butt Hinges

On flush-mounted doors, butt hinges are normally fastened to the side of the door and the inside edge of the case or facing. They are commonly recessed or mortised in place so the door will fit closer to the facing or case side. A butt hinge can also be installed on a door that completely overlaps the casework. It is fitted on the backside of the door and the front of the facing or case side as shown below. The hinge pin is then visible only from the side of the piece. This is a common method of hanging the front on small chests, stereo cabinets or bedside tables.

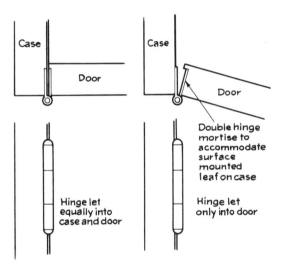

On flush-mounted doors, butt hinges are normally mortised so that the door will fit as closely as possible to the case. Hinge leaves can be recessed half-and-half in the door and case, or recessed entirely into the door.

Top right: Butt hinges can also be surface-mounted on flush doors.

Right: On doors that completely overlap the front facing or side of a cabinet, butt hinges can be installed so that pins are visible only from the side.

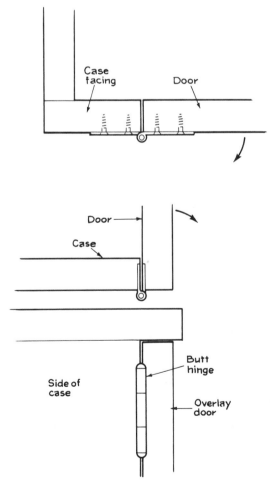

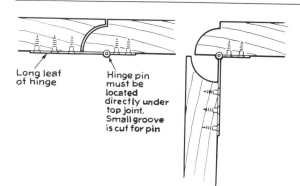

Long leaf of hinge

Hinge pin must be located directly under top joint. Small groove is cut for pin

Drop-leaf hinges are commonly used on table leaves and other items that swing down.

Making a Mortise for a Hinge Leaf

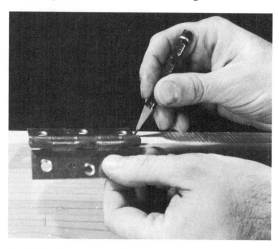
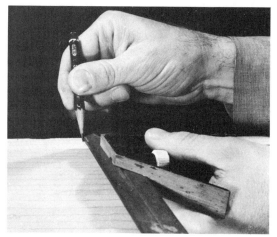

Left: Mortises for small cabinet hinges can be made with a sharp chisel. First step is to position hinge on door and mark the length with a sharp pencil. *Right:* Using a try square, mark straight across the stock as shown. Then use a marking gauge or try square to mark width and depth of backside cut. *Bottom left:* Use a chisel to mark the outline of the mortise. *Bottom right:* Then make several scoop cuts to loosen material. Later, use a paring cut from the side to remove the material and clean out the mortise.

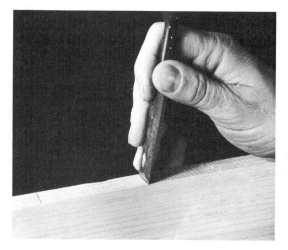

Piano hinge. The piano hinge, or continuous hinge, is used in the same way as a plain butt hinge, but is installed along most of the length of a door or leaf. It is commonly used on such items as drop lids on desks that require a great deal of holding power. It is available in long lengths and is normally cut to size with a hacksaw.

Drop-leaf hinge. A drop-leaf or backflap hinge is wider (in proportion to its length) than the standard butt hinge, and is used for drop-leaf tables and other lids that are hinged to swing down. One side is longer than the other, and the long side is positioned to reach across the joint of the drop lid.

To install a drop-leaf hinge, it is first positioned with the long side on the drop leaf portion and the short leaf on the stationary portion. The pin must be in line with the top cut on the joint to make a smooth, even-looking joint. Although these hinges are not mortised in place, you will have to cut a small groove so the hinge pin can fit snugly in place against the underside of the table edge.

Mortising Butt Hinges. Butt hinges are normally mortised or recessed in place. This can be done with a chisel or with a router and a special template. On a box, the hinges are usually set in from the edge a distance about equal to their own length, but on doors they are usually spaced a bit more away from the ends.

Hinges are usually fitted to the door first, then the door and hinges fitted in the casework. Position the hinge in place on the door and mark its length with a sharp pencil. Using a try square, mark straight across the stock. Then use a butt-marking gauge or try square to mark the backside cut. The depth of the cut will depend on whether the hinge is to be let into the casework and door equally, or mortised into the door and surface-mounted on the casework.

Use a chisel to cut the mortise to the correct depth, first cutting straight down to mark the hinge outline. Then make several scoop cuts to loosen the material to be removed. Use the chisel in a paring cut to remove the material from the mortise, leaving a clean, flat-bottom mortise.

Surface-mounted hinges are often used for decoration on casual styles of furniture. Shown is an oak linen cupboard (c. 1906) with copper T-hinges. *Metropolitan Museum of Art, Gift of Cyril Farny, 1976.*

Cutting a good mortise is very important to hanging a door properly. This often takes a bit of trial and error, especially the first time, to insure that the door hangs straight and true.

Ornamental Surface-Mounted Hinges

These are made to be fitted to the outside of the door and cabinet. They include the basic strap hinge, and other shapes such as the H-hinge, butterfly, and Cross Garnet. The design of the basic strap hinge and other similar shapes provides extra support for wide doors. These hinges are available in a number of decorative finishes, surfaces and colors. Because they are not mortised in place, the door must fit flush with the cabinet, furniture side, or facing. They are quickly and easily installed.

There are also surface-mounted hinges that are offset to fit the lip or overlay cabinet doors used on kitchen cabinets.

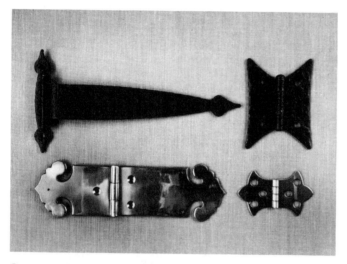

Ornamental surface-mounted hinges for flush doors are available in wrought iron, brass, and other finishes, and in a variety of shapes and sizes.

Above right: Surface-mounted hinges are also available with a ⅜-inch offset for use on lip and overlay doors.

Right: On this cabinet, wrought-iron finish H and H-L hinges are mixed and matched.

Cabinet (Semi-concealed) Hinges

These hinges are especially designed to fit the standard-size lips or rabbets on cabinet doors. Usually only that portion of the hinge that is fastened to the cabinet facing is visible, or in some cases only the pin portion of the hinge. The opposite leaf of the hinge is fitted to the backside of the cabinet door.

These hinges are available to fit several types of doors. The *lip door hinge* is commonly used on kitchen and vanity cabinet doors. The hinges are offset to fit the ⅜ × ⅜-inch lip on the back of the doors. *Semi-concealed overlay door hinges* are much like a butt hinge except that they have only one leaf. The leaf is attached to the back of the door, and the hinge pin fastened to the front casework or facing. The *wrap-around hinge* is used for flush doors of ¾-inch stock. A hinge pin and small leaf are attached to the casework, so it looks like a butt hinge from the front. But the back leaf wraps completely around to the back edge of the door to provide more support. *Offset hinges* are quite similar to the wrap-around, except that they are fitted to rabbeted doors.

Semi-concealed hinges are very rarely mortised in place on cabinet doors. The offset caused by the hinge thickness is barely noticeable due to the lip or overlap of the doors they are used on. However, larger versions of these hinges can be mortised in place to provide added support for heavy doors. Again, the best method of installation is to fasten them to the door, fit the door in place, then fasten the hinges to the case, making sure the door swings freely and is situated squarely in the opening.

Large leaf of semi-concealed hinge for a lip door is fastened on back of door. Only the hinge portion is visible from front of case.

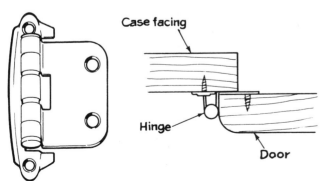

Cabinet doors which partially overlap case facing can be fitted with semi-concealed overlay door hinges. Hinge pin is fastened to case facing, and long leaf is attached to door.

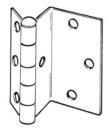

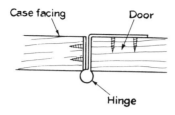

Wrap-around hinges are used on flush-mounted doors. Heavy wrap-around hinges for larger doors can be mortised into the door and surface-mounted on the case as shown below.

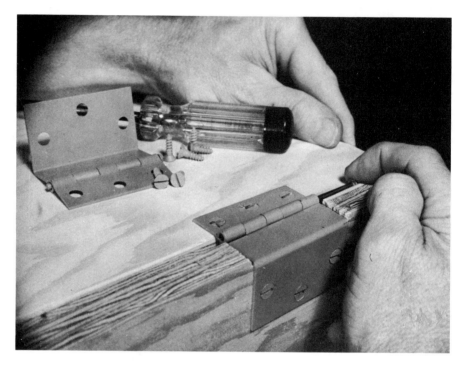

Concealed Hinges

In addition, there are several types of hinges that are designed to be inconspicuous or even invisible. This is a useful feature on projects where the presence of a door is to be de-emphasized.

Invisible Hinges. There are also hinges that are designed to be entirely invisible when installed, such as the Soss invisible hinge. These are installed by cutting mortises in the door and the case side and fitting the hinge in the mortise.

Pivot Hinges. These are installed on the top and bottom edges of the door and case. They are also called knife hinges because of their opening action. Only a thin edge of metal is visible when the door is closed.

Knobs and Pulls

There is a wide variety of items available in this category of hardware. They are available in all types of sizes and materials including porcelain, metal, and wood. They are installed simply by boring a hole through the door or drawer front and fastening a threaded bolt through the hole and into threads cut in the end of the knob. If the bolt isn't long enough to reach entirely through the door or drawer front, a hole must be counterbored in the back. Incidentally, if you are installing knobs or pulls in a number of doors or drawers of the same size, you can use a simple jig such as shown on page 207 to locate the screw holes.

Some knobs will have wood-screw threads fastened to their ends and are simply screwed in place. These are typical of small hardware such

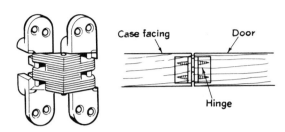

Soss invisible hinges are mortised into the door and case side so that no part of the hinge is visible from the outside.

Pivot hinges can be installed on doors which completely overlap face of cabinet. Only a thin wedge of metal is visible from outside of cabinet. This type of hinge will require mortising if used on the middle of a door as shown above.

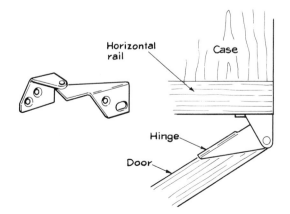

Pivot hinges which mount on horizontal rails of cabinet are also available.

There are many different styles of pulls for cabinet doors and drawers. Heavy doors and drawers warrant two screws or bolts per pull.

Specialty hardware companies supply many types of period hardware. For this reproduction piece, Chippendale-style pulls with matching lock escutcheons were used. *Trimble Sharder, Nashville, Tennesee.*

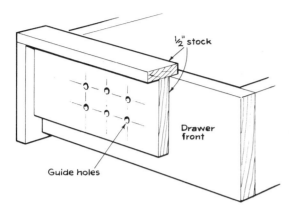

A shop-made jig will speed up installation of knobs or pulls when you have a number of drawers or doors of the same size.

as for jewelry boxes. Knobs may also have escutcheon plates that can be put behind them to add a decorative look to the hardware. This is particularly true on the larger hardware, such as on Spanish furniture styles. Old-time porcelain knobs are installed by running a screw-bolt from the front of the knob through the door and fastening with a washer and nut on the back. The screw is part of the decorative appearance of the knob.

Pulls are also available in a wide variety of sizes and styles. There are pulls that suit kitchen cabinet styling and pulls that can be used to suit traditional antique style or reproduction pieces of furniture. Pulls normally are installed by boring two small holes for the holding screws which are screwed in from the back or inside of the door or cabinet. Some pulls may also have escutcheon plates. Finger-hole pulls are normally flush mounted on sliding or by-passing doors, and are made of plastic or metal. They are fitted into a mortise or recess cut in the front side of the door and are held in place with tiny brads or screws.

Door Catches

Most furniture and cabinetry have catches on the doors to keep them closed. Again, there are many different styles, including a "touch latch" that automatically locks the door yet starts it to swing open when the front of the door is touched in the location of the latch.

The most common type of latches are the magnetic and spring or roller catches. Either type is merely fastened in place on the inside of the cabinet or furniture case, and the corresponding latch piece, whether it be a metal plate for the magnetic latch or a spring clip for the roller or spring catch, is fastened with screws to the door. About the only problem in installation is making sure that the two pieces line up properly, so they will meet when the door is shut to hold it securely in place.

There are also spring-loaded cabinet door

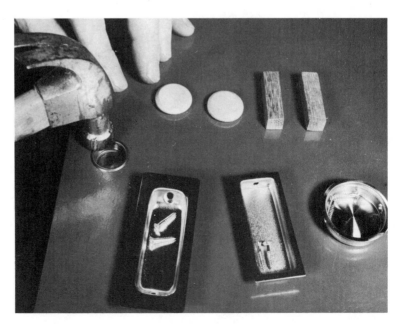

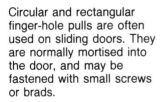

Circular and rectangular finger-hole pulls are often used on sliding doors. They are normally mortised into the door, and may be fastened with small screws or brads.

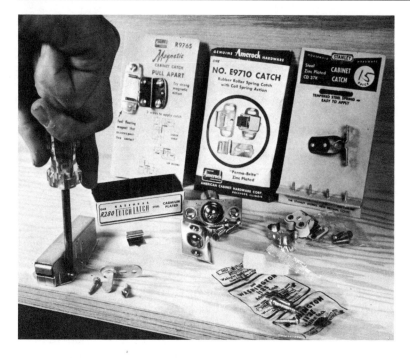

Door catches are available
with magnetic, roller spring,
or touch latch mechanisms.

Catches should be mounted out of the way inside
the cabinet. Make sure both parts align when door
is shut.

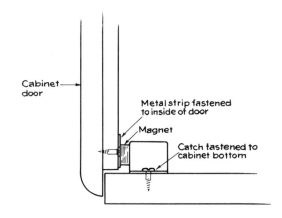

Cabinet door

Metal strip fastened
to inside of door

Magnet

Catch fastened to
cabinet bottom

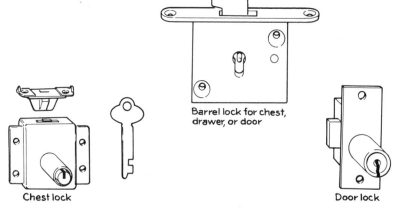

Chest lock

Barrel lock for chest,
drawer, or door

Door lock

Many types of small locks
are available for use on
drawers, doors, jewelry
boxes, and chests.

Mail-order woodworking supply houses carry a large variety of specialty hardware items for specific jobs. One example is this cedar chest hinge. It holds the lid of a chest upright when it is open, yet prevents it from banging shut when the lid is closed.

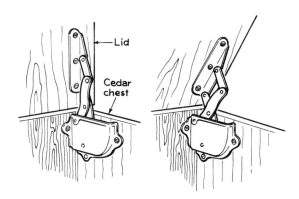

hinges that eliminate the need for catches. When the door is opened past a certain point, the hinges automatically hold it open. A gentle push is all that is needed to start the door swinging shut. The hinges slowly close the door much in the same manner as a door-closing device on a screen or storm door. Once the door is shut it is held securely in place; no other catches are necessary.

Door Locks

Locks are very seldom installed on kitchen cabinet doors or drawers. However, quite a few furniture pieces do have locks, including desks, bureaus, and some bedroom furniture. Drawer, box, door, and chest locks are all mortised in place into the furniture.

Miscellaneous Hardware

In addition to the standard hardware items mentioned, there are a number of unusual and specialty items for furniture and cabinet construction, including extension table slides for use in adjustable leaf tables, hardware to make the post and rail joints of bedsteads de-mountable, Lazy Susan bearings for revolving turntables, and heavy-duty rocker and swivel hardware for platform rockers.

14

Carvings, Moldings, and Other Decorations

Carving is one of the most ancient woodworking arts, and it is still a necessary as well as enjoyable aspect of cabinetmaking. Elaborate carvings of fruit, flower, and animal forms are a prominent feature of Gothic, Tudor, Baroque, and other traditional furniture styles. In the furniture styles originated in the past two hundred years, on the other hand, carvings have been somewhat less fanciful and scaled-down in size. The work of Duncan Phyfe and other master cabinetmakers of the nineteenth century, for example, is characterized by restrained, delicate carvings which are integrated with the lines of the furniture.

There are basically two different types of wood carving methods used on furniture and cabinetry. The first is employed on a structural part of the item, such as the arms of a Danish modern chair, or the ball-and-claw feet of English period furniture. The second type is an "add-on" feature that is glued in place, such as the panels on a door or drawer front.

Luckily, today's furniture and cabinet builder doesn't have to be a master wood carver to be able

Elaborate carvings are a prominent feature of many traditional furniture styles. Shown here is a carved rosewood table with marble top by J. H. Belter, c. 1861. *Museum of the City of New York.*

Carvings may be either a structural part of the furniture, or an added detail such as this rooster carved in mahogany by a Philadelphia cabinetmaker (c. 1770). *Metropolitan Museum of Art, Friends of the American Wing, 1975.*

Scaled-down adaptions of Baroque and Rococo carvings were often used in the 19th century to complement the simple, classical lines of Empire-style furniture. Side chair with harp motif (c. 1815) is by Duncan Phyfe. The maple side chair at right (c. 1820) has a slat formed with delicately carved leaves. *Museum of the City of New York.*

Many different types of embossed wood carvings, crosscut and embossed moldings, and scalloped trim pieces are available to the home craftsman. These can be simply glued in place to create the effect of hand-carved designs.

Luckily for today's furniture and cabinet builder, there are many types of carved panels to simulate the look of hand-carved panels. Some of these are available in wood, and others in wood-grained plastic.

to embellish his handmade furniture with beautiful carvings and decorations. There are hundreds of stamped and machine-made carvings and carved moldings available from leading woodworking supply houses. These can be glued in place to create almost any "style" of furniture from Spanish to traditional. The better machine-made carvings will also have an exaggerated grain pattern that creates quite a realistic wood grain effect. A great deal of the stylish furniture seen today utilizes polyurethane formed "carvings" that look so much like real wood you can't tell the difference unless you cut into them with a sharp knife. Many of these formed carvings are also available to the home craftsman.

By choosing different carvings you can make simple box furniture such as bedroom chests, enclosed end tables, or even kitchen cabinets look like Spanish, French Provincial, Italian, Mediterranean, Traditional, or other furniture styles. In many cases, however, the woodworker may wish to carve his own panels. Or it may be necessary to render such items as a ball-and-claw foot to match an existing set of furniture. In any case, wood carving is not that difficult for most woodworkers, although it does take some special tools and a little practice. There are several different

methods of wood carving. Let's start with the simplest.

Tools

A great deal of wood carving can and has been done with nothing more than a sharp pocketknife. However, most furniture carving requires special tools. Depending on what type of carving you are doing, you might need special chip-carving chisels, a gouge chisel set, wooden mallet, spokeshave, drawknife, inshave, rasp—and files of all kinds, a rotary rasp for a power drill, and a small electric hand grinder. Although not a necessity, a set of tiny linoleum-carving knives can really come in handy for finishing intricate work. These come in shapes similar to, but smaller than their larger cousins, the sculpting gouges.

Of course, for any serious woodcarving you'll need a set of carving chisels and a wooden mallet. A good set of chisels will include square and skew chisels of different sizes, as well as gouges of different sizes. You'll want at least one large, fairly flat gouge, probably one inch or larger. This is used for roughing out; it takes a pretty big bite, removing a rounded chip. You will also want a

Tools needed for carvings can vary a great deal, depending on what types of carving you will be doing. For gouge or relief carving, you'll need gouges and a mallet in addition to carving chisels. (Regular chisels are also useful in many projects.) *Leichtung.*

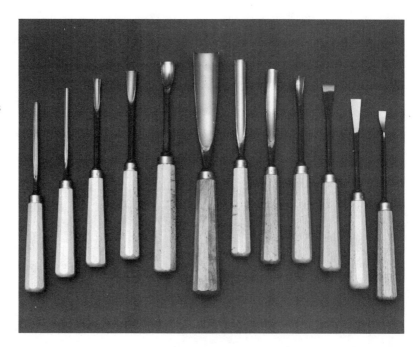

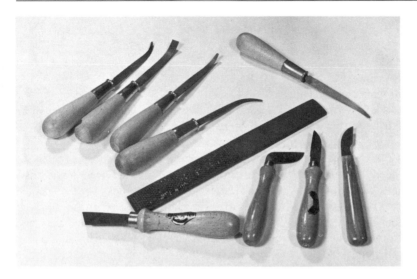

Other specialty tools used in carving include rifflers, rasps, files and chip-carving knives.

smaller straight gouge, about ⅜ inch, and a half-inch bent gouge. If you plan to do any lettering work, you'll want a tiny straight gouge, sometimes called a veiner chisel. Although not a necessity, a good set of bent rifflers, or carving files, will come in handy for smoothing chisel marks in hard to reach areas. These come in all different sizes and shapes and are usually equipped with a handle.

You will need a wooden carver's mallet—probably a 16-oz. size to start with. If you're doing delicate carving you might also need a smaller 13-oz. mallet. You would use a 21- or 32-oz.

carver's mallet for heavy sculpting and removing large amounts of material.

One problem with all carving mallets is that they are made of heavy dense wood, and have a tendency to dry out and check rather quickly if not cared for properly. When the mallet is not in use, it's a good idea to wrap it in a plastic sack with a tiny piece of damp sponge inside.

With these basic tools you'll be able to handle almost any wood carving problem, but you will also need clamps. Nothing is more exasperating than to try to carve an object not held securely, so make sure you have a good vise that is fastened

A small hand grinder can be used for a lot of wood carving.

to a heavy table or bench. For flat, "low-relief" work such as wooden plaques, a great helpmate is a bench hold-down. These are special clamps that are used to clamp the work solidly on the table or bench. Of course, C-clamps also can be used to hold work to the table.

Tool Maintenance and Sharpening

A good set of carving tools is a pretty fair investment; so care for them properly. They should be stored in a wooden case specially made for them, or rolled up in a cloth case. They should never just be thrown together in a drawer or they will become dulled and chipped. An occasional light spray of some penetrating rust-preventive oil such as WD-40 will do wonders to keep them in good shape.

All woodworking tools must be kept as sharp as possible, and this is doubly important for wood carving tools. A dull chisel not only makes for extra work, it takes out a ragged looking chip and can be dangerous. It will slip and cause a bad accident, rather than digging in and cutting a clean chip.

To keep your tools sharp you will need a good bench stone, and special gouge slips for honing gouges and other curved carving chisels. You should have a Crystolon bench stone for rough honing, and a good India or Arkansas stone for that final razor sharpness. The bench stone should be securely clamped to the bench and kept well oiled. The tools are stroked across the hone with firm, even strokes. If you can get one, an old-fashioned razor strop can be used to remove the "wire-edge" left from honing and can put that final keenness on the edges of your tools.

Chip Carving

Chip carving is just what it sounds like—carving out small triangular chips of wood to create a pattern. Chip carving is probably the easiest type of carving for the beginner to master, yet an experienced carver can also create beautiful and elaborate designs with this simple wood carving technique. Chip carving provides an excellent method of decorating chest fronts or even panels for doors. Chip carving can be done with chisels, a sharp utility knife, chip-carving knives, or even a sharp razor blade, depending on the proficiency of the carver. Using a sharp pocketknife or utility knife is a good way to learn chip carving. Once you learn the basics of making the cut, you can proceed to carving gouges.

Chip carving relies on geometric shapes. The first step in mastering this carving technique is to learn to carve a triangle. Draw a small triangle on a piece of soft white pine or basswood, tilt the

Chip carving is probably the easiest method for the beginner to master, and it provides some excellent designs for cabinet and furniture fronts. A sharp pocketknife can be used for chip carving.

Chip carving relies on geometric shapes. To cut a triangle, the knife is held at a 15° to 20° angle, and the three cuts made as shown.

knife about 15° to 20°, and cut from point A to point B (see photo). Then, holding the knife at the same angle, make a cut from B to C, then from C back to A. If the slope of the knife and the size of the triangle are correct, you will have cut out a small wedge-shape chip. These are actually small compound triangles cut in the wood surface. Experiment to find the right angle and triangle size to make a perfectly carved chip. Then, by varying the type of triangle and adding triangles

together, you can make a design. An advanced chip carver will probably want two knives—a striking knife and a slicing knife.

In addition to the triangles, you will need to make V or line cuts. To lay out this cut, mark the outside edges of the cuts, then mark a centerline. Cut with the knife angled so the cuts will meet at the bottom on the centerline. Taper the cut at the ends. A stopped line cut is made in the same manner, except it is stopped with a straight down,

V- or line cuts are also used in chip carving. Lay out the design as shown, then cut with knife held at an angle so the cuts meets at the centerline of the design. The ends can be tapered or stop-cut.

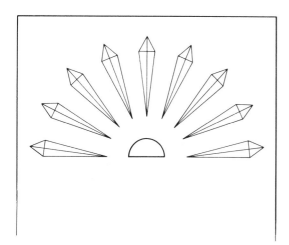

By varying the design and adding several together, you can create an unusual decoration for an arched door.

or vertical, cut at the ends. An excellent carving technique for decorating arched doors is the fan shaped design using a variety of triangle shapes.

Incised Line Carving

Incised line carving is done in much the same manner as chip carving, except in most cases a small V- or U-shape chisel (called a *veiner* or *parting* chisel) is used to make the cut. The line can be a geometric or a natural shape. Common examples of this are carved lettering and carved borders on molding. (See photos on page 218.)

When using small veiner or gouge chisels to make an incised line, work carefully and slowly. Don't allow the chisel to run out of line and follow the grain of the wood instead of your outline. It's a good idea to make cuts in several light successive passes, instead of cutting to full depth in one sweep. If the chisel continues to run out on a diagonal cut, make a stopped cut in the center, then start again after you get past that point. These V-shape lines can also be cut with a sharp knife, but the cuts won't be quite as regular.

Intaglio Carving

Intaglio carving utilizes both chip carving and incised-line methods plus a few of its own techniques. Intaglio carving carves the object in reverse, as in relief carving; but the pattern is cut *into* the wood—the opposite of relief. Intaglio carving is an excellent method of carving chest door fronts and other items. A common type of intaglio carving is often seen on old butter molds.

Incised-line carving is usually done with small V- or U-shape chisels.

Lettering is a common application of incised-line carving.

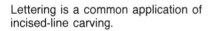

Intaglio carving is a combination of chip carving and incised-line. It is commonly seen on old-fashioned butter molds.

In relief carving, the background is cut away so the carving stands out. This 17th-century oak chest has drawers and framework carved in low relief. (This type of work is also called *stamping*.) *The Metropolitan Museum of Art, Rogers Fund, 1908.*

Relief Carving

There are two different types of relief carving, low relief and high relief. *Low relief* is carved quite shallowly, and often the surrounding surface is left fairly close to the carving. *High relief* is often carved by cutting away almost all of the background to achieve a full "round" type of carving.

In relief carving the subject is outlined using a "stop cut." This cut is made with the chisels and gouges held perpendicular to the surface of the wood and driven straight down into the wood, outlining the subject with a deep cut. A large, straight gouge is then used to remove background from around the subject. For a primitive look, the background can be left as is with the chisel marks of the chips showing. Or the background can be stippled with a nail set, or treated in other ways.

The first step in relief carving is to outline the object, cutting perpendicular to the design with appropriately shaped chisels and gouges.

Relief Carving (Cont'd.)

Then the background is cut away with gouges and a mallet until it is fairly smooth.

Finally, the design is rounded and shaped.

In *stamping,* another type of low-relief carving, the edges of the design are left flat and the background cut away very shallowly. (This was a popular method with Jacobean furniture builders as well as Scandinavian and North Italian carvers.) The background of a stamped design can be stippled with a nail set, as shown above at right.

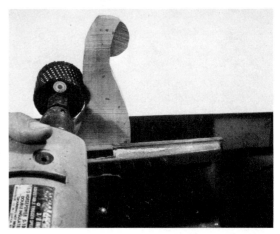

A rasp attachment in a power drill can sometimes be used to rough out full-round carved items. It removes a lot of material quickly.

Pierced-relief carving is a technique traditionally used on mirror frames. Shown is an 18th-century Chippendale-style mahogany mirror. *The Metropolitan Museum of Art, Sansbury-Mills Fund, 1952.*

With the subject area standing out from the surface of the wood, its edges and surfaces are then rounded to produce a look of depth. With careful attention to detail and a little thought, the depth can be given a bit of exaggeration, making the design appear more full and rounded than it actually is.

One style of low-relief carving is not really carving but stamping. It was practiced by the Scandinavian and North Italian carvers to produce a work called strapwork or ribbon carving. In this method the background is cut away very shallowly, then a decorative metal punch is used to stipple or roughen the background and provide a contrast between the background and the relief carving. Stamped patterns were also commonly used on Jacobean and some Early American furniture. In this type of carving, the pattern is left flat, rather than rounded or carved.

In high-relief carving, the background is carved away, and the design almost undercut but not completely separated as it would be for in-the-round carving. High-relief carving takes a great deal of skill, practice, and time, yet it results in some of the most beautiful carving in the world. Usually low-relief carving is used as a fur-

niture decoration, while high relief is used more as sculpture or for decorative items. However, there is a great deal of variation and overlap between the two. Almost any tool can be used for roughing-in the subject. The final modeling should be done with a single sharp tool that fits the contour of the item carved, so you get a final polished cut that won't require sanding. The direction of the grain is extremely important in high-relief carving. It's easy to break a piece by pushing too hard against the grain, causing the chisel or knife to jump and slice through or split the piece.

One type of high-relief carving often used, especially on items such as fancy carved mirrors and name crests, is pierced-relief carving. In this method, the carving goes completely through the background and leaves small holes in the surface. This is also often used for decorative screens and other similar items.

High relief is most often done quite realistically, which takes the most time and skill, while low-relief and other geometric types of carvings are done with more artistic license. In many instances you will need to combine all of the techniques to achieve your desired results.

Moldings play an important part in furniture and cabinet building. On this 17th-century chest, carved moldings are combined with decorative split turnings. *Museum of the City of New York.*

Gouge Carved Moldings

A different type of gouge used in somewhat the same manner as for chip carving can produce some highly decorative and unusual moldings or borders. These designs are achieved with two basic cutting techniques. The first simply creates a small depression in the surface. This is done by holding the gouge vertically over the surface and cutting and rolling it as you make the cut to scoop out a perfect circle, or "dot." The second type of cut is a groove made much in the same manner as the veiner V-cuts. In most instances on softwoods you push the gouge with one hand while guiding it with the other, but on hardwoods you will probably have to use a wooden mallet. Combinations of different techniques can be used to make up any number of different patterns.

Simple straight-line gouge cuts, as well as more elaborate carvings, can be used to embellish moldings.

Machine-made Moldings

There are a number of manufactured moldings that can be bought and used to embellish a piece of furniture. In addition to specialized moldings, there are also a number of standard millwork moldings that can be applied to decorate furniture. By combining the various moldings you can create various designs. Of course, in many cases the particular moldings will have to be hand-made, and this can be done in a number of ways, depending on the molding and what it is used on. For instance, the top molding on a grandfather clock must be cut out with a bandsaw, then molded with a shaper. Elaborate moldings can be made by combining machine molding with carved or gouged molding, and even by gluing on "fretwork," or pierced pieces, to make a design. In Chapter 24, the use of the various moldings as millwork is discussed. In this section I'll discuss moldings for furniture and cabinetry.

Planer Cutting

Probably the simplest method of cutting molding is with a surface planer, such as the Belsaw unit. With this particular unit molding knives are fitted in the revolving head and the stock is pushed through the planer, resulting in the finished molding. Using this particular machine you can surface-plane and mold an edge, or even two edges, on stock simultaneously. There are many standard molding knives available, and by using the different knives or by combining cuts you can achieve many different types of designs.

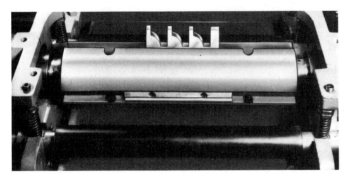

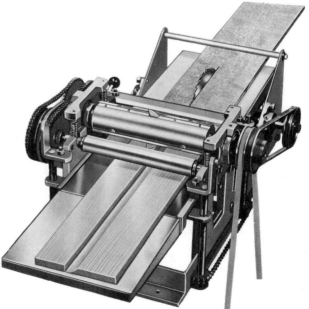

Probably the easiest way to cut moldings is on a surface planer. There are many different molding knives available for this use.

On some planers, stock can be surface-planed and edge-molded in one operation.

Cutting Moldings on a Table Saw

The most common type of home-shop molding cutter is a molding head which is used on a table or radial arm saw. Picture frames, trim of all sorts, and table edges can be shaped in this way. The better molding heads come with an assortment of cutter blades, in sets of three, that are fastened in the head by means of set screws. A molding head's capability is a bit more limited on the table saw than on the radial arm saw, so let's start with the table saw.

When using a molding head on a table saw, you will usually need an auxiliary table or table insert as well as an auxiliary fence. The auxiliary table is used to minimize the opening around the molding head, and the auxiliary fence shields the cutterhead and protects the regular fence. You can make a fence quite easily that will slip down over the existing fence, or you can screw wooden strips to each side of the existing fence. Hold-down arrangements are usually necessary to stabilize work against the impact of the molding head; a tenoning jig in particular is useful for many cuts.

There are a great many different cutters avail-able, most of which conform to standard shaper cutters. Some knives, such as the tongue-and-groove or glue joint, are to be used full profile. Others, such as the quarter round, or cove, can be used for partial cuts. Or you can combine cuts from different types of cutters to make almost any molding shape.

Small strip moldings can be made by molding an edge of a board, then rip cutting the strip off. Or you can make a strip-molding jig for such things as screen molding to hold the thin strips in place while they are being shaped. This technique is especially good when you have a number of strips to shape.

Use all safety precautions anytime you're using a molding head. It's a good idea to make light cuts, gradually deepening them to full depth as desired. In most cases depth of cut should be from ⅛ to ¼ inch in hardwoods, and not more than ⅜-inch deep in softwoods. Don't hurry or force the stock into the cutterhead.

Naturally, with-the-grain cuts will be smoothest. Cross-grain cuts on wide boards are made in the same manner as cuts with the grain, but it is a good idea to use a push stick to complete the cut

Machine-made Moldings (Cont'd.)

Molding heads used on table saw or radial arm saw come with a variety of cutters. Cutters are fastened on the head with set screws. Shown at right are a few of the standard cutters which can be used on a molding head.

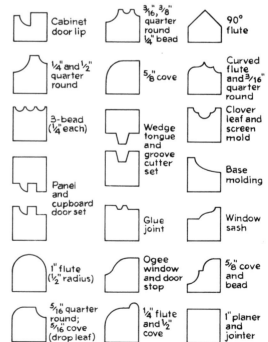

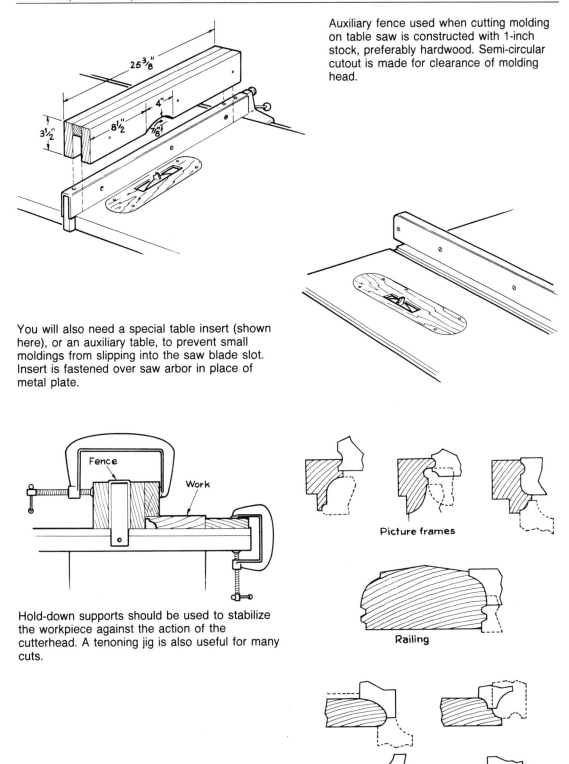

Auxiliary fence used when cutting molding on table saw is constructed with 1-inch stock, preferably hardwood. Semi-circular cutout is made for clearance of molding head.

You will also need a special table insert (shown here), or an auxiliary table, to prevent small moldings from slipping into the saw blade slot. Insert is fastened over saw arbor in place of metal plate.

Hold-down supports should be used to stabilize the workpiece against the action of the cutterhead. A tenoning jig is also useful for many cuts.

An unlimited number of molding configurations can be made by combining different cutters and using different cutterhead projections. Shown are a few of the possibilities.

Picture frames

Railing

Table edges

Machine-made Moldings (Cont'd.)

Thin molding strips can be made by first cutting molding on side of wide stock, then ripping the pieces to desired thickness.

An alternate method of shaping thin strips is to use a jig fastened to auxiliary fence with clamps or screws. Piece is pushed into jig and pulled out at other end—or it can be pushed through with next piece.

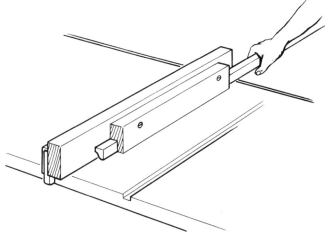

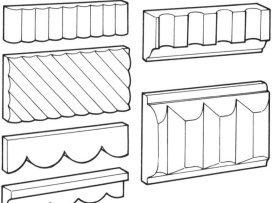

Crosscut moldings are some of the most unusual. They are easier to cut on a radial arm saw, but can also be done on a table saw.

to prevent splintering the wood at the end. Cross-grain cuts on short narrow stock should be cut using the miter gauge on the saw to hold the stock securely. Larger pieces, whether cut across grain or with the grain, can be laid flat on the table or stood on end.

Always make the cut on the side that is nearest the fence, rather than running stock between cutterhead and fence, so any variation in stock thickness won't matter. Anytime the molding runs entirely around a piece, always make the cross-grain cuts first, then cut with the grain. These latter cuts will remove any slight splintering left by the cross-grain cuts.

Cross-cut Moldings. These are highly ornamental moldings that often give the appearance of being hand carved. They are easiest to cut on a radial arm saw, but can also be done with a table saw. By varying the molding cutter shapes you can get a variety of cuts. On the table saw, the cuts are spaced using a guide board fastened to the stock. The guide board has regularly spaced slots cut in its back to fit a special fence fastened to the miter gauge. The fence has a metal pin— a cut-off nail—that fits in the saw slots.

After cutting crosswise, the molding can be ripped into narrower strips or further shaped by cutting it lengthwise on the stock. Setting the miter gauge at an angle produces angled moldings or creates diamond effects.

Another quite similar molding is a standard dental molding. It can be made using the same spacer pins. However, a regular saw blade is used to make the cuts in wide stock; then the stock is ripped into thin pieces and glued in place to form the molding. When ripping the thin pieces you will probably wish to make a special auxiliary

When making molding cuts across the face of stock, a special guide is needed to hold the stock and space the cuts. The guide board is tacked to stock and placed against auxiliary fence. Work is then pushed over molding head with miter gauge.

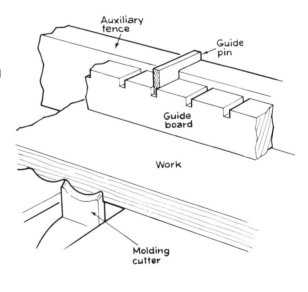

Dentil molding

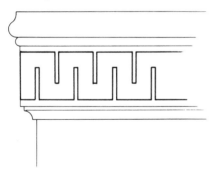

Dentil molding is commonly used on period furniture. It is cut with regular saw blade on wide stock, using spacer pins, and the stock is then ripped to thin widths.

When ripping thin pieces such as dentil moldings, an auxiliary table can be devised as shown to prevent the pieces from dropping down into the saw blade slot.

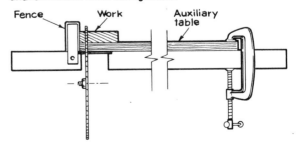

table to prevent the small pieces from being pulled down through the opening in the table insert. Merely clamp the top in place with the saw blade lowered below the table. Turn on the saw and raise the blade until it comes through the wooden stock in the exact place you wish to get the thin widths.

Cutting Coves. A quite unusual type of molding can be made by cove cutting on the table saw, using a regular saw blade. This is done by clamping a wooden auxiliary guide fence at an angle to the saw blade, then pushing the stock over the saw blade repeatedly to make successive light cuts. The angle determines the width of the cove, while the height of the saw blade provides the depth. It is helpful to remove some stock with regular saw cuts before beginning the cove cuts. The first cut must be made with the saw blade no more than an eighth of an inch above the table. Raise the blade no more than ⅛ inch for each successive cut. You can determine the proper fence angle by use of a parallel rule. Merely set the rule at the cove width desired, and place it in position over the blade set at the desired cove depth. Angle the rule until both edges of the blade

Machine-made Moldings (Cont'd.)

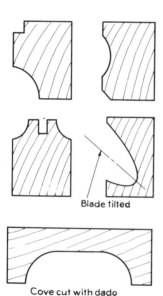

Blade tilted

Cove cut with dado

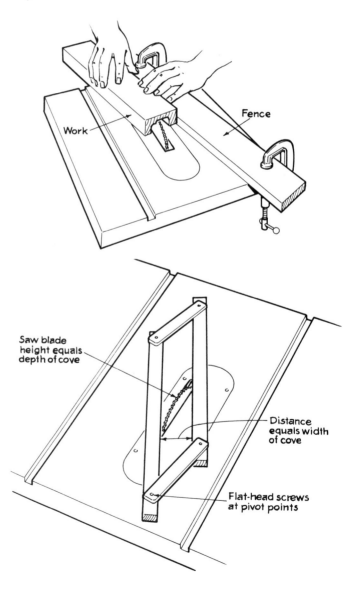

Work

Fence

Saw blade height equals depth of cove

Distance equals width of cove

Flat-head screws at pivot points

A variety of shaped cuts can be made with cove cutting techniques. Cove is cut by pushing stock against saw blade at an angle instead of straight on: the depth of blade and angle of fence determine shape of cove. Successive light cuts are made until the proper depth is achieved. (Blade can be tilted to cut irregular shapes.)

A special parallel rule can be made to help determine the proper angle for coving.

just touch the inner edges of the frame. Mark the angle on the table top—this is the angle of the auxiliary fence. You will have to move the fence in or out according to the distance between the stock edge and the cove edge. It is best to use a small sharp saw—a six-inch saw provides the best cove shapes.

Cutting Moldings on Radial Arm Saw

Molding heads can also be used on a radial arm saw, which is a bit more versatile in operation than a table saw. Most standard molding work will require the saw to be set up for horizontal sawing. You will have to make an auxiliary fence

and table as shown. The table is necessary to protect the original table on deep cuts, and on cuts where part of the cutterhead is below the work. The auxiliary fence shields the molding head and supports the work after it has passed the cutter. The techniques of setting the molding head and establishing the pattern are the same as for the table saw. Again, it is necessary to make repeat passes, cutting only a small amount each time. To make the cuts, slowly push the stock against the fence and into the cutter. Use push sticks and hold-downs whenever practical. It's a good idea to wear a face shield or goggles when doing any type of molding work to protect your eyes from flying chips.

Molding head on radial arm saw is a bit more versatile than on table saw. (Note: Guard has been removed for photo—always use special cutterhead guard for your saw.)

As with table saw, an auxiliary table and fence must be used for molding operations on radial arm saw.

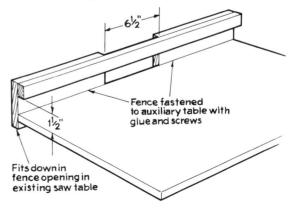

Use a push stick to push the narrow cross-grain cuts through. Narrow moldings can be cut on wide stock, and the strips then rip-cut off. However, if a number of strips are to be molded, it will be worthwhile to make a special jig as shown.

One advantage of a radial arm saw is that you can do circular or irregular shapes by using special jigs. This is important when making molding for rounded pieces, such as the tops of grandfa-

ther clocks. When using an irregular-shape jig, make sure you use a special cutterhead guard as well to cut down exposure to the cutterhead. You can also make molding cuts on flat panels. And by tilting the molding head you can achieve even greater variety of cuts.

Cross-stock moldings can also be made using the molding cutter on a radial arm saw. Because the molding head has a tendency to grab, this

Machine-made Moldings (Cont'd.)

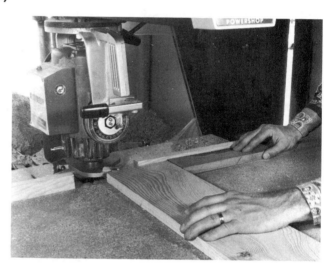

When cutting edge molding across the grain of stock, use a push stick to help hold the stock straight and to prevent splintering at the end.

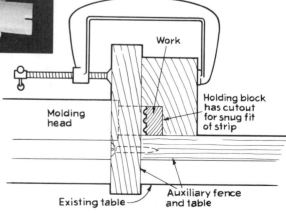

Hold-down supports should be used when cutting moldings whenever practical. A strip-holding jig can be set up as shown to cut small thin moldings.

Work

Holding block has cutout for snug fit of strip

Molding head

Existing table

Auxiliary fence and table

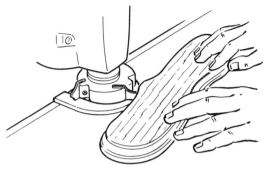

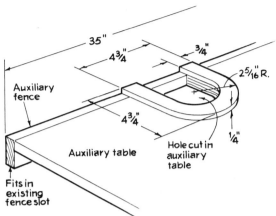

An advantage of the radial arm saw is that it can be used to mold irregularly shaped pieces. For this type of work, a special guide jig is set up as shown.

Crosscut molding can also be done on the radial arm saw. Cuts are not made full depth, but in a succession of light passes.

By tilting the radial head and running stock through in rip fashion, you can create an even wider variety of moldings.

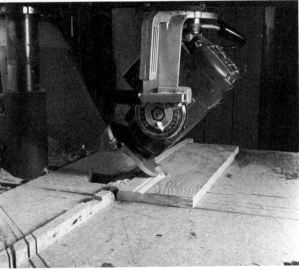

type of cutting should be done slowly and by making several light successive cuts to the final depth. Then rip the strips to the desired width.

Cutting Moldings on a Shaper

Of course the simplest method of cutting molding

is to use a shaper. There is a larger variety of molding cutterheads available for a standard shaper, and this allows more flexibility. In addition, the shaper turns with a higher speed and provides a somewhat smoother cut than table and radial arm saws. Using special jigs, you can also cut moldings on irregular-shape pieces.

Machine-made Moldings (Cont'd.)

A shaper provides another excellent method of making moldings. It can be used to mold the edges of irregularly shaped panels.

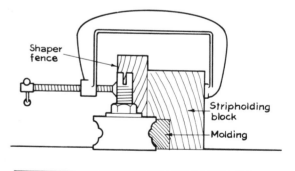

As with radial arm saw and table saw, hold-down supports should be used when cutting moldings on shaper. Strip-holding jig is set up as shown.

15

Working with Glass and Plexiglas

Glass

Furniture makers as far back as the fifteenth century used glass and mirrors to enhance their work, even though it was very costly and available only in small sizes. Modern processes produce fine, inexpensive glass that can be used to even better advantage by the cabinetmaker or furniture builder. It takes a little practice to learn how to cut glass, but once the technique is mastered it is easy to do.

There are several types of glass used in cabinets and furniture. Regular *sheet* glass, or window glass, can be used for cabinet doors, picture frames, and table tops in addition to windows. It comes in thicknesses from 1/16 inch (for small picture frames) to nearly a half inch. The thicker, double-strength sheet glass is also called "crystal" glass. *Plate* glass has basically the same composition as sheet glass, but its surfaces are ground and polished to eliminate distortion—the best grades have no distortion at all. Plate glass for home use is 1/8- or 1/4-inch thick; and commercial plate glass can be as thick as 1 1/4 inch. It is a little harder to cut than sheet glass. *Glareproof,* or picture, glass is slightly frosted to eliminate light reflection. When this glass is placed on a picture, the image is sharp and glare-free. Picture glass is extremely brittle, so it is best to practice glass cutting with less expensive sheet glass. *Mirrors* have many applications in furniture and cabine-

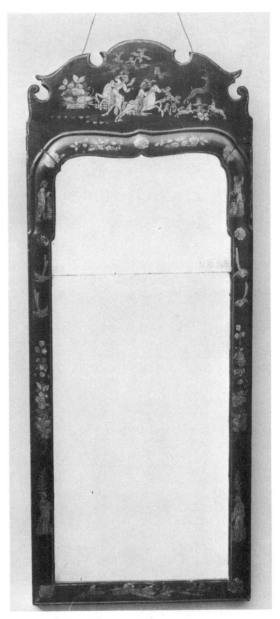

For centuries, glass and mirror stock was extremely expensive, and available only in small pieces. Shown is an English lacquered pine frame (c. 1725) with two-piece glass insert. *The Metropolitan Museum of Art, Rogers Fund, 1925.*

A visit to a glass shop will reveal that there are many different types of glass—shown are just a few. From right to left: Glare proof, single strength, double strength, plate, safety, ⅜-inch-thick tinted plate, textured colored, textured opaque, textured clear, wire reinforced, plate mirror, and tinted gold-veined mirror.

The ideal glass for displaying valuable pictures is glare-proof glass. An object placed some distance behind this glass appears fuzzy. When placed directly behind the glass, however, an image is perfectly clear.

Leaded glass for cabinet doors can be custom-made by a glazier or stained-glass craftsman, or purchased through a cabinet supply house.

try. They are often used, for instance, on the back wall of a display cabinet to reflect a collection of china or other items. Mirror stock is cut in the same manner as sheet glass. In addition, there are many different decorative varieties, such as smoked, scored, textured and tinted glasses. You can also have leaded glass designs executed by a glazier or stained-glass craftsman.

Cutting Glass

"Cutting" glass or mirror stock is actually done by scoring it and then breaking it along the scored line. One of the most important things in cutting glass is to have a flat, smooth surface to work on. A table top, workbench, anything will do, as long as there are no globs of paint, chunks of wood, or other debris that might crack the glass while you're working on it. If you can find a table with a good square edge, so much the better.

Cutting a Straight Line. Clean the glass thoroughly with a bit of glass cleaner, then lay it down flat on the work surface and mark both ends of the cut with a felt tip pen. Find a good straightedge to use as a guide for the glass cutter. A carpenter's square, T-square, or smooth-edged straight board can be used. (A wood straightedge is less likely to slip during the cut than a steel one.) On long cuts, you can place a stop block at one end and use your hand at the other to hold the straightedge securely. The cutter to be used should first be lubricated by dipping it in house-

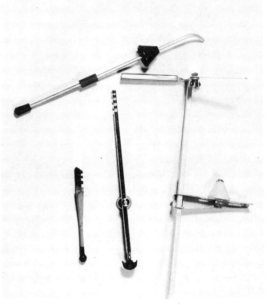

Some of the tools for cutting glass: A normal glass cutter (left, below); a circle cutter (middle); a bottle cutter (right); and a tapper (top).

When not in use, or before cutting glass, a cutter should be soaked in lightweight household oil. Or the cutting wheel can be sprayed with WD-40.

hold oil or by dusting it a bit with WD-40 or a similar lubricant.

I think the biggest secret to cutting glass successfully is confidence. If you feel hesitant, you can't make the scoring stroke properly. Just set everything up, then *do it!* The cutter should be held firmly between the fingers, with the handle straight up, the cutting wheel down on the glass, and the edge of the cutter tightly against the straightedge. Then with a smooth, even stroke, bring it back along the glass. Never repeat a stroke with the cutter. This only makes the glass

Scoring and Cutting Straight Lines

Using a good straightedge (preferably of wood), grasp the cutter as shown and make a firm single stroke to score the glass.

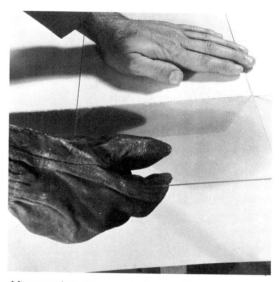

After scoring, an expert glass cutter merely snaps off the excess glass by positioning the scored line flush with a table edge and pushing down sharply.

A much safer method is to tap on the underside of the glass, following the scored line, until the piece drops off in your hand.

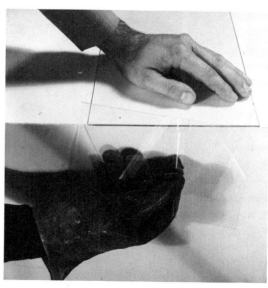

chip and can cause it to fracture away from the scored line. One of the biggest problems is in starting the cut evenly at the top of the stroke. One way to do this is to make an initial very short forward stroke on the edge before you start to bring the cutter toward you for the main cut.

To make a good scored line, the cutter should make a complete cut without any skips. If the cutter skips at any point you won't be able to break the glass smoothly, and the glass may even fracture in the wrong place because of the pressure applied in snapping. Glass scoring does take a bit of practice and patience, but once you learn the knack of it, you'll be amazed at how easy it is. Incidentally, glass isn't all the same; even the same types will have some pieces that are brittle and more easily shattered than others.

After the line has been scored, the next step is to break the glass on the scored line. This should be done as soon as the line is scored. One method, which again takes a bit of practice, is to position the glass on a flat surface with the scored line just hanging over the edge. Hold the glass flat on the table surface with one hand and give the portion hanging over the edge a quick downward snap with your other hand. This trick works about 99 percent of the time, after a little practice, but occasionally it will fail for even the expert. Inci-

dentally, you should always wear heavy gloves for this type of operation to prevent cutting your hands on sharp edges.

A safer and more predictable method of cutting glass is to position it with a bit more of the scored line hanging over the table edge. Rap on the underside of the scored line with the heavy ball end of the glass cutter. As you proceed along the line you will notice a sharp crack shooting along it ahead of the tapping ball. Make sure you hold the protruding portion, because it will usually fall off in your hand before you reach the end of the line. If it doesn't, place the scored line directly over the table edge and use a downward snap as shown at the top of facing page.

If the glass fractures out of line, as happens when a portion of the line is skipped or when the overhanging glass doesn't have enough weight to break off on its own, you will have to snap off the protruding pieces with a pair of wide-jaw flat pliers. This should be done only after the underside of the scored line has been tapped with the ball end of the cutter. Position the pliers over the glass, making sure their jaws don't extend over the scored line, and snap downwards to remove the glass pieces. This will usually only remove small pieces at a time, and you will have to continue along the line to remove all the material.

Small slivers or areas which didn't break evenly can be snapped off piece by piece with wide, flat-jawed pliers, or with the slots in a glass cutter.

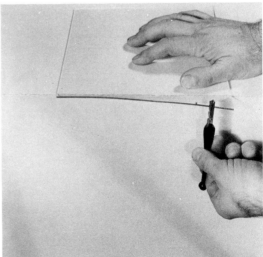

Cutting Circles and Ovals

This circle cutter comes with an adjustable head that enables it to be used as a straight-line cutter as well. Also included are extra cutting wheels.

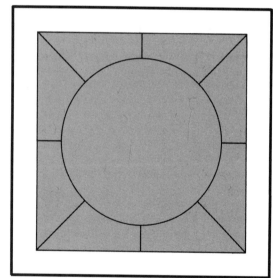

After circle has been scribed, straight-line cuts are made as shown, and the outside pieces broken off.

Shown below are center marks used in scribing arcs to make up an oval. As with circle, outside straight lines are then scribed and the pieces broken off.

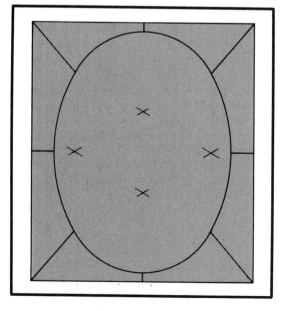

Cutting Circles and Ovals. You can easily cut circles and even ovals in glass with a special cutting tool. This tool is fitted with a suction cup and a cutter on a pivoting rod. Set the pivoting rod for the radius of the cut (distance is measured from center of pivot to center of cutting tool). Moisten the rubber suction cup and place the cutter in position. Hold the knob on top of the suction cup to prevent the tool from moving, and use your other hand to push the cutter-head around in a circle in one single sweep. After making the circle cut, adjust the cutter to make it a "straight-line" cutter. Make a series of outward radial cuts from the scored circle to the edge of the glass. As soon as possible after making the cuts, tap gently on the underside of the glass to allow the pieces to drop loose. Each outside piece should easily break out, leaving a perfect circle. If you wish to smooth the edge, use a bench stone, emery cloth, or even a file.

An oval is cut in much the same manner, except that you must first draw an oval with a draftsman's compass on a piece of paper. Also mark the center positions of the arcs making up the oval as shown. Position the circle cutter on each center mark to cut the individual arcs, making sure the scored lines meet properly. Again score radial lines outward to the edges of the glass and gently tap the glass to break out the pieces. You'll have to smooth up the "corners" where the arcs meet to make a perfect oval.

Installing Glass and Mirrors

Glass and mirrors can be installed in a rabbeted frame and held in place with molding, just as is done with other types of panels. There are also special plastic clips that screw into the wood surface of the frame and lip over the glass panel to hold it in place. When glass is installed in a picture frame, small brads or glazier points can be used to fasten the assembly (usually a sandwich of glass, picture, and heavy cardboard backing) against the front edge of the rabbet. The nails or points are driven sideways into the frame about every six inches.

Mirrors can also be fastened with a screw and plastic rosette. A carbide-tip bit in a drill press is used to bore the screw holes in the back of the mirror. A small dam of glazing putty is first built around the area of the hole, then filled with turpentine for lubricant. Use the slowest speed on the drill press to make the hole, and apply very little pressure. This job takes a bit of patience and a light touch, and it's a good idea to practice on several scrap pieces before attempting a large mirror.

Etching

There are many applications for this technique. It can be used to make a mirror look antique by bordering it with scrolled leaves and flowers, to inscribe a special design on glass panels, or even to apply monograms to glass tumblers. When I was in college, etching was a common shop project. At that time, we used a complicated acid solution, plus asphaltum to block out the area. When I discussed this method recently with a local druggist, he suggested an even simpler method. The only materials needed are hydrofluoric acid and common paraffin.

Hydrofluoric acid is not much in demand, and you'll probably have to have your druggist order it for you. *Caution:* Used improperly, hydrofluoric acid can be very dangerous. The liquid itself or even the vapors can cause severe burns which may not be immediately painful or visible.

A gun that drives in glazier points makes it easy to install glass in frames.

It may be fatal if swallowed. In case of contact, very carefully follow the instructions printed on the label of the container. Wear a rubber apron and rubber gloves, have plenty of ventilation in the room, and don't breathe the fumes. Because hydrofluoric acid eats through glass, it must be stored in a container of another material, normally plastic. Naturally, it should be stored out of the reach of children.

Don't let the precautions scare you away from trying this enjoyable project. Just remember the rules and treat the chemical with proper respect.

The method of etching a design on glass is simple. The first step is to coat the glass with melted paraffin. Melt the paraffin in a double boiler arrangement so there will be no danger of it catching fire. Brush the melted wax onto the glass. Make a stencil of the design and position it in place over the wax. Then, using a small sharp knife, cut through the wax to the glass following the lines of the stencil. You can also cut the design free-hand if you desire. Remove the material between the lines and make sure you have a neat, clean-cut design, with all bits and pieces of wax removed. You can use a tiny cotton swab and a bit of acetone to clean the area thoroughly.

Position the glass in place with the design facing up. Using a plastic eye dropper, or the applicator in the container, drop just enough acid into the design to fill it. Don't apply so much that a lot of the acid runs—just enough to completely cover and fill the design cut in the paraffin.

Allow the acid to etch the glass for six to twelve hours, depending on how deeply you want it etched. If you want it etched quite deep, you may even leave it overnight. Do this in a place where the glass won't be disturbed, and where pets and children can't get to it.

When the acid has crystalized and etched into the glass, carefully peel the paraffin away. Using rubber gloves, hold the glass under cool tap water and rinse the acid off. Then wash the glass with hot soapy water.

Plexiglas

In recent years acrylic sheet has been discovered by furniture builders. While it doesn't appeal to many traditional cabinetmakers, it is now commonplace in factory-made furniture.

Plexiglas is the brand name for acrylic sheet manufactured by the Rohm and Haas Company. It is a rigid, resilient acrylic plastic that is available in a range of thicknesses, in colorless sheet, transparent tints, translucent and opaque colors, and in a hammered glass pattern. It can be used for many of the same applications as glass, and a few in addition. Because it is shatter-resistant, it can be used on items where glass panes might be dangerous. Unlike glass, it can be bent in a home shop; and it can also be sawed, drilled, and cemented like wood or soft metal.

There are more than forty standard colors of Plexiglas available. These include a wide range of transparent and opaque tints and colors, several solar control tints (smoke tones), and eight textured surface patterns. It can be purchased at leading hobby craft stores, building supply dealers, hardware stores, paint stores, and glass and wallpaper outlets. Plexiglas distributors are listed in the Yellow Pages under *Plastics: Rods, Tubes, and Sheets.*

There are two formulations of Plexiglas sold in the consumer market: Plexiglas G and Plexiglas K. *Plexiglas G* is the general purpose material for creative crafts projects and safety glazing. *Plexiglas K* is the more economical safety glazing grade. It has most of the characteristics of Plexiglas K, but cannot be solvent cemented.

Clear Plexiglas is available through retailers in the following sizes and thicknesses:

Plexiglas G (safety glazing and decorative grade)

⅛″ Thickness	¼″ Thickness
18″ × 24″	24″ × 48″
24″ × 48″	36″ × 36″
26″ × 26″	36″ × 48″
28″ × 30″	
30″ × 34″	
36″ × 36″	
36″ × 48″	

Plexiglas K (safety glazing grade)

.080″ Thickness	0.10″ Thickness	⅛″ Thickness	3/16″ Thickness
18″ × 24″	18″ × 24″	18″ × 24″	24″ × 48″
20″ × 32″	20″ × 32″	24″ × 24″	30″ × 34″
24″ × 48″	24″ × 48″	26″ × 28″	36″ × 48″
26″ × 28″	26″ × 28″	28″ × 30″	
28″ × 30″	28″ × 30″	30″ × 34″	
30″ × 34″	30″ × 34″	36″ × 36″	
30″ × 36″	30″ × 36″	36″ × 38″	
32″ × 40″	32″ × 40″		

This Parson's table was constructed with transparent bronze Plexiglas. The simplicity of the table's design permits a great deal of flexibility in terms of size. One of the pillow-topped ottoman cubes shown was made with the Plexiglas left over after cutting out the table legs. Another 3×4-foot sheet of material was used to build the second cube.

Plexiglas can be drilled for installation of hardware, as for the project shown at left.

Plexiglas sheet was strip-heated and bent to form the bathroom shelf unit shown here. The towel bar is solvent-cemented to the bottom shelf, and remaining Plexiglas scraps have been used to make an attractive soap container.

Scribing and Breaking Plexiglas

Regular Plexiglas up to ¼-inch thick can be scribed and broken along a straight line with basically the same technique used for cutting glass. All that is needed is a special plastic-scribing tool, a straightedge, and a length of ¾-inch wood dowel for use in breaking. Textured Plexiglas and Plexiglas thicker than ¼ inch should be cut with power tools.

The backer sheet should be left on while scribing and breaking. Using the straightedge as a guide, place the scribing tool at the edge of the material. Apply firm pressure on the tool, and draw the cutting point the full width of the material. Repeat the cut five or six times for thicknesses from ¹⁄₁₀- to ³⁄₁₆-inches, and seven to ten times for ¼-inch stock.

To break, place the scribed line face up over the wooden dowel. Hold the long end of the sheet

Cutting, Drilling, and Bending Plexiglas

Above: Regular Plexiglas up to ¼-inch thick can be scribed and broken in much the same manner as regular glass. Use a plastic scribing tool and a good straightedge to make the cuts. (Backing is left on for all cutting and drilling operations.) To break Plexiglas, place the scribed line over a ¾-inch diameter dowel and apply pressure on the short side of the break as shown. Reposition hands in back of the break as it progresses down the line.
Below: Textured Plexiglas and material over ¼-inch thick has to be cut with power tools. Use a finish saw blade or a plastic-cutting blade, and hold the material firmly while cutting. Curved and straight lines can be cut with a fine-tooth blade on a saber saw or band saw.

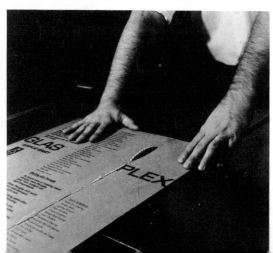
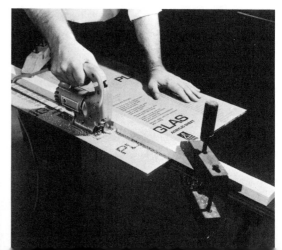

with one hand, and apply downward pressure on the short side of the break with the other. The hands should be kept together, and should follow about two inches behind the break as it progresses along the scribed line.

Cutting Plexiglas with Power Tools

Straight cuts can also be done with a circular saw. Use a special plastic-cutting blade, or a steel crosscut blade that is recommended for finish cuts on plywood, veneer or laminates. The blade should have at least six teeth per inch. Set the blade height just a little above the top of the sheet to prevent chipping. Feed the sheet slowly, and hold it down firmly while cutting.

Curved shapes can be cut with a fine-tooth blade on a saber saw or band saw. To cut very thin stock, a saber saw blade with at least thirty-two teeth per inch should be used. For stock $3/16$

Cutting, Drilling, and Bending Plexiglas (Cont'd.)

Plexiglas can be drilled with a metal-cutting bit in a power drill or standard twist drill. The material should be backed with soft wood and securely clamped while drilling.

A strip heater for bending Plexiglas along a straight line can be constructed very inexpensively. The strip-heater element comes with complete instructions for building the heater—additional materials needed are plywood, aluminum foil, and asbestos paper.

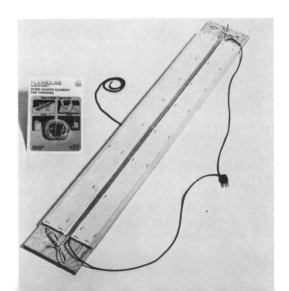

inch or thicker, the blade should have at least fourteen teeth per inch. Band saw blades should have at least ten teeth per inch. Either of these tools can also be used for straight cuts.

Drilling Plexiglas

Plexiglas can be drilled with either a standard twist drill or a power drill, using bits intended for metal. The sheet should be backed with soft wood and securely clamped or held.

Finishing Edges

Plexiglas edges are finished to insure breakage-resistance, and also to provide a smooth surface for glue joints. First, the corners are rounded and any uneven cuts smoothed with a medium- or fine-tooth metal file. The edges are then scraped with a thin metal straightedge, such as the back of a hacksaw. Next, edges are sanded with increasingly finer grits of "wet or dry" sandpaper (150–320 grit). They should not be rounded, as

Finishing Plexiglas Edges

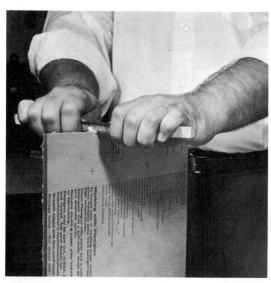

Plexiglas edges are smoothed in three stages to insure breakage resistance and to provide a smooth glue joint. First, corners are rounded and uneven cuts smoothed with a fine-tooth metal file. File marks are removed by scraping the edges with a sharpened metal blade—the back of a hacksaw blade is being used here.

Below left: Next, to improve the appearance of the edge and prepare it for cementing, sand with progressively finer grits (150–320) of "wet or dry" sandpaper. Be careful not to round the edges, as this will result in bubbles in the cemented joint.

Below: For a transparent, high-gloss edge, continue sanding with increasingly finer grits (400–500) of "wet or dry" paper. Then buff the edge with a muslin wheel dressed with a fine-grit buffing compound.

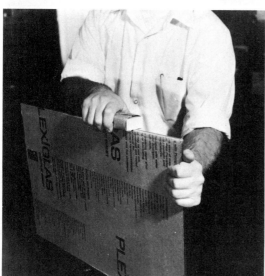

Joining Plexiglas Sheets

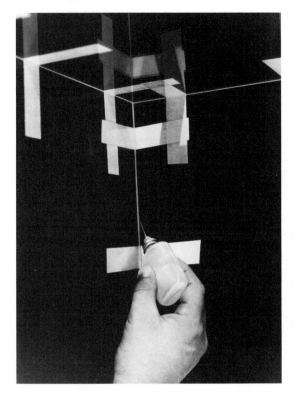

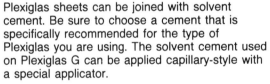

Plexiglas sheets can be joined with solvent cement. Be sure to choose a cement that is specifically recommended for the type of Plexiglas you are using. The solvent cement used on Plexiglas G can be applied capillary-style with a special applicator.

The thickened solvent cement used on Plexiglas K sheets is applied with the joint held horizontally. This type of cement can also be used to fill in scratches. (Allow 24 hours drying time between applications.)

this will result in bubbles in the cemented joint. To make a transparent high-gloss edge, continue sanding with finer grits of "wet or dry" paper (400–500 grit); then buff with a plastic buffing kit, or other muslin wheel dressed with fine-grit buffing compound.

Joining Plexiglas

Plexiglas G can be joined at the edges with solvent cement. There are several types of solvent cement suitable for this purpose; be sure to choose a cement and applicator specifically recommended for use on Plexiglas. After the edges have been finished to the final stage, remove the protective backing paper. Assemble the pieces, and hold them together with masking tape. The project should be turned so that each joint is horizontal while applying the cement. *Caution:* Solvent cements are toxic and flammable. Use them in a well-ventilated, flame-free area, and keep them away from children.

A Plexiglas K project can be put together with thickened solvent cement. Again, be sure to choose a cement that is specifically recommended for Plexiglas K. (Any cement suitable for use on Plexiglas K can also be used on Plexiglas G, but not the reverse.)

Plexiglas can also be contact-cemented to other materials. There are several household cements that are recommended for this purpose, and floor tile and countertop adhesives can also be used. The joints can be covered with pressure sensitive plastic tape or other materials.

PART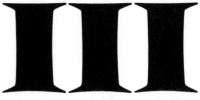

Finishing

16

Surface Preparation

A common shortcoming of many craftsmen is the failure to prepare a surface properly prior to applying a finish. No matter how fancy the wood used in a project and how carefully it is built, the result can still be quite shabby if the wood is not properly prepared before the finish is applied. There are no shortcuts. It takes plenty of time and elbow grease, no matter whether the wood is white pine or oak or the project a simple foot stool or a full set of kitchen cabinets.

The first step in achieving a good surface preparation is to use the proper machining and cutting tools, kept well sharpened. Sharp cutting tools leave a "burnished" surface on the wood that provides a smoother surface than even the best sanding can duplicate. The use of a jointer or planer to smooth all surfaces before construction begins is an important element in surface preparation. The final cutting of hardwoods should be

Heavy sanding of a coarse-textured wood such as oak will result in an uneven surface, because some wood cells are softer than others. This is why proper surface planing and cutting is essential.

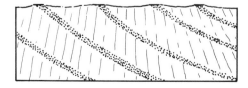

done with a fine-tooth hollow-ground blade or plywood blade. This is especially important when working with coarse-textured woods such as oak, ash, or walnut because these woods can be damaged by heavy sanding. Proper machining before using the wood insures the best surface.

Filling Holes and Patching Defects

In most woodworking projects you will have holes or defects that will need to be patched or filled. This is especially true in projects that are assembled with nails or screws. When screws are used in furniture projects they are usually countersunk and covered with wood plugs, which are then cut off flush with a chisel and sanded smooth. Nails, on the other hand, are usually "set" or driven just below the surface of the wood with a nail set, and the holes then filled with Plastic Wood, wood putty, or a similar substance. This filling is usually left just a bit higher than the surface of the wood. After it has dried a belt sander can be used to smooth it down flush with the wood surface.

All cracks must be filled as well, and it's best to apply the filler across the cracks to work it into them, rather than with the cracks. Incidentally, the belt sanding operation is often used on cabinet projects not only to remove excess filler, but also to cut all surfaces of the front solid-wood facers to a smooth, even surface.

If the wood surface is to have a stain and a clear finish, the wood fillers must match the surrounding wood surface or they will stand out when the finish is applied. Most wood putty fillers are available in a number of colors to match standard wood tones. However, if you need to, you can often make up a custom color by adding some very fine sanding dust from the wood being

249

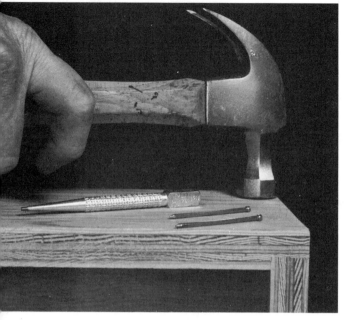

When nails are used to fasten pieces together, they are set below the surface with a nail set.

The hole is then filled with Plastic Wood or other filler. All other surface defects such as cracks are also filled in at this time.

If the surface is to be stained, wood filler should match the surrounding wood. It can be tinted with artist's oil colors if a special tone is needed.

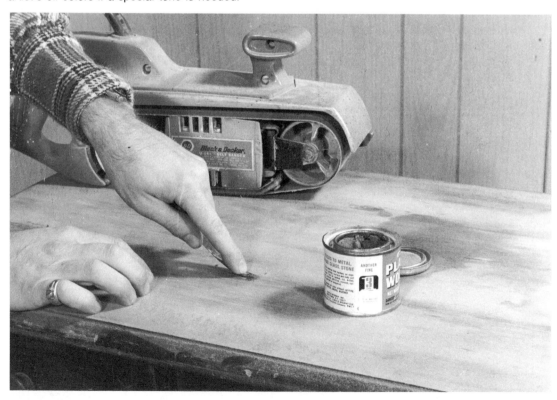

patched to natural-color wood putty. A filler such as Plastic Wood can also be tinted with ordinary artist's oil colors. (If it becomes hardened, merely use a bit of lacquer thinner to soften it back to workable shape.)

An alternative to this type of patching is to use shellac stick or other professional refinishing tools to patch the holes after the wood surface has been finished, but this is a tough job even for professional refinishers.

It's a good idea to smooth and sand all pieces as much as possible before assembly, as they will be much easier to sand at this time. Sanding is equally important on the inside surfaces of items. A good cabinet or furniture builder makes sure the inside surfaces of a furniture piece or cabinet are well sanded as well as the outside.

Before you start to sand the surface, remove all pencil marks by erasing them. It's almost impossible to sand out a pencil mark, especially in soft-woods such as white pine. Grease or other dirt should be washed off with lacquer thinner; otherwise the heat generated by sanding can drive the grease down into the wood cells.

Any pencil markings on a project should be erased—don't attempt to sand them off.

Removing Glue

The number one problem for most woodworkers is glue that has been left on the surface of the wood. When stain or finish is applied over a glue stain, the area shows up as a glaring patch or smear. The first rule is to wipe off all excess glue as soon as the item is clamped securely. If your fingers or tools become coated with glue during assembly, be sure to wipe this off as well so that it doesn't get on the wood. When gluing joints such as a mortise-and-tenon, apply only enough glue to coat the surfaces to avoid squeeze-out.

It is important to remove glue squeeze-out immediately after clamping a joint.

In most cases, especially on hardwoods, it is almost impossible to hand-sand out a glue smear. The best method is to use a sharp chisel to "cut" away the glue. The chisel can also be used in small, hard-to-get-at places which can't be reached with a sander. Large flat areas such as glued-up table tops can be sanded with a belt

In some cases, excess glue cannot be sanded away and will have to be cut off with a sharp chisel.

sander to remove a glue line. However, any object that can be run through a surface planer will have the best glue line removal and resulting finish.

Production Sanding

It is best to sand such items as cabinet or furniture door or drawer fronts before installation. In many instances a sort of production-line setup can be used to shorten sanding time. For instance, with all items stacked on a table, each piece can first be belt sanded to remove any irregularities, and then finish-sanded with a pad sander. A special molding-shape sand block can be used for final sanding of molding. A vise or clamp or L-shape holding cleat can be used to hold the pieces in place for sanding.

When you have a number of items to sand, it's a good idea to sand them production-line fashion. For instance, all belt sanding is first done on all pieces, then the finish sanding as shown. Here, a vise is used to hold the pieces for sanding.

Cabinet Scrapers

An old-fashioned tool that is little known by today's high speed craftsman is the cabinet or hand scraper. This was once the only tool available for achieving a smooth finish on wood surfaces, and it can't be improved on today. However, the job is entirely a "hand tool job," and it takes quite a bit of practice to learn to use the scraper and keep it properly sharpened. A hand or wood scraper is actually a piece of high quality steel that has one cut edge burnished, or rolled over, to produce a fine scraping tool. The scraper can be either pushed or pulled; most craftsmen find the pulling stroke easiest. The scraper is held at about a 75° angle and pulled toward you to produce a polished final surface.

Actually, the hardest part of using a scraper is not in operating it, but in sharpening it. The first step is to place the scraper in a vise, and with a good, mill-cut file, file the edge flat and square. Round the corners just a bit so they won't be so dangerous or cut into the wood surface. Use a fine honing stone to remove any wire edge from either side. Then use a steel burnisher, which is made especially for this job, to burnish the edges to

about an 85° angle, rolling it over to make sort of a "hook" on the edge. Sharpened this way, the tool will peel off a fine wood shaving as it is pulled. With the edge kept properly burnished it can be used many times before it will have to be resharpened.

Selecting Abrasives

Sandpaper is actually not made of sand. It is called "coated abrasive" in the industry, and is made from one of four different materials. Flint and garnet papers are made from natural materials which are mined; silicone carbide and aluminum oxide papers are made from manufactured materials. Coated abrasive papers are made by grinding the materials into fine pieces, then sifting them through graded screens to obtain uniform-size particles. The particles are then glued

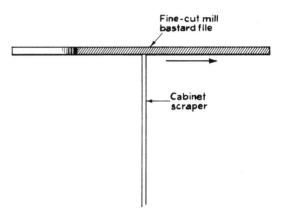

First step in sharpening a cabinet scraper is to draw-file the edge flat.

Then a burnishing tool is used to pull over and burnish the edge, leaving a fine hook-like cutting surface.

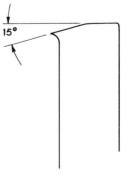

An old-fashioned cabinet scraper will produce a glass-smooth surface.

to a backing material of paper or cloth. The papers are graded according to the size of the particle. There are a great number of different papers available, and choosing the right paper for the right job is very important.

What confuses the issue is that there are three methods of stating grades for sandpaper. The old method, which is still used by some manufacturers, is the 0 system, which is similar to the method used in steel wool. The second system—and the one relied on by most cabinetmakers—designates the paper by the number of openings per linear inch in the grading screen. Some of the more economical papers, particularly flint paper, are usually specified just by description, as "coarse" or "super fine." The chart illustrates the relative coarseness and the grades for each type of sandpaper.

In addition to the different types shown in the table, sandpaper is made in "open" coat and "closed" coat types. Open coated sandpaper is normally used for heavy sanding jobs and has only about 70 to 75 percent of the backing covered with particles. This prevents the paper from becoming clogged too quickly.

Sandpaper comes in a large variety of abrasive grits, particle sizes, and types of backing for use in hand and machine sanding.

Sandpaper

Particle Sizes	Flint	Garnet	Aluminum Oxide	Silicone Carbide	Most Common Uses
Extra Coarse		16 20 4 3½	16 20 4 3½	12 16 20	Paint and varnish removal, floor sanding, etc.
Very Coarse	Extra Coarse	24 30 36 3 2½ 2	24 30 36 2 2½ 2	24 30 36	
Coarse	Coarse	40 50 1½ 1	40 50 1½ 1	40 50	Rough sanding, paint and finish removal
Medium	Medium	60 80 100 ½ 0 2	60 80 100 ½ 0 2	60 80 100	Preliminary sanding on rough wood and general sanding
Fine	Fine	120 150 180 3 4 5	120 150 180 3 4 5	120 150 180	Final sanding on bare wood before applying finish
Very Fine	Extra Fine	220 240 280 6 7 8	220 240 280 6 7 8	220 240 280	Dry sanding between finishing coats
Extra Fine or Super Fine		320 400 9 10	320 400 9 10	320 360 400 500 600	Wet or dry polishing

Flint Paper

Flint is the most economical sandpaper and is light tan in color. It is used primarily for such jobs as removing paint and varnish, where the paper clogs easily and must be discarded quite often.

Garnet Paper

Garnet paper is one of the most commonly used sandpapers in woodworking. It is red-brown in color and is quite a bit more durable than flint paper. The reason is that the abrasive particles are actually pieces of hard crystal instead of stone as on the flint paper. Garnet paper is especially good for hand sanding and costs more than flint paper.

Silicone carbide is the hardest sandpaper abrasive. It is frequently used for final sanding between finishes.

Garnet paper is the most commonly used sandpaper for hand sanding.

Aluminum Oxide

A manufactured abrasive, this sandpaper is a brown material that will sometimes appear light brown in the finer grades. It is quite a bit more expensive than the natural-abrasive papers, but will last a lot longer. It is available in both paper and cloth backing, and is an excellent choice for power sanding equipment.

Silicone Carbide

This is the hardest abrasive, almost equaling the hardness of diamond, and as a result it is the longest lasting and the most expensive. It is blue-black in color and comes on paper or cloth backing. It can be had in almost all grits from super fine to coarse, and is used almost exclusively for the final sanding of wood or metal surfaces. It can be used wet or dry and is excellent for sanding between finishes.

Emery Cloth

Emery cloth is a hard, dull black abrasive on a cloth backing. It is primarily used for working rust and scale from metal or smoothing it down for a finish. It can be used either wet or dry.

Steel Wool

Steel wool isn't ordinarily used for surface preparation of wood because the tiny particles of metal have a tendency to pull out and stick in the crevices and grain of the wood. However, the finer grades are often used to burnish the final coats of a finish.

Like sandpaper, steel wool is available in different grades, ranging from 0000, which is the finest grade available, to No. 3, which is extremely coarse. Most woodworking steel wool will be 0000, 000, or 00.

Steel Wool

Classification	Coarseness	Most Common Uses
0000	Super Fine	Final rub down after all finish coats have been applied
000	Extra Fine	Smoothing between finishing coats
00	Fine	Rub down between coats of finish and to dull a glossy finish
0	Medium Fine	Common grade for general smoothing and for stripping finishes
1	Medium	Household and woodwork cleanup; also paint removal and metal cleaning
2	Medium Coarse	Seldom used on furniture
3	Coarse	Seldom used for any woodworking

Steel wool is rarely used for surface preparation because it leaves slivers of steel in the grain. It is more commonly used for polishing finishes.

Abrasive papers come in sheets and belts to fit power sanding equipment. Normally you won't have to use a full sheet when hand sanding or for most finishing sander equipment. You can either cut the sheet or tear it, after folding and scoring, into the sizes you need. Or you can fold it, opening up the folded paper to a new surface whenever you need it.

How To Use Abrasive Papers

Almost all sanding, whether it is power or hand sanding, is done in steps, starting with a coarse grit and proceeding to a fine paper. The grade of coarseness depends on the material. A properly planed surface of hardwood can be sanded with a 150 or 180 grit paper and then be ready for a finish; all that is really needed is a light sanding. On the other hand, cross-grain tool marks in hardwoods may require some really heavy power tool sanding to remove the marks, and this might necessitate 40 to 50 grit paper. When changing from one grit up to the next, finer grit, never change more than two 0 numbers. Otherwise you will have trouble removing sanding marks left by the coarser grade. With good craftsmanship and sharp tools you normally won't have to use anything coarser than medium or 60 to 100 grit except for such things as edge shaping with sanding belts.

The number one rule of proper sanding is *always sand with the grain.* This is especially important when you get to a place where two pieces of wood meet with the grain running in different directions, as on the rails and stiles of a panel door. If using power equipment, make sure not to overrun and allow the sanding belt to cut cross-grain marks on one of the pieces. In many cases this type of joint will have one piece that is just a bit higher than another. In this case, you may have to cut across the grain with a belt sander to make the two surfaces flush. If so, you will then have to cut the marks out by sanding with the grain, using the same grit paper.

There are basically two methods of sanding: by hand and with power sanders. Each has its ad-

All sanding should be done with the grain.

You can also use a piece of plywood as a sanding block. For most sanding operations a backing of rubber or felt will help a great deal.

vantages and disadvantages. Naturally, power sanding can save time, especially with extremely hard woods such as oak or maple. On the other hand, a power sander can do a lot of damage if not handled properly. A power belt sander can very quickly cut through the thin veneer of a hardwood plywood to the underlying crossband. This mistake on the top of a desk or table top can ruin a fine project that has taken a lot of time to build—and you can't patch it.

When sanding fairly broad flat surfaces by hand, always use a sanding block of some sort. One of the best is the small rubber block shown. You can also quickly and easily make your own sanding block. It's best to have the surface under the paper backed with rubber or a piece of felt.

Hand sanding of a broad, flat surface should be done with a sanding block. The easiest to use are those with a rubber backing.

Small hard-to-get-at places can be sanded with any number of different sandpaper-holding devices. For instance, dowels wrapped with sandpaper can be used to sand the inside of holes and circular cutouts. Small pieces of sandpaper rolled up into narrow strips can be used to sand cracks and the inside edge of turnings. To get into an especially tight area, you can use a narrow strip of sandpaper glued to a thin piece of wood.

Smaller pieces can be sanded by first gluing a full-size sheet of sandpaper to a wood slab. The slab can be clamped to a table top and the work taken to the sandpaper, in reverse of normal sanding procedure.

When sanding by hand with a pad you must apply plenty of pressure to get the sandpaper to cut properly. Power sanding equipment should never be forced, but its action will rock a small workpiece. For this reason, small workpieces should be anchored during the sanding operation. A tabletop stop block or an old-fashioned bench hook will serve in many cases. Or you can simply place the item in a vise. When sanding the edges of a board, it's a good idea to clamp a couple of pieces of scrap stock along the edge to prevent the sandblock from rounding the edges. However, all corners and edges are rounded slightly. This not only makes them less dangerous to people, but also allows them to hold a finish better than a sharp edge.

While sanding, rub your hand over the sanded surface very lightly as you go so you can feel your progress. Watch the edges for wood splinters that might catch in the sandpaper and tear away. This is especially important on woods such as white pine, yellow pine, or fir.

In most professional shops a specific sanding schedule is followed. An example is shown here,

and raise up so that they can be removed with a very light sanding with extremely fine sandpaper. This is called "raising the grain" and is the final sanding operation for quality finishes.

Once the project has been thoroughly sanded, inspect it carefully in good light for any shiny spots or places that might not have been sanded completely. A piece of nylon can also be run over the surface to detect rough spots. Once the surface has been sanded try not to touch it with oily or greasy fingers or leave any other marks that will prevent stain or finish from adhering to the surface.

Cabinet Finishing

Operation	Method or Tool	Particle Type and Grade	Form
Sanding drawers	Belt sander or stationary sander	40, 50, or 60 garnet cloth	Belts
Flush-cut backs, facers, sides, remove glue lines	Portable belt sander	80 or 100 aluminum oxide cloth	Belts
Rounding edges	Hand-held sanding block	100, 120, or 150 garnet paper	Sheets
Final finish sanding and touch-up	Vibrating or oscillating finish sander	120, 150, or 180 garnet or aluminum oxide finishing paper	Sheets

as suggested by a leading abrasive manufacturer. (See also the photos on following pages.)

There is a great deal of controversy over the right grit paper to use for the final sanding operations, and you will probably have to make up your own mind on this matter following your own experience. In some cases you may wish to apply a coat of sanding sealer before the final sanding operation, or you may wish to apply it after the application of the stain, depending on whether the wood is to be finished natural or stained. Some stains won't take well over a sanding sealer.

All dust should be removed from the project with a vacuum cleaner. A soft cloth can be used to loosen stubborn areas. Then lightly dampen the entire surface with a sponge or soft cloth to raise the tiny wood fibers that have been forced down flat and are only partially cut away from the surface. The dampness causes these to swell

Tack Cloth

If you're ready to apply the finish, the next step is to remove the rest of the sanding dust. However, if you won't be applying the finish for a day or two leave this step until just before the finish is to be applied. Although you can't see it, there is a fine film of dust adhering to the surface and this must be removed before a finish can be applied. This is done using a tack cloth. You can purchase a tack cloth or make your own quite easily.

To make your own, dampen a cloth with water and wring out all excess water, then pour a bit of turpentine on it and wad and roll the cloth around to assure that it is well coated with turpentine. Wring out any excess. Then pour a bit of varnish on the rag and place the rag in a plastic bag. Knead the rag in the bag until the entire rag is well soaked with varnish and an even yellow brown all over. Now place in a glass jar with a lid on it and allow it to "age" for about a day.

To use the tack cloth, merely wipe it lightly over the wood surface to remove all dust, dirt, sanding dust, and debris just before the application of the finish. Don't handle the wood with your bare hands once this operation has been done or you will leave fingerprints that can prevent a good finish. Keep turning the tack cloth to provide a clean surface, continually picking up material. Don't allow the tack cloth to rest on the surface or you will leave a spot that won't take finish as well. Store the tack cloth in a closed jar.

A Typical Sanding Schedule

Sanding schedule for an item such as a kitchen cabinet would start with belt-sanding all glue lines away. Be very careful when sanding plywood—a power sander can quickly cut through the thin veneer.

Then sand the facers flush with a belt sander, going with the grain of each facer or strip.

Next, a finish sander is used to sand all flat surfaces, including the facers.

Typical Sanding Schedule (Cont'd.)

Edges are lightly rounded by hand sanding.

Sanding dust is removed by vacuuming.

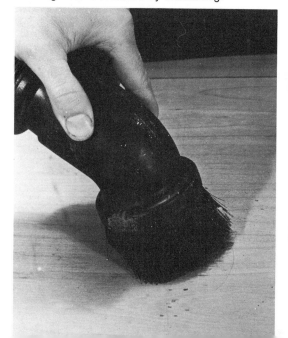

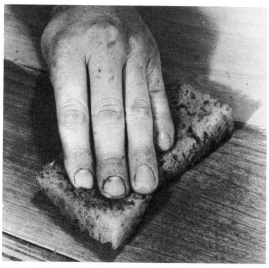

Then a damp sponge is rubbed over the surface to raise the grain.

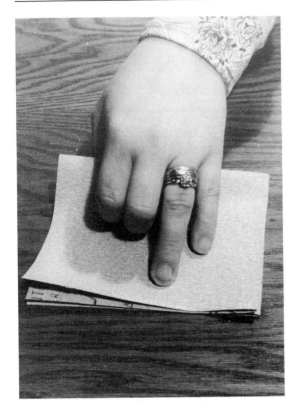

After the surface has dried, extremely fine sandpaper is used to cut away the raised-grain whiskers.

Just before surface is to be given a finish, it is wiped lightly with a tack cloth to remove dust and sanding debris.

You can make your own tack cloth by dampening a rag in water, then in turpentine, and working a small amount of varnish into it. Allow it to set overnight.

17

Applying Finishes

The final appearance of a furniture project will be greatly influenced by the type and quality of finish that is applied. The previous chapter emphasized the importance of good surface preparation prior to applying the finish. Choosing the correct finish and applying it properly is just as important. There is a great deal of lore on the subject of finishes, and an abundance of different finishing products. As a result, many craftsmen are somewhat perplexed when it comes time to tackle the final stage of a project.

Actually, achieving a high-quality finish on a properly prepared wood surface is quite easy, but there are a number of steps that must be followed. The first is the choice of finish. There are many different kinds and brands of stains, sealers, and varnishes on the market. Some of these can be combined, while others are not compatible at all. This chapter will cover each of the important and commonly used finishes and how they must be applied to achieve a professional quality finish.

Finishing Steps

1. Application of stain (if a different wood color or highlighting of the grain is desired).
2. Application of a sealer (used on coarse-textured woods, in particular, to allow an even application of stain or finish. Also needed to prevent some types of stains from bleeding into and clouding the finish).
3. Application of a filler (used on large-pore woods such as oak to provide a smooth, even surface for the finish).
4. Application of the final finish.
5. Sanding, rubbing or buffing between finish coats to smooth the surface for succeeding coats.
6. Applying paste wax and buffing after the last coat of finish.

In many instances you will not need all of these steps. For instance, on some woods and for some projects you will not wish to stain before application of the finish.

Stains

Stains are coloring agents that are applied on wood to enhance the appearance. They may be transparent or semitransparent, and there are four basic types: penetrating oil, nonpenetrating oil, water or alcohol, and stain sealers.

The choice of the type and color of stain is dependent on the kind of wood, the grain of the wood, the amount of grain you wish to let show through, and the style of the project. Many styles of furniture are stained in pretty much standard patterns. For instance, most French Provincial furniture is stained with a light brown to tan coloring, or painted. On the other hand most Spanish-style furniture is stained dark brown to near black. Early American-style furniture made with maple or other hardwoods is usually stained with light-color stains to bring out the grain of the wood. A dark, fairly opaque stain might be used if the wood is pine.

Choosing an appropriate stain is important. In many cases a certain type of stain is traditionally used, such as the light maple stain on this Early American-style dining table set.

Painted finishes and stenciled designs are used on primitive Early American styles.

Stains are available in every wood hue imaginable, ranging from extremely light blond to ebony. They are also available in every color of the rainbow. Color stains can be used to provide some unusual accent pieces, as well as to simulate some of the very primitive Early American furniture which was stained with different colors to hide the bland grain of the pine.

Finishing Sequence

If stain is to be applied, it is normally applied first. In some cases a light sanding sealer is applied before the stain.

If a sealer is needed, it is then applied over the stain.

The filler is next. (Sometimes filler is applied mixed with stain as shown.)

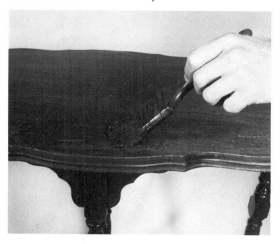

Then the finish is applied, following instructions given. A simple wipe-on clear finish is being applied here.

Sanding, rubbing, or buffing is done between coats as needed.

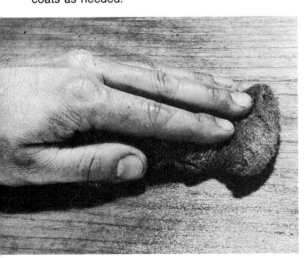

In most instances, a paste wax is applied over the final coat.

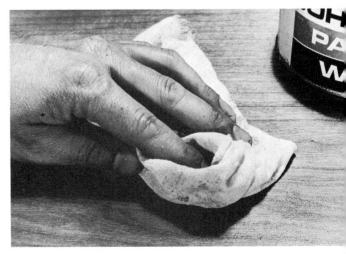

Nonpenetrating Oil Stains

These are also called *wiping* stains because of the manner in which they are applied. They are made with a linseed oil base, and although they will penetrate the wood pores to some degree, the majority of the stain stays on the surface of the wood. The excess is wiped off with a soft cloth, and the amount of wiping determines the amount of stain that is left and its hue or darkness. Because nonpenetrating stains are fairly opaque, they leave the surface of the wood somewhat cloudy. They are, however, an excellent means of evenly staining a piece of wood that has uneven light and dark areas in it, because you can control the color or darkness of areas by wiping off less or more stain. Nonpenetrating stains can also be mixed together, and again, the amount of wiping can be varied to make the application match almost any existing hue or color. Because they use a linseed oil base, you can even add artist's oil pigments to the stain, or make up your own stain by mixing pure boiled linseed oil with artist's oil colors or colors-in-oil. For this reason, these stains are an excellent choice for matching kitchen cabinets or other built-ins with existing paneling or plywood veneers.

Nonpenetrating stains are often used to create the dark, massive look of Spanish-style furniture.

Nonpenetrating oil stains are often used in conjunction with a filler material for open-pore woods such as oak. One excellent use of these types of stains is to create the dark, massive Country English pine furniture that is stained almost black or the similar almost-black tone of Spanish oak furniture.

The stain is available in many different tones. Before use, it must be stirred well to mix the

Nonpenetrating or wiping stains are easy for the beginner to apply. They are brushed on, and excess stain is then wiped away with a soft cloth. The amount of wiping determines how dark or opaque the stain will be.

Since wiping stains are made with a linseed oil base, you can add "colors-in-oil" to change the tint.

settled color particles with the linseed oil base. When the stain is well mixed, additional coloring is added if needed, then a good large brush is used to spread it on in a full, thick coat. If extremely dark coloring is desired, apply the stain again, making sure you get a rich coat. Then wipe all excess stain off the brush, and use a "dry brush" and with-the-grain strokes to smooth the coloring and blend it well. Keep removing drips of stain from the bottoms of chair rungs, undersides of table tops, etc., as the stain collects to avoid leaving dark splotches in these areas. My favorite applicator for this method of applying, blending and wiping stain is a foam pad. These produce an extremely smooth stain job.

Another method—and probably the most common—is to apply the stain in a full coat, allow it to dry for a few minutes or until it starts to turn a bit dull, then wipe off the excess stain with a cloth such as burlap. By the amount of pressure and wiping you can vary the amount of stain that is left on the wood surface.

Penetrating Oil Stains

Penetrating oil stains are commonly made with a much lighter base such as turpentine and so can be sprayed on as well as brushed. The thinner base enables the stain to penetrate the wood pores and produces a more transparent stain. Penetrating stains are sometimes called *non-grain-raising,* because they won't raise the grain of the wood as do water- or alcohol-base stains. They can be used on raw wood or on wood that has been sealed. Wood that has been lightly sealed will often allow for a more even coloring than raw wood, because the light base of the stain will penetrate the softer springwood portions of medium- or coarse-textured woods much more quickly than the harder areas.

Penetrating stains can be applied with a brush or spray gun. Because the stain penetrates fairly fast, and thereby dries quickly, you have to brush it on rapidly so that no brush marks will show when brush strokes "dry" before the next overlapping strokes can be made. For this reason, a spray application usually produces the best results.

Penetrating oil stains can usually be finished over within six hours, while nonpenetrating oil stains will require at least twelve hours drying time before a new finish can be applied.

Penetrating oil stains are made with a thin base such as turpentine and can be sprayed on as well as brushed. This type of stain penetrates quickly and must be brushed on very rapidly to prevent streaks and overlap marks.

Water Stains

Water stains are purchased in powder form and dissolved in hot water to make the colors you need. These stains can be brushed or sprayed on. Because the vehicle containing the stain is extremely thin, they will soak into the wood quite rapidly. Unless you're pretty fast when applying them with a brush, they can result in a streaked, uneven stain unless you quickly flood the surface and allow the excess to run off. Because of this problem, water stains are more frequently applied with a spray gun than with a brush.

Apply the stain in a full, wet coat with a spray gun, brush, or rag, going with the grain. Excess stain can be removed with a rag or, better yet, a sponge brush stroked in the direction of the grain.

The water in the stains will raise the grain in the wood, so the surface should be sponged with warm water before the stain is applied. Add a bit of Dextarin or starch gum (found at most wallpaper stores) to stiffen these grain fibers that are raised by the water. Then after the wood surface has dried thoroughly, sand off the tiny fibers with fine sandpaper. A wash coat made up of equal parts of sanding sealer and lacquer thinner can also be applied before the stain to help cut down on the grain-raising problem.

One of the disadvantages of using water stains is that they must dry for at least 24 hours before the finish can be applied. Water stains are extremely transparent, and if you don't achieve a dark enough appearance the first time, just let the stain dry, then give the surface another coat.

Vinyl Stains

Vinyl stains are relatively new and are somewhat similar to vinyl paint, except they are transparent. They clean up with water, and you'll find they're one of the easiest types of stains to use. They also have no odor, are nonflammable, and will dry in about one hour. There is no thinning or mixing necessary. Vinyls will raise the grain of wood to some extent, but probably not enough to require additional sanding. They are available in a number of wood tones, plus decorator colors.

After the wood surface has been sanded smooth, the stain can be applied with a rag,

Vinyl stains are one of the easiest to apply, and they produce a good looking, transparent tone.

sponge, roller, brush, or spray gun. While the stain is still wet, wipe off any excess with a damp absorbent material, such as a soft cloth or sponge. Again, make the final wiping strokes with the grain of the wood. Allow to dry one hour, then apply the finish.

Stain Sealers

Probably the easiest type of stain to use is the stain sealer group. This is a one-coat product that both stains and seals at the same time. In some cases it is all that is used to finish a project, but an additional coat of finish will provide more protection. Stain sealers are excellent for staining large projects such as built-ins, room trim, or doors. They are available in a wide variety of wood tones and colors. Many of them penetrate to some degree, which allows them to actually become part of the wood. This makes them an excellent stain for such things as baseboards which take a lot of abuse.

Using these stains is simple. Make certain the wood surface is clean, dry, and carefully sanded. Choose the wood tone or color you need or mix some together to achieve a special tone or color. Then apply the first coat on the raw wood with a clean brush or cloth. Let it stand for five to fifteen minutes. Then remove the excess with a clean cloth and allow to dry overnight. A second coat can be applied if necessary. A special natural filler can be used to lighten the color.

After 24 hours apply paste wax, and polish to a soft finish. If a harder surface is desired, use a compatible clear finish.

Stain sealers are not to be confused with varnish stains. The latter are actually a varnish base to which a dark stain coloring has been added. They're almost impossible to use, even by the experts, because they must be brushed on perfectly evenly, using just the right amount of varnish, or streaks and globs of stain will discolor the wood surface.

Alcohol Stains

Alcohol stains can be used on shutters, louvers, picture frames, moldings, wicker, and rattan—any detailed surface. Their advantages are that they dry in 30 minutes and stain and seal the surface in one application. They're easy to use, and no wiping is necessary. They are applied from an aerosol can, and so can be used whenever brushing is difficult; for quick touch-ups and for finishing small pieces.

When spray-staining new wood, be sure the wood is clean, sanded, and dust-free. Spray with rapid, uniform strokes, and overlap strokes to assure an even coat. Apply additional coats for the desired depth of color and uniformity. Do not sand, and allow the stain to dry for at least 30 minutes. Then finish with a compatible finish. At least three coats of finish are necessary.

Shading and toning with spray sealer stains is an easy way to restore previously stained furniture and cabinetry. The spray stain must be darker than the base color for this type of blending. The stain is applied with rapid strokes from the center to the edges of an area where shading and toning is desired. Build up deeper shades slowly—stain dries fast so that isn't too difficult. Spray moving away from the darker area until you obtain a gradual blending from dark to light. (Practice on scrap wood first to develop a good technique.)

General Staining Tips

The quality of a staining job depends on several things. First, the brush or cloth used to apply the stain must be clean and free of dirt, debris, or thinner that might not be compatible with the stain. I like to use a sponge brush for applying most stains because it loads up with more stain and seems to provide a much smoother coating than does a bristle brush. Make sure you have the correct solvent on hand to clean brushes and containers, and above all, make sure the surface of the wood is correctly prepared as explained in the previous chapter. Read manufacturer's directions and shake or stir the stain according to directions

Stain sealers are a surface coating with both stain and a bit of sealer. They are excellent for large projects such as kitchen cabinets, and are probably the easiest type of stain to apply.

before use. If mixing up a stain color, make sure you have enough mixed to do the job. You can almost never recreate the same color without a great deal of experimenting. Try the stain on scrap wood before proceeding to the final job.

One of the problems with staining is that the appearance of the wet stain on the wood is often quite different from that of the dry stain, and the application of finish will cause further changes. It's a good idea to first try out both the stain and finish on scraps of wood of the same type used in a project.

When staining such items as tables and chairs, turn them upside down and stain the bottoms of the rungs and similar areas first, then stand the piece upright to complete the staining job. When staining a large project such as a chest, do only one side or section at a time. When a surface is fairly large, apply the stain as quickly as possible so there won't be any drying lines where the brush strokes overlap. Use the brush in long, smooth strokes, going with the grain for the entire length of the surface, to smooth out the stain. In almost all cases it's much easier to wipe off

excess stain than to add more after the material has started to get tacky.

Sealers

In many hardwoods, the springwood sections have a softer composition than the summerwood, and this means that applications of stain and finish will be absorbed unevenly. Several hardwoods, notably oak, also have unusually large pores which will absorb more stain or finish than the surrounding wood. The effects produced by uneven absorption are desirable for such effects as "antiqued" oak, but in most instances you will want to apply a "sealer" coat over the wood surface before applying stain so that the stain can be applied more evenly. Wood sealers are sometimes applied after the stain coat as well to prevent the stain from bleeding through into a finish coat.

Paint finishes require a sealer too, and in this case it should be a special primer-sealer which is suited for opaque coating.

Sealers are especially important on the end grain of wood, because most stains penetrate

A sealer can be applied before the stain coat to allow the stain to take more evenly, and it may be used after the stain as well to prevent the stain from bleeding into the finish. Sealers are also applied to seal and "level" rough surfaces—a sanding sealer is often used for this purpose in professional cabinet shops.

these areas much more readily than the rest of the surface. Sealer can also be used to seal off darker-colored areas of a piece of wood. For instance, a dark portion of the piece can be given a light sealer coat so that stain won't penetrate that portion as deeply as it penetrates the raw wood, resulting in an easier stain-blending job.

Wood that has a sealer coat is also much easier to sand smoother with very fine abrasives. Special *sanding* sealers are used for this purpose. These materials close the wood pores and cause the minute particles of grain that have been loosened by wet sanding to rise up. Very fine sandpaper is then used to cut off the raised wood fibers and create a smooth surface for the stain or final finish. In the case of wood having extremely large pores, the pores must also be filled with a *filler,* which will be discussed next.

Sealers are available in several different solvent bases, and the sealer used must be compatible with the materials that will be used for the stain and final finish. Sealers and finishes that are not compatible can result in a mess. For instance, lacquer applied over a varnish sealer will bubble and blister.

The most commonly used sealers are: *shellac*; *varnish* thinned with turpentine or synthetic thinner; *commercial sanding* sealer, which usually consists of a vinyl base and is used under varnish; and *lacquer sanding* sealer, which is used under a sprayed lacquer finish.

Sealers must be applied in a light wash coat. Most commercial sealers will already be thinned to the proper consistency, but follow the directions on the can for proper thinning procedure.

To apply the sealer with a brush, flow it on in a full generous coat, paying special attention to end grain. In fact, you will probably have to recoat the end grain several times to get it well sealed. Brush out the sealer coat, stroking with the grain. Some absorbant woods may require a second coat. Once the sealer coat has dried thoroughly, use extremely fine finishing sandpaper or steel wool to smooth the wood surface. Go lightly, and don't sand to the point of cutting any sealer off the surface, or you will end up with a patchy stain job. Since the surface of the dried sealer won't be as shiny as the final finish, you can't see what you have cut through as readily as you can when touch-sanding the final finish coats.

This is one little chore that should be practiced a bit on scrap lumber before it is done on a finished project.

Some sealers can also be sprayed on, and, in fact, this is probably the most common method of applying the sanding sealers. Varnish sealers are among those that cannot be sprayed.

Wood Fillers

Although a sealer will fill the pores of most woods, woods such as ash, walnut, and, especially, oak require additional filling. This is done with a coat of paste wood filler. There are also liquid wood fillers on the market, but they're nothing more than thickened finish material such as varnish and won't do nearly as good a job as will the old-fashioned paste. The paste is made up of finely ground quartz crystals in an oil base. It is usually a greyish tan, but is also available in most of the common wood hues.

In most instances you will want to seal the surface before applying the wood filler. This provides a smoother surface for the filler, and allows it to dry more evenly. When applied to raw wood, filler has to be built up to fill the pores, and it takes more time for these built-up areas to dry properly.

Normally, the natural grey-tan wood filler is colored by mixing a bit of nonpenetrating oil stain with it to make it the color desired. Then the combined stain and wood filler can be applied in one coat. However, it's a good idea to follow manufacturer's directions for tinting specific wood fillers. The wood filler-stain combination must be quite a bit darker than the desired final result; it will dry quite a bit lighter because of the filler material.

Most fillers will require a thinner in addition to the stain coloring agent. They should be thinned with turpentine or the material specified by the manufacturer to the consistency of thick cream.

Apply the filler liberally, brushing it on *against* the grain. Use a brush to work the filler well into the pores of the wood. In most cases wood filler dries fairly slowly, so you have time to make sure the entire surface is well smeared.

As soon as the surface of the filler begins to dry or becomes dull, wipe off the excess filler with a

Application of a wood filler is a necessary step in finishing large-pore woods such as oak, unless a penetrating oil finish is to be applied. Fillers are usually mixed with stain and brushed on in a full wet coat, then allowed to partially dry. Excess filler is then wiped across the grain with a coarse cloth, and finally wiped lightly with the grain.

coarse material such as burlap. Wipe across the grain to force the filler down into the pores; then wipe lightly with the grain. Once the filler becomes too dry, it's almost impossible to wipe it off unless you use a thinner, and then you begin to defeat your purpose. So make sure that all excess is removed before it begins to dry. Allow it to dry thoroughly—usually about 12 hours—before applying a stain or finish coat.

If you wish to recreate a "silver" or "limed" oak finish, apply a dark stain to an open-pore type of wood. Then apply the light colored filler over the dry stain and remove the excess.

Finishes

There are many different kinds of finishes on the market, some very old and some the result of today's advanced technology. Choosing the correct finish for a project is sometimes fairly difficult. The type of project and the uses it will be put to, the woods used, and the skill needed to apply a particular finish will all play a part in determining the correct finish to choose. The most commonly used finishes include: shellac—once the old standby; French polish; penetrating oil finishes; rubbed oil finishes; polyurethane clear varnish; alkyd varnish; counter, or bar-top, varnish; epoxy-ester; clear finish; and lacquer. All are good finishes in their own way, but not all are good in all cases. For instance, a kitchen cabinet front which will be subjected to a lot of abuse and water spotting should be finished with a good water-resistant finish such as lacquer or alkyd or polyurethane varnish. The tops of most tables should be finished with a water- and alcohol-resistant lacquer. A piece of Danish Modern furniture, on the other hand, looks shabby and cheap with a high-gloss finish. The normal finish for this type of sculpted wood is a penetrating oil finish. Many pieces of Early American furniture are finished with a hand-rubbed, old-fashioned oil

A tabletop or other furniture item that is subject to abuse should have a finish that is resistant to alcohol and water. A lacquer finish is often used on such items.

finish, followed with paste wax to create the traditional finish.

The skills and finishing tools of the craftsman will also have something to do with determining what type of finish will be used. If a craftsman is skilled with a spray gun, he will probably finish most of his projects with lacquer, as it's fast drying, easy to apply, and provides a good, tough finish. The craftsman without a spray gun will probably use varnish or oil finishes for most jobs.

Shellac

Although shellac is an old-time finish, it is seldom used as a final finish today. It is one of the most economical finishes, but it doesn't provide the protection of lacquer or varnish, and it shows water spots. The most commonly used shellac for finishing is white shellac, although orange shellac is also used when it's necessary to darken a wood surface. The biggest problem with shellac is that it doesn't have a very long shelf life. Once it ages it will stay tacky rather than drying quickly. Most manufacturers put a date on the shellac can, and you shouldn't use shellac that is over five months old. If you're in doubt about the drying quality of the shellac you can try it on a scrap board. It should dry to the touch in 40 to 45 minutes. If it takes longer, the shellac is not good as a finish material.

Shellac is applied in a series of light coats, as are most finishes. Probably the biggest advantage to the use of shellac is its speed and ease of application with a brush. Since it is about the consistency of water, it goes on quickly and easily. It won't bubble on the surface as varnishes do.

Before applying shellac make sure the wood surface is smooth and clean. Shellac won't stick to an oil surface, so make sure all fingerprints have been removed. Then apply a light sealing coat of shellac and wait for about an hour for it to dry. Lightly sand and remove any sawdust or shellac powder and repeat as necessary. After the last coat (there should be no fewer than three coats), allow the shellac to dry for 24 hours, then lightly sand or buff with steel wool to smooth the last coat. Then apply a good full coat of paste wax. This is rubbed to a soft sheen with extra-fine steel wool, followed by a buffing with a soft cloth.

French Polish

French polish is the finish found on many fine antiques. It is a bit more durable than shellac, yet it will still water spot. Probably the biggest disadvantage to French polishing is the painstaking work involved in applying the finish. It isn't easy even for the pros. But it's the only finish to use when duplicating a type of furniture that traditionally used that finish. French polish should be used only on raw wood or wood that has been stained with a water-base stain.

You can utilize padding lacquers, which are a modern version of French polish, or you can make your own polishing material using white shellac to which a tiny bit of boiled linseed oil is added. Apply by dipping a rag in the mixture and forming it into a ball, then apply the material in light strokes, going with the grain. Allow this to dry, then lightly sand smooth with extra-fine sandpaper or steel wool. Add a bit more linseed oil to the mixture for the next coating and apply it in the same manner, this time rubbing a bit more vigorously. These steps are then repeated as needed. To intensify the shine that will start to come up, the finish is rubbed more vigorously. This is a hard job that will really get to your arm muscles after a time, but is the only method of applying the finish. The difficulty is in getting the finish rubbed evenly over the entire surface so you don't have shiny and dull spots. Applied correctly and evenly, the finish will provide a beautiful warm glow that really looks great on "antique" style furniture.

Penetrating Oils

Probably the easiest finish to apply is a penetrating oil with a resin base. These will usually provide the most consistently good-looking finish without nearly as much hassle as other finishes.

Penetrating oil finishes are exactly that: they penetrate the wood surface rather than lying on top of it as do other finishes such as varnish and lacquer. One of the main advantages of this type of finish is that a minor scratch will not show at all. Because they are relatively fast drying and don't have a surface gloss, there is less likelihood that dust will settle on the finish while it is drying.

A penetrating resin finish is the easiest to apply, and one of the most durable. It looks well with any wood where a natural look is desired, and is particularly good for large-pore woods such as oak and walnut.

using. Allow stain to dry for at least 24 hours.

The finish is usually applied with a brush or cloth, but a spray can also be used. The surface should be completely flooded with the finish. Allow this to penetrate for about 30 minutes and keep reflooding any areas that start to dry out. Then merely wipe off the excess to leave a dry, finished surface. Apply a second coat, allow another 30 minutes for penetration, and wipe this off as well. On plywood the second coat should only be allowed to penetrate for about 15 minutes. And that's all there is to it.

One caution is that the surface *must* be wiped dry and clean within an hour of the initial application or the surface will become tacky. Tackiness can be remedied by applying more fresh resin and allowing it to sit for about 15 minutes before wiping off the excess.

Varnish

Varnish is probably the most common and popular type of wood finish and has been so for many years. Today there are many different types of varnish made from both natural and synthetic resins. Varnish is one of the hardest finishes to apply, yet one of the most durable.

Properly applying varnish requires scrupulous attention to surface preparation and dust problems. Varnish is always applied with a brush, and the skill used in applying the finish can make the difference between a good-looking finish and a sloppy one. It is one of the most durable wood finishes, and is used on such things as bar tops, gym floors, and boat spars. The main disadvantage of using varnish is that it takes a long time to cure, or dry, and this may allow a great deal of dust to settle on the surface and roughen it. For this reason, varnish should be applied whenever possible in a dust-free finishing room rather than in the main shop.

Although there is a wide variety of varnishes available, there are two main types—*natural,* or oleoresinous, and *synthetic.* Natural varnishes are made of natural resins held in an oil base, and can be thinned with turpentine. Synthetic-resin varnishes are manufactured with various chemicals. Some of them can be thinned with turpentine and others require special reducers. Many

Another advantage is that because there is little surface coating in this type of finish it won't crack, peel, darken, or craze.

There is no sheen or glossy shine to this finish. It is quite often used on Danish Modern and other pieces of today's "sculpted" furniture, and it looks well on any type of wood from walnut to oak. The resins in the finish penetrate deeply into the wood pores and fill them to provide a smooth "suede" finish. Because these penetrating resins act as a sealer, you should not use any sealer or filler in addition.

Penetrating oils are available either clear or in a variety of stain colors, and the latter provide a means of staining and finishing at the same time.

Some penetrating oils have an oil rather than resin base, and these can be used when durability is less important.

Although the finish is extremely easy to apply, the wood surface must be absolutely smooth and silky to the feel because there is no way to cover up irregularities as you can with surface coatings. You also should not sand between coats when applying this finish.

After sanding the wood surface thoroughly, remove all dust with a vacuum cleaner. If a separate stain is desired, you can use an oil-base stain or one compatible with the brand of finish you are types of synthetic varnishes are available only to industrial finishers.

Varnishes are also available in a wide variety of surfaces; generally, flat, satin, and glossy finishes. The degree of shine is regulated by the use of a flattening agent such as calcium or zinc stearate.

Natural varnishes. Natural varnishes can be broken down into three classifications, depending on their oil content: they are referred to as short-, medium-, and long-oil varnishes. Marine and spar varnishes are the *long-oil* type. They have more oil in relation to their resins and require more drying time. These varnishes are very heavy-bodied and viscous; the extra-long drying time allows for a more durable, tougher and more elastic type of finish. Tung oil is also added to these varnishes to help make them weatherproof.

The *medium-oil* varnishes are the floor and interior-trim varnishes. They dry somewhat faster than the long-oil types, but are still more elastic and slower in drying than the short-oil types.

Short-oil varnishes are the ones used for finishing furniture. They form an extremely hard, brittle surface and can be polished to a high gloss. Because there is less oil in the base, the varnish is quite a bit thinner and penetrates farther into the wood surface than the long-oil varnishes.

Synthetic varnishes. *Polyurethane* varnish is the synthetic-resin varnish used for furniture and cabinets, and it is the varnish most commonly used by the home craftsman. It is an extremely versatile varnish and is almost an "all around" finish. It is mar-resistant enough to be used on floors, yet thin enough for furniture finishes. A tough, fast-drying finish, it dries to an extremely clear, transparent coating.

Phenolic-resin varnishes are thermosetting; that is, they are cured by heat to form a hard, baked-on surface. They are commonly used on commercial bar tops and restaurant tabletops. *Epoxy* resins are two-part coatings and are the hardest varnish available. They are water-resistant and are often used on boats. *Alkyd* varnishes have good weathering properties and so can be used for outdoor projects.

Applying Varnish. A sealer coat must always be applied before the varnish. It is especially important to apply sealer to an oil-base stain coat. A sealing coat of shellac is sometimes used to prevent the oil from the stain from dissolving in the varnish and clouding the surface. Allow the sealer to dry, then sand lightly with 400 grit sandpaper before applying varnish.

As mentioned before, varnish is one of the most difficult finishes to apply. It must be brushed on just right. You also have to pay special attention to dust, dirt, and other materials in the brush and the varnish. The work area should be warm and dry. If the area is cold, the varnish may take several days to apply; if it is damp, natural varnishes can "bloom." A sunlamp placed a safe distance away from the surface can be used to help hasten drying time in a cold room.

All brushes used in applying varnish should be of good quality and extra clean. Bristles that come loose from the brush can be extremely hard to remove from a varnished surface, and particles of dried varnish or other materials will cause a rough, sloppy-looking varnish job.

Any varnish from a can that has been opened, or used before, must be strained through a fine-mesh material such as nylon hosiery to remove dried particles of varnish and other impurities. Then pour the varnish into a clean container for application of the finish. A varnish application container should have a steel wire across its top as a strike wire. This allows you to remove excess varnish and bubbles picked up with the brush. Dip only the tip of the brush in the varnish, then lightly drag it against the strike wire to remove excess varnish.

Apply the varnish in smooth, light strokes, *always overlapping from the preceding brush stroke.* Don't force the brush down or bend the bristles excessively; use as smooth and light a stroke as possible.

The biggest problem in applying varnish is the bubbles that result. You will never be able to eliminate them all, but you can prevent many of them. Stir varnish very, very slowly to avoid creating bubbles. Also, as noted, do not overwork the brush.

Use a tack cloth before applying each varnish

(*Text continues on pg. 278.*)

Applying Varnish

Strike wire
soldered
in place
to can

Before applying varnish, make sure that the sealer or lacquer coat is completely dry. Apply the varnish with a light, even stroke, always overlapping from the preceding stroke.

One of the main problems in varnishing is the bubbles that arise when the solution is stirred and applied. A varnish applicator can should have a steel strike wire attached so the brush can be passed across it to remove excess varnish and bubbles.

After the surface has dried, lightly sand with 400 grit sandpaper.

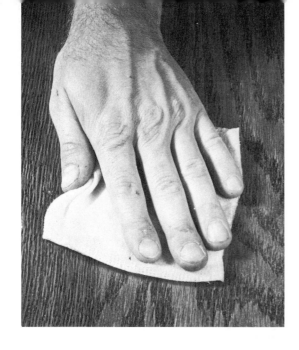

Before applying next varnish coat, use a tack cloth to remove all dust and grit from the surface.

Succeeding coats of varnish are then applied. It takes several coats of varnish to create a good-looking finish.

After the second coat of varnish has been applied, a rubbing compound of Ivory soap and water can be spread and rubbed with 6/0 wet-or-dry sandpaper to level and smooth the surface for succeeding coats.

coat to remove pieces of sanding dust and grit that may accumulate on the wood surface.

After an entire surface has been properly coated, remove almost all varnish from the tip of the brush and using very light smooth strokes, gently brush the varnish and level it down. If possible go across an entire surface with one stroke. Each coat of varnish that you apply should be applied with this same procedure.

When the varnish has dried completely, use extra-fine steel wool or finishing sandpaper to cut down the bubbles and level the surface of the finish. Then again use a tack cloth to remove all dust and debris, and recoat as necessary. If the surface requires more smoothing after the second coat, a protective sludge of Ivory soap and water can be spread and 6/0 wet or dry sandpaper used to level the surface. After the final coat has dried, apply a paste wax and buff with fine steel wool. Allow to dry thoroughly, then buff with a soft cloth.

Additional Notes on Applying Varnish. Probably the most common mistake the beginner makes with varnish is overloading the brush and then scrubbing the material onto the wood surface. The main rule is to do as little brushing as possible. The more you stroke with the brush, the more tiny bubbles you will create in the coating, and the rougher the coating will be when it dries.

Allow each coat plenty of time to cure. In most cases varnish will dry to the touch in about 8 to 12 hours, but it usually won't be entirely cured for 24 hours. High humidity or cold temperatures may lengthen the curing time to several days, and some varnishes, such as marine varnish, may require several weeks to cure.

You can test a varnished surface by pressing your finger against the surface on the underside of a tabletop or other place where it won't show. Then wipe away the fingerprint. If you can't wipe it away entirely, the varnish is still tacky.

Small dust particles and other debris can be removed from a wet or partially dried surface with a tiny paintbrush that has been dipped in varnish and allowed to get a bit tacky.

When varnishing large objects, do only a portion at a time, but always cover each surface to prevent overlaps caused by applying wet varnish

onto cured varnish. If possible, position the object so the varnishing surface is horizontal to prevent sags and drips.

Lacquer

The finish preferred by most cabinetmakers and fine furniture builders is lacquer. A good-quality lacquer properly applied will provide a finish that will resist water, alcohol, and hard abuse, and look like a million dollars.

Lacquer is a chemical finish that was discovered after the First World War. It is basically a combination of guncotton (nitrocellulose) and resin gums, with solvents added.

There are many different kinds of lacquer, including the well-known automobile finishes, spray lacquer in aerosol cans, and brushing lacquer. The lacquer we're concerned with is furniture-finishing lacquer. It is available in several formulas to produce a glossy finish, a flat finish, or any kind in between. The types of lacquer used by professionals for most furniture and cabinets are known as water white, clear, satin-finish, or egg-shell finish lacquers. These will dry with the least amount of color change to the wood.

A good lacquer finish does require plenty of work in preparing the surface. The wood should be sanded as smooth as possible using progressively finer grits of paper. The last paper should be an extremely fine cabinet-grade, open-coat finishing paper; preferably a silicone carbide.

After the surface has been sanded as smooth as possible, it must be sealed. This can be done with lacquer diluted half and half with lacquer thinner or a special lacquer sanding-sealer. The sealer is applied in full coats, but in a dusting spray. After the final coat of sealer, an extremely fine sandpaper should be used to knock off the raised grain and smooth the finish. When you do this, the entire lacquered surface will turn a chalky white, but the surface will clear up with the next coat of lacquer. After the surface is completely smoothed, wipe the surface clean with a dry, clean, lint-free rag. Some professional finishers use an air-hose with an air chuck to remove dust and lint before each lacquer coat.

Lacquer must always be thinned with lacquer thinner before application. For best results use a

Most professional shops finish with lacquer, using spray equipment. The method is fast and provides a hard and durable surface.

lacquer thinner recommended on the lacquer can. For most spraying the lacquer should be thinned with 25 to 35 percent thinner, depending on the application. Sealing coats require 50 percent thinning.

Spraying lacquer requires a compressor and a spray gun, and also a good mask. Lacquer or lacquer-thinner fumes are extremely dangerous and can be explosive, so wear a mask and shut down all gas-operated equipment such as furnaces (even pilot lights). You should also watch out for static electricity. You must have some means of venting the dangerous fumes out of the building. One good method is to have a separate room for spraying with its own ventilation fan; preferably an explosion-proof fan.

The spray gun can be either a bleeder or non-bleeder, but an external-mix nozzle works best with lacquer. The nozzle should be adjusted so the spray pattern is rectangular. The air compressor unit must be capable of obtaining at least 40 pounds per square inch, and preferably 60.

Place the item to be sprayed in a clean, dry area. If possible have it on a rotating stand.

Dilute the lacquer according to the instruc-

Very fine steel wool or finishing paper is used between succeeding coats of lacquer to smooth and level the surface.

tions of the manufacturer and apply in thin dusting coats. Spray across the grain first, then with the grain. Overlap each spray stroke at least 50 percent and make sure to keep the spray gun parallel to the surface and no less than eight inches away. Keep the gun moving. Because lacquer is applied in dilute form, the main problem is avoiding runs. This is why each application must leave only a light dust on the surface. You can spray over a wet coat with other dusting coats, as long as you don't overload the surface.

After at least two hours drying time, the lacquer can be sanded very carefully with 5/0 extremely fine cabinet paper or fine steel wool. Then apply succeeding coats as needed. If you have a gun which is used for lacquer only, clean it thoroughly after use, then leave it about half full of lacquer thinner.

To give the final coat of lacquer extra protection, as well as a bit more sheen, apply a couple of coats of paste floor wax, and buff it with extremely fine steel wool.

A finish like this will withstand everyday use and when the glass coasters are forgotten you won't worry; the ring will wipe off.

Troubleshooting Lacquer

Problem	Cause	Prevention
Blushing	Excess moisture	Use lacquer retarder and avoid spraying on muggy, humid days
Orangepeel	Airgun is too far from surface, or not enough air pressure	Adjust gun
Pinholes	Lacquer too thick	Thin lacquer.
Sags and runs	Gun too close to surface, gun allowed to remain still	Use gun properly

Hand-rubbed Linseed Oil Finishes

One of the oldest and most traditional methods of finishing a woodworking project is the hand-rubbed oil finish. Today's new easy-to-apply finishes have almost completely replaced the old, hard-won finish, but it is still the one to use for extremely fine furniture. Some of the newest finishes on the market are based on the old-style finish. They require less work than the old method, though, and produce a somewhat different result.

A hand-rubbed oil finish may be applied to furniture to give it real protection. The finish is extremely water-resistant, will hold up to hot dishes, and because it runs deep into the wood, will not show scratches as surface finishes do.

The old-fashioned oil finish requires little in the way of materials, little in the way of knowledge, but a lot in the way of elbow grease, which is one of the reasons it is no longer so popular. On the other hand, to the admiring craftsman, the fine mellow look of the old hand-rubbed finish just can't be beat.

The finish does not work well on some walnut pieces because it can turn the wood almost black. (Test it on a piece of scrap stock before using.) Although it can be applied over a stain, it cannot be used over wood filler; the latter will merely leach into the oil. For this reason, hand-rubbed oil finishes are not normally applied to large-pore woods like oak.

The wood surface should be thoroughly sanded, cleaned of all sanding dust, and stained if you desire, before applying the oil. To make sure you've removed all dust and sawdust from the surface, go over it thoroughly with a tack cloth.

When it comes down to the exact method of applying the finish, it seems there are just about as many methods as there are old-timers who used them. For instance, many people suggest that the oil be heated and applied hot. I have found no difference in ease of application or results, and heating linseed oil on a stove is dangerous business. If you do decide to try this method, make sure you have the finishing material in a double-boiler arrangement to prevent the possibility of igniting the oil. The oil works best when applied at a room temperature of around 65 to 70 degrees F.

The method long used to apply this finish required as many as 25 different coats of oil, and it took as long as a year to apply. However, this was primarily due to the crude linseed oil used. Today, using pure boiled linseed oil, much the same results can be obtained by applying about a

Hand-rubbed oil finishes were once a popular method of finishing. They require little in the way of equipment and material, but a lot of elbow grease.

The pure boiled linseed oils available today make the job easier than it used to be, but it may take as many as a dozen coats and 6 weeks to apply a rubbed oil finish. Each coat is allowed to penetrate for about 15 minutes, rubbed vigorously, and allowed to dry for two days or more.

dozen coats over a period of four to six weeks. You can use either straight boiled linseed oil, or two parts boiled linseed oil mixed with one part pure gum turpentine to shorten the drying time.

The oil can be applied with a brush or a folded cloth well saturated with oil. If the wood surface is the top of a table or other similar large surface, the folded cloth is best. If the surface is rounded or has intricate details or carvings, a brush is easier for the initial application of the oil. Some craftsmen prefer to use their hands.

After you're sure the entire surface is flooded with plenty of oil, allow about 15 minutes for the oil to soak into the wood pores, then wipe off all excess oil. Be sure to wipe around carved areas too. Then rub the wood vigorously with a clean cloth, a small portion at a time. You'll have to rub hard and fast to create the friction and heat needed to "drive" the oil into the wood surface and bring out the luster associated with this type of finish. After rubbing the entire piece thoroughly, making sure there are no areas with any surface oil, allow the finish to dry for at least 2 days. Then apply the second finish, exactly as the first. Again, allow a couple of days drying time, then apply the next coat of oil. Keep applying the oil, wiping off all excess, and rubbing the surface hard and fast to create the sheen until there are no dull spots left on the surface. A minimum of a half-dozen coats should be applied.

If you've missed a spot and it has become tacky, apply more oil, allow a few minutes for it to loosen the tackiness, then rub the area vigorously with a rough cloth such as burlap.

To give the finish even more shine, rub down the last coat with pumice stone and oil. Then wipe with a clean cloth and rub hard with extremely fine steel wool, followed again by a clean cloth.

Incidentally, anytime you're rubbing down a piece of furniture with steel wool, make sure the wool is new. Old or rusty steel wool will break readily and leaves a litter of fine metal pieces to catch and collect in corners and crevices. A piece of new steel wool should stay together until it is so packed with rubbed-off finishing material that you will have to discard it.

One of the most common ways in which this old style of finish has been used is in the finishing and refinishing of gunstocks. Because they're submitted to all kinds of weather, this was the standard finish on guns for many years. Today, plastic varnish and synthetic finishes that are impervious to water and cold are used because of the ease in applying them at the factory, but many hobby gunsmiths stick to the hand-rubbed oil finish. When applying an oil finish to an old stock, remove old finish with paint and varnish remover or by thoroughly sanding the article. Then wash the wood with alcohol and start applying the finish. Because of the work involved in applying a hand-rubbed oil finish, it's a good idea to start out on a small piece such as a gunstock so you can get an idea of the amount of work, time, and patience required to do the job.

In addition to the hand-rubbed oil finish, there are many new oil finishes on the market that are quite similar, but that don't require nearly as much work. These are the penetrating oil finishes described earlier, and they are applied in just the same way but in fewer coats and with much less effort in rubbing the finish to its final luster. Some woods such as teak or aramanth are so hard and oily that they will not take anything but a penetrating oil finish very easily. In fact, they may not take a plain linseed oil finish. The solution is to use one of the oil finishes which is especially formulated for these hard, dense, and oily woods.

Whether you use one of the newer oil finishes or try your hand at the hand-rubbed linseed oil, you'll be applying a finish that is both practical and beautiful. If you try the old method, you'll not only be tasting a bit of the effort the older craftsmen had to make, but also learning some of their patience.

Enameling Furniture

"Old-fashioned" enameled furniture has come back into style. Available in bold, exciting colors and gleaming high-gloss and semi-gloss sheens, enamels "shine" in almost any setting. As with other finishes, keep good surface preparation foremost in mind. Even minor surface defects are apt to stand out on enameled furniture, due to the thinness and gloss of the finish coat.

If you're working on an old piece of furniture and it's in good condition, start by removing old wax, polish, grease, or dirt with mineral spirits. It is also wise to prepare the old surface so that the new coating will adhere properly. Brushing on a preliminary surface conditioner is one way to improve adhesion. Let the conditioner stand on the surface for as long as the instructions indicate. Then apply a fresh coat of paint. Sanding the surface lightly with a fine grit sandpaper and then dusting is another way to improve adhesion.

If old furniture is cracked or peeling, it should be completely stripped of its old finish. Use a good paint remover and follow the directions carefully. Be sure to work in a well-ventilated room. Fill any holes or cracks with Plastic Wood or water putty and let them dry thoroughly. Finish by sanding the surface as smooth as possible.

Now apply the enamel undercoat. Sand again before the top coat is applied.

Unfinished furniture is usually factory sanded. But it's a good idea to sand it lightly before you apply the enamel undercoat. If you apply a second coat, sand lightly between coats.

Selecting a Quality Paintbrush

Pay for a good quality paintbrush and you'll always save. It will hold more paint, show fewer brush marks, enable you to paint smoothly and with a minimum of effort, and will last for years if cared for.

Good brushes have a number of characteristics in common. They all have bristles that are "flagged" or split on the ends. The more "flags" the better, as they help retain paint. When buying a paintbrush, test for "bounce" by brushing bristles against the back of your hand—the bristles should feel springy and elastic. When the brush is gently pressed on any surface, the bristles should not fan out excessively.

Check the setting of the bristles too. They should be solidly set so that they will not fall out. Jar the brush and fan the bristles; any loose bristles will be apparent. The brush's metal band, called the ferrule, is important too. Stainless steel and aluminum ferrules are generally used on the better brushes because of their greater resistance to corrosion.

Finishing Children's Toys and Furniture

Each year children are made seriously ill and sometimes permanently harmed by eating or chewing on paint-covered items. Usually these are window sills or other woodwork that has been painted with old-fashioned lead-base paint. But in some cases toys have been covered with other dangerous coatings by unsuspecting craftsmen.

If you do build toys for children, or furniture which may be used by children, make sure the finish is safe. Check the finish-can label carefully.

If you want a subtle color, try painting the toys with poster colors diluted with water, then var-

A nontoxic paint or clear finish should be used when finishing children's toys or furniture. Read the label on the can to make sure the finish is safe for this use.

nish over the colors when they're dry. You can also use most latex colors, but most of these produce a flat, dirt-catching surface which is hard to clean.

Furniture for children's rooms can be painted with an enamel clearly identified for such use, or finished with a good spray lacquer. Most of the resin finishes such as varnishes, penetrating oils, and lacquers are safe (after they are thoroughly dry), but make sure to check the label before using.

Probably the best finish for toys used by toddlers is no finish at all, because you can bet they will chew on the wood. Toys such as wooden blocks and bathtub boats can simply be made of a good dense hardwood, sanded as smooth as possible. The surface can be rubbed with olive oil or salad bowl finish, or left as is. Leaving toys unfinished certainly doesn't detract from a child's enjoyment of them.

Spray Finishing

A great deal of the furniture and built-ins today are finished with sprayed-on materials. For small projects you can use aerosol cans; but in most instances the use of a spray gun and compressor will be necessary. Choosing the correct equipment is extremely important for easy and proper furniture and cabinet finishing.

Spray Guns

There are two styles of spray guns on the market today. One is a self-contained gun with a tiny diaphragm-type compressor built right into the handle of the gun. This is fine for spraying paints and stains, but it won't work for spraying lacquer and other finishes. The other type of gun is connected to a separate air compressor, and this is the type used for furniture finishing.

There are two types of spray guns used for spraying finishing materials. The first is a *bleeder* gun, in which the air flows continuously through the gun although the finishing material flows through the gun only when the trigger is pulled. These are normally used with small diaphragm compressors because they can quickly empty an air tank. The air in a *nonbleeder* gun is fed from a tank. The air and paint are controlled by the trigger and are released only when the trigger is pulled.

There are also two different methods of feeding the material through the gun. The first is *pressure* feeding. The air is fed directly into the liquid and forces it up through the fluid tube to the nozzle. This type of feed is usually used for fast spraying of heavy liquids such as paint. The other type of feed is a *siphon* feed. In this type of gun, the air flows across the fluid tube to create a vacuum so that atmospheric pressure will force the liquid up the tube. The siphon feed creates a finer atomization of the materials and results in a smoother sprayed finish. The better spray guns can be used for either pressure or siphon feed by opening or closing a vent on top of the gun cup.

The type of nozzle on the gun also makes a difference in the type of material that can be sprayed. There are two different types of nozzles: external and internal mix. *Internal-mix* nozzles are most commonly used for spraying heavy liquids and on pressure-feed guns. *External-mix* nozzles are used for lightweight materials such as lacquer. They can be used with either pressure or siphon guns, although they do a better job on siphon guns.

To sum up, the furniture finisher really needs two guns: a pressure-feed gun with an internal mix nozzle for spraying paint and other heavy materials, and a siphon-feed gun with an external nozzle for spraying lacquers, etc. There is another reason why most cabinet shops keep at least two separate guns. No matter how carefully you clean a paint gun, there will still be traces of paint in it. If you use it for lacquer or other transparent materials, you will have tiny bits of paint in the finish. Most professional shops keep "lacquer" guns that are used only for that clear finish. When purchasing a gun, make sure that the nozzle can also be adjusted to create both horizontal and vertical spray patterns.

Compressors

Be sure to select a compressor that is compatible with your gun or guns. The most important thing is that the compressor match the standard cubic feet per minute (SCFM) rating of the gun. The higher the SCFM rating, the more air moves through the hose to the spray gun. The introduction of more air breaks up the finish material density to produce a lighter finish. (A high SCFM is also necessary for use with air tools.)

Another important factor in choosing the compressor is the pressure, or force (in pounds), per square inch (PSI) that the compressor delivers to the gun. A higher PSI permits use of heavier-bodied paints without thinning, and also allows a wider range of adjustments.

For lacquer and other high atomization spraying, the best choice would be a ¾- to 1-hp compressor which delivers at least 6.9 SCFM at 40 PSI.

Spray Finishing

Finishing with spray equipment isn't particularly hard to do, but it does take some practice. The first step is to thin the material so it will work properly in the spray gun. This should be done

A good compressor is important in applying spray finishes. It must be able to deliver at least 40 pounds of air pressure per square inch if it is to be used with lacquer and other fine furniture finishes.

Before spraying a finished project, test-spray a piece of cardboard or scrap stock to make sure the mixture has proper viscosity.

following manufacturer's directions for the specific finish. In fact, getting the proper viscosity of the finish materials is probably the hardest part of spray finishing. If the spray material isn't the correct viscosity, it won't spray properly: too thin and it will dry in the air before it contacts the surface, resulting in a rough, "orange-peel" finish. If the mixture is too thick, the spray gun won't be able to spray the material at all, and the gun will quickly clog up. A tool called a viscosimeter will help a great deal. This is a small cup-like gauge that will quickly tell you the thickness of the solution. It then tells you how much to thin the material so it will spray properly.

Always work in a well-ventilated area and wear a protective shop mask to filter out harmful paint fumes. When spraying materials such as lacquer, make sure all pilot lights and other flames are extinguished.

After determining that the material is correctly thinned, check your pressure gauge and make sure you're using the correct pressure for the ma-terial to be sprayed. Then spray test a piece of cardboard or waste stock to see if the gun is operating properly and if the viscosity is correct.

Adjusting the Gun

The finish solution and air must be properly balanced to get the correct mixture for a finish. This is done by turning the adjustment screws on the top of the sprayer. One controls the amount of air in the mix, and one the amount of finish. This can also determine whether you get sagging, caused by too much material and too little air, or "orange peel," too much air and too little material.

Then, holding the gun parallel to the surface and just to one side, pull the trigger to start the spray. Bring the gun across the surface in a smooth swing and keep it parallel with the surface. As you go past the edge release the trigger to stop the spray. A common mistake made by beginners is to swing the gun in an arc. This results in a build-up of material in the center.

Adjust air and material mixture to achieve the correct density of spray.

Spray with a smooth, even motion, keeping the gun parallel to the surface. Start spraying before you reach the surface, and don't release until past it.

If possible have the surface of the object vertical so you can keep the gun in an upright position. Sometimes this isn't possible, but in these cases make absolutely sure that the gun doesn't leak or drop blobs of finish onto the freshly sprayed surface.

It's a good idea to spray all edges and corners, then spray the main portion of the surface. Always overlap each pass. This is best done by aiming the center of the spray pattern at the edge of the last pass. Hold the gun from 6 to 9 inches from the surface, depending on the pressure and type of material used. Always keep the gun moving to avoid too much build-up of material with resulting runs and sagging.

Apply the finish in thin coats; don't try to get a full finish coat in one application. In fact, the more coats that are applied and worked down, the deeper and finer the finish will be. The first coats should be thinned a bit more than the later coats. Mask surrounding areas to prevent overspray.

And lastly, clean the gun thoroughly. A gun that is allowed to sit with finish material in it will clog and become extremely hard to clean. The best method is to remove the cup, fill it with the appropriate thinner, and spray this through the gun. In most cases this is all that will be needed, but you may also want to remove the nozzle components and clean them.

Aerosols

Aerosol spray paints are perfect for painting objects that need smooth, even finish coats. But a really smooth aerosol paint job calls for slick technique. To get a perfect finish from your next aerosol painting project—try these tips:

When you're ready to begin spraying, hold the nozzle of the container parallel to the surface being painted. Ideally, the can should be 10 to 12 inches from the surface. Don't hold it too close—overpainting, dripping and running will result.

Use rapid, smooth, dusting strokes as you spray. If you stop the movement of the can or stroke too slowly while spraying, streaking may occur.

"Freezing on the button"—holding the nozzle down too long—is a mistake frequently made by

Aerosol spray color lacquers are good for small projects, and come in a wide variety of colors. For best results, hold the can about 12 inches from the surface, and use rapid dusting strokes to apply the finish.

Some exotic woods such as teak and aramanth are difficult to finish. The best choices include a penetrating resin or special finish made just for these hard, dense, oily woods. Lacquer can also be used if sprayed on in very thin coats.

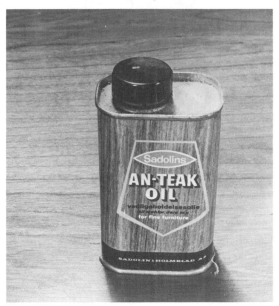

novice spray painters. This can cause dripping and running. Release the pressure on the button just before ending each stroke—the trick is to follow-through.

Finishing Rare Woods

Some of the most beautiful woods—teak, rosewood, amaranth—are also some of the hardest to finish. Their natural oils are retained even after they have been thoroughly dried and cured, and these oils can cause all kinds of finishing troubles.

Regardless of the finish that is to be applied, the first step for oily woods is to wash them thoroughly with denatured alcohol (ordinary shellac thinner). Use a stiff-bristle brush and flood the area with alcohol. Repeat this operation at least two times, using clean alcohol each time. Allow the wood to air-dry between each alcohol bath. Don't heat it or set it in the sun to dry, as this will only bring more oil to the surface.

After removing the oil from the wood surface, the wood may be finished in one of several ways. Probably the easiest to apply is a penetrating oil finish. This type of finish provides a non-glossy look that complements the beauty and grain of the wood. Several coats of finish should be applied, buffing each with a soft cloth.

You can spray on a lacquer finish, but it must be applied in very thin coats. One unusual way of finishing these woods is to merely apply wax, such as a quality paste floor wax, buffing between coats with steel wool and buffing after the last coat with a soft cloth. A stain-filler should be used to fill the open pores first.

Varnish can be applied as a finish, but a thin wash-coat of sealer made up of thinned-down varnish or shellac must first be applied. This coat is then cut down to the wood surface by sanding, and the final varnish coat applied.

Finishing Serving Dishes

Items that will be used for preparing or serving food such as butcher blocks, countertops, and salad bowls should be finished with nontoxic materials. There are two methods of doing this. Special salad bowl finishes are available from woodworking supply houses, or you can simply use olive oil and rub it thoroughly into the wood surface much in the same manner as you would a penetrating-oil finish.

Polishes and Waxes

Polishes and waxes come in three forms: paste, liquid, and aerosol. Paste wax is a concentrate used where protection is important, as on antiques, checked wood, or soft leather. To improve checked wood surfaces, apply wax to a small area with fine steel wool, rubbing with the grain. Polish immediately while the wax is still moist.

Liquid polishes are available in several types. The familiar red-oil polish is formulated for wooden furniture and floors. It restores and polishes both light and dark wood. To use this polish, pour a few drops on a slightly damp cloth and apply with gentle strokes. Buff with a clean, dry cloth.

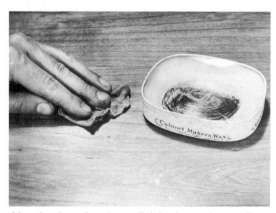

After furniture has been finished, wax is usually applied to provide added protection.

If there are any checks or splits in the grain, the surface can be improved by rubbing wax into the area with fine steel wool.

Another liquid polish, sold under many brand names, is "lemon oil." It has yellow coloring and a lemon aroma, and is used the same way as red-oil polish.

Cream polish is another cleaner-polish. It is excellent for Danish Modern furniture or any dull or natural finish. It cleans without shining. Cream polish also can be used on "antiqued" finishes, laminated plastics, and metal and vinyl surfaces. It is excellent for stainless steel, chrome, and enameled wood.

"Kitchen waxes" are a liquid, but in heavy-duty form. They are made specially for cleaning and polishing in the kitchen.

The most popular polishes with the homemaker who is "easy-care" oriented are the aerosol "dusting" sprays. They are generally a formula of waxes and oils with silicones added. Many also have lemon oil. These waxes should be used sparingly, according to instructions. Usually they say to spray the furniture very lightly and evenly, then polish with a clean, dry cloth.

A streaked or dulled effect may result when an aerosol polish is used over an oil or paste-wax finish, or when liquid polish is used over wax. This can be corrected by complete removal of the polish with a cloth dampened in mineral spirits, then repolishing to restore the finish.

All major aerosol polishes contain silicone. Some refinishers claim that varnish removal is difficult when silicone polishes have been used, but modern varnish removers have eliminated this problem to a large extent.

Never "dry-dust." Wiping a surface on which grit and dust have collected can cause minute scratches. Dust with wax to moisten the surface and pick up grit without scratching.

There are wax finishes which produce the satiny patina important in finishing antiques or reproductions. You also can make your own wax finish: Apply penetrating wood sealer to the raw wood and allow to set 10 minutes. Wipe off the surplus, and let the sealer dry 24 hours. Rub lightly with steel wool, then apply paste wax with a steel-wool pad, rubbing with the grain. Buff shiny, then apply a second coat of wax with the cloth used for buffing.

For matching the right polish or wax to your particular finish, follow the recommendations in the chart.

Recommended Treatment

Finish or Surface	Dusting	Cleaning	Protection
Wood—high luster (lacquer, varnish, etc.)	Spray wax	Liquid polish (red oil or lemon oil)	Paste wax
Wood—low luster (penetrating oil finish)	Cream polish	Oil cleansing foam	
Other wood—			
Antiques			Paste wax
Antiqued (painted)		Liquid polish (red oil or	Cream polish
Unfinished	Spray wax	lemon oil), kitchen waxes	Wax finishes
Worn finishes			Paste wax
Checkered finishes			Paste wax
Painted			Paste wax
Other materials—			
Plastic laminate	Spray wax	Kitchen waxes	Cream polish
Marble	Spray wax		Paste wax
Leather upholstery	Spray wax		Cream polish
Vinyl upholstery	Spray wax		

Rubbing Down Finishes

The majority of finishes require some rubbing down. Rubbing produces almost the entire finish with French polishes, and it's done to a lesser degree with penetrating oil finishes. For the most part, finishes such as lacquer and varnish can be given a deep professional appearing sheen by properly rubbing them down. Some special finishes such as "piano" finish are formed by applying many, many coats of lacquer and rubbing them down between coats with successively finer materials.

Steps in Rubbing Down

Normally, sandpaper is not used for the final rubbing down steps because it cuts too rapidly, but in the case of a rough surfaced finish you may have to use sandpaper for the first step. If this is the case, use only 400 grit wet-or-dry silicone carbide paper. The paper should be allowed to sit in a bowl of warm water for a few minutes before using. On a shellac finish, the sandpaper is normally used dry; otherwise water will penetrate the finish.

The next step is to use pumice stone powder and oil or water. Water is usually preferred because oil leaves a film that is sometimes hard to remove. In any case, sprinkle a bit of FFF pumice powder onto the surface of the finish. Then sprin-

kle water over the powder and use a felt rubbing pad in a circular motion to rub the surface. Start with enough pumice powder to finish the job; adding new pumice will only cause scratches in the surface because the new powders haven't been "cut-down" by the scrubbing action. Cover the entire surface, then give a final rubbing, going with the grain and paying special attention to areas such as facings where stock runs at cross angles. Use a soft clean rag to wipe off a small area and determine if you have rubbed the surface enough. Be absolutely sure that you have covered

Some special finishes are created with elaborate rubbing down techniques. A piano finish, for example, is made by rubbing in many coats of lacquer with increasingly fine abrasives. Here, pumice powder and water are being rubbed with a felt block.

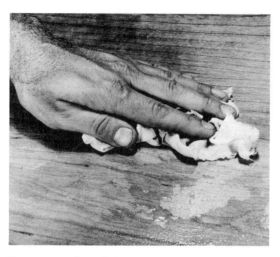

For an even finer finish, rottenstone if used after the pumice and buffed with a soft cloth. The final step is to apply paste wax and buff.

all portions of the surface equally, or you will end up with dull and shiny spots and an uneven surface. Once you're satisfied that you have rubbed the surface to a consistent sheen, remove all debris with a soft moist cloth followed with a soft dry cloth to buff it clean and dry. In most cases this step is all that will be needed to produce a soft, even sheen to the surface. If you would like a deeper, shinier surface such as a piano finish, then the same step is repeated with rottenstone. This is a powder similar to pumice only much finer. Rottenstone may be used with either water or oil as a lubricant, and a soft cloth pad is used for rubbing. Then the surface is cleaned thoroughly.

The last step is to apply paste wax to the surface and buff it with a soft cloth. You may also wish to apply furniture polish over this.

PART IV

Projects

18

Furniture Projects

Building furniture is one of the most satisfying and challenging aspects of woodworking. In this chapter, I have tried to select projects with typical construction elements so that you can use the same methods described here as a guide in building furniture of your own design. For instance, the same method used in constructing the casework for the first project, the French Provincial dresser, can also be used to build other types of casework furniture such as stereo cabinets, gun cases, dining room buffets, and many others. Also, you can change the style of the dresser merely by altering the leg-and-frame construction and varying the decorations on the doors and the top, as shown in the drawing on page 295.

French Provincial Dresser

A hand-crafted bedroom suite of beautiful hardwood is one of the finest and most useful projects a craftsman can undertake. The classic French Provincial dresser shown will provide a satisfying challenge to even the most experienced woodworker. Although pieces such as the dresser appear complicated, they are fairly simple if you break them down into their component parts—in this case, the leg-and-rail unit, the case, and the top. By tackling each part separately, and taking it step by step, the construction will not be nearly as difficult as it may look.

The furniture shown is made of cherry and finished with a clear lacquer. Another standard French Provincial finish is white paint accented with gold gilding. If you choose this type of finish, the furniture can be constructed of quality white pine or, better yet, maple or birch. Pecan is also sometimes used in today's French Provincial-style furniture.

This French Provincial dresser is not difficult to build if you work on each component part separately. The parts are leg-and-rail unit, the case, and the top.

CASE

Sides, ¾ × 16½ × 26″ plywood, 2 req'd
Back, ¼ × 26 × 52⅛″ hardboard, 1 req'd
Bottom, ¼ × 16 × 51½″ hardboard, 1 req'd
Top facer, ¾ × ¾ × 52⅛″, 1 req'd
Bottom vertical facer, ¾ × 2 × 9″, 1 req'd
Middle vertical facer, ¾ × 2 × 8″, 1 req'd
Top vertical facers, ¾ × 2 × 5¼″, 2 req'd
Corner posts, 1½ × 1¾ × 26″, 4 req'd

WEB FRAME

Front pieces, ¾ × 2 × 53½″, 4 req'd
Back pieces, ¾ × 2 × 53½″, 4 req'd
Side pieces, ¾ × 2 × 14″, 8 req'd

LEG-AND-RAIL ASSEMBLY

Legs, 3 × 3 × 6″, 4 req'd
Front rail, ¾ × 4½ × 52″, 1 req'd
Back rail, ¾ × 2 × 52″, 1 req'd
Side rails, ¾ × 3¼ × 16″, 2 req'd

TOP

Top, ¾ × 19½ × 55½″ plywood, 1 req'd
Side edging pieces, 1½ × 3 × 26″, 2 req'd
Front edging, 1½ × 3 × 62″, 1 req'd
Back edging, 1½ × 3 × 62″, 1 req'd

DRAWERS

Drawer fronts (inner), ¾ × 8⅞ × 24⅞″ plywood, 2 req'd
Drawer fronts (inner), ¾ × 7⅞ × 24⅞″ plywood, 2 req'd
Drawer fronts (inner), ¾ × 16⅛ × 5″ plywood, 2 req'd
Drawer front (inner), ¾ × 5 × 15⅜″ plywood, 1 req'd
Drawer-front frame (bottom), ¾ × 2½ × 8⅞″, 4 req'd
Drawer-front frame, ¾ × 2 × 20″, 4 req'd
Drawer-front frame (middle), ¾ × 2½ × 7⅞″, 4 req'd
Drawer-front frame, ¾ × 1¾ × 20″, 4 req'd
Drawer-front frame (top), ¾ × 2¼ × 5″, 6 req'd
Drawer front frame, ¾ × 1¼ × 10⅞″, 4 req'd
Drawer front frame (top center), ¾ × 1¼ × 11⅝″, 2 req'd
Drawer sides (bottom), ½ × 8⅞ × 16″, 4 req'd
Drawer sides (middle), ½ × 7⅞ × 16″, 4 req'd
Drawer sides (top), ½ × 5 × 16″, 6 req'd
Drawer backs (bottom), ½ × 8¼ × 24⅞″, 2 req'd
Drawer backs (middle), ½ × 7¼ × 24⅞″, 2 req'd
Drawer backs (top), ½ × 4⅜ × 16⅛″, 2 req'd
Drawer backs (top center), ½ × 4⅜ × 15⅜″, 1 req'd
Drawer bottoms, ¼ × 15⅝ × 24⅜″ hardboard, 4 req'd
Drawer bottoms, ¼ × 15⅝ × 15⅛″ hardboard, 2 req'd
Drawer bottom, ¼ × 14⅞ × 15⅝″, 1 req'd
Drawer guides, ¾ × 2 × 16¼″, 7 req'd

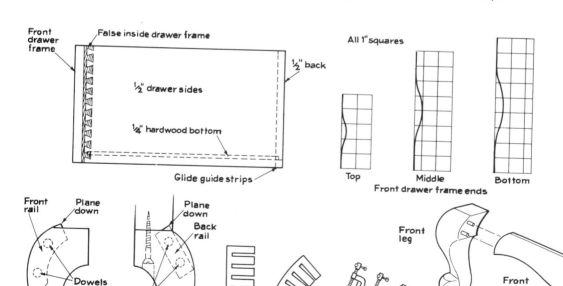

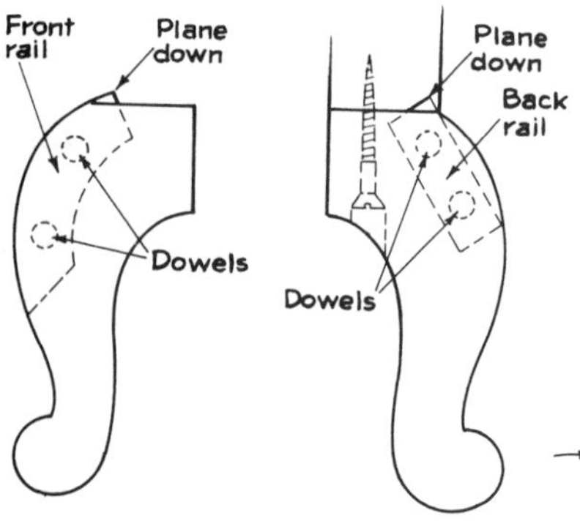

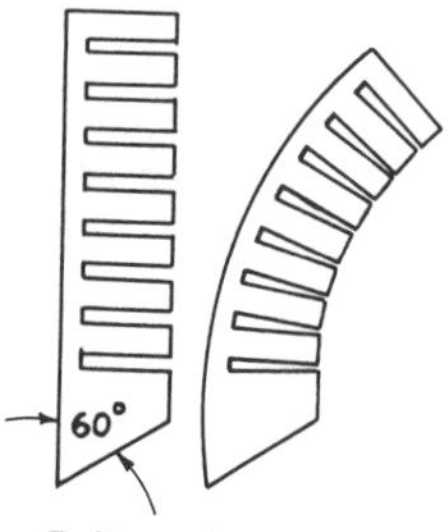

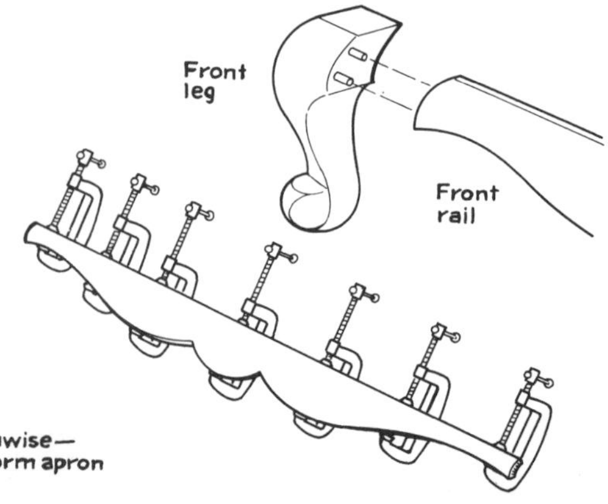

Construction

The first step in construction is to enlarge the squared drawings for the cabriole legs, the bottom rails, the top edging pieces and the drawer-frame pieces on one-inch-square paper. Transfer the drawings to heavyweight paper and cut patterns for each.

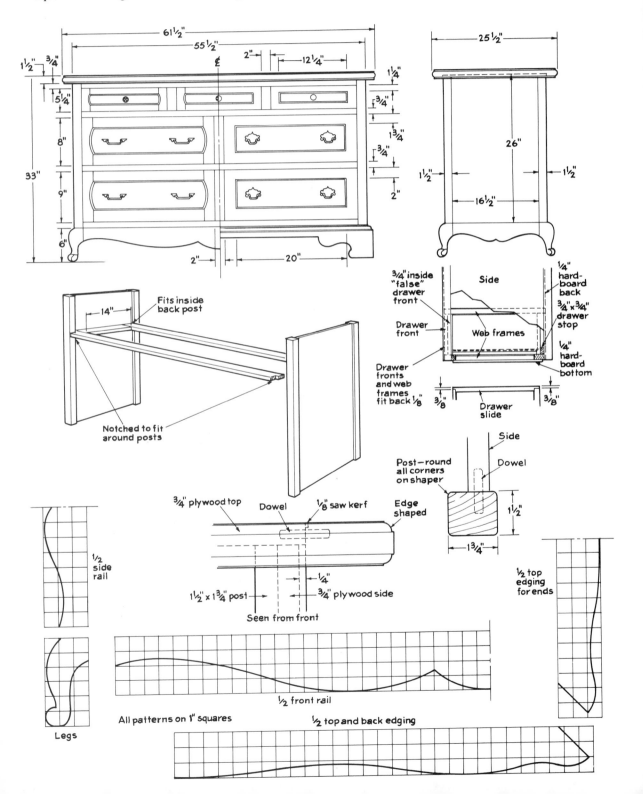

Fits inside back post

Notched to fit around posts

3/4" inside "false" drawer front

Side

1/4" hard-board back

3/4" x 3/4" drawer stop

Drawer front

Web frames

1/4" hard-board bottom

Drawer fronts and web frames fit back 1/8"

Drawer slide

Post—round all corners on shaper

Side

Dowel

3/4" plywood top

Dowel

1/8" saw kerf

Edge shaped

1 1/2" x 1 3/4" post

1/4"

3/4" plywood side

Seen from front

1/2 side rail

1/2 top edging for ends

1/2 front rail

All patterns on 1" squares

1/2 top and back edging

Legs

Cutting the Legs

Glue together ¾-inch-thick pieces to make 3 × 3-inch solid wood blocks, or cut from 3-inch solid stock if you have it. Enlarge the leg drawings to 1-inch squares and make patterns from heavy paper or cardboard. Trace the pattern on one side of the block.

Using a band saw, or a coping saw if you're using hand tools, cut through the outlines on one side of the block.

Turn the block over and trace the leg pattern on the adjacent side.

Legs. The cabriole legs are cut from 3 × 3-inch solid wood blocks which can be made up from ¾-inch-thick pieces. The first step is to glue up the material, or cut larger blocks to the correct size. Then joint all four sides of the block smooth, and make sure the top is also cut smooth and square. Position the leg pattern on one side and mark around it with a sharp pencil. Turn the leg and mark the leg pattern on the adjacent side. Using a band saw, cut around the leg outline on the first side. Then tape the cut-off pieces back on the block and cut around the leg outline on the

Use masking tape to bind the cut pieces back together, then turn the block and cut through the lines on the second side.

The resulting rough cabriole leg.

Below: To taper the leg further, it is marked with a pencil down each side and rough edges are cut away with the band saw or coping saw.

Above: A hole is bored in the inner side of the leg and a lag screw (with the head cut off) is turned into the hole. This can be held in a vise to hold the leg for final shaping and sanding.

second side. The result is a "rough" cabriole leg.

To complete the slim foot design, the sides of the foot must be cut away on the band saw as shown to produce a "tapered" look. Then a hole is bored in the side of the leg and a lag screw (with the head cut off) is turned in place. This can then be clamped in a vise and used to hold the leg securely while the final shaping is done. The front part of the foot is rounded with a wood rasp or Surform tool, and the inside cuts smoothed and rounded slightly to complete the leg. Then sand to smooth all contours.

Making the Rolled Rails

Rails. The front and side rails must be bent. The first step is to trace the pattern for the rails onto the stock. Then they are cut to the proper shape on a band saw with the table tilted. Cut the rail pieces a bit long to allow for final trimming. After the rail is cut to shape, the lengthwise kerfs are made with a fine-toothed saw blade on a radial arm saw. Soak the wood overnight in a tub of warm water, allow to dry for about an hour, then force white glue down in the saw kerfs. Using a number of clamps, slowly bend the wood to make up the curved rail. Allow to dry overnight.

Leg to Rail Joints. The legs and rails are held together with dowels. The holes are first bored in the sides of the legs; then dowel centers are used to locate the dowel locations in the rails after they are trimmed to the right length. This is one of the most difficult and critical steps in assembling the

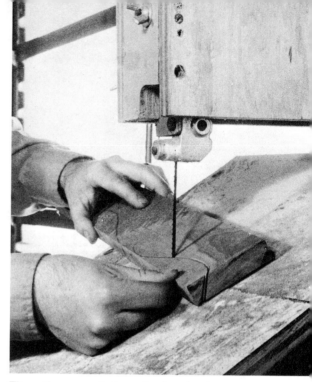

The rails are made by enlarging the drawings on 1-inch squares and making a pattern, then drawing the outline on the rail stock. The cuts can be made on a band saw with the table tilted to 45° as shown, or with a coping saw.

Each rail is kerfed on the back side with a radial arm saw, as shown here. The kerf in the ¾-inch stock is cut to within ⅛- or ¹⁄₁₆-inch of the bottom side. (It's a good idea to experiment with a similar piece of wood.) Then the pieces are soaked in water, dried, and glue is applied in the kerfs so the pieces can be bent. Pieces are bent to shape by applying clamps along the entire length as shown in the drawing on page 294.

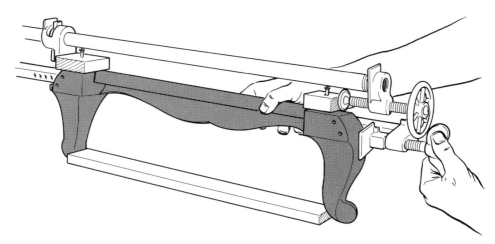

Locate and bore holes for dowels in legs and rails. When gluing, follow directions carefully to make sure leg and rail joints are not pulled out of place by clamps. Blocks are screwed to the tops of legs to provide clamp-holding locations, and spacer block is placed as shown.

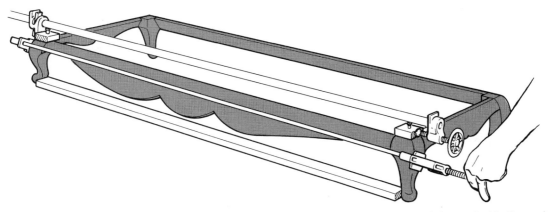

Front and back rails are glued and clamped the same way. Again, a spacer block is used at bottom of assembly. The back rail is merely a flat board, but is placed at an angle similar to that of front rail.

piece. Both legs must fit the rail squarely, without twisting to one side or the other. Because there is no reference to work from, this must be done entirely by eye. The best method of locating the rail in respect to the legs is to lay the legs down in place flat on a smooth surface, then place the rail between them in the correct position. Tap on the legs lightly to mark the location of the dowel-center finders in the rail. Double check the location. Bore these holes, then glue the dowels in place and clamp a side rail and two legs together. Because there are no flat spots for the clamps to fit, you will twist the legs out of square unless special clamping methods are used. Screw a cou-

ple of blocks to the top of the legs as clamp holders. Then place a spacer block between the lower parts of the legs. With clamps on top and bottom, tighten lightly one at a time until the unit is square and true.

After both side units have been glued, you can then use the same procedure to clamp and glue the front and back rails in place. The back rail is a flat board, but it is placed in position at an angle as shown. When clamping the front and back rails in place, make sure the unit is placed on a smooth, flat surface and is square and true. Too much force on one clamp may pull one leg up and make the frame tilt out of square.

Building the Case

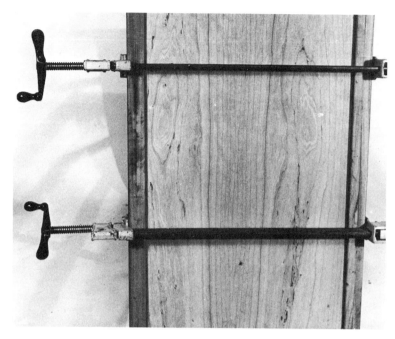

The sides of the case are cut from ¾-inch hardwood-face plywood which matches the solid wood of the piece. The corner posts are cut to shape, then doweled and glued in place to the side pieces.

The web frame pieces are cut to size, then are doweled and glued together. The frame is then attached to the sides with glue and countersunk wood screws. Be sure the screws are the correct length so they won't protrude through the outer surface of the sides.

Case Construction. Now the hardest part of the project is done. The next step is construction of the case, and this is a standard "box" construction project. The sides are first cut from hardwood-faced plywood with a plywood blade. (If using a portable circular saw, cut with the front face down. If using a table saw, place the good face up.)

Cut the four corner posts to the correct size, joint all four sides, then round the corners on a shaper. The posts are fastened to the sides with

dowels and glue. Make sure to wipe all glue away from the joints as it will be hard to clean out later on. After the sides have been thoroughly glued, cut the web frame pieces and dowel and glue them together. Note that the front frame pieces are made of hardwood, but a more economical wood can be used for the side and back pieces. The front pieces are notched to fit around the corner posts, but the back pieces fit inside the back posts. The side pieces are counterbored with screw holes for fastening to the case sides before the

A flathead wood screw is driven into the bottom center facer, which will separate the two bottom drawers. The clamp holds the frame while the glue dries.

With the case turned on its back, the front facers are cut to fit, then glued and screwed in place.

frames are assembled. After the frames are dry, glue is placed on their ends and they are positioned on the case. Clamps are used on both sides to hold them and they are fastened in place with wood screws driven into the case sides. Make sure the case is square before fastening the frames in place. A wooden brace is temporarily nailed across the back to hold the case square until the back is installed. This will be the last step.

With all frames installed, turn the case over on its back and cut and fit the front facings. To fit

these properly, cut one end smooth with a fine-tooth blade in a radial arm saw. Then hold the stock in place against one end of the case. Mark the length with a fine pencil and cut with a fine toothed saw. Then place glue on the ends, position the facer in place, and clamp it solidly. Flat-head screws are then driven in through the web frames and into the facers to hold them securely.

A top filler strip must also be installed on the top web frame at this time, and it is held with glue and wood screws from the underside.

The case is now ready to fit on top of the leg-and-rail assembly. Note the use of a brace attached diagonally across the back to hold the case square.

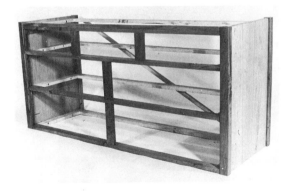

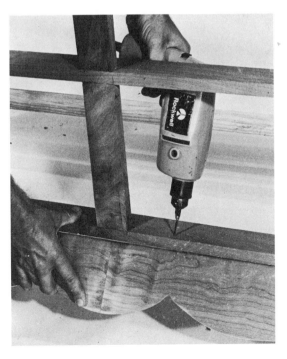

The case is positioned on the leg-and-rail assembly and screws are driven down through the bottom frame pieces into the rails. Long screws are also driven up from the underside of each leg.

Making the Top

Enlarge the drawings for the edging pieces on 1-inch squares to make patterns for cutting. Cut and sand the edging pieces, and miter the ends at 45°.

A decorative saw cut is made on the inside top edge of each edging piece, as explained in the text. Then shape the outer edges of the pieces on the shaper.

Top. Now the basic case is finished and you're ready for the third part, the top. The first step is to cut the plywood center to the correct size. Take extra care to avoid splintering the edges—the top of the plywood edge will be exposed due to the decorative saw cut which will be made in the aprons. Again, use a plywood blade and cut with the good side down if using a circular saw. Masking tape can also be placed over the cutline to help prevent splintering of the face veneer.

The top edging is made from 1½-inch-thick material; you may have to glue up narrower pieces to make this stock. Joint the back edge of the stock, and cut the front edge to shape on a band saw.

It is almost impossible to make a perfectly even joint between plywood and solid wood, because the laminations in the plywood have a tendency to push the dowels up or down a bit. Sanding down the joint only results in more problems, as you can very easily cut through the thin face veneer of the plywood. For this reason, a decorative cut is made along the straight back edge of the edging pieces to eliminate the need for a per-fect joint. The kerf should be ⅛ inch deep and the width of a saw blade. (Use a wooden auxiliary fence when cutting it on a table saw.)

After shaping and miter-cutting the edging pieces, glue and dowel them to the plywood top. Make sure to clamp all four pieces at the same time, and use clamps on each corner to insure that they are held flush as well. Allow the assembly to dry overnight.

Edging pieces are attached to the plywood top with dowels and glue. Bar clamps hold all four edge pieces to the plywood at the same time, and C-clamps are used to hold the mitered corners flush. Use protective cloth pads with the clamps to protect the wood edges.

A dampened cotton swab and damp rag can be used to clean glue out of the decorative saw cuts and from the joints.

Making the Drawers

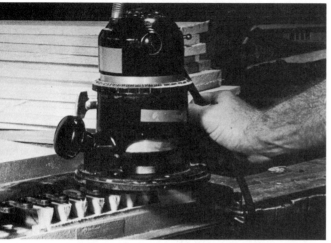

Cut all pieces for the drawers including ¾-inch false fronts. A ¼ × ¼-inch rabbet is cut in the front, back and side pieces to take the ¼-inch hardboard bottom. Dovetail joints are cut in the false fronts and sides. Here an accessory dovetail jig is used with a dovetail bit in a router.

Drawers. While the top is drying, you can start assembling the drawer fronts. These consist of a hardwood frame which is fastened over a hardwood-face plywood front. Cut the rounded side pieces of the frame; then glue and dowel them to the straight pieces. When the frames have dried thoroughly, mold the inside edges with a shaper or router.

The drawers are constructed with ½-inch pine or sycamore drawer stock. The sides are joined to the back and front with dovetail joints. The ¼-inch hardboard bottom is held in place in dadoes cut in the sides, back and front. After all drawers have been constructed, they are fitted in place in the cabinets and wood center guide strips are cut and fitted in place.

Assembly. With all drawer guides fitted in place, turn the top upside down on a smooth flat surface. You can use an old blanket to prevent scarring the plywood surface. Place the case portion upside down on the top, and fasten the two together with screws driven through the web

Assemble the drawer pieces to see how they fit. Make any necessary adjustments, then glue and join them together. The ¼-inch hardboard bottom is placed in position, the drawer squared up, and the back piece fastened with glue and flathead screws. Then guide strips are cut and fitted in place on the drawer bottoms.

The drawer fronts are made by doweling a solid wood frame together. The two curved end pieces are first cut with a band saw or coping saw; then the inside of the frame is molded on a shaper as shown, using a guide pin and collar set.

The plywood drawer front is fastened to the wood frame with glue and flathead wood screws. Be sure the screws are short enough so they don't protrude through the front of the frame.

The drawer guides are fastened in place on the front edge of the web frame.

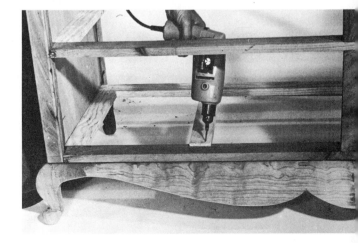

Drawers are placed in position on the guides. Make sure they fit flush with all edges of the front facers.

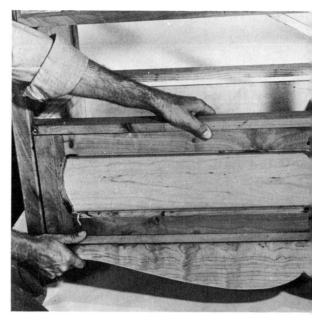

frames and into the edging pieces. Since a piece of furniture of this type is often picked up by the top edge, it must be securely fastened in place.

The last construction step is to cut the back from ¼-inch hardboard and secure it in place with roundhead screws.

Sand the entire piece thoroughly, and apply your favorite finish. A good lacquer finish sprayed on and sanded thoroughly between coats will provide a professional-looking finish. Finally, fit the hardware in place.

Then the back of the drawer guide is fastened in place with small wood screws. Drawer should be in position as each guide is fastened to insure correct alignment.

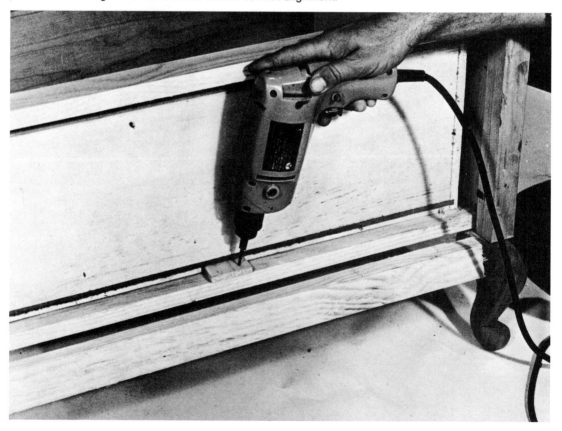

The top is attached by turning it upside down on a flat, level surface and placing the case on it. Carefully align the two, then drive screws through the web frames into the top edging pieces.

The ¼-inch hardboard back is cut, fitted in place, and fastened with roundhead screws.

Mediterranean-Style Bedside Tables

Night stands can be decorative and practical—or they can be a nuisance. These stands were designed with enclosed cabinets below to hold books, magazines, and all the bedside paraphernalia that we seem to collect. They could also be used as end tables for a couch or, with holes cut in their sides, as stereo speaker enclosures. If used as a bedside table, the stand should be designed so that the top is a bit lower than the top of the mattress; I've been poked in the face more than once by a table top that protruded above bed height. The tables shown were designed so that the tops end ½ inch below the top of a kingsize bed mattress on a box spring and standard frame. You may wish to alter the dimensions somewhat if the top of your mattress is higher or lower.

Construction of the units is simple box assembly. The sides and top are cut from ¾-inch oak veneer plywood. You may prefer, however, to make the cabinets from solid wood. If so, dowel and glue up the pieces to make the width needed.

Mediterranean-style night stands of solid oak and oak-veneer plywood are sized so the tops are slightly below bed height.

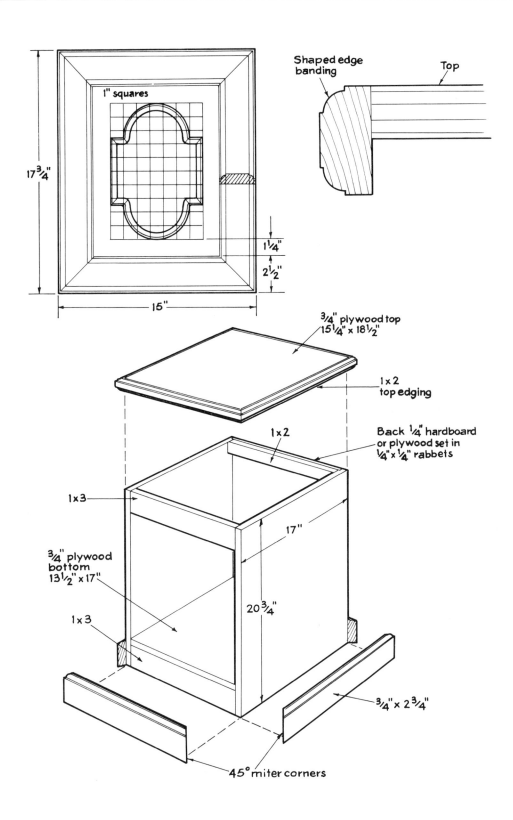

1" squares

Shaped edge banding

Top

17¾"

1¼"

2½"

15"

¾" plywood top
15¼" x 18½"

1 x 2
top edging

Back ¼" hardboard
or plywood set in
¼" x ¼" rabbets

1 x 2

1 x 3

17"

¾" plywood
bottom
13½" x 17"

20¾"

1 x 3

¾" x 2¾"

45° miter corners

Construction

Cut the side pieces to size from ¾-inch hardwood veneer plywood, and the bottom from ¾-inch fir plywood. Cut a ¼ × ¼-inch rabbet along the back edge of each side piece and along the back of the bottom piece to accept the ¼-inch back. Then cut the top and bottom 1 × 3 braces. The back brace, cut from a 1 × 2, also has a ¼ × ¼-inch rabbet to accept the back. Fasten the top braces in place by nailing and gluing the plywood sides to them. Then install the front bottom brace in the same way, making it flush with the front edges of the side pieces.

Use a square to mark the location of the plywood bottom on each of the side pieces; then glue and nail the bottom in place.

Turn the cabinet on its front and cut the ¼-inch hardboard or plywood back to fit. Use a carpenter's square to make sure the cabinet is square; then fasten the back in place using small flathead nails and glue.

The bottom molding pieces can be cut by ripping a 1 × 6 into two equal widths. Then shape the top edge of each piece with a shaper or molding head on a table saw or radial arm saw. Cut the side pieces straight on the back and with a 45° angle miter on the front ends, and fasten them in place with glue and No. 8 finishing nails. Cut the front bottom molding piece with a 45° miter on each end and carefully fit it in between the two side pieces, again fastening with glue and finishing nails.

Cut the ¾-inch hardwood-veneer plywood top. It should protrude ⅛ inch on each side and 1½ inches at the front, and should be flush with the back end of the case. Cut the molded edges on the 1 × 2 top edging pieces. These strips are then cut to size just like the bottom molding pieces; straight-cut at the back and with 45° miter

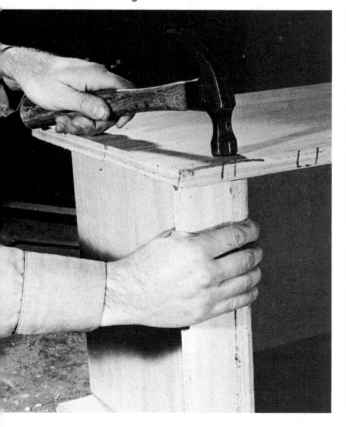

The basic construction of each stand is a simple box. Here, the bottom is being fastened to the sides with glue and nails.

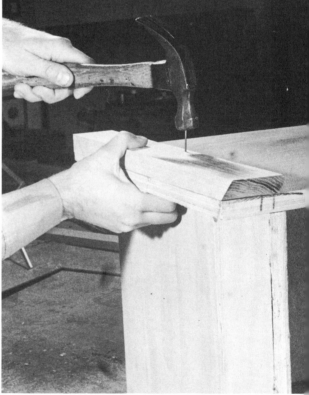

The three bottom molding pieces are miter cut at a 45° angle on the front corners. Then they are glued and nailed in place.

The frame pieces for the doors are edge-molded on both sides, then rabbeted to accept the center panel. After the frame has been glued and clamped, the base panel and decorative center panel can be fastened in place with glue and screws from the back.

cuts at the front. They are fastened in place with glue and finishing nails. Then set all nails with a nail set and fill the holes with wood putty. Allow to dry and thoroughly sand the entire cabinet.

The door is a typical frame-and-panel construction with an outside frame of ¾-inch-thick stock and a base panel of ¼-inch hardwood-faced plywood. A decorative center panel of solid wood is glued and screwed to the front of the ¼-inch base panel.

The frame is made by first routing a ¼ × ¼-inch rabbet along the edge of the 1 × 3 stock to hold the center panel. Then the front edge of the stock is molded, and the stock cut to size and miter cut. It is then assembled just like a picture frame. One of the best clamps I have used for this job is the Porta-Press frame-and-panel clamp by Universal. It makes easy work of gluing up a complete frame, and insures a square, correctly assembled frame. After the frame has set, the base

The stands shown were given a coat of dark brown stain and finished with lacquer.

The doors are then hinged to the cases. (One door should swing right, and one left.) Skotch fasteners were used to reinforce the mitered corners.

panel is glued in place. The decorative center panel is cut to shape with a band saw or saber saw, then the edge molded on a shaper. It is then centered in place and fastened to the base panel with glue and screws from the back.

The door hardware is then installed, the door hinged in place, and a magnetic catch located at the bottom edge to hold the door closed. The doors on the separate stands are hinged to swing in opposite directions. The stands shown were given a coat of dark brown stain and finished with lacquer.

Family-Size Harvest Table

Most factory-built furniture is designed to accommodate a typical-size family, and this sometimes presents a problem for larger households. The harvest table shown is designed for a large family. It will seat four adults on each side, and if a chair is used at each end, ten adults can be accommodated. The table height is 29 inches, which allows for use of standard-size purchased captain's chairs. (The design of the table also allows the chairs to be pushed in under the ends of the table when not in use.)

The table and benches are constructed with 1¼-inch (⅘) white pine and 2×4s of white pine.

Most large building-supply and lumber dealers carry both types of lumber, but if you live in a rural area you may have to do a bit of searching for the 2×4s.

Construction

The first step is to cut and lay out the ⅘ material for the table and bench tops. The table top is made up of six 5⅝-inch pieces, and each bench is made up of three 4⅞-inch pieces. Cut all pieces to the correct width, leaving an extra ⅛ inch or so to allow for jointing the edges. Before jointing the edges, check your jointer to make sure it is cutting a perfectly square edge; otherwise, you will end up with a warped table top or one with

One advantage of building your own furniture is that you can scale it to suit your needs. The table shown was designed for a large family: It will seat 10 adults quite easily.

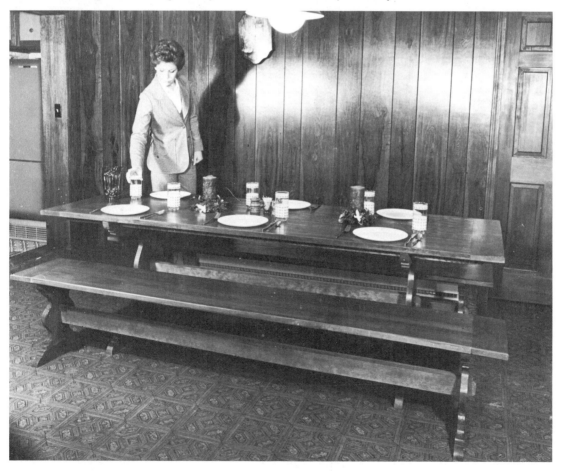

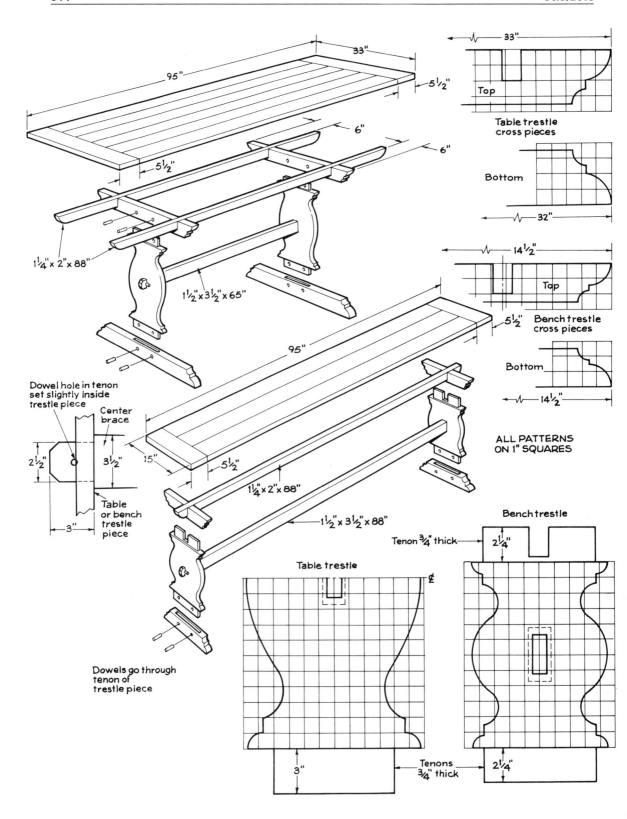

33"

Top

Table trestle cross pieces

Bottom

32"

95"

33"

5½"

5½"

6"

6"

1¼" × 2" × 88"

1½" × 3½" × 65"

14½"

Top

5½"   **Bench trestle cross pieces**

Bottom

14½"

ALL PATTERNS ON 1" SQUARES

Dowel hole in tenon set slightly inside trestle piece

Center brace

2½"

3½"

3"

Table or bench trestle piece

95"

15"

5½"

1¼" × 2" × 88"

1½" × 3½" × 88"

Tenon ¾" thick

Table trestle

¢

Bench trestle

2¼"

2¼"

Dowels go through tenon of trestle piece

3"

Tenons ¾" thick

TABLE

Tabletop, 1¼ × 5½ × 84", 6 req'd
Top ends, 1¼ × 5½ × 33" (cut to fit), 2 req'd
Trestle pieces, 1¼ × 12 × 28", 2 req'd
Trestle crosspieces (top), 1½ × 3½ × 33", 2 req'd
Trestle crosspieces (bottom), 1½ × 3½ × 32", 2 req'd
Under-top braces, 1¼ × 2 × 88", 2 req'd
Center brace, 1½ × 3½ × 65", 1 req'd

Dowels, ⅜ × 3", 30 req'd
Dowels, ⅜ × 1¾", 8 req'd
Dowels, ⅜ × 3½", 2 req'd

BENCHES

Bench tops, 1¼ × 4½ × 84", 6 req'd
Top ends, 1¼ × 5½ × 13½ (cut to fit), 4 req'd
Trestle pieces, 1¼ × 9 × 16½", 4 req'd
Trestle crosspieces, 1½ × 3½ × 14½", 8 req'd
Under-top braces, 1¼ × 2 × 88", 2 req'd
Center braces, 1½ × 3½ × 88", 2 req'd

Dowels, ⅜ × 3", 30 req'd
Dowels, ⅜ × 1¾", 8 req'd
Dowels, ⅜ × 3½", 4 req'd

Stock for the table and bench tops is cut ⅛-inch large on each side. Then the edges are smoothed on a jointer.

open cracks. Cut the boards to the proper length with a fine-tooth blade in a radial arm saw or table saw.

Clamp a straightedge to a large table top or weight it down on a smooth floor surface, and butt the ends of the pieces on this as you lay them together to form the table top. This insures that the glued up pieces will meet flush on the ends. Turn every other piece over to alternate the grain direction (see illustrations on pages 94 and 104). With all pieces laid together, check for ripples or open joints. You may have to joint one or two pieces again to eliminate these.

Doweling and Gluing the Top. Mark the locations of the dowels on the boards, and number each piece so you can reassemble them in the same order. Cut ⅜-inch dowel rod into 3-inch

The edges of outside table and bench pieces are finished with a chamfer. Mark the chamfer cuts with an adjustable square; then cut them with a good jack plane.

lengths to make up the dowels. Cut a glue slot along the edge of the dowels to make them easier to install, and round all of the ends. Each dowel hole should be 1¾ inches deep. (See Chapter 5, pages 91–94, for details on using a doweling jig.) After the dowel holes have been drilled, apply glue in all dowel holes along each board and along the edge of the board. Tap the dowels in place in each consecutive board to get them started. Then, using a minimum of four clamps, pull the pieces together on a smooth, flat surface. Tighten each clamp gradually so the pieces go together evenly. When the top is clamped securely, check to make sure it is perfectly flat. Allow to dry overnight. The bench tops are assembled in the same manner.

Stock for the table and bench tops is doweled and glued together. (Use a doweling jig to insure that dowel holes are aligned precisely.) You will need some extra long bar clamps to clamp the table top lengthwise.

The end pieces of the table and bench tops are glued and doweled to the tops in the same way. (Mortise-and-tenon joints could also be cut on these pieces with a shaper blade on a radial arm saw, but holding the heavy table top in place for sawing would create a problem. The under-the-table braces provide enough support that the stronger joint is not necessary.) A set of pipe clamps at least 9 feet long will be needed to hold the end pieces to the top while the glue dries. Again, clamp the assemblies on a flat solid surface. The end pieces will have a tendency to buckle and turn up, so the ends should also be pulled down flat with clamps.

After the glue has dried thoroughly, remove the clamps and belt sand the tops, going *against* the grain first, then with the grain. Then go over the end pieces with the grain to remove the cross-grain sanding marks on these pieces. To make the chamfers on the edges of the tops, draw a line $\frac{1}{16}$ inch from the edge, using an adjustable square. Use a hand plane to cut the chamfer, cutting the long sides first, then across the ends to remove any splintering. Go over all surfaces thoroughly with a finishing sander to remove all belt-sanding marks. This last step can't be stressed too much. Every rough sanding mark will show up after finish is applied.

The end pieces of the table and bench tops are then doweled and glued to the assembled tops. An additional handscrew clamp is used to pull the end piece down flat. (To create the impression of a mortise-and-tenon joint between the end piece and top assembly, decorative plugs can be inserted about 2 inches from the end.)

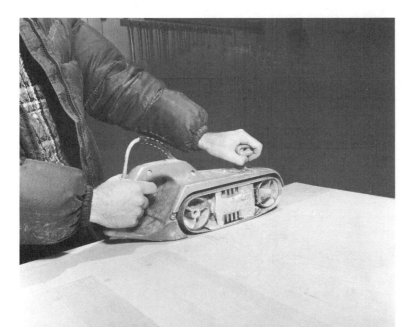

After the glue has dried, the entire top is sanded smooth.

The bench and table trestles and trestle crosspieces are cut out on a band saw.

Trestle Legs. Enlarge the squared drawings for the curved trestle pieces on one-inch-square paper and cut these from ¾ stock. All of the pieces can be cut on a band saw, even a small one. If you're using a small band saw, trace the cutline on each side of the stock, and turn the stock over when cutting is obstructed by the neck of the band saw. With all end pieces cut, mark for the mortises and bore starting holes, then cut them out with a saber saw. It's a good idea to cut the mortises somewhat small, then finish with a wood rasp or chisel.

The curved edges of the pieces can be sanded with a flap sander in a portable electric drill or radial arm saw, or with a sanding drum in a radial arm saw or drill press. The main thing is to get all cross marks sanded off the edges, as these will show up when the table is stained. The tenons on the ends of these pieces can be cut with a dado blade on a radial arm saw or table saw. They should be ¾ inch thick. The tenons won't have to be sanded or smoothed since they will not show, and the roughness helps provide a tooth for the glue.

The tenons on the trestle pieces can be cut with a dado blade on a radial arm saw.

Enlarge the squared drawings to make a pattern for the top and bottom crosspieces of the trestles, and cut these out with a band saw or saber saw. The edges of these pieces should also be sanded to remove across-the-grain cut marks. The mortises in these pieces can be roughly cut with a ¾-inch Foerstner bit in a drill press. First, mark a centerline to locate the holes, then mark the ends of the cuts. Bore overlapping holes to make the cut. Use a wood rasp to smooth up the inside cuts just enough so that the tenons will fit snugly. The ends of the mortises will not have to be squared up because the top corners of the curved pieces will cover this portion. When all trestle pieces fit smoothly on the crosspieces, glue and clamp them together.

Dowels are inserted into the trestle pieces so that the trestles will be securely fastened to the crosspieces. After the glue has set, use a ⅜-inch Foerstner bit to bore through the mortise-and-tenon joints. Set the depth stop on the drill press so that the bit will come through just enough to punch a marking hole on the bottom of the stock. Then turn the stock over and finish the hole from the other side to prevent splintering out the wood. Cut wooden dowels to 1¾-inch length, but don't round the ends or make a glue channel in these. Apply glue and push them into place with a drill

The tenons should be left rough—not sanded—to make a good glue joint with the mortised crosspieces.

When the crosspieces fit properly, they can be glued and clamped to the trestles.

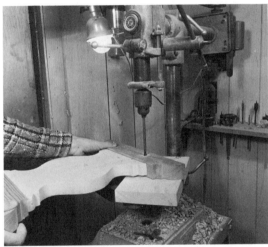

To strengthen the joint between the trestles and crosspieces, holes are drilled through the crosspiece as shown, and dowels inserted through the tenon.

so that they are flush with one side of the stock. The protruding ends can be sanded off with a belt sander after the glue has dried.

The tops of the table trestles are mortised to make cross-lap joints with the two 78-inch-long braces that fit under the table top, and each bench trestle is also mortised to accept a brace.

Braces. Cut the under-the-top braces for the table and benches and round their ends as shown in the drawing on page 314. Then cut the mortises in the crosspieces with a dado blade.

Cut the center crossbraces for the table and benches to size, and plane and sand them smooth. The longer cuts for the tenons at each end can be made with a dado blade, and the narrower cuts with a fine-tooth backsaw and chisel. Sand these areas smooth and trial-fit the pieces in the mortises on the trestles. Mark each tenon at the point where it comes through the trestle mortise, and bore a ⅜-inch hole at this point for the holding pins. Position the bit so that just a fraction of the hole falls behind the marked line to provide for a tight-fitting pin.

Assembling and Finishing. Turn the table top upside down on a smooth surface. Position the trestles and the under-the-top braces in place on the table top and mark their locations. The tres-

Trestles are fastened to table and bench tops with countersunk No. 10 1¾-inch wood screws.

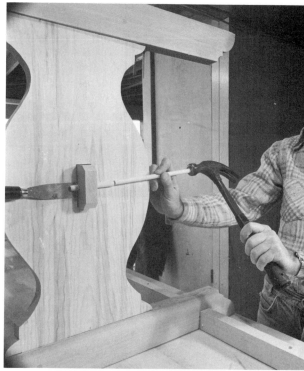

Finally, the cross braces are fitted in the mortises in the trestle pieces. A 3½-inch length of dowel (slightly flattened on each side) is used to lock each brace in place. Use a putty knife as shown to keep the hardwood dowels from marring the pine.

tles are fastened to the top by driving screws up through the trestle crosspieces as shown. The bench tops and trestles are assembled in the same way.

To finish the table and benches, sand all portions with a fine-grit paper and make sure all glue runs have been removed. Then stain to suit. A dark walnut-type stain looks good on this type of wood.

The table shown was first given 13 coats of lacquer, and was sanded between each coat with 420-grit sandpaper. This was followed by two more coats of lacquer, each buffed with 0000 steel wool. Then four coats of paste floor wax were applied, again buffed with fine steel wool, and finally a coat of furniture polish.

Drop-Lid Desk

One of the problems with a desk is the clutter that inevitably gathers on top of it. A drop-lid desk like the one shown is one solution. The bottom of the unit has plenty of drawer space, while the top portion has a number of cubbyholes and small drawers to hold unsorted mail, pencils, stamps, and other small items. D-grade white pine was used for the entire construction of the desk shown except for the bottom and back of the case. The lumber was doweled and glued to make up the width of stock needed and was stained an almost-black brown. White porcelain knobs complete the Country English styling.

The desk is made in three sections. First, the bottom case is assembled, then the top cut-away portion, and finally the pigeonhole divider section for the top portion.

Construction

The wide pieces of the construction (sides, desk top and drop lid) must be glued up from narrower stock. Cut the lumber slightly longer than the dimensions shown in the drawing to allow for slight misalignments, and glue and dowel the pieces together. (A doweling jig makes this job much easier.) Turn the stock so that the end grain direction is alternated on adjacent pieces as shown on page 94. Trim the stock to exact dimensions after the glue has dried thoroughly.

In assembling the desk, finishing nails or screws can be used as fasteners if the desk is constructed with pine. (Nail holes are later filled with Plastic Wood, and screw holes with wood plugs.) If using a hardwood, you may prefer to glue the entire desk together, using glue blocks on the inside corners to strengthen the construction.

This drop-lid desk provides a good way to hide home office clutter. The pigeonhole divider in top section has space for neat storage of mail and other papers, and the space between dividers provides enough room to store a full-size calculator and a small lamp. When open, the lid provides a large work area.

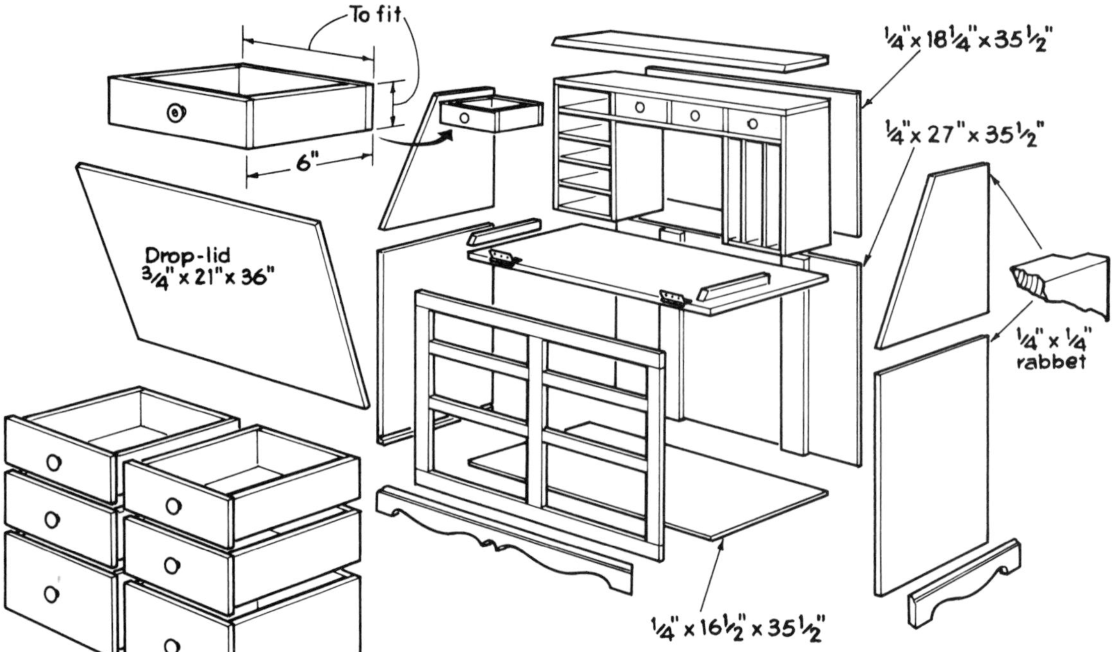
To fit
6"
Drop-lid
3/4" x 21" x 36"
1/4" x 18 1/4" x 35 1/2"
1/4" x 27" x 35 1/2"
1/4" x 1/4"
rabbet
1/4" x 16 1/2" x 35 1/2"

Half pattern— front apron

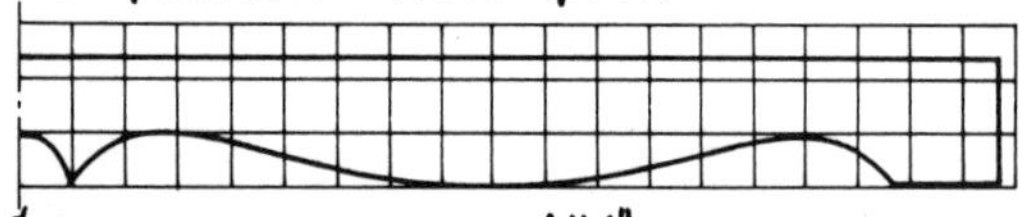

All 1" squares

Full pattern— side aprons

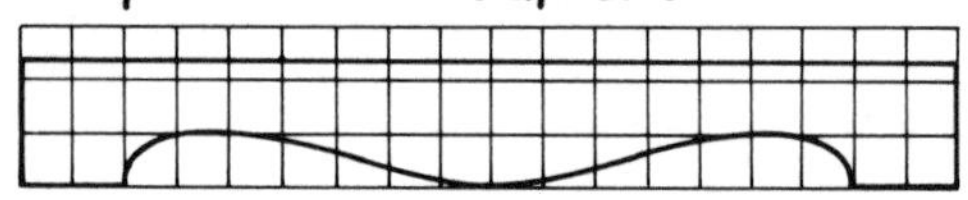

Divider section

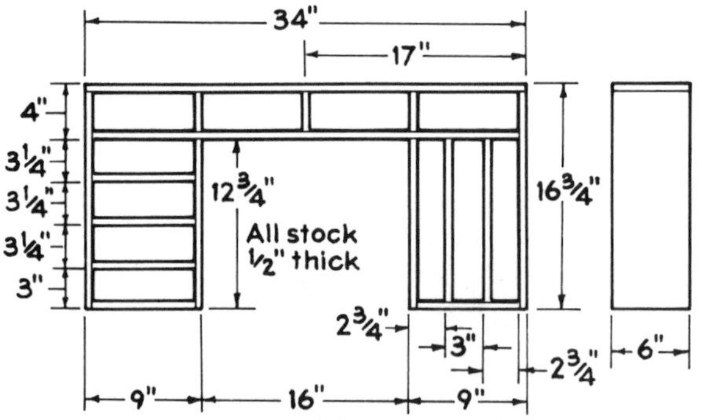
34"
17"
4"
3 1/4"
3 1/4"
3 1/4"
3"
12 3/4"
All stock
1/2" thick
16 3/4"
2 3/4"
3"
2 3/4"
6"
9"
16"
9"

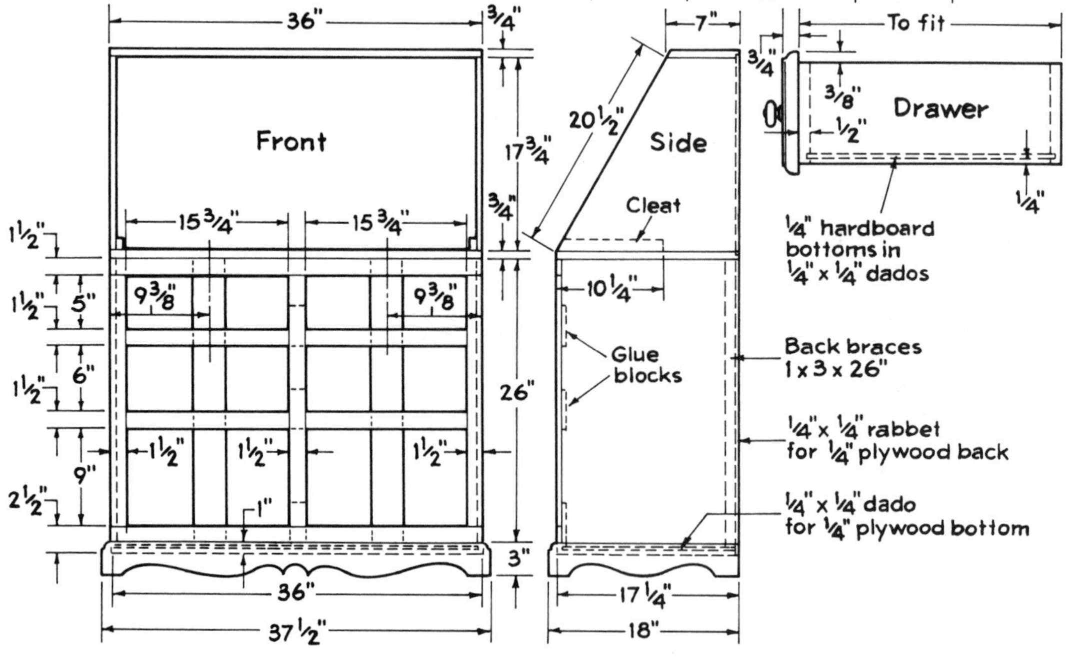
36"
3/4"
Front
17 3/4"
3/4"
15 3/4"
15 3/4"
1 1/2"
1 1/2"
5"
9 3/8"
9 3/8"
1 1/2"
6"
26"
1 1/2"
1 1/2"
1 1/2"
9"
2 1/2"
1"
3"
36"
37 1/2"
7"
20 1/2"
Side
Cleat
10 1/4"
Glue
blocks
17 1/4"
18"
To fit
3/4"
3/8"
Drawer
1/2"
1/4"
1/4" hardboard
bottoms in
1/4" x 1/4" dados
Back braces
1 x 3 x 26"
1/4" x 1/4" rabbet
for 1/4" plywood back
1/4" x 1/4" dado
for 1/4" plywood bottom

BOTTOM CASE

Sides, ¾ × 16¾ × 27", 2 req'd
Bottom, ¼ × 16½ × 35½" plywood, 1 req'd
Back, ¼ × 27 × 35½" plywood, 1 req'd
Horizontal front facers, ¾ × 1½ × 36", 2 req'd
Vertical front facers, ¾ × 1½ × 23", 3 req'd
Divider facers, ¾ × 1½ × 15¾", 4 req'd
Side aprons, ¾ × 3 × 18", 2 req'd
Front apron, ¾ × 3 × 37½", 1 req'd
Back braces, ¾ × 2½ × 26", 2 req'd

Drawer fronts, ¾ × 5¾ × 16½", 2 req'd
Drawer fronts, ¾ × 6¾ × 16½", 2 req'd
Drawer fronts, ¾ × 9¾ × 16½", 2 req'd
Drawer sides, ½ × 5 × 16½", 4 req'd
Drawer sides, ½ × 6 × 16½", 4 req'd
Drawer sides, ½ × 9 × 16½", 4 req'd
Drawer backs, ½ × 5 × 15¼", 2 req'd
Drawer backs, ½ × 6 × 15¼", 2 req'd
Drawer backs, ½ × 9 × 15¼", 2 req'd
Drawer bottoms—¼" hardboard, cut to fit
  drawers

TOP SECTION

Sides, ¾ × 16¾ × 17¾", 2 req'd
Top, ¾ × 7 × 36", 1 req'd
Bottom, ¾ × 16¾ × 36" (cut slightly oversize), 1
  req'd
Back, ¼ × 18¼ × 35½" plywood, 1 req'd

DROP-LID

¾ × 21 × 36", 1 req'd

TOP DIVIDER SECTION

Top horizontal piece, ½ × 6 × 34", 1 req'd
Horizontal piece, ½ × 6 × 33½", 1 req'd
Vertical pieces, ½ × 6 × 16¼", 2 req'd
Vertical dividers, ½ × 6 × 12¾", 2 req'd
Vertical dividers, ½ × 6 × 12¼", 2 req'd
Horizontal dividers, ½ × 6 × 8½", 4 req'd
Vertical dividers, ½ × 6 × 3½", 3 req'd
Drawers—½" material cut to fit
Drawer bottoms—¼" hardboard cut to fit

HARDWARE

Knobs—11 white porcelain knobs
Drawer slides—6 sets
Hinges—2 small butt hinges or piano hinge
Drop-lid support chain

The Bottom Case.   Cut a ¼ × ¼-inch rabbet on the side pieces to accept the back, and a ¼ × ¼-inch dado for the bottom. The bottom and back of the case are cut from ¼-inch plywood. Glue and nail the back to the sides, and then fasten in the bottom, using a nailing cleat between the back and bottom. Then fasten the 1 × 3 back braces to the back. (These will serve as an anchoring point for the drawer guide runners.)

While the glue is drying, cut out the front facers. Install the top and bottom horizontal facers first. The facers can be installed with glue and No. 8 finishing nails or wood screws. The vertical facers are installed next, then the divider facers are carefully measured and cut to fit between. Use backer blocks to reinforce the joints between the horizontal facers and dividers in the center of the case. (The front facers can also be assembled with glue and half-lap joints, and the entire front simply glued in place on the sides.)

Stock for the sides, top and lid of the desk is doweled and glued to make up the widths needed. (See Chapter 5, pages 91–94, for details on using a doweling jig.)

Clamp glued and doweled stock together with bar clamps.

After the bottom case has been assembled, the front facers are installed and clamped.

Divider facers are installed with glue and nails; then backer blocks are inserted behind them for additional support. Clamp the assembly until glue is dry.

When the facers are in place, the top can be fastened onto the assembly with glue and wood screws. (The screws will later be concealed by the top part of the desk.) The best method to make sure that the top fits flush with all sides of the unit is to cut it about $\frac{1}{32}$ inch larger around the perimeters, then sand it flush with the sides and front with a belt sander.

Enlarge the squared drawings for the side and front aprons on one-inch-square paper to make a pattern for the aprons. Cut out the side aprons first with a band saw or saber saw, and shape their top edges with a shaper or router. Sand the bottom edges of the aprons with a drum sander attachment on a radial arm saw or drill press, or on a belt sander as shown. Install the aprons with nails and glue, or by installing glue blocks on the underside.

The front apron is treated a bit differently. Cut the stock to the proper width and shape the top edge. Then miter cut the ends at a 45° angle and test the fit before cutting out the bottom edge.

Apron pieces are cut on a band saw and the curved portions smoothed on a belt sander.

The front apron piece should be test-fitted before the bottom edge is cut.

The Top Section. Make the angled cuts on the side pieces as shown, and cut the top piece to size from a 1×8 board. The back of this section can be constructed with ¼-inch plywood or with 1×8s as shown. If 1×8s are used, fasten the back to the sides by nailing through the sides with No. 8 finishing nails. If plywood is used for the back, cut a ¼×¼-inch rabbet in the side pieces and glue and nail the back to the sides. Test the fit of the top section on the bottom case before proceeding.

Cut the holding cleats to size from 1×1 stock and predrill them in several places to accept #6 1-inch screws. Taper the ends of the cleats to match the taper of the side pieces. Then glue and screw these pieces to the inside edges of the assembly.

Carefully measure the inside dimensions of the top section before constructing the "pigeonhole" divider section. Using No. 8 nails and glue, cut

The side pieces for the top section are cut with a taper in front.

The pigeonhole section for the top is assembled with glued and nailed butt joints.

out and assemble this section to suit your individual needs.

Now put the top and pigeonhole sections in position on the bottom case. Make a light pencil mark around the inside edges of the holding cleats to mark the position. Apply glue to the underside of the unit and glue and screw it in place.

Drop Lid and Drawers.   Cut the drop lid to size and miter cut the top and bottom edges to fit. Thoroughly belt sand both sides of the lid before setting it aside.

The sides and backs of the drawers are cut from ½-inch drawer stock, and the bottoms from ¼-inch hardboard. The drawer fronts are cut from ¾-inch stock to match the aprons. The

Then the drawers are constructed. Drawer fronts can be edge-molded on a shaper as shown, or with a router.

drawer fronts are cut ¾ inch larger in each dimension than the openings (⅜ inch larger on each side). They protrude ¾ inch in front of the case, the same amount as the aprons. A decorative cut is made around the drawer fronts with a router or shaper.

Cut a ¼ × ¼-inch dado in the side and back pieces of each drawer, ¼ inch up from the bottom edge, to accept the ¼-inch hardboard bottom. Glue and nail the front to the sides; then fasten in the back and slide in the bottom. Hold the drawer assembly with a clamp until it is dry.

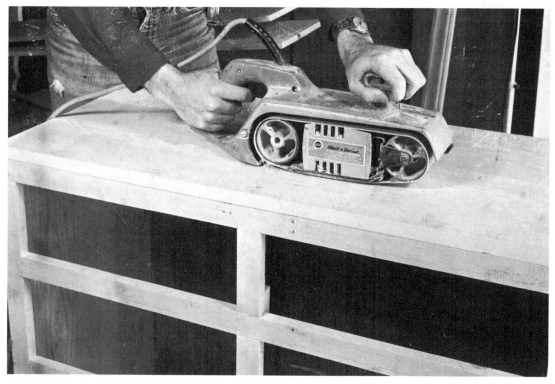

Before fastening the top section to the case, go over all surfaces thoroughly with a sander.

The pigeonhole divider section can then be fastened to the top section.

After the assembly has been stained and finished, drawer hardware can be installed.

The drawers for the top portion are made the same way. (Thinner stock could be used to construct these small drawers if desired.)

Finishing. After all the parts have been assembled, except for the drop lid, set all nails or cover screw heads with wood plugs. Go over all the exterior surfaces thoroughly with a belt sander and make sure that all glue marks and lines are removed. Use a finishing sander to do the final sanding. Mortise the drop lid and the top for the hinges.

Stain all of the exposed surfaces to suit. A varnish or lacquer can be used as finish. (A spray-on lacquer was used on the project shown.) Apply an extra coat of finish on the desk top, where wear will be the greatest.

Now the drawer slides and pulls can be installed and the drawers inserted. Screw in the hinges for the drop lid, and install a brass chain between the top section and the lid as shown.

Finally, a brass chain is installed to hold the lid level in the open position. (Special drop-lid hardware could also be used.)

Heritage Cradle

This cradle is styled in a "Country English" manner and features raised panels inset in rail and stile pieces, plus simple wood turnings. The support stand is characterized by very simple and plain lines.

The support stand is held together entirely with pinned mortise-and-tenon joints so that it can be disassembled for storage. The tenons of the uprights (M) are fitted into the mortises in the stands (O), and the stretchers (N) are fitted into the mortises of the uprights. Pins (P) are driven through each mortise and into the tenons that protrude from the stretchers. If these mortise-and-tenons are carefully made and the pins hammered in lightly, the cradle stand will be as sturdy as if it were glued and screwed together and will support the cradle for all the "gentle rocking" mother desires.

Because it is difficult to avoid glue squeeze-out on raised panel assemblies, no glue is used on the cradle body. The elements of the body are held together with mortise-and-tenon joints and screws. The cradle is held on the support stand with "support pins" (Q) which are pushed through the upright supports (M) and through the end pieces (L) of the cradle.

Building this cradle is not a job to be attempted in only one weekend or without a little previous woodworking knowledge. Assembling it is as tricky as fitting together an intricate puzzle. Because no glue is used in fastening the cradle, each

The heritage cradle features graceful raised panels and simple wood turnings. The stand which holds the cradle is fastened with pinned mortise-and-tenons on the supports and stretchers.

By merely tapping out the pins, the entire cradle support stand may be disassembled and placed inside the cradle for storage.

The support pins of the stand are made to fit snugly in the uprights. There are no nails or screws in the stand, but if the mortise-and-tenons are carefully made, the stand will hold the cradle securely for generations to come.

piece must fit perfectly, and this requires a lot of careful cutting and fitting.

Although the project isn't large, it eats up a lot of material because of the amount of cutting and fitting required. Almost any wood will do, but it looks best when made with a dense, uniformly textured hardwood such as walnut, cherry or hard maple. Even these woods may have some soft pieces, so carefully pick out the hardest pieces of the material you have to choose from. The cradle shown was made with walnut "recycled" from an old church pew. The wood shows a beautiful grain and figure that is impossible to buy today.

A. Side rails, ¾ × 1⅞ × 29½", 6 req'd

B. Side uprights, ¾ × 1⅞ × 17", 4 req'd

C. Side panel dividers, ¾ × 1⅞ × 7¾", 6 req'd

D. Side panels, ¾ × 6⅜ × 7⅞", 8 req'd

E. End stretchers, ¾ × 1⅞ × 20½" (cut to fit), 6 req'd

F. End uprights, ¾ × 1⅞ × 17", 4 req'd

G. End panels, ¾ × 6 × 17½", 2 req'd

H. Bottom support strips (side), ¾ × ¾ × 32", 2 req'd

I. Bottom support strips (ends), ¾ × ¾ × 16", 2 req'd

J. Bottom, ½ × 16⅝ × 32¾" plywood, 1 req'd

K. Turnings, 1 × 1 × 5" block, 16 req'd

L. End top piece, ¾ × 6 × 12", 2 req'd

M. Stand uprights, 1⅝ × 3½ × 33", 2 req'd

N. Stand stretchers, 1¼ × 2½ × 40¾", 2 req'd

O. Stand bottoms, 1⅝ × 3½ × 24", 2 req'd

P. Pins, ⅜ × ¾ × 6", 4 req'd

Q. Support pins, 1¾ × 1¾ × 5" block, 2 req'd

R. Molding, ¾ × ¾ × 96" (cut to fit)

S. Brass strip, ¾" × 36" (cut to fit)

Construction

After all the wood has been surface-planed to the proper thickness, begin cutting out the raised panels. A ¼ × ¼-inch rabbet must first be cut along the back edges of the panels. The angled cuts on the fronts of the panels can be made with a panel-raising cutter on a radial arm saw as shown, or with a regular saw blade on a table saw. The edges of the panels should be ¼ inch thick after the rabbets are cut and the fronts raised. It is important to give the panels—and all other pieces —a good sanding before assembly; the scooped

surfaces will be almost inaccessible once assembly is complete. Be sure not to round the corners in sanding, as this will make the joints loose.

Cut the rails (A,E) and stiles (B,C,F) to width and length, then cut the ¼ × ¼-inch rabbets indicated by the dotted lines in the drawing. A 10° angled cut is made on the ends of pieces E and F. Note that ¼ × ¼-inch tenons are cut along the length of the crosspieces (A,E) to fit into the rabbets cut in the uprights (B,F). The short spacers (C) between the panels have tenons cut on their ends to fit into the crosspieces (A).

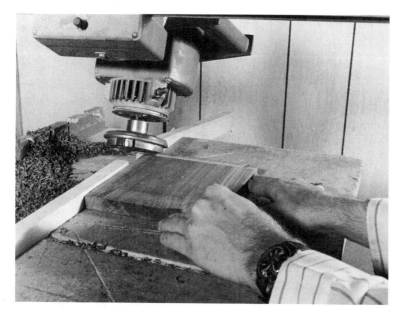

Here, the raised panels are cut on a radial arm saw using a panel-raising attachment. They also could be cut on a table saw or by hand with a Surform tool. A ¼ × ¼-inch rabbet is cut into all four inside edges of each panel.

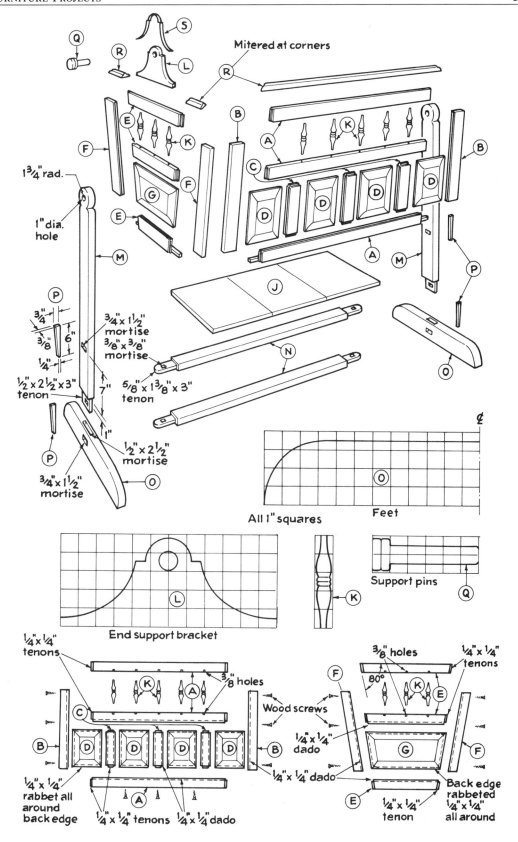

Mitered at corners

1¾" rad.

1" dia.
hole

¾"
4

⅜"

¼"

½" x 2½" x 3"
tenon

¾" x 1½"
mortise
⅜" x ⅜"
mortise

⅝" x 1⅜" x 3"
tenon

6"

7"

1"

½" x 2½"
mortise

¾" x 1½"
mortise

Support pins

All 1" squares   Feet

End support bracket

¼" x ¼"
tenons

⅜" holes

Wood screws

¼" x ¼"
rabbet all
around
back edge

¼" x ¼" tenons   ¼" x ¼" dado

¼" x ¼"
dado

¼" x ¼" dado

⅜" holes

80°

¼" x ¼"
tenons

¼" x ¼"
tenon

Back edge
rabbeted
¼" x ¼"
all around

Turn the small spindles (K), then lay out the sides of the cradle and carefully fit all pieces together to insure that the joints will be good and tight when the cradle is assembled. If the joints fit perfectly, start assembling the cradle by screwing the uprights (B) to the crosspieces (A). When these are in place, drive screws through the crosspieces (A) into the panel spacers (C). Remember to recess the screw heads; these will later be covered with wooden plugs cut from scraps of the wood you're using.

The end pieces are assembled in the same way as the sides. The sides are then screwed to the ends, again with all screw heads recessed. Next, screw the top pieces (L) in place. These must be fitted exactly in the center of the end assemblies, or the cradle won't hang properly. Cut the brass strips to length and fasten them in place over the top pieces (L) with small brass screws. To make the brass strips fit tightly, press them down into the corners with a hardwood block and hammer them into place.

The molding (R) shown is clover-leaf or "screen-door" molding cut with a molding knife set in a planer. The molding could also be cut with a molding blade on a table saw or with a shaper or router. (Always cut this type of molding on the edge of a board that is wide enough to handle safely; then rip to the proper thickness.) The molding is mitered at the corners and applied with No. 4 finishing nails. The heads of the nails are recessed and Plastic Wood or a similar filler applied over the heads.

The bottom support strips (H,I) are cut to size and screwed in place ¾ inch up from the bottom edge of the cradle. Then the bottom is cut to size and screwed in place. A 3-inch-thick piece of solid foam rubber can be cut to fit the contours of the cradle to make a soft yet firm "mattress" for the baby.

Sand the finished cradle as smooth as possible, then set it aside until you finish the support stand. There should be no joints requiring filling, but if there are any, fill them with Plastic Wood stained to match the wood you're using.

Support Stand. The cradle support stand is quite simple to build, but it does require some careful fitting of the mortise and tenon joints so that the cradle will be held solidly and securely.

The panel edges fit into ¼ × ¼-inch dados in the edges of the cross rails and upright panel spacers. All screw heads in the cradle are recessed and later concealed with wooden plugs made from scraps of a similar wood.

All pieces of the cradle are held together using screws (no glue, because it would be difficult to keep glue out of the cracks in the raised panels). The screws are recessed and their heads covered with walnut plugs tapped in place. Then plugs are cut flush with surface as shown and sanded smooth.

Cut all pieces for the stand to rough size. The bottom pieces (O) can be cut on a band saw or with a saber saw. Sand all edges thoroughly. The ends of the uprights (M) can be rounded with a Foerstner bit. When the bit point starts to come through, turn the wood over and drill from the opposite side to insure there will be no splits around the hole.

Very carefully mark the tenons on the uprights (M). These can be cut with a dovetail handsaw or by making repeat cuts on a radial arm saw. With the tenons properly cut, mark the mortises and drill a hole at each end of the mortise outline. Then, supporting the tenon from underneath with a scrap block of wood, cut out the mortise with a sharp chisel.

Carefully mark the mortises on the stands (O) and cut these out, again using a drill and chisel. Note that the side mortise runs through the top mortise on each stand.

The tenons on the stretcher pieces (N) are cut in the same way as those on the uprights (M), but the entire stand should be assembled before the mortises are cut on the stretchers. Place the up-

rights (M) in place on the stands (O), then insert the tenons of the stretchers (N) in the mortises and hold the pieces in position with a long clamp. Now the mortises can be marked in the protruding stretcher tenons. Cut these mortises just a little deeper towards the inside of the tenon so that when the pins are driven in place they will be jammed tightly against the uprights and feet, thereby insuring a solid stand. This step requires a lot of cutting and trial fitting; don't be surprised if you have to do it over several times to get a good fit. The proper fit is of the utmost importance.

When everything fits properly, disassemble and sand the pieces as smooth as possible, making sure not to round the corners or edges of joints.

Turn the support pins (Q) to the proper size and shape. These should fit snugly in the uprights (M) and more loosely in the top pieces (L) of the cradle so that the cradle can swing freely. These pins can be calipered as they are turned to insure an exact fit, and the measurements should allow for final sanding and application of a finish.

Because of the crevices and corners of this pro-

The cradle is held by 1-inch-thick support pins which are turned on the lathe. The pins should fit tightly in the uprights of the stand but more loosely in the top pieces of the cradle to allow the cradle to swing freely.

A brass strip is fitted over the top edge of the cradle and screwed in place to give added strength and a "fail-safe" system should the wood break.

A quality penetrating oil is suggested as a finish for this piece because of its many crevices. (Lacquer or varnish must be sanded after application, and the crevices would make it difficult.) Select a finish that is safe for children.

ject, a finish such as a penetrating oil works better than a surface finish such as lacquer or varnish. (The latter must be sanded after application, and it's almost impossible to properly sand all the crevices.) A good application of penetrating oil will permeate into the corners, insuring an even coating of finish overall. Any finish used must be safe for children, and should be applied several weeks in advance of use of the cradle to allow time for the solvents to evaporate.

TOP

Top, 1¼×5×72″, 4 req'd
Top edging (back), ¾×2½×69½″, 1 req'd
Top edgings (side), ¾×2½×19″, 2 req'd

LEGS

Legs, 3½×3½×28″, 4 req'd

POST-AND-RAIL ASSEMBLY

Top aprons, ¾×5×10½″, 2 req'd
Top apron, ¾×5×63″, 1 req'd
Lower stretcher, 1¼×3×63″, 1 req'd
Lower stretchers, 1¼×3×10½″, 2 req'd
Top facer strip, ¾×¾×63″, 1 req'd
Bottom facer (and drawer support), ¾×2×63″, 1 req'd

Vertical facer blocks, ¾×2×3½″, 5 req'd

Dowels, ⅜×1½″, 32 req'd

Chair buttons, 16 req'd

Wood screws, No. 10×2″, 32 req'd

DRAWERS

Drawer fronts, ¾×4¼×14″, 4 req'd
Drawer backs, ½×3×12¼″, 4 req'd
Drawer sides, ½×3⅜×13½″, 8 req'd
Drawer bottoms, ⅛″ hardboard, cut to fit
Drawer slide spacers, ¼×1×4¾″, 16 req'd
Drawer slide spacers, ¼×1×13½″, 8 req'd
Drawer slides, ¾×1×13½″, 4 req'd

Trestle Desk

This sturdy child's desk is patterned after the Early American trestle-style desks and is made from the traditional material—white pine. However, it has been stained a dark brown for a "country pine" styling. The desk is large enough so that two youngsters can work at the same time, and sturdy enough to withstand rough-and-tumble activities.

Most of the desk is of white pine. The legs are turned from 4×4 posts (3½×3½-inch actual dimensions). Because white pine in the dimensions needed for the posts was not available locally, clear, heart-grade redwood was used instead. If the desk is to be stained dark, painted or antiqued, the darker hue of the redwood won't matter. However, if you wish to stain the desk in the traditional light stain of Early American pine furniture, you will have to acquire the 4×4 stock in pine, or glue up the posts from smaller pieces.

Redwood and pine are both extremely soft and take a bit of care in turning. For best results, use extra sharp tools and turn the pieces at a relatively low speed. Using only cutting tools rather than scraping tools will also help prevent chipping and tearing of the softwood fibers.

The top of the desk and the bottom stretchers are made from 1¼-inch (5/4) white pine stock,

Sturdy trestle desk provides a good piece of furniture for a boys' room. It is made of white pine and finished in primitive Early American style, with dark stain.

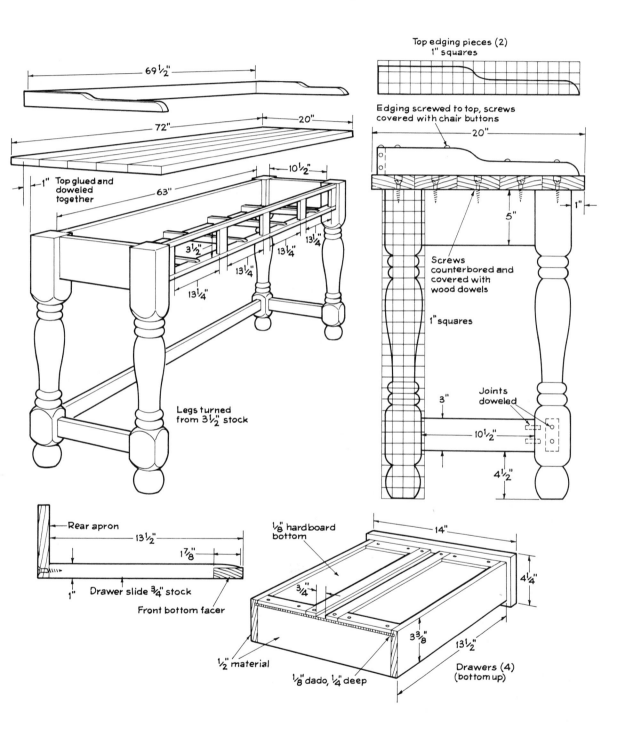

69½"

72" 20"

10½"

1" Top glued and doweled together

63"

3½"

13¼"

13¼"

13¼"

13¼"

13¼"

Legs turned from 3½" stock

Top edging pieces (2)
1" squares

Edging screwed to top, screws covered with chair buttons

20"

5"

1"

Screws counterbored and covered with wood dowels

1" squares

3"

Joints doweled

10½"

4½"

Rear apron

13½"

1⅞"

Drawer slide ¾" stock

1"

Front bottom facer

⅛" hardboard bottom

14"

3/4

4¼"

½" material

3⅜"

13½"

⅛" dado, ¼" deep

Drawers (4)
(bottom up)

which provides an excellent work surface and a sturdy construction. This lumber is available from most leading building-supply and lumber dealers.

Construction

Enlarge the squared drawings to one inch per square and trace them off onto a piece of stiff cardboard to provide a profile pattern for the legs. After turning each leg to the proper size and shape, sand it smooth while it's still in the lathe, using small strips of medium fine sandpaper.

The top of the desk is made with 5-inch pieces of ¾ white pine stock, doweled and glued together. Alternate the grain direction of the pieces so the top won't warp. While the top is setting up, you can glue up the leg assembly.

Cut the top aprons and the bottom stretchers. The top aprons are cut from white pine of ¾-inch thickness, and the bottom stretchers from ¼ pine. Dowel and glue these in place on the legs. Make sure to assemble and clamp the leg assembly on a flat surface so it will sit squarely when the glue has set and the clamps are removed. You will need a couple of long pipe clamps to glue the two leg assemblies, and it may take a bit of help to get the long stretcher and apron glued and clamped properly. Wipe away all glue runs with a cloth that has been dipped in warm water and wrung out; otherwise, the runs will show up later in the stain. (Glue runs, after they have dried, are almost impossible to remove from around the edges of joints such as those between the bottom stretchers and legs.)

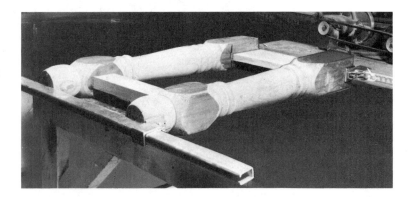

The turned legs of the desk are doweled and glued to the side aprons and stretchers.

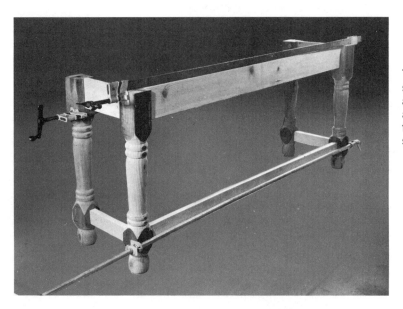

Then the long apron and stretcher pieces are doweled and glued to the leg assemblies. Make sure the frame is absolutely level and square while clamping.

The long horizontal front facers are glued and doweled to the legs; then the facer blocks are glued and nailed to the strips as shown.

After the leg assembly has dried, cut the front facing pieces to size. Note that the bottom facing strip also serves as a support strip for the drawers; it is set horizontally and is glued and doweled to the legs. Position the two short end facer blocks in position next, and glue and screw them to the legs. Then position the top facer strip on these and glue and screw it to the end blocks. Again, wipe away all excess glue, and make sure that all facer edges are flush.

Sand the bottom edges of the glued up top with a belt sander to remove any dried glue and provide a smooth surface for the glue joint with the leg assembly. Cut the ends of the top square and position it on the leg assembly to mark where it fits. Remove the top, and apply glue to the top edges of the leg assembly. Then put it back in place and fasten it to the leg assembly with screws driven down through the top. The screw holes are counterbored and later filled with lengths of ⅜-inch wood dowel. The dowels are glued in place and left protruding above the surface of the top; after the glue has dried they can be sanded down flush with the top. Smooth down the entire top with the belt sander, then follow with a fine finishing sander.

Bevel all edges of the top with a small plane or Surform tool, then use a finishing sander to round all edges and corners. This beveling makes the piece more durable and safer for youngsters, and is also traditional in Early American furniture.

Top Edging Pieces. Enlarge the patterns for the side edging pieces on one-inch-square paper and cut them out with a band saw or saber saw. Then cut the back piece to size. The edge pieces are installed by first boring a pilot and shank clearance hole for each screw, and finally a ½-inch counterbore ½ inch deep. After the pieces have been glued and screwed in place, decorative wood furniture buttons are tapped in place to cover the holes. In most cases you won't have to glue the buttons in place; in fact, gluing will leave a thin white glue line that can't be removed.

Drawers. A decorative cut is made along the edges of the drawer fronts with a cove cutter in

The top is fastened to the frame with glue and countersunk screws. Screw holes will later be filled with dowel plugs.

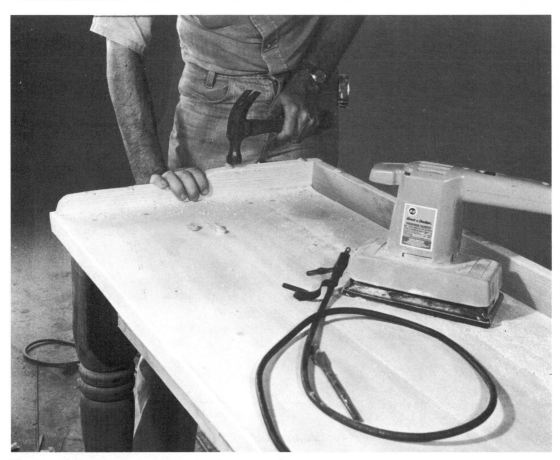

The top edging pieces are fastened to the top with countersunk screws. Decorative wood buttons are used to cover the screw holes.

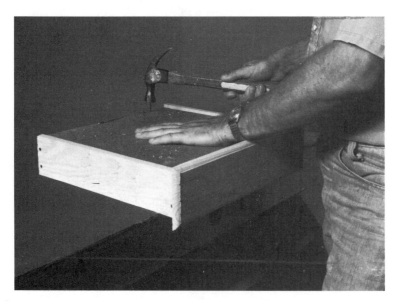

Edges of the ¾-inch-thick drawer fronts are shaped with a cove cutter on a shaper or router. Sides and backs of the drawers are assembled with standard ½-inch drawer stock.

a router or shaper. Assemble the drawers; then add the drawer guide strips to the back edges. The drawers are guided with center runners made of strips of white pine. The runners also act as center braces and help strengthen the front of the desk. To install, cut the pieces to length and width and trial-fit each piece in place. Round the front ends on a band saw and trial-fit again. They should fit snugly but not so tightly that they push the front out of alignment. Apply glue to both ends of each runner and place in position. Use a tiny brad to fasten the front end in place; then place the finished drawer in place and move it around until the front fits flush with no large cracks on any side. Now the location of the back end of the runner can be marked. Fasten the back end in place with a counterbored screw covered with a chair button.

Sand the entire piece to smooth all corners and remove glue lines, etc. Then stain and finish to suit.

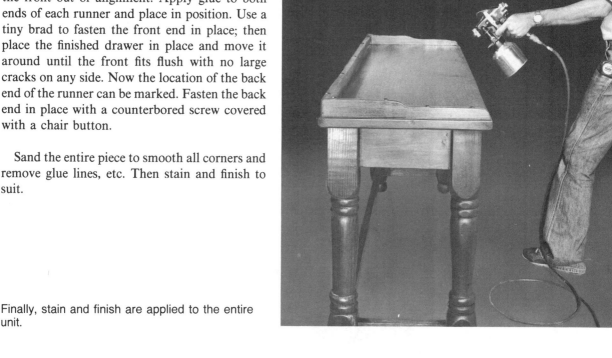

Finally, stain and finish are applied to the entire unit.

A Boy's Bedside Table

Little boys are notoriously rough on furniture, and this project was designed with that in mind. The stand is a simple project; if you have power tools, it will take about an hour to build. The use of 1¼-inch (5⁄4) white pine makes the construction extremely sturdy. This type of lumber is often seen in informal American furniture. It is available at most building supply dealers, but it may have to be ordered.

The stock for the stand shown was a full 14 inches wide. If you can't acquire stock in that width, narrower pieces can be doweled and glued up to make the wide stock.

Construction

The first step is to cut the sides, bottom, and top to size on a radial arm saw or table saw. Using a belt sander or jointer, smooth all edges of the stock. Cut the 1 × 2 braces for the top front and back to size and sand their edges as well.

The table can be fastened together with glue and nails or screws, and the holes concealed with wood putty or wood dowel sections.

Using a carpenter's square, draw a line 2 inches

Bedside table for a boys' room is constructed with sturdy 1¼-inch-thick white pine. This stock is often used for casual furniture.

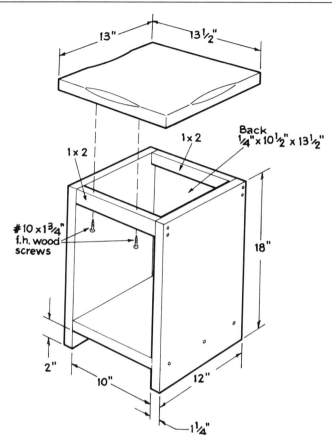

13" 13½"

1×2

1×2   Back
       ¼"×10½"×13½"

#10×1¾"
f.h. wood
screws

18"

2"

10"   12"

1¼"

The stand is put together
with glued and screwed butt
joints. The edges can be
shaped and rounded with a
Surform tool.

up from the bottom edge of each side piece. Align
the bottom piece with these lines, and fasten the
sides to the bottom. Then fasten in the top braces,
fill the nail or screw holes with wood putty, and
allow to dry. Use a belt sander to sand the surface
smooth.

Lightly sand the front and back edges to insure
that they are as smooth as possible. Then turn the
assembly upside down and center it on the top
piece. Mark the position of the sides and back on
the bottom of the top piece. Using a screw-starter
bit, bore two holes for a No. 10 1¾-inch screw
in each support piece. Fasten the top in place with
screws, but no glue. (The screws will hold the top
securely in place, and it's hard to remove glue
squeeze-out from the inside of the project.)

Turn the table over on its face to rout or chisel
a ¼ × ¼-inch rabbet on the inside for the ¼-inch
plywood back. Cut the back to size and fasten it
in place with No. 4 ½-inch screws.

Sand all edges smooth and round them
slightly. Then rasp the top edges as shown in the
drawing. This adds a bit of decorative flair to the
piece and makes it look a little more "professional." The shaping can be done with a Surform
rasp or, better yet, a Surform attachment in a
portable electric drill, followed by a sandpaper
flap wheel. Be careful not to hold the drill in one
place too long, or you'll cut away too much material. Sand the table thoroughly with 200 grit
sandpaper, and stain and finish to suit. A clear
lacquer finish was used on the table shown.

Space Table

The pure simplicity of this little table allows it to blend in with almost any style of interior design. Although not difficult to build, it is an exercise in angle cutting. Because the wood grain itself provides the "character" of the table, select a beautifully figured hardwood-veneer plywood such as the walnut shown.

Construction

Begin construction by ripping the side pieces to the correct width. Use a piece of scrap stock to determine the exact saw setting for a 30° angle cut, and cut both edges of each side piece at this angle. Cut the top edge of each side piece at 45°. Apply glue to the edges of the side pieces and hold them in place with a band clamp until the glue dries.

Decorative space table is constructed with hardwood-veneer plywood.

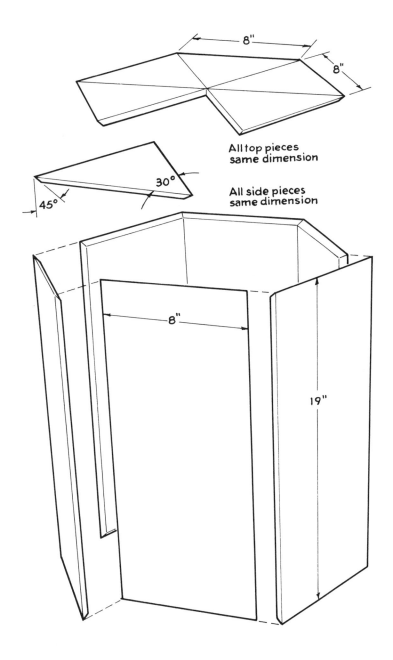

8"

8"

All top pieces
same dimension

30°

All side pieces
same dimension

45°

8"

19"

Each side and top piece for the table is cut at a 30° angle to make up the hexagon. The top edges of the side pieces and the bottom edges of the top pieces are cut at a 45° angle.

Joints of the table are glued and doweled. Use clamp pads to avoid marring the veneer surface.

The top can be made by cutting six triangular pieces to size as shown, or by cutting one hexagonal piece after carefully measuring across the tops of the assembled sides. If you cut the six pieces, lay them out so that the grain runs toward the center of the table. Cut the outside edges at 45°. Drill dowel holes in the edges and insert the dowels before gluing and clamping the pieces on a flat surface. Allow the top to dry overnight; then glue it onto the side assembly.

The table shown was finished with a penetrating-oil sealer.

19

Kitchen Cabinets and Vanities

Building kitchen cabinets, bathroom vanities, and other built-ins is one of the most important facets of woodworking. This type of woodworking can prove invaluable for the homeowner and is a full-time career for many craftsmen. Custom-made cabinets can not only add real value to a home, but also make it more beautiful and practical and personalized. And, of course, the savings realized from doing the job yourself is extremely important. One big advantage of constructing the kitchen cabinets yourself is that you can custom design them to suit your stature. If you are small you can make the countertops a bit lower, and if you're tall, you can add a bit of height to prevent backache from too much bending over at the sink. Remember, however, that any extreme changes may lower the resale value of a home.

Although the construction of kitchen cabinets may seem like a huge undertaking, especially for the beginning craftsman, it really is quite simple, and a great learning phase of woodworking that can be extended into the construction of fine furniture as skill and knowledge increase. Construction of even the largest and most elaborate set of kitchen cabinets is nothing but a step-by-step method of constructing various elements or units, then assembling them together.

Kitchen Cabinets

One of the most important aspects of building kitchen cabinets is designing them so they can be practical, efficient, yet good-looking and easy to construct. Although there are only five basic kitchen designs, the variations are endless. They may be designed with pure convenience in mind for today's busy working woman, or they may be designed for gourmet cooking with places for the extra utensils needed for that hobby.

Design and Layout of the Kitchen

Regardless of the design of the kitchen, it must be planned for convenience. One of the most important things in kitchen layout is efficient use of the cabinets to cut down on unnecessary steps or other tiring work. There are three basic work areas in the kitchen. The first is the refrigerator and food storage area. This should include not only the refrigerator, but a pantry cabinet or storage area for groceries coming into the kitchen. A corner cabinet with rotary shelves is an excellent choice for storage of canned goods, etc. A full-size walk-in pantry can be utilized for larger scale storage. Make sure to observe which way your refrigerator door swings and allow clearance for the door to swing when designing the cabinets.

The second area of the kitchen is the cooking area. There is a wide choice of stove-oven ranges available, or you can also install a cooking top that fits right into the countertop and add a separate oven.

The third area is the clean-up area. In this area the sink cabinet provides storage for supplies and tools used for preparing foods and for clean-up after meals.

In most instances a triangle is utilized to help establish the layout of the kitchen. The total length of the triangle between the three areas should be no more than 22 feet for an efficiently designed kitchen. This is then used to establish the five basic kitchen layouts.

The first is the *in-line* shape with all the cabinets and appliances in a line against one wall. This is primarily used in apartments and other

The motif of kitchen or bathroom cabinets is determined by the design of the doors and drawers. Frame-and-panel doors are extremely popular for both types of cabinets, and they're less prone to warp than solid doors.

areas where space may be limited. It may also be used to allow for a dining area on the opposite wall. The in-line arrangement should only be used on short walls, as stretching the cabinets down a long wall will mean more steps and an inefficient kitchen.

Another popular layout of kitchens is the *corridor* or pullman style, in which the storage cabi-

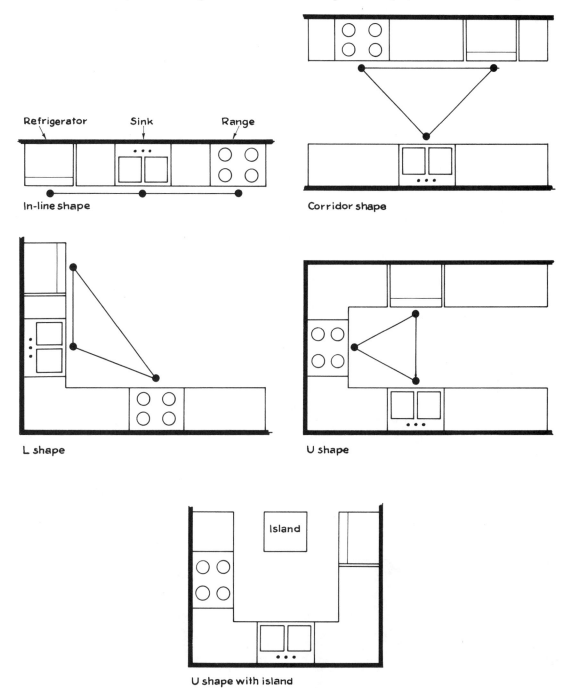

Refrigerator   Sink   Range

In-line shape

Corridor shape

L shape

U shape

U shape with island

There are three basic work areas in the kitchen: the cooking, clean-up, and storage or refrigerator areas. In designing a kitchen, appliances and cabinets should be arranged so that the sum of a triangle drawn between the three areas is between 12 and 22 feet.

nets, countertops and equipment are lined up on facing walls. This is primarily used in a long, narrow room or in a kitchen with a dining area at one end. This type of kitchen must be at least eight feet wide to allow sufficient floor space in the corridor.

The third design, the *L*-shape kitchen, is quite popular for larger kitchen areas. It arranges the counters and appliances along two adjacent walls. This places the work triangle where it is not crossed by traffic, and is one of the most efficient designs. Space along the other two walls can be used for an eating area, laundry or family room arrangement.

The *U*-shape kitchen is an extension of the L-shape and is even more efficient as it provides more space in a smaller area. It is extremely useful in smaller kitchens. Placing one of the work areas on each wall with proper counter and storage space by each is extremely convenient. Rotating shelves in the corner cabinets makes good use of those areas. The peninsula kitchen is a variation of the U-shape kitchen and is quite often used to provide a room divider or bar between the kitchen and family room or dining room.

The fifth type is the *island*. This is a cabinet placed in the center of the kitchen, with other appliances and cabinets arranged in a U or L shape around it. This cabinet may feature a stove or cutting table for the gourmet cook.

In addition to the basic layouts shown there are an infinite number of variations and combinations that may be used to fit a particular kitchen and the homeowner's needs.

Cabinet Designs

In addition to the standardized layouts of kitchens, the cabinets themselves are pretty well standardized. They consist of four basic types: wall, base, oven or tall units, and specialty units such as desks. By combining these four standard types you can make up almost any type of combination you need.

Cabinet sizes are also pretty well standardized

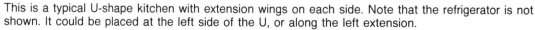

This is a typical U-shape kitchen with extension wings on each side. Note that the refrigerator is not shown. It could be placed at the left side of the U, or along the left extension.

There are basically four types of kitchen cabinets: Base, wall, tall storage or oven, and specialty such as desks. This kitchen features all four cabinet shapes.

to suit standard appliance sizes. The most common width of wall cabinets is 30 inches, and standard depth is 12 inches. They can range in height from 12 inches to 30 inches, depending on the ceiling height and how low you desire them to hang. Base cabinets are usually 36 inches high including the countertop, and 24 inches deep from the front edge of the countertop to the wall. Oven or tall units are usually 84 inches high, but shop-made cabinets can be built to reach a higher ceiling.

Slide-in ranges, separate cooking tops, eye-level ovens, and even free-standing ranges are de-signed to be "built-in" with the cabinetry, and your plan should make the most of this feature. For instance, a dishwasher can be installed under a countertop, and cabinets built to fit around a free-standing oven or refrigerator. (To make a dishwasher more inconspicuous, you can face it with a panel to match your cabinets.)

The spaces over refrigerators can usually accommodate 12-, 15- or 18-inch high cabinets, depending on the height of the refrigerator and the ceiling. The cabinets directly over ranges or cooking tops will normally be 15 to 18 inches high, allowing for a range hood to be installed in them.

Most appliances are designed for the "built-in" look, and kitchen cabinets should be planned with this in mind. Also, be sure to allow plenty of counter space around work centers.

Cabinet Clusters

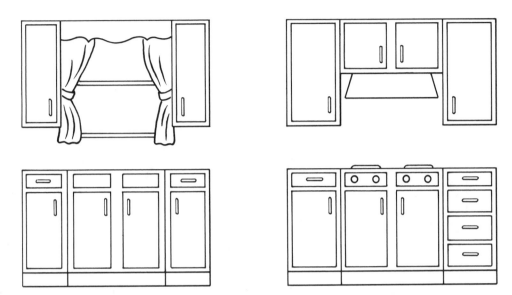

The sink area shown at left can be the basis for an L-shape or U-shape kitchen. Just add a refrigerator and range. If the cooking-top cabinet (shown at right) abuts an outside wall, you can save on materials needed for exhaust venting. Another advantage of a short venting system: It can be cleaned of accumulated cooking grease, which becomes a fire hazard.

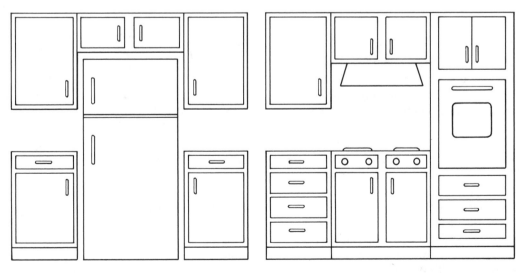

Even a refrigerator can be "built in" with surrounding cabinets as shown at left. If space is more limited, cabinets can be eliminated on the hinge side of refrigerator but counter space should be provided at least on one side. The cook top-oven center shown at right features an oven cabinet with storage space. Again, if the cooking top is next to an outside wall, the exhaust-vent line can be desirably short.

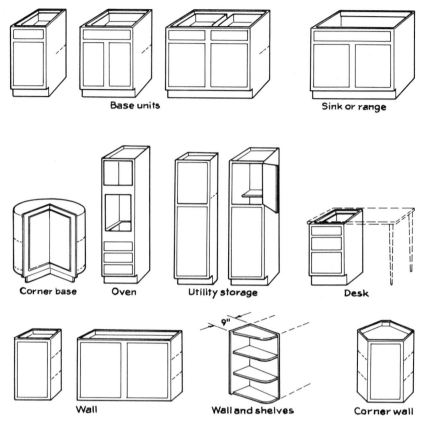

An alternative to building your own cabinets is to purchase them and install them yourself. There are many different styles available—shown are a few of the basic units.

Drawing a Floor Plan

Before you begin to think about construction you should carefully measure the kitchen and make an accurate floorplan drawing to scale as well as an elevation sketch of the proposed cabinets. This will save a lot of confusion later on. With this method you can accurately determine if the kitchen of your dreams will turn out that way.

The floor plan should be done on grid paper. But first, starting at one corner of the room, carefully measure it with a good steel tape and draw a rough, free-hand sketch. It's a good idea to measure everything in inches, and you should measure at about countertop height from the floor. Measure all major appliances and around every door and window. Always measure outside of window and door casings and make a note of the casing width.

After measuring, make a second check of your measurements. Indicate all existing electrical outlets, plumbing pipes, radiators or other items that may affect the location of equipment or which you may wish to change. Then transfer this rough sketch to a grid to make up the scale drawing.

You can also measure the ceiling height and make up a scaled elevation drawing of the cabinets. This will help a great deal in determining exactly how they will look in accordance with the room size.

When making the drawing, allow ¼ to ½ inch of additional space for dishwashers, ranges, trash compactors, washers, freezers or other appliances. You should also allow a minimum of 3 inches additional space for the refrigerator.

Remember that kitchen cabinets not only provide storage space but also counter working space. Minimum counter spaces are considered to be 24 inches on each side of the sink, and 15 inches by the door-opening side of a refrigerator or next to a built-in oven. In many cases you will also want to replace older appliances, and if you do, make sure to make the appliance openings large enough for today's larger appliances.

Some other design suggestions by a professional cabinet builder are: Make sure you utilize all existing space. Don't end a cabinet just short of a corner of a room. If a dishwasher is to be installed make sure it is next to the sink to conserve piping. If you don't install a dishwasher, leave a 24-inch space on one side of the sink cabinet so one could be installed later if desired.

In addition to the standard kitchen cabinet units you can also equip your cabinets with special convenience accessories such as vegetable bins, pull-out bread box, sliding towel bars, cutting boards, drawer dividers, glide-out trash receptacles, and shelf kits.

Materials

In most cases, kitchen cabinets are constructed with plywood. Hardwood-veneer plywood is used for areas that will be exposed, and softwood plywood or particleboard for the unexposed sections. The solid wood facing strips in front are often of the same type of wood as the plywood veneer so that they can later be finished to match it. (Commonly used hardwood plywoods are oak, hickory, ash, pecan, maple and birch.) Pine facers may also be used, but the wood is quite soft and won't take the abuse that the harder woods will. The cabinet back is usually ¼-inch plywood or hardboard. Countertops are constructed with plywood or particleboard and surfaced with plastic laminate or ceramic tile.

Construction

There are two basic methods of constructing kitchen cabinets. The first is to construct the cabinet piece-by-piece on the job, a technique that was once popular but is rarely done today, except for special cabinets that must be fitted into unusual places. The second method is to construct the cabinet in the shop. This is probably the most efficient method, as well as the easiest, and it results in the best cabinets.

Although cabinets were once constructed piece-by-piece and built in on the job, the best method for producing good, sturdy cabinets is to build them in the shop in larger sections, then assemble them in the kitchen.

Regardless of the design of the cabinets, the construction is pretty basic. The decor that personalizes the cabinet is primarily in the doors and the drawer fronts. The construction methods shown here were developed in my father's cabinet shop years ago and have been a proven method of building good solid cabinets. The cabinets are also rodent-proof and easy to build without a large number of production type tools.

Base Cabinets. Custom-constructed base cabinets are usually made in one single length for each wall, except when the unit would be too long to be handled properly. Where two base cabinets meet at a corner you have several options. Since the corner treatment may determine the length of the straight-line cabinets, this decision should be made before beginning construction. See the discussion of corner treatments on pages 367–69.

The first step is to cut the 2×4 bottom risers to the correct length. Then cut the bottom from one piece of ¾-inch fir plywood or particleboard. If the cabinet will have exposed ends, a ¼ × ¼-inch rabbet should be cut in the bottom to accept the back. If the bottom is longer than a single sheet of 8-foot plywood, join separate lengths over the 2×4 supports. The bottom is fastened to the 2×4s with No. 8 cement-coated nails and glue.

Cut the end panels. If both ends are to be unexposed, cut them from fir plywood or particleboard and glue and nail them in place. If an end will be exposed, the inside edges of both ends should have a ¼ × ¼-inch rabbet to accept the ¼-inch plywood back. Cut a decorative kickboard notch in the exposed end with a saber saw, then glue and nail to the bottom with No. 8 finish nails.

Cut the ¾-inch plywood dividers for each section. These should be cut ¼ inch narrower than the sides if the sides are rabbeted. A ¾ × 6-inch notch is cut in their top back corners in which to fit a nailing brace. Turn the construction over and fasten the dividers to the bottom with glue and cement-coated nails.

Construction and installation of the front framing pieces is fairly simple if you follow a step-by-step procedure and carefully trial-fit each piece in place as you assemble it. Standard facers

are hardwood 1×2s (actual dimensions ¾-inch thick and 1¾-inch wide), but the dimensions of the facers can be varied to suit your needs.

The first step is to cut the two horizontal facer boards. Joint both edges of each board smooth. Glue and nail the top facer in place on the sides of the cabinet. All facers are installed with glue and No. 8 finish nails which will later be set and the holes filled. If hardwood is used, it's a good idea to predrill the nail holes to prevent splintering out the wood. If the side of the cabinet will be exposed, the facer is nailed so that its outside edge is flush with the outside edge of the cabinet end. If the cabinet is to be set against a wall, the cabinet is usually made about a half-inch shorter in length and the facer strips allowed to protrude by that amount. This allows you to trim the facer strips to match the angle of the wall if the wall is not perfectly plumb.

Then the bottom facer strip (cut a full-inch wide) is installed. The left and right vertical facer strips are installed next. These must fit between the two horizontal facers, so their ends should be cut smooth with a hollow-ground saw blade to insure a good joint. The stock is held in position after one end is cut, and the opposite end marked. Then the second cut is made and the piece trial-fitted before it is glued and nailed in place.

The same procedure is used to fasten vertical facers to the dividers of the cabinet.

The drawer openings are now covered with facers. These fit between the top and bottom facers and must fit snugly. If you follow the procedure described and carefully fit each piece, you can easily achieve a good professional-appearing cabinet front. Joint all edges of the facer strips before installing them, and make sure all stock is exactly the same thickness. Otherwise, you may have some problems in making the pieces fit flush on the front of the cabinet. Glue and nail the facers in place by driving nails through predrilled holes in the vertical facers. In many cases there will also be a complete row of drawers across the top of the cabinet. This means that there will be points where two facers meet on an upright, and it's not possible to fasten them as securely. In this instance, a backer block is glued and tack-nailed in place behind the drawer facers to help support them.

Next, cut the kickboard piece to length and nail it to the bottom risers.

After installing all facers, set all nails with a nail set and fill the holes with Plastic Wood or wood putty. Allow it to dry, and sand the facer portion of the cabinet. Sand the sides lightly to make sure the side facer strips are flush with the plywood sides. Be very careful not to oversand

this area and cut into the plywood.

Stand the cabinet up and install the 1×6 back brace. Now the back can be fastened on.

Cut 1×2 cleats from a softwood such as pine, and glue and nail them to the inside top edges of the cabinet. Then bore ¼-inch holes in them. These will later be used as pilot holes for the screws that fasten the top in place.

Constructing a Base Cabinet

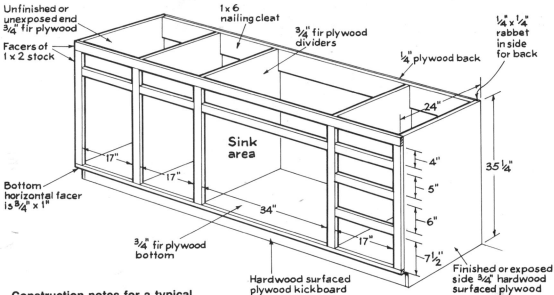

Construction notes for a typical base-cabinet construction: A. Sink opening width should be twice as wide as other divisions to accommodate double doors. B. In most instances it's best to limit a cabinet's length to 8 feet, and join smaller units on the site if necessary to make up a longer length. However, you can install a longer unit by joining the bottom plywood pieces on a 2×4 brace. C. There is a 2×4 support nailed beneath plywood bottom on each end and under each divider. D. All facers are ¾-inch thick solid hardwood stock and should be surface planed at the same time to assure uniform thickness. E. All front facers are of 1×2-inch stock. The bottom horizontal facer, however, is cut to 1-inch width.

The first step in construction is to nail the bottom piece of ¾-inch plywood to the 2×4 risers, using cement-coated nails.

Constructing a Base Cabinet (Cont'd.)

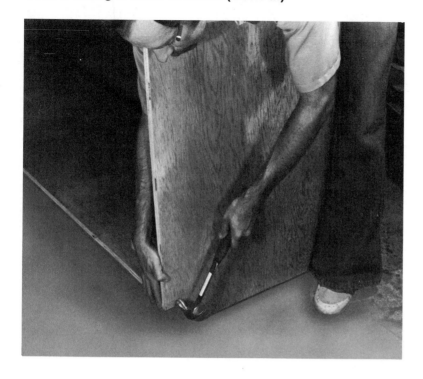

Then nail the ends in place with No. 8 finishing nails. (You can set their heads later.)

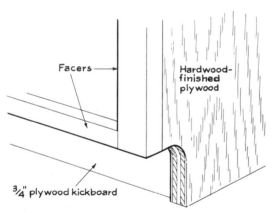

A decorative notch can be cut in the exposed cabinet end. Notch is cut a little shallower than depth of kickboard.

Install the ¾-inch plywood dividers with the cabinet lying on its back, using glue and cement-coated nails.

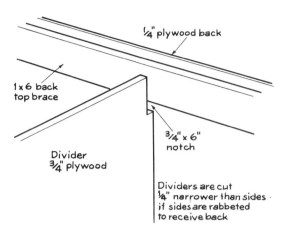

¼" plywood back

1 x 6 back
top brace

¾" x 6"
notch

Divider
¾" plywood

Dividers are cut
¼" narrower than sides
if sides are rabbeted
to receive back

Dividers are notched to allow for the 1×6 bracing to be installed later.

With the cabinet still on its back, install the front facers, starting with the top horizontal facer. Check the placement of the center dividers with a ruler when fastening them in place to the top facer to make sure they join at right angles.

Bottom horizontal facer is cut and nailed in place to the edge of the ¾-inch plywood bottom.

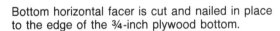

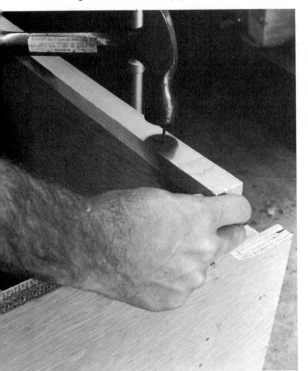

The top edge of the bottom facer must be kept flush with the top edge of the plywood bottom.

Constructing a Base Cabinet (Cont'd.)

Then the vertical side facers are cut to fit between the horizontal facers. Each piece must be carefully fitted.

Note that each vertical facer is cut so that it barely fits between the top and bottom facers, to make the best possible joint at each place.

Vertical facers are then nailed in place with No. 8 finishing nails.

Finishing nails are also driven up through bottom and top facers into each side facer to prevent them from tipping in and out.

Then vertical divider facers are installed. Make sure to position them squarely. They are nailed onto the ¾-inch plywood dividers and also from the top and bottom facers to keep them from tipping.

Drawer facing strips are then installed with glue and nails. Nails are driven through the vertical side and divider facers into the divider strips. These strips must fit snugly, but not so tightly that they force the vertical facers out of line. Clamp holds strips in place until they are nailed solidly.

Constructing a Base Cabinet (Cont'd.)

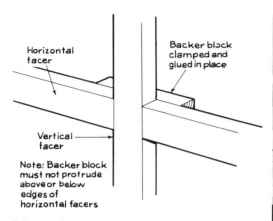

Horizontal facer

Backer block clamped and glued in place

Vertical facer

Note: Backer block must not protrude above or below edges of horizontal facers

A backer block, cut from the same stock as facers, is installed to reinforce horizontal facers which meet at a vertical facer. Backer block must fit exactly and not protrude above or below edges of horizontal facers.

Next, install the kickboard.

All nails are set and the holes filled with wood putty.

Stand cabinet up to glue and nail the 1×6 back support cleat into place.

Then the ¼-inch plywood or hardboard back is installed. Use a square to make sure the cabinet is square. Then nail back in place with No. 4 cement-coated nails.

Cleats to support the countertop are glued and nailed in place with cement-coated nails.

Finally, holes are drilled in the cleats to accept wood screws that will hold the top in place.

Doors and Drawers. With the basic cabinet assembled, the next step is to construct the doors and drawers, and these are the elements that will determine the design of the cabinet. Doors and drawer fronts can be routed or shaped, surface-planed, sawn for a panel effect, or complete with raised panels. The easiest type of drawer or door for most people to build and install is the ⅜-inch lip type. The lip construction allows more leeway for errors and doesn't require as precise fitting as other types. See Chapters 7 and 8 for details on constructing and fitting doors and drawers.

Kitchen sink cabinets often include a false drawer front to help vent moisture that condenses on the pipes beneath. This is constructed in the same way as the drawer fronts; then a radial arm saw or table saw is used to cut the stopped slots.

Doors and drawers should be fitted in place before the finishing operations take place. When they fit properly, the doors, drawers and cabinet facers can be stained and finished, and the pulls, knobs, and other hardware installed.

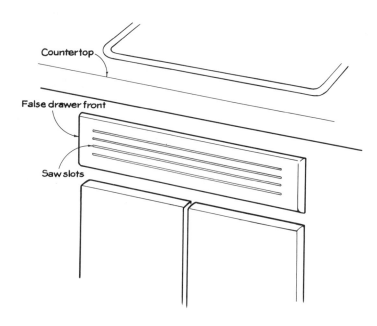

Sink cabinets often include a slotted false drawer front to promote ventilation of the pipes beneath. Slots can be cut with a radial arm saw or table saw. (Details on door and drawer construction and installation are given in Chapters 7 and 8.)

Slide-out storage trays are a useful feature in many cabinets. Trays can be installed with either side- or bottom-mounted hardware, in the same way as regular drawers.

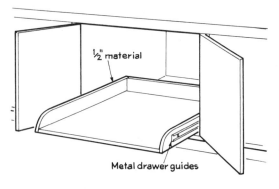

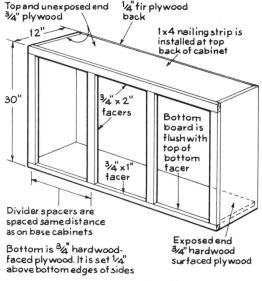

Top and unexposed end ¾" plywood

¼" fir plywood back

12"

1 x 4 nailing strip is installed at top back of cabinet

30"

¾" x 2" facers

Bottom board is flush with top of bottom facer

¾" x 1" facer

Divider spacers are spaced same distance as on base cabinets

Bottom is ¾" hardwood-faced plywood. It is set ¼" above bottom edges of sides

Exposed end ¾" hardwood surfaced plywood

Note: Height may vary from 8" to 36" depending on style and location of cabinet

Shelves are installed with shelf strips or similiar hardware

A typical wall cabinet construction. The construction materials are basically the same as for base cabinets, except that the bottom as well as any exposed sides are of hardwood-faced plywood.

Wall Cabinets. An important consideration in planning wall cabinets is the layout of divider facers on any base cabinets that will be beneath them. If the wall and base cabinets make an identical run, the wall cabinet dividers should be spaced the same way as those on the base cabinets.

Wall cabinets are a bit easier to construct than base cabinets. The first step is to cut the sides and bottom of ¾-inch hardwood-face plywood. Then cut the top from ¾-inch softwood plywood. The back edges of all these pieces must have a ¼ × ¼-inch rabbet cut in them to accept the ¼-inch plywood back.

Glue and nail the top, bottom and sides together. The bottom of the cabinet is set up ¼ inch from the sides so that it can be fastened flush with the 1-inch thick bottom facer.

Then turn the cabinet on its front to install the back nailing cleat, square up the cabinet, and glue and nail the ¼-inch plywood back in place with small cement-coated nails.

The installation of front facers depends on what type of doors and shelf system will be used. If dadoes are cut in the sides or cleats fastened in to provide for adjustable shelves, the vertical side facers will be omitted. (See Chapter 9 for details on installing shelf systems.)

After the interior shelving arrangements have been made, the cabinet is turned over on its back and the front facer strips carefully fitted and installed, just as with the base cabinets. All nails are set and filled, the doors constructed, and the assembly stained and finished.

Corner Cabinets. When two base cabinets meet at a corner, there are several ways to treat the corner. The easiest method is to simply join the cabinets together, leaving just a bit of space between for filler strips. A portion of the corner can then be utilized for storage and might contain a rotary tray accessory. The back walls should be covered with plywood sheets, and all joints between the cabinet sides and backs sealed to make the units rodent-proof. A second option is to construct a separate corner cabinet and join the other two base cabinets to it. Metal circular shelves can be cut to fit the contours of the cabinet, and the front edges of the shelves attached with brace plates to both doors. A push on either door will then bring out the revolving shelves. The third possibility is a larger corner cabinet construction. This takes up a great deal more floor space, but the larger door area makes it easier to get to items stored back in the corner. (See the illustrations on following pages.)

Corner Cabinets

Fasten plywood sheets to wall

Facer runs all the way through

Top brace

Bottom runs all the way through on this side

Solid ¾" plywood side

Filler strips cut ¾" wider than facers and fastened to horizontal facers with glue and screws

The easiest way to deal with a corner is to simply join two base cabinets as shown. However, the space in the corner will be largely wasted because stored items would be difficult to reach.

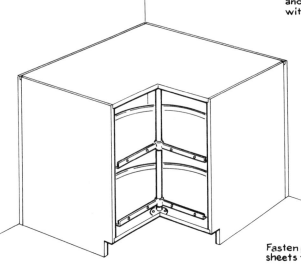

For ease of access and relatively full utilization of corner space, you can install a corner cabinet with Lazy Susan turntable shelves, shown above. The base plate for the Lazy Susan is installed at the front corner. Door panels are then mounted to base plates on the shelves as shown at right. These panels rotate inside the cabinet as the shelving circumference is rotated past the door opening.

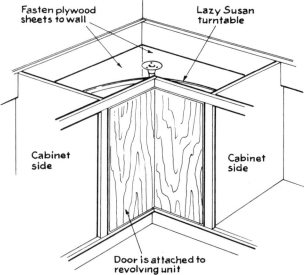

Fasten plywood sheets to wall

Lazy Susan turntable

Cabinet side

Cabinet side

Door is attached to revolving unit

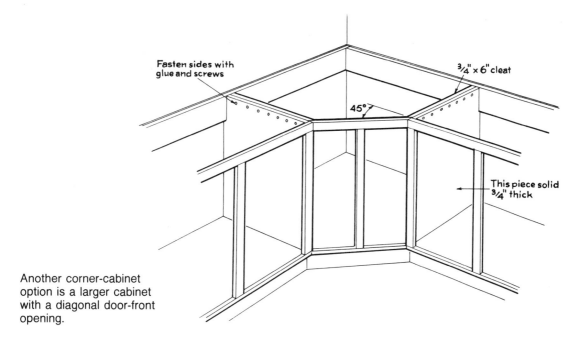

Fasten sides with glue and screws

3/4" x 6" cleat

45°

This piece solid 3/4" thick

Another corner-cabinet option is a larger cabinet with a diagonal door-front opening.

Installation of Cabinets

Whether you construct your own cabinets or use factory-made ones, the installation is basically the same. The base cabinets are usually installed first, but you can also install the wall cabinets first. If you install the base cabinets first, you will have to lift the wall cabinets up over them. However, the base cabinets also provide a convenient support for the wall cabinets. If the wall cabinets are installed first, you can construct a support that extends from the floor.

If you're remodeling an old kitchen, the first step is to shut off the water to the sink and disconnect the stove and refrigerator. Then move these entirely out of the room so you will have plenty of working room. Remove all old cabinets, tops, baseboards, molding, and anything else that will be in the way of the new cabinets. Then patch any walls that need fixing. This is also a good time to make sure the bottom corner of the walls and floor is well patched.

To install the new cabinets, first locate the position of all wall studs where the cabinets are to be installed. Mark their locations so they can easily be seen when installing both the base and wall cabinets. Remove all baseboards and other items that might be in the way of the cabinet installation. Then locate the highest point on the floor with a level and make a mark. This is important for both installation of the base and later the wall cabinets. Use the level to mark the true vertical and horizontal level lines on the walls as well. Test the corners for squareness and note any irregularities.

If the assembly includes an L-shaped or U-shaped corner cabinet, start the installation in a corner. Slide the cabinets into their approximate position. If using separate units, fasten them together with screws, spacing the screws at both top and bottom to hold the units securely.

Make sure all cabinets are in the correct position, then check for levelness with the level laid from front to back of the cabinet. Pull the cabinet out and insert wedge-shape shims between the wall and cabinet if necessary to compensate for unevenness in the wall. Then turn the level to check for levelness along the length of the installation. Starting at the low point of the floor, insert shims as needed between the cabinet bottom and the floor. Take your time with this operation and make sure you have the cabinet properly leveled and shimmed solidly in place. This is one of the most important aspects of cabinet installation and can make the difference between a high quality set of cabinets and one that is frustrating to work at because of an unlevel top.

After all cabinets have been leveled both from front to back and lengthwise, fasten them to the

(*Text continues on pg. 372*)

Installing Cabinets

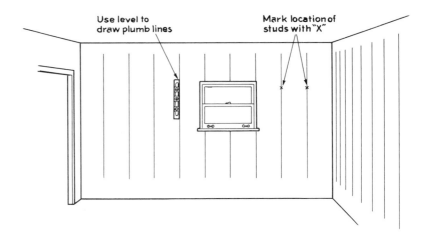

When installing new cabinets, it's best to move all appliances out of the room so you'll have plenty of working space. Locate and mark the positions of all wall studs where cabinets are to be installed, and draw a plumb line at each stud location.

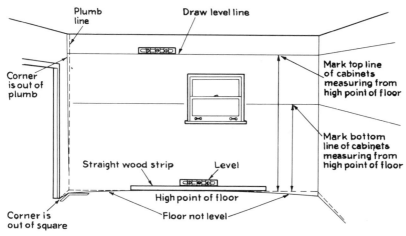

Plumb the corners of the room as well, and mark the high point of floor. Then mark the top and bottom edges of wall cabinets, measuring from high point of floor.

Put the base cabinets in place, and check the level across each cabinet as shown at left. Insert shims between wall and cabinet if necessary to set cabinet level. (Wooden shingles make excellent shims.) Then turn the level lengthwise on cabinet, starting at high point of floor. Insert shims as needed to bring lower portions up to level. When all cabinets are level, they can be fastened to wall studs with 2½-inch No. 8 wood screws through the top support cleat and cement-coated nails through the plywood back.

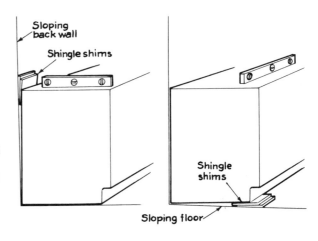

Wall cabinets are usually installed after the base cabinets are in so that support jack can be set on countertop. However, jack can also be constructed to extend from floor if wall cabinets are to be installed first.

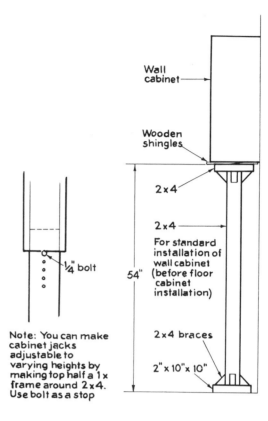

Wall cabinet

Wooden shingles

2 x 4

2 x 4

54" For standard installation of wall cabinet (before floor cabinet installation)

2 x 4 braces

2" x 10" x 10"

¼" bolt

Note: You can make cabinet jacks adjustable to varying heights by making top half a 1 x frame around 2 x 4. Use bolt as a stop

Below left: With adjoining wall cabinets supported by a jack, fasten them loosely together with screws driven through the facers. This temporary fastening makes it easier to level them with shims. *Below middle:* Check for levelness across the cabinet bottoms, and insert shims as necessary under the support jack to bring them to the level line. *Below right:* Check the front of the cabinet for plumbness, and insert shims between wall and cabinet if necessary. When cabinet is perfectly level and plumb, fasten it to wall studs with screws through the nailing strip as well as cement-coated nails through the plywood back.

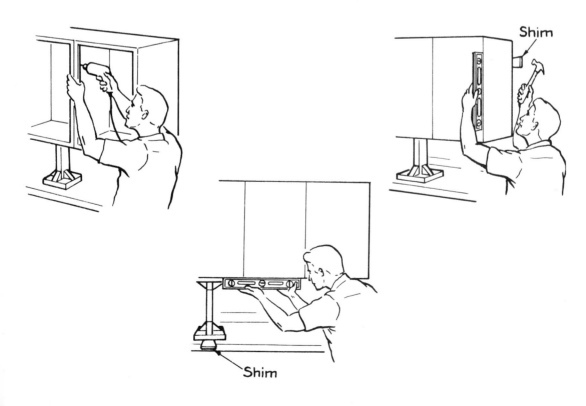

Shim

Shim

Installing Cabinets (Cont'd.)

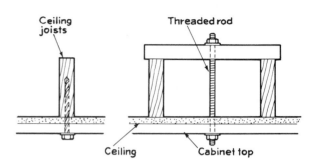

Overhead storage cabinets can be suspending from the ceiling. They must be securely bolted directly to the ceiling joists. If tops of joists are exposed, additional framing can be laid across the top to create a stronger support as shown at right.

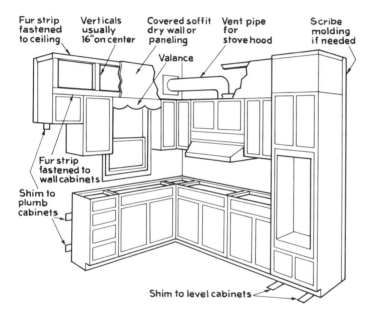

Notes on cabinet installation:
A. When all cabinets have been leveled and fastened to wall studs, use a chisel to trim the shims flush with the cabinets. B. A valance strip such as shown can be installed to conceal a fluorescent light fixture, or simply for decoration. It is usually cut to size after the side cabinets have been installed. C. When ceiling height is more than 84 inches, soffit panels are often installed over the wall cabinets. Soffit is constructed by fastening furring strips to the ceiling joists and to the tops of wall cabinets. Vertical strips are then fastened in at 16-inch intervals and the soffit panels attached.

wall studs with 2½-inch No. 8 wood screws. These are driven through the top back brace piece and into the studs. Then use cement-coated No. 8 nails to fasten the back into the studs as well.

Using a chisel, cut off the shims flush with the edges of the cabinet both on floor and wall. Then cut quarter-round molding and install to fill in and conceal the crack between the cabinet and the floor.

The wall cabinets are then installed by using special cabinet "jacks" as shown on page 371 to hold the wall cabinet 18 to 19 inches above the countertop. The jack can also be made adjustable as shown to vary the height, as when the cabinets must be installed up against a soffit.

Starting at one end or corner cabinet, position

it in place on the braces and make sure it is square and level and plumb. Then fasten in place with cement-coated nails driven through the plywood back and into the studs. (If the cabinet has a hanging cleat, use screws to fasten it to the wall studs.) Install the next adjoining cabinet in the same manner, joining them together as needed to make up the cabinet run, and again making sure you keep them all level and plumb by using shims as needed. Make absolutely sure the cabinet is installed level horizontally, or the doors won't work properly. Then check for plumbness at the front as you go.

When installing oven cabinets, follow the directions of the manufacturer of the oven on constructing and installing that particular cabinet.

Overhead storage cabinets can be a useful addition in kitchens provided with a bar window. Cabinets can be either fastened to ceiling joists or wall-mounted with a soffit above, as shown here, depending on ceiling height.

Above all make sure this cabinet is level and that the oven cutout is level.

Additional Notes on Installation

There are a few common problems that arise in cabinet installation, and these can usually be solved quite easily. The first and most frustrating problem is misaligned doors. Very few rooms have perfectly level and plumb floors and walls, and even a slight unevenness will cause problems in operating the doors and drawers. For this reason, pay particular attention to the level and plumbness during installation. If a door still doesn't open smoothly, you can usually correct the problem with additional shims between the cabinet and the floor or wall. If this doesn't help, you

may have to remove the doors and realign them to get them to work properly.

Another common problem is a drawer front that doesn't fit flat against the facings. This is usually caused by the drawer hardware shifting a bit. Readjust the nylon roller support to allow the drawer to fit back evenly with the facings. If a drawer rubs on the lower rail of the facers, this is usually caused by absent nylon rollers or out-of-adjustment rollers. Again check and realign.

One of the worst problems and one that has been experienced at one time or another even by professional cabinet-makers is a set of cabinets slightly too long to fit between the walls. If you have provided the cabinets with extended facers, this won't be a problem. But if the side facers fit flush with the sides you will have to tear up and redo one side.

Constructing the Countertop

Many craftsmen like to construct the countertop after the base cabinets have been installed. This way, measurements for the countertop can take into account any shims or other adjustments that have been made in installation, and the countertop constructed to cover any out-of-squareness, extra wide cracks between the wall and cabinet back, or other irregularities. However, it is easier to construct the top in the shop, then install it on site.

Countertops may be covered with either plastic laminate or ceramic tile. There are two basic tops that can be utilized for plastic laminate. The first is a "cove" top or one that has a rounded backsplash and front edge. This type of molded top cannot be constructed in the shop. It is usually ordered from building supply dealers or cabinet shops to fit the cabinet, and generally comes complete with a plastic laminate of your choice installed. The second type of base is one you construct yourself with plywood or particleboard. The basic construction is the same whether you plan to cover it with plastic laminate or tile.

The first step is to cut the top from ¾-inch softwood plywood or particleboard. It should be cut about ¼-inch wider than the cabinet, and its dimensions may also take into account any irregularities created during installation of the cab-

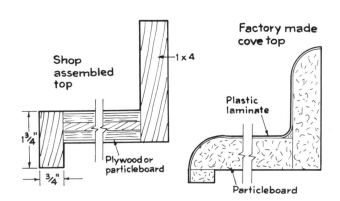

There are two basic countertop styles, standard and cove top. The standard-construction tops can be made in the shop. The cove tops must be ordered to fit.

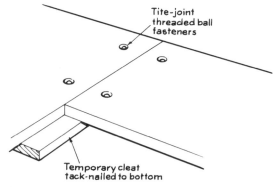

The two pieces of an L-shape counter can be fastened with Tite-joint fasteners (see page 53). Dowels and glue may also be used. A temporary cleat is tack-nailed to the joint to hold the pieces in place until they are installed.

When the countertop has been assembled, it is installed with screws driven through the ¼-inch pilot holes predrilled in the cabinet cleats.

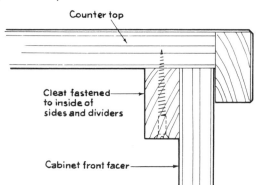

inet. Then cut a front facer strip of ¾-inch soft-wood lumber such as pine and nail and glue it in place as shown. (Alternate methods of treating the edge are shown in Chapter 12.) A backsplash piece can be fastened in place as well. Apply plastic laminate to the top as shown in Chapter 12.

If the countertop is to make a turn, as on an L-shape cabinet, join the two pieces solidly with Tite-joint fasteners as shown.

Installing the Countertop

Place the countertop in position on the cabinet and fasten it in place by driving screws up through the predrilled wood cleats on the cabinet

sides and dividers. Be sure not to drive the screws so far that the screw points protrude into the top surface.

Butcher Block Top

A butcher block countertop can be constructed by laminating strips of hardwood such as maple. This is a very decorative top, and practical as well. It is constructed with 1- or 2-inch maple strips and assembled as shown. Allow the glue to dry thoroughly, then use a belt sander or planer to smooth it down. This type of top is usually finish-sanded, then rubbed with vegetable oil. No other finish is used.

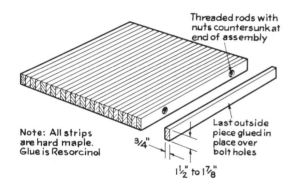

A butcher block countertop or countertop insert has many uses. Top can be assembled with strips of maple or other suitable hardwood.

Constructing Vanity Cabinets

Although vanities can be built in place, the best method, as in constructing kitchen cabinets, is to build them in your shop, then install them in place after they're finished. The countertops are usually installed after the cabinet is in place. The main thing in an installation of this kind is to measure very carefully in the planning stage. In addition to room clearances, the width of the entryway door as well as of any halls you might have to carry the unit through is important, particularly if the vanity is one of the longer double-sink units.

Start with a simple drawing of the unit planned. The example shown is fairly typical, and also shows the solution to a common problem. The cabinet is angled so it can fit against a door, yet it provides full-depth storage along most of its length.

A vanity can be built with solid wood or a combination of solid wood and plywood. If a vanity installation is surrounded by three walls, as it commonly is, the entire vanity can be made from economical softwood plywood except for the front. The front can be made of hardwood, a hardwood plywood, or white-pine plywood if it is to be painted. The front facings should be made of solid wood.

The basic construction of a vanity is the same as that described for kitchen cabinets. The ¾-inch plywood or particleboard bottom is first fastened to 2×4 risers. Then the ends are fastened in place and any dividers fastened to the bottom. If using solid wood for the ends, you will have to dowel and glue pieces to make up the wide stock. The 1×2 facers are carefully measured and trial-fitted before they are fastened in place so that they will not force the assembly out of line. Then the back nailing brace is attached, the frame checked for squareness, and the ¾-inch plywood back fastened in place. Nailing cleats are attached to the ends and dividers to anchor the countertop.

There are several materials available for use as vanity countertops. In addition to ceramic tile and the custom-made or shop-made plastic laminate tops mentioned earlier, there are a few newer materials that are increasingly being manufactured for home use. Cultured marble tops are now available in many colors and in quite a large range of standard widths and lengths. These can be purchased with a single or double lavatory bowl already molded in. Some manufacturers will custom-build a top to size. Corian countertops are similar in appearance to cultured marble, but the material can be cut with regular power woodworking tools. Corian can be purchased in sheets, or as a countertop assembly with backsplash and single or double bowls molded in.

Bathroom vanities are constructed in the same manner as kitchen cabinets. Shown is a fairly typical construction with a double-door sink partition.

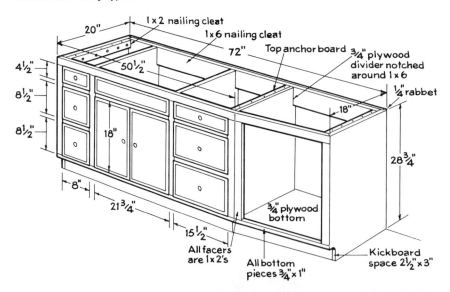

As with kitchen cabinets, the principal design feature of a vanity is the style of the doors and drawers.

There are many types of ready-made countertops for use on vanity cabinets. Shown is a cove top with marble-pattern plastic laminate applied.

PART V

The Cabinetmaker's Workshop

20

Planning a Workshop

The woodworker who merely wishes to keep a few tools on hand for occasional home repair jobs or to build small projects doesn't need a spectacular workshop. In fact, the kitchen table often suffices, as can a basement corner. The serious cabinet and furniture builder, on the other hand, needs a good-size workshop with a full complement of tools. In the following chapters, the hand and power tools that are needed for advanced woodworking are itemized. This chapter will concentrate on the shop itself: its location and layout. The shop discussed here is designed primarily for the advanced woodworker whose hobby is furniture or cabinet building, or for the one-man commercial cabinet shop.

Because of the expense involved, very few people build a workshop when just beginning to work with wood. Most folks have to grow into such a need, accumulating tools and cabinets as they progress. This often makes for a haphazardly designed, inefficient shop. Even if you don't have all the power tools and cabinets you need at the start, it's a good idea to sit down and make a working drawing of the shop you ultimately want to have. You can then work towards that overall plan, purchasing tools or building storage cabinets, tables, and workbenches as you go along. The end result will be an easy-to-use, efficient workshop.

Location

The first step in planning the shop is the location. There are two places that are most often used—the basement or a portion of the garage. Although both are common, they have a few disadvantages. In the basement, unless it is a walk-in type, you will have a bit of trouble getting large materials in and even more trouble getting large pieces of furniture or built-ins out. An attic is even worse. I have heard of shops set in an attic, but have never seen one that was practical. (I once built a speed boat in an attic, after having determined that the boat would fit through the window. But I hadn't noticed the power lines outside that obstructed the window. I had to hire a crane to come and lift the boat out of the window and over the power lines.) A second disadvantage of a basement is often humidity. This can really play havoc with metal tools, and in some locales tools can be ruined in a couple of weeks. If you must use a basement as a workshop, make sure there is plenty of ventilation to prevent moisture problems. One advantage of the basement shop is that it is temperate: cool in summer, warm in winter, and you won't have to provide supplemental heat.

A garage is also often used, but sometimes this means leaving the car out in the weather. Another problem with garage workshops is that they are frequently situated close to the street, and opening up the garage door while working exposes tools to the view of passersby.

A better choice would be a separate room of the house, perhaps a remodeled porch. However, the best choice for a shop is a separate building. Not only does this keep the sawdust and mess away from the house, but it can also usually be designed for your particular needs. One of the disadvantages of a separate building is that you will need to run wires for electrical power to it and provide separate heating or cooling.

The separate outdoor shop should be a minimum of 24×24 or 24×30 feet. This provides enough room for most power tools, storage of materials, and work space.

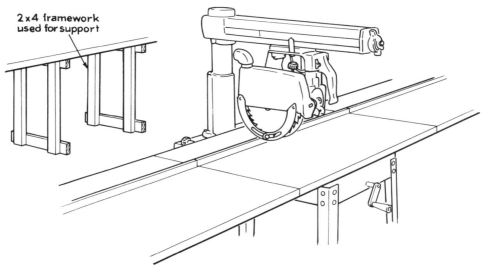

2 x 4 framework
used for support

Tools which are used extensively should be set up to their best advantage. Since a radial arm saw is primarily used as a cut-off saw, the shop layout should allow space on both sides of it for extension tables.

Table saws are primarily used for ripping. A table extension placed in back of the saw will enable you to rip even large panels by yourself. Table can also be wired and used as a work surface with other tools (see pages 393–95).

Layout of the Shop

Once you have determined the right location for your shop, the next step is the shop layout. Even the biggest shop can be frustrating if it is not designed for efficient use of tools and easy transporting of material in and out of the shop. On the other hand, a small shop can be extremely efficient if designed properly.

One of the most important aspects of the shop layout is proper placement of the stationary tools. Each should be usable without having to move it, and also should not obstruct the use of another tool. Workbench and work tables should be exposed to natural light whenever possible. It's a good idea to make a ¼-inch scale drawing of the shop, then make scale cutouts to represent the tools. Place these on the drawing of the floor plan and move them around until you find the best place for them.

Probably the two most important tool placements for a cabinet shop are the radial arm saw and the table saw. Each of these tools does a specific job better than the other, and each should be set up permanently so it can be used most efficiently. The radial arm saw should be set against one wall with table extensions on either side. This allows you to use the saw for cut-off work and to hold long stock in place without having to have someone hold one end.

The table saw is most often used for ripping boards. It should be placed in the center of the room with a work table behind it which is the same height as the saw table. Long stock or sheets of plywood can then be ripped quite easily because they're supported by the work table as they come off the saw. The work table can also be used for assembling items when the table saw is not in use. It's a good idea to wire the table with electrical outlets, making it a "hot table."

Tools that are not used so frequently, such as a planer, can be placed near a garage door or other door opening. Long stock can be pushed into the tool from outside or extend outside through the door if necessary.

Ideally, a shop should be set up so the materials

A planer can be located near a door opening so that long stock can extend outside. An alternative is to set up collapsible sawhorses with roller supports when the tool is in use.

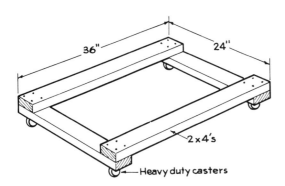

A shop-made dolly makes the transport of materials and large projects much easier.

come in one door and are stored near that door so you don't have to thread bulky materials around the tools. Finished projects should be completed near another door, so you can then move them out easily without having to move tools or materials. A simple shop dolly can really take the hassle out of moving large projects such as cabinets. The dolly can be made of four 2 × 4s as shown, with casters installed on the bottom.

It's best to work under plenty of natural light. This means you need large windows, even at the expense of some wall space. Of special importance is to have a workbench situated near a north window. This provides even lighting without the glare that comes from the other directions. Naturally, you will need large doors to move items in and out, and if they're screened they can do double duty in warm weather by letting light in. Many shops have garage doors on one end for ease in getting out large projects. If you use these, you may wish to choose those that are translucent for more light. Of course, another alternative for natural lighting would be to install translucent plastic panels in the roof of the shop as well.

Wiring

A full woodworking shop requires a well designed electrical set up. This will probably be a matter of personal choice to meet your particular needs. However, one thing to remember is to provide plenty of extra capacity for the future. Even if you don't have some of the larger tools, such as a planer, you may acquire them in the future, and having to add circuits or install a larger fuse box can be a problem.

Although the electrical requirements of a full woodworking shop are somewhat greater than those for a hobby shop, the three basic requirements are the same. To be safe and efficient it must have proper lighting, adequate power, and the system must provide for proper grounding of all tools.

Naturally, the location of the shop will be significant in determining the electrical lighting requirements. If the shop is located in a dark basement, it will require more lights than a remodeled garage or porch with many windows. There are two basic ways to install artificial lighting: you can flood the entire shop with light, using fluorescent lighting strips or panels, or you can install a few main lights, then provide fixtures over individual tools. I prefer using as much natural light as possible, with a main light and individual lights over the tools used as needed. However, the fluorescent lighting plan is probably a much more economical system. If using separate lights for the individual tools, the lights should be situated to best illuminate each type of tool. All lights in the workshop should be covered with a protective shield. There should be plenty of lighting over the workbench and work tables.

Whether the workshop is attached to the house or not, it should have its own service center panel (fuse or circuit breaker box). The service center for a woodworking shop should be no smaller than a 100-amp, 240-volt panel. This not only provides an adequate number of circuits but will also handle overloading when starting heavy motors such as the 3- or 5-horsepower motor used on a planer or other heavy woodworking tool. Some tools, such as a planer with a 5-hp motor, will run better on a 240-V circuit.

Probably the most frustrating thing for a

A basement shop can be lighted with low-cost fluorescent fixtures. This shop also has strip plugs on the wall to provide a large number of receptacles around the room.

Individual lights may also be required for some tools.

The shop should have its own service center panel, with a capacity of at least 100 amps.

woodworker is to have to repeatedly unplug one power tool to plug in another. A well-designed workshop will have outlets spaced no less than 6 feet apart around the entire room. There should also be strip outlets located under the front side of the workbench and on any worktables. This lets you plug in several small portable tools such as drills or power screwdrivers. Each of the outlets must be grounded, and above all don't break off the grounding ear of tool cords. Unless the shop is pretty fancy, surface-mounted receptacles will do quite nicely. One thing that should be avoided is a tangle of extension cords on the shop floor. Not only is this dangerous from the electrical standpoint, but you could trip and fall while a power tool is running, with disastrous results. It's not a bad idea to install an outside receptacle next to the door in case you later want to build larger items outside. In this case, make sure the receptacle is protected by a ground fault unit to prevent the possibility of electrical shock when using tools in damp weather.

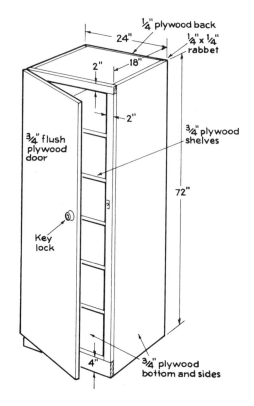

Tool Storage

Anything from second-hand desks and old lockers to custom-built cabinets with dividers and drawers can be used for storing tools. Old metal

Metal gym lockers make good storage cabinets for portable tools and other shop items. A cabinet can also be constructed for this purpose as shown.

A machinist's chest can be constructed for storage of small items such as chisels and calipers.

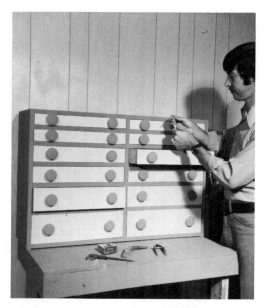

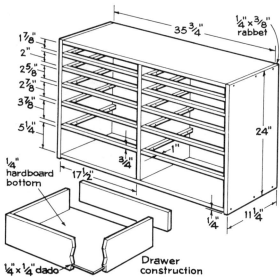

Drawer construction

Portable electric tools can also be stored in individual cases.

gym lockers are excellent for portable power tool storage. They often come in units of 4 to 6 lockers, and they can be bolted to the wall.

Many hand tools can be hung on hooks above the workbench. This includes saws, hammers, screwdrivers, and chisels. Special racks and cases can be made to hold specific tools. Drawers in the workbench can hold items such as planes. One excellent tool storage unit is a machinist's chest.

This can be a shop-made item, and it can be used to hold special tools such as tap-and-die sets or veneering equipment. In many cases, the stands of larger stationary tools can also be equipped to hold the special jigs and tools needed for those specific tools. A pegboard tool rack can hold many items such as clamps. The pegboard hooks can then be rearranged as you add more tools to your shop.

Hand tools should be stored in a wall display rack so that they're out of the way, yet within easy reach.

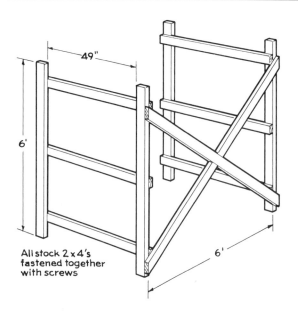

49"

6'

6'

All stock 2 x 4's
fastened together
with screws

A shop-made storage rack will hold plywood panels securely, and will keep them from warping.

Material Storage

Proper storage of lumber is extremely important. Not only must it be stored in a dry, cool place, but it should be well supported and aired so it won't warp or twist. A rack for plywood, hardboard, and other similar large 4×8 sheets of material can be constructed as shown. If the ceiling of the workshop is left unfinished, a rack to hold lumber and moldings can be built by fastening 2 $\times$ 4s to the ceiling joists. This keeps the different types of stock separated and well supported.

Probably the biggest material storage problem is presented by nails and screws and other similar items, and there are almost as many methods of storing them as there are individual shop owners. There are small chests with many individual drawers available for this purpose, or the items can be stored in jars on a shelf. Cardboard boxes

can also be used, and of course these should be labeled on the outside.

And last, paint storage. Solvents and paints should be kept in a separate room, preferably the finish room, and placed on wood shelves, with finishes, stains and specialty items stored separately. In addition, you will wish to have a storage place with drawers in it for storage of small cans of paint, brushes, and other painting and finishing equipment.

Workbenches and Work Tables

You need at least two work areas in a shop; actually the more the better. But you must also remember to leave a portion of the floor clear so you can assemble large cabinets and furniture pieces. The ideal situation for a one- or two-man

A rack for storing lumber and moldings can be constructed by fastening 2×4s to ceiling joists.

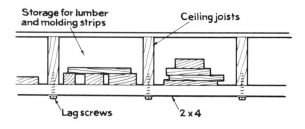

Storage for lumber
and molding strips

Ceiling joists

Lag screws   2 x 4

A workbench should provide some storage space, as well as table room for assembling projects. This European-style purchased bench has two woodworking vises and pop-up "dogs" to hold stock being planed or sanded.

shop seems to be a large workbench and a center worktable with a work surface of 4×8 feet. As mentioned before, this can also be an extension table for the table saw, wired with plug-ins on all sides. The table in my shop also has some permanent tools fastened to one side; a dovetail jig on one corner, and a belt/disc sander on the other.

Cabinet-Style Workbench

The workbench shown on pages 390–93 is made to hold a large assortment of tools, to keep them out of the way of dust, dirt, and moisture. Its top provides a sturdy work surface with plenty of space for laying out projects. The top also has a row of bolt heads for bench hold-downs. These are recessed into the bench top, but may be pulled up in a minute. The bench has a woodworking section on one end and a metal-working section on the other.

The metal-working section features a huge "railroad" vise as well as drawers for socket sets and wrenches. The woodworking end of the bench features a heavy-duty woodworking vise which also has a pull-up "dog." Additional pull-up metal dogs can be fitted into the top so that stock can be held between a dog and the vise.

Construction of the case. The workbench cabinet is constructed in much the same way as the cabinets shown in Chapter 19. One difference is that the assembly is "stress braced" so that it can withstand the impact of hammering and sawing without twisting or shaking. (See page 392.)

The shop-made cabinet-style workbench has a ¼-inch hardboard top which can be replaced when it is damaged.

Workbench has a woodworking vise on one end, and a machinist's vise on the other.

Pop-up dogs can easily be inserted in the table to hold stock being worked on.

To construct the basic case, first glue and nail the 2×4 risers (0) to the bottom, keeping the two end risers flush with the bottom on the outside and back edges. Then fasten the ends (A) to the risers and to the bottom. Use a carpenter's square to make sure they are square with the bottom.

Cut and fasten in the top back brace (G), making sure it is flush with the back and top of the end pieces. Turn the cabinet on its back to install the dividers, facers, and braces. Before installing the dividers, cut a $\frac{3}{4} \times 3\frac{1}{2}$-inch notch in the tops to fit around the back brace.

The easiest way of insuring a good fit of the facers is to cut and install the outside vertical and horizontal pieces first (H, M, L); then carefully trial-fit and cut the rest of the facers and dividers (I, J, K, and N). A cutout can be made in the facer under the vise (N) to allow your vise bars to slide under the bench top.

The upright braces (D) are fastened in first, with notches cut in the four back braces as shown. Then the horizontal braces (E) are cut and fitted between, and finally the diagonal braces (Q) are fastened in place. Check as you fasten each brace in place to make sure that you don't "rack" the base out of square with the braces. Cut and fasten the kickboard to the risers. Now the assembly can be turned over and the back fastened in with glue and screws.

Interior Partitions. The center section of the workbench can be fitted with a shelf installed about halfway up, and the shelf space can be sectioned off with hardboard partitions to form "cubbyholes" for specific hand power tools (such as a router, circular saw, electric drill, and sanders). Each section should also be large enough to hold the accessories used with each tool.

Doors and Drawers. Cut a $\frac{3}{8} \times \frac{3}{8}$-inch rabbet all around on each door so that the doors can be fitted with standard lip-door hinges. The drawer fronts can also be rabbeted and trial-fitted at the same time. Then cut an additional $\frac{1}{2}$-inch

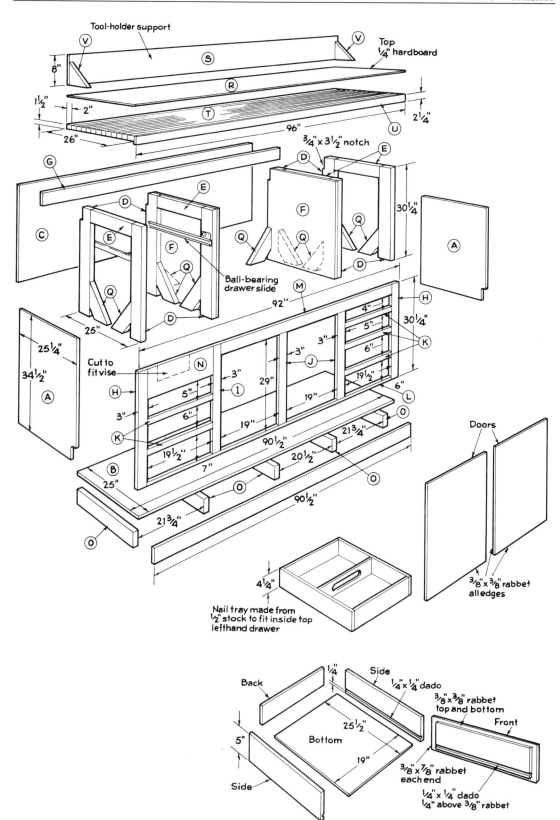

Tool-holder support

Top
¼" hardboard

8"

1½"
2"
26"
96"
2¼"

¾" x 3½" notch

30¼"

Ball-bearing
drawer slide

92"

25"

30¼"

4"

5"

6"

19½"

25¼"

34½"

Cut to
fit vise

29"

3"

3"

3"

19"

19"

6"

5"

3"

6"

19"

90½"

19½"

21¾"

25"

7"

20½"

90½"

21¾"

4¼"

Nail tray made from
½" stock to fit inside top
lefthand drawer

Doors

⅜" x ⅜" rabbet
all edges

¼"
Side
Back
¼" x ¼" dado

⅜" x ⅜" rabbet
top and bottom

Front

25½"

5"
Bottom

19"

⅜" x ⅞" rabbet
each end

Side

¼" x ¼" dado
¼" above ⅜" rabbet

CASE

A, Ends, ¾"×25¼"×34½" plywood, 2 req'd
B, Bottom, ¾"×25"×90½" plywood, 1 req'd
C, Back, ¼"×34½"×90½" plywood, 1 req'd
D, Upright braces, 2×4×30¼", 8 req'd
E, Horizontal braces, 2×4×18", 4 req'd
F, Dividers, ¾"×25"×30¼" plywood, 4 req'd
G, Brace, ¾"×3½"×90½", 1 req'd
H, Facers, ¾"×3"×30¼", 2 req'd
I, Facer, ¾"×3"×29½", 1 req'd
J, Facers, ¾"×3"×26¼", 2 req'd
K, Divider strips, ¾"×1 ¾"×19½", 5 req'd
L, Facer, ¾"×¾"×86", 1 req'd
M, Facer, ¾"×3¼"×63½", 1 req'd
N, Facer, ¾"×7¾"×19½", 1 req'd
O, Risers, 2×4×23", 5 req'd
P, Kickboard, ¾"×3½"×90½", 1 req'd
Q, Braces, 2×4×12", 10 req'd

TOP

R, Top, ¼" hardboard, 26¾"×96", 1 req'd
S, Back support, ¾"×8"×96", 1 req'd

T, Top, 1½"×2"×96", 13 req'd
U, Facer, ¾"×2¼"×96", 1 req'd
V, Braces, ¾"×6"×10", 2 req'd

DRAWERS

Fronts, ¾"×5¾"×20¼" plywood, 2 req'd
Fronts, ¾"×6¾"×20¼" plywood, 3 req'd
Front, ¾"×7¾"×20¼" plywood, 1 req'd
Front, ¾"×4¾"×20¼" plywood, 1 req'd
Bottoms, ¼"×19"×25½" hardboard, 7 req'd
Sides, ½"×5"×25⅝", 4 req'd
Sides, ½"×6"×25⅝", 6 req'd
Sides, ½"×7"×25⅝", 2 req'd
Sides, ½"×4"×25⅝", 2 req'd
Backs, ½"×4½"×18½", 2 req'd
Backs, ½"×5½"×18½", 3 req'd
Back, ½"×6½"×18½", 1 req'd
Back, ½"×3½"×18½", 1 req'd

DOORS

Doors, ¾"×19¾"×27" plywood, 2 req'd

rabbet on the sides of each drawer front to accept the sides.

The drawer sides are cut with a ¼ × ¼-inch dado, ¼ inch up from the bottom edge, to accept the bottoms. Assemble the drawers, making sure that the drawer sides and backs are flush at their top edges. After they have been squared up, slide in the hardboard bottom of each drawer, and tack it to the drawer back. The top lefthand drawer can be fitted with a lift-out nail tray as shown.

Heavy-duty side-mounted metal drawer slides can be installed on the vertical brace pieces (D), and for additional support, support blocks can be nailed in under the slides at the back. A monorail drawer slide could also be used, but will not supply the support needed for very heavy items.

Top. The strips for the top (T) are sawn from 2×6s; each of the 13 strips is 2 inches wide and 1½ inches thick. Glue and clamp the strips together with heavy-duty bar clamps, alternating the grain direction of each piece to minimize warping. The front facer (U) is then glued and screwed in place on the front.

The glued-up top is then fastened to the cabinet base by driving long screws down through the top and into the 2×4 cross braces (E). The top can

be sanded smooth, or planed with a long hand plane.

To provide a good work surface and one that can be changed as often as needed, a sheet of ¼-inch hardboard is cut and fitted down over the bench top, and fastened on with small nails.

The tool holder (S) is cut and screwed to the workbench. Various holding devices can be hung on it as desired.

Finally, to make the bench more convenient, an electrical outlet can be fastened on each end, close to the front edge. These are wired to a short cord which may be plugged into the nearest outlet.

An acrylic enamel can be used to finish the bench, as shown, or a natural wood color finish.

Hot Table

For several years I worked in a cabinet shop, and the majority of my time was spent working at one of several 4×8-foot tables positioned down the center of the shop. Not only were these large tables easy to work on, but they also had an extra dividend: they were wired with electrical receptacles on all four sides. With two or three portable

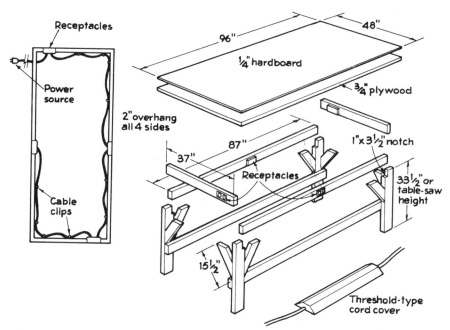

A large hot table provides an excellent work area for assembling many different types of projects. The table can also serve as a back-up table for a table saw.

electric tools plugged in, we had a small "assembly line" type of operation going. When I started my own home workshop, the first thing I did was build my own "hot table." Like the ones I worked at previously, this one is also 4×8 feet and wired with electrical receptacles on all four sides. In addition, one end of the table is positioned against the table saw to serve as an extension table.

The top of my table is made of ¾-inch plywood. Over this I tack down a piece of ¼-inch hardboard. When the hardboard becomes stained or chewed up, I merely remove it and replace it with a new piece of hardboard.

The first step in building the hot table is to cut the leg pieces and apron and brace pieces to the correct length. They are all made from 2×4s. If you plan on using the table in connection with your table saw, cut the table legs so that the table will sit flush with the saw table top.

The apron pieces on the long sides are fitted in notches cut in the 2×4 legs, providing more holding strength for the table top. After cutting all pieces to size, and cutting the notches in the legs, assemble the side frames, using glue and long round-head screws sunk in countersunk holes. With the side frames assembled, stand

them up, and have someone hold them in position while you screw the cross aprons and cross braces in place on the ends. Make sure the table is sitting square, then position the 45° angle braces in place and fasten them.

Fasten the ¾-inch-thick 4×8 plywood top to the legs and aprons, using flathead wood screws countersunk to the surface of the plywood. Paint or stain the table as desired and tack on the final ¼-inch hardboard top with small flathead brads.

You can turn the table down on one side, or leave it standing upright to install the electrical wiring, whichever is easiest. Mark the locations of the receptacle boxes. Drill holes in the locations of the four corners of each box with a ¼-inch drill; then insert a saber saw and cut out the box openings in the aprons.

Fasten the boxes in place using screws, and run the wiring from box to box. Install the electrical receptacles, connecting the white wires to the silver terminals, and the black wires to the brass terminals. Make sure the receptacles are properly grounded by connecting the ground wires to the grounding screw on each receptacle, and run a short ground wire to a grounding screw on each box. If you're lucky and have a shop with floor receptacles, it's merely a matter of running a wire down the inside of each leg and leaving enough cable to reach the receptacle. (A plug is then installed on the end of the cable.) However, you will probably have to run across the room to connect to a receptacle. In this case, heavy duty extension cord cable is used. Merely connect a simple plug on a short piece of cable running from the first receptacle. Make up a good heavy duty extension cord, and be sure it is properly grounded, and of just the right length to reach the wall receptacle. To prevent tripping over the extension cord, you may wish to encase it in a home-made "threshold" type of board. It can also be taped to the shop floor with aluminum duct tape.

Once you work at one of these tables, you'll be spoiled. Not only does the electrical power on the table help, but "working in the round" is much easier for many projects.

Finishing Room or Booth

Ideally, a cabinet or furniture shop should have a separate spray room. If you will be working with varnishes and other slow-drying brush-applied finishes, you will absolutely have to have a separate room to keep dust from the shop from settling on the finish.

If you will be using fast-drying spray finishes such as lacquers, a spray booth can also serve the purpose. The booth can be constructed by simply putting up a couple of room dividers. This arrangement will keep overspray to a minimum and prevent paint and finish from getting on surrounding tools and materials.

Any finishing room or booth should have explosion-proof lights and an exhaust fan that will not ignite volatiles—any sparks can ignite finish vapors. One advantage of a separate finish room is that you don't have to worry quite as much about the danger of a furnace pilot light igniting.

Fire Protection

By its very nature a home workshop can be the worst fire hazard in your home. Fires in workshops, particularly in basements or attached garage shops, can mean the loss of your entire home and also of the precious lives of your family. The accumulation of dust and wood products, combined with the flammable solvents in paints and finishes, makes the home workshop an especially hazardous fire problem. Your insurance agent will be the first to acknowledge that fact.

Fire Prevention

Here are some "do's and don'ts" for workshop fire protection that might save your life.

The first rule is to turn off all pilot lights in furnaces, water heaters, etc., when spraying such volatile materials as lacquer or when applying flammable adhesives. Open windows or doors and allow for plenty of ventilation. If possible, set up a room separate from the rest of the shop for this type of work, and make sure it has plenty of ventilation.

One of the most common fire hazards is gasoline. Gasoline may be one of the best materials for cleaning machinery or engine parts, but if you do use it, use it only outside and away from any buildings.

Another common problem is with old paint or finish-loaded rags. Such oily rags can start a fire by spontaneous combustion, and should always be kept in a closed metal barrel or can, preferably outside the building.

Gasoline, benzine, naptha, and similar solvents should never be stored in the house since they give off vapors which might be ignited. Paint, varnish, turpentine, and other finishing materials must be kept in closed metal containers and away from any heat. Read the label on a can before using the product.

Another thing to watch out for is faulty wiring on motors. Workshop motors collect a lot of dust, both on the outside and inside, and a short can literally cause the motor to explode.

Keep the floor of your shop clean. A heavy collection of dust, wood chips, and sawdust is an invitation to a fire. Above all: Cigarettes and workshops don't mix. All it takes is one forgotten cigarette to ignite a pile of sawdust.

Fire Extinguishers

There is a great deal more to putting out a fire then just sloshing water on it. Some fires, such as those burning on oil or grease, are only spread by

Every shop should be equipped with fire extinguishers. They should be inspected regularly to insure they are in good working order.

the use of water. Water on an electrical fire can cause an electrical shock.

One of the most important things you can do to provide fire protection for your home workshop, and the rest of your home as well, is to provide fire extinguishers. You should have at least two extinguishers in the workshop: one located just inside the shop door, and one over the workbench.

There are three basic types of fire extinguishers, for the three classifications of fires. *A* rated extinguishers are for ordinary materials such as paper and wood. *B* rated extinguishers are for fires burning on gasoline, oil, grease, and other flammable fluids. The *C* extinguisher is rated for electrical fires. Most manufacturers offer a single

extinguisher rated for both B and C type fires, and this type will also take care of A fires.

In addition to the letter classification, extinguishers are also rated according to the coverage they provide. Home-rated extinguishers normally run from 1 to 10. The higher the number, the greater the coverage.

Check your extinguishers according to manufacturer's instructions—at least once every six months—and make sure they're properly charged and ready for use.

In addition to the extinguishers in your shop, you should also have one handy in the kitchen for grease fires, and one in the basement and recreation room. Make sure they're easy to reach, fastened to a wall near a doorway, and that everyone in the household knows how to get to them and operate them.

Fire Drills

When most of us think of fire drills, we think of those exciting few minutes we got out of the humdrum of school work. But fire drills are just as important in the home as in public buildings.

To help make your family fire conscious, conduct regular planned fire drills and go over the basics of escape. Survey your home to determine the quickest escape route and always know an alternate route in case the first is blocked.

The most important step in fire survival is to evacuate your house immediately. Walk in a crouched position, cover your mouth and nose, and be sure to close the door behind you. Never stop to pick up belongings; seconds count in a fire. Always call the Fire Department as soon as you have safely left the house.

Many of us workshoppers invest in thousands of dollars worth of tools, but often forget and ignore the few dollars spent for fire protection equipment that could mean our homes and lives.

21

Hand Tools

A good assortment of hand tools is an absolute must for any cabinet or furniture builder. The tools should also be top-quality, name-brand tools. Cheap bargain-bin tools break quite easily, won't hold an edge, and in fact can cause a bad accident. Good tools will naturally cost a great deal more, but with normal care they will last a long time. In fact, most of them will probably last several lifetimes. I have hand tools that are three generations old and still in fine shape. It's a very nice feeling to work with a tool that belonged to your grandfather.

In my opinion everyone should start his woodworking career with nothing but hand tools; no power tools of any kind allowed. It is naturally much easier to work with power tools after the basics of the craft are learned with hand tools. And also, the same methodical techniques needed for hand tools are normally carried over to the use of power tools, resulting in good and conscientious craftsmanship. Much of the finer cabinetry was done long before the invention of electricity, and the proof is in museums all over the world. This book is primarily a construction book on cabinetry and furniture, so we won't delve too deeply into all the intricacies of each hand tool. However, a brief description of those most commonly seen in cabinetmaking shops and how to use them follows.

Hammers

Many times it seems that you cannot have enough hammers in the cabinet shop. No matter how many you have, they always seem to be at the opposite end of the shop from where you're assembling an item. Hammers come in many different shapes and sizes, but the hammer most commonly used for cabinetry, millwork, and furniture building is a standard 16-oz. claw hammer. It can be used to drive small brads and heavy nails, and the curved claw provides easy nail pulling. There are two other common hammer sizes: the 13 oz. which is ideal for light work such as assembling drawers; and the large 20 oz. hammer

The hammer used for most cabinetry and millwork is a standard 16-oz. claw hammer. A heavier 20-oz. ripping hammer with a straight claw is handy for prying off form boards and for heavy-duty nailing jobs.

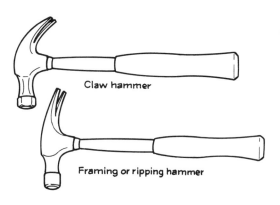

Claw hammer

Framing or ripping hammer

which is most commonly used for house framing. The latter type of hammer is also available with a ripping, or straight, claw. The ripping claw can be used to pry up boards, and it's very handy when removing molding for installation of a cabinet or built-in, or any other heavy chore.

Good hammers have a forged head with a crowned, or slightly curved, face. Cheap hammers are made with cast-iron heads and usually the face is flat. They are often found in bargain bins with the heads painted black or red. The metal on the head will also be rough—not smooth like that of a forged head. The crowned head on a hammer is designed to present more surface to the nail with a normal arm swing, which helps to drive it in straight. A head with a flat face will bend many more nails. Also, the crowned hammer head can be used to drive finish nails right down to the wood surface without any denting, whereas the flat-face head will always leave a dimple in the wood.

Hammers are available with three different kinds of handles: wood, fiberglass, and steel. All three are excellent, and which you prefer is merely a matter of personal opinion. Hammers are quite personal to most craftsmen, and when they find one that "feels just right" they can become quite jealous of it, especially when someone wishes to borrow it. The main thing in the "feel"

is the balance; some craftsmen prefer a hammer with more weight in the head, and this usually means a wooden handle. Others prefer more of the weight back in the handle, in which case a steel hammer would be the best choice.

There is little maintenance to a hammer; merely keep it lightly oiled with WD-40 or a similar lubricant to prevent rusting. A hammer is a simple tool, and yet hard to use well. Even a small child can often pick up a hammer for the first time and drive small nails. At other times, because of the angle of the swing, or the type of wood or nails, even the pros can have a pretty rough time of it.

Grasp the handle near its end but so it feels balanced in your hand. Then position the nail in place with the other hand and give a light tap to set it in place. Swing from the shoulder with a good arc of the arm and let the hammer do the work. The most common mistake of beginners is to grasp the hammer handle near the head—this makes for much harder work. If the nail bends when driven part way, you must remove it. This can be done with the claw. A long stubborn nail can be removed more easily by first placing a block of wood under the claw. Or you can hook the nail between the claws and turn the head over sideways to force it out.

There are also a couple of "old-timer" tricks that can make driving nails much easier, especially in tough woods. The first is to use a bit of beeswax on the tip of the nail. When driving nails in hardwoods which may split, the best bet is to predrill the nail holes using a bit slightly smaller than the nail size.

In addition to the hammers mentioned, you may also have use for some special hammers, such as tack hammers for driving tacks in upholstery. Most of the better tack hammers have a magnetic head, which makes it easy to hold the tacks for driving. You will probably also wish to include a ball peen hammer for metal work such as straightening a hinge, etc.

A claw hammer face can shatter or chip, so never use a woodworking hammer on metal, and never use a ball peen hammer for driving nails.

Another handy hammer is a plastic- or rubber-faced mallet. This is excellent for driving parts together that are to be doweled and glued. The rubber or plastic face won't mar soft woods. You

The face of a quality hammer is curved to help direct the force of a hammer blow, so it is less likely that a miss-hit blow will bend the nail. Also, the crowned head allows you to drive a nail flush with the wood, whereas a flat-face hammer will leave a dimple.

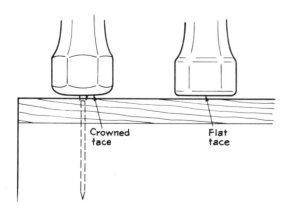

Crowned face

Flat face

will also probably wish to include a wooden mallet for use with chisels and gouges. It's commonly sold with wood carving tools.

Most fiberglass and steel handles won't have to be replaced, but a wooden handle will sometimes break. To replace it, cut off the handle at the bottom of the head, then bore holes down from the top of the head through the remaining wood portions, being careful not to bore into the steel wedges. Drive out the pieces, shape the new handle to fit in the head, then cut off the excess and drive the wedges back in place from the top.

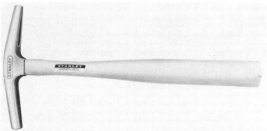

In addition to claw hammers, you will probably also need a tack hammer for upholstery work and other small jobs.

A plastic- or rubber-faced mallet is used when driving dowel-joined wood pieces.

A wooden mallet is commonly used when working with chisels and gouges.

A ball peen hammer is used for metal work, such as bending hinges or reworking tools.

Saws

You will need a variety of handsaws for the cabinet shop. Purchase only top quality saws; cheap saws won't hold their sharpness long and some may even break. The better saws today are taper ground—the teeth are a bit wider than the saw's back, making it much easier to use. New saws also have a bit of blade crown which provides for faster cutting. The crown can be seen by holding the saw up to the light and sighting down the teeth. The crown will come just about in the middle of the saw blade. Saws are available with either plastic or wooden handles; most craftsmen prefer the wooden handles.

The two most commonly used saws are the crosscut and the rip saw. Crosscut saws are used to cut stock across the grain, and rip saws to cut stock with the grain. Never use a rip saw for crosscutting or vice versa. Not only is it hard on the saw, but it can ruin a fine piece of wood.

The teeth on a crosscut saw are bevel-filed so that they act like tiny skew chisels to cut away the material. A rip saw, on the other hand, has teeth that act as vertical chisels that come straight down on the work. In both saws, alternate teeth are "set," or made to point away from each other, to provide clearance for the saw in the cut.

Both saws are available in several different sizes; the most common are the 16- and 26-inch lengths. The number of teeth per inch determines the fineness of cut. Naturally, a saw with more teeth per inch will cut more slowly than one with less, but the cut will be smoother. The most commonly used crosscut saw has eight points, or teeth, per inch. Ten- and 12-point saws are used for finish work. A rip saw will normally have only 5½ teeth per inch.

To use a crosscut saw, grasp the handle firmly with the thumb and forefinger on opposite sides of the saw. Then position the saw on the "waste" side of the cut line—don't saw directly on the line. Use the thumb of the free hand to steady the saw blade and guide it when beginning a cut. Use a light pull stroke to get the cut started—if you push down, you'll only cause the blade to jump, and you might get a nasty cut on your thumb. Once the cut is started, cut on the downward stroke only. Keep the saw at about a 45° angle to the work surface face, and saw with light but firm, smooth strokes. Try to use most of the saw blade to prevent early dulling of the center of the blade. Make sure you keep the saw square with the work surface and follow the line carefully.

A rip saw is used in much the same manner, except that the cut is started at the very tip of the saw blade using light strokes. Once the cut has

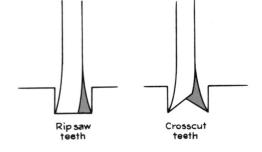

Handsaws are available in several different lengths and point sizes. A standard crosscut saw—for cutting across the grain of wood—is used for 90 percent of woodworking shop chores.

A rip saw has relatively large teeth with deep gullets between to clear away sawdust. Crosscut teeth are smaller and set at a more pronounced angle.

Rip saw
teeth

Crosscut
teeth

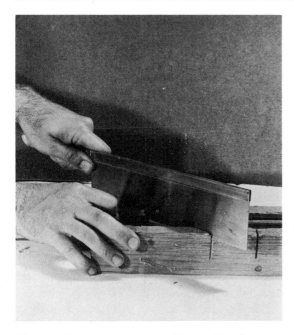

Miter and back saws are used for making fine joint cuts.

Even finer cuts can be made with a dovetail saw.

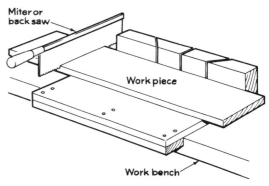

A bench hook is often used to hold work being cut with a back saw. (Bench hook can also be adapted for use as a miter box.)

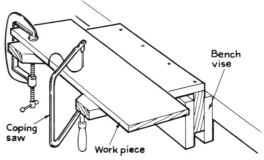

A coping saw is used for cutting scroll work and other irregular shapes. Work to be cut with a coping saw can be clamped to a special L-shape jig with a V-shape cutout for the blade.

been started, use long easy strokes and the entire blade. Normally the angle used when ripping is less, about 60°.

In addition to the standard crosscut and rip saws you will also wish to have a variety of special saws for cabinetry and furniture work. *Miter* and *back* saws are similar to standard crosscut saws except that they have a stiff reinforcement along the back. Miter saws are available up to 30 inches long, and only in finer cuts such as 11 to 12 teeth per inch. Back saws run a bit shorter. These saws are primarily used for final finish cuts and are used by holding the teeth horizontally over the work rather than at an angle. They are commonly used in miter boxes to cut millwork joints and other joints where the cut must be true and

straight. In fact, the smoothest, finest joints are made using a miter or back saw rather than power equipment. Incidentally, if you don't have a miter box, you can make one quite easily (see Chapter 5, page 81). Or you can adapt a bench hook for use in cutting miters.

A *dovetail* saw is a small back saw with a thinner blade and finer teeth. This type of saw may have as many as 15 points per inch. It is used to cut dovetail joints and can be used for cutting veneer, although a regular veneer saw works better.

You will also need a *coping* saw or fret saw for cutting irregular shapes. This has a very fine ⅛-inch-wide blade which can be used for cutting almost any type of curve or for cutting molding.

A keyhole or compass saw (not shown) can be used to cut an opening in a wall or similar surface. The point is used to start the hole.

The blade can be set in any direction to make sharply angled cuts. It is best used with a shop-made "saw clamp," an L-shape jig fitted into a vise. The top of the jig is notched to provide working room for the saw blade. The work can then be clamped to the piece to secure it and prevent it from chattering.

In addition, a *compass* saw is often a useful item. This has a pointed end so that it can be used to start and cut holes in walls, as when installing kitchen cabinets.

Planes

Years ago, planes were extremely important to the cabinet or furniture builder. With today's power tools most of the jobs that were formerly done with planes can be done more quickly and, in many cases, more accurately with power tools. However, learning to plane a surface smooth, square up the ends of stock and cut bevels with planes will make a much more appreciative craftsman. And there is a multitude of small jobs that are easier to do with a hand plane.

There are several different types of planes, and each one does a specific job. It's a good idea to have at least one of each of the three most common types. Many planes are available with either wood or metal bodies. Most craftsmen like the feel of a wooden plane, but they usually cost a great deal more than the metal ones.

The *block* plane is the smallest, and is often kept right at the workbench to quickly cut down a joint or smooth up an edge while fitting pieces together. The block plane is normally 7 inches long, but there are models as small as 3½ inches. The blade is set at a shallow angle, so the plane takes off very little material. It can be used for cutting across the grain and for cutting chamfers. These are extremely handy little tools, and once you own one, you'll find many, many different uses for it.

The next size is the *jack* plane, also sometimes called a bench plane. Most jack planes are 14 inches long, but there are several other sizes. It is a general purpose plane, and its length enables it to be used for almost any planing job. Similar to it is the smoothing plane, which is usually somewhat shorter, about 9 inches long.

The *jointer* plane is the longest. It is usually 20 to 24 inches long. In the past, this was the plane that was used to surface materials. Today, the most common use is in jointing edges of boards that are to be joined together. It will also make quick work of planing the edge of a door.

In addition, there are special planes for rabbeting, routing and other tasks. Many of these specialty planes have been pretty well displaced by

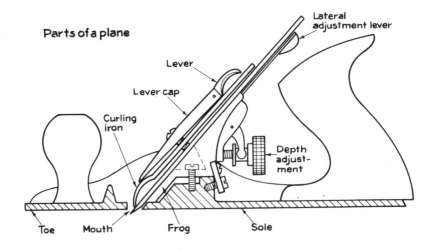

Parts of a plane

Lateral adjustment lever

Lever

Lever cap

Curling iron

Depth adjustment

Toe   Mouth   Frog   Sole

A block plane is used to cut chamfers on the edges of stock, or to smooth end grain.

The jack or bench plane is a general purpose plane. It is usually about 14 inches long.

power tools, and are not widely available anymore.

The most common specialty plane is the *router*. This can be used for making smooth-bottom dadoes, grooves, and similar cuts. A smaller version can be used for very narrow routing work such as making cutouts for inlays or letting in lock plates. The *rabbet* plane is used for cutting

A router plane is used to form a dado after the side cuts have been made with a saw.

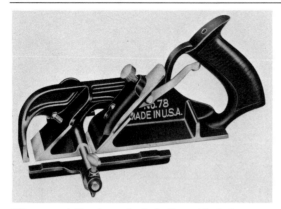

Other specialty planes include the rabbet plane . . .

Bull nose rabbet plane . . .

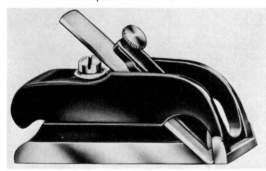

And dado plane.

rabbets or fillisters, and there are several different sizes and types. One variation is the *bull-nose* plane, which can be used on inside surfaces because its blade is right at the end of the plane. The *box* plane is a small blade mounted on a swivel handle. It can be used to remove defects in a surface before refinishing. A *compass* plane has a curved bottom that can be adjusted to different curvatures by turning a knob on the front of the plane. A *circular* plane is quite similar except that it can be used on both concave and convex surfaces.

Choosing the correct plane for the job is important. As a rule, use the largest plane you have when planing any broad surface. A longer plane will bridge over the low spots more easily, and you won't get the dips and high spots possible with a smaller plane.

A plane has to be adjusted properly, and the blade kept smooth and sharp. With a little practice, adjusting a plane is easy, but for the beginner it can be quite frustrating. The plane iron, which does the cutting, should project through the hole just a little. If it projects too much, the plane will dig in and be hard to push. Too little, and the plane won't cut. The iron should also be parallel with the bottom of the plane; if twisted to one side

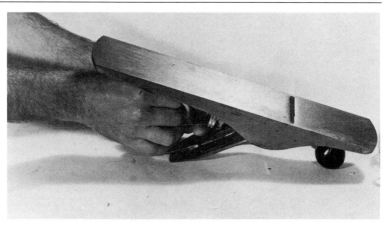

To be effective, a plane must be kept in adjustment. With the plane turned over, adjust the iron to be parallel with the bottom, and check its projection.

or the other it will dig in on one side. To adjust the plane, turn it upside down. While sighting across the bottom, turn the adjusting nut until the blade projects just a little. If the blade is canted, move the adjusting lever to the right or to the left to straighten it.

Larger planes such as the jack and jointer have a double iron. This is to stiffen the cutting iron; it also causes the shavings to curl up and out of the plane. (This is not needed on block planes because they are normally used across grain or for very fine cuts.) The double iron is adjustable, so you can control the thickness of the shavings. Normally the second iron will be about $\frac{1}{16}$-inch back from the edge of the plane iron. After making this adjustment, make sure you get the cap

tightened securely in place so shavings won't be forced between the two.

After you learn how to adjust a plane, using it is quite simple. The material must be held securely in place with a vise, bench hook, or clamp on a worktable top. Grasp the front knob with your left hand, with your fingers up on top of the plane and out of the way. Grasp the back handle with your right hand. As you start the planing stroke apply pressure with the left hand. But as you progress through the planing stroke start applying more pressure to the right or back hand, and finish the stroke with most of the pressure on the back hand. This will prevent digging in at the end of the stock. When planing across the grain on the end of stock, it's a good idea to plane the

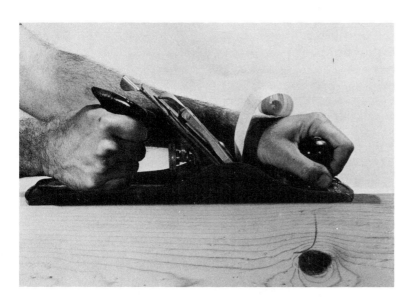

Planing motion begins in a long, smooth stroke, with pressure applied on the front. At the end of the stroke, pressure is transferred to the back of the plane.

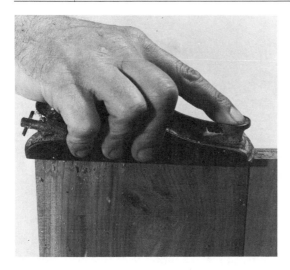

A piece of waste stock tacked to the end of workpiece prevents plane from splintering stock as it passes the edge.

A shop-made vise can be constructed to hold stock for planing. Shown is a top view.

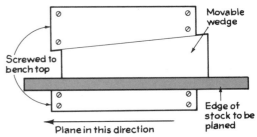

cross-grain cuts first, then follow with the long "with-the-grain" cuts to remove any splinters that may result from the cross-grain cuts. An alternative is to clamp a scrap block in place against the edge of the stock; this will prevent splintering the end of the stock.

Edge planing must always be done with the grain. If the plane digs in too deeply yet the blade is not set too deeply, the problem is that you're going against the grain. Start at the opposite end of the stock. This is much more of a problem with some softwoods, such as fir and pine, than with most of the hardwoods.

Always lift the plane after each forward stroke. Dragging it back across the wood surface will soon dull the iron. Check the surface that is being planed from time to time so you can keep it square. Use a straightedge to make sure there are no dips or high spots.

When planing across a wide surface use the largest plane you have and plane at about a 45° angle (to the grain) for the initial roughing cuts. Then you can turn and go across this at 90° angles in the opposite direction to further "surface plane" the stock. Final cuts are with the grain.

Planes should be carefully stored to prevent their blades from dulling. Also, a bad injury can result if you happen to run your hand across one in a drawer. Whether you store them in a drawer or in a rack on the workbench, the blade should be covered with a thin piece of wood.

Several related tools that I have found a great deal of use for are the drawknife, spokeshave and inshave. The *drawknife,* as its name suggests, is drawn rather than pushed across a surface. It is excellent for carving the rough edges of stock that is to be turned on the lathe. A *spokeshave* can be pushed or pulled, and its design makes it ideal for planing curved edges. Its blade is adjustable, so it can be used to make rough or very fine cuts. An *inshave* looks something like a drawknife, but its blade has a more pronounced curve. It can be used for such tasks as sculpturing chair seats or scooping out bowls.

A drawknife is useful for many trimming jobs.

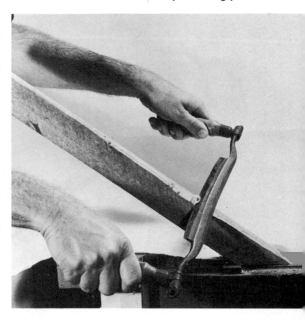

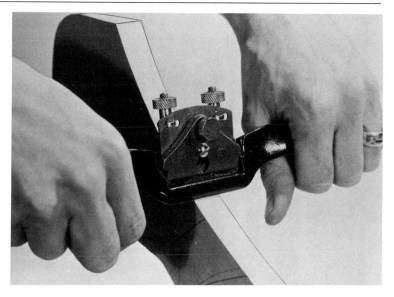

A spokeshave can smooth a curved edge.

Chisels and Gouges

A woodworking shop wouldn't be complete without an assortment of chisels and gouges. Chisels normally have straight blades, whereas gouges have curved or V-shape blades. Again, purchase only good brand-name tools that will retain their edge. A dull blade will force you to push and strain, which often results in an accident.

The type of handle a chisel has determines its use as much as anything. There are three basic handle styles. The *tang* style is used on chisels that are not meant to be driven with a hammer. The chisel blade tapers into a prong which is

A full assortment of chisels and gouges is a necessity for any woodworking shop.

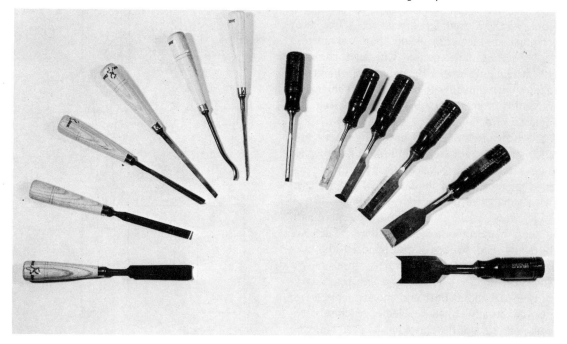

It's a good idea to purchase chisels in sets like this. Note the variety of sizes.

driven into a wood handle or encased in a plastic one. The *socket* type is used for light mallet work. Its blade ends in a socket which receives a wood handle with steel cap. The *heavy-duty* type has a continuous steel shank fitted with a steel cap and wood handle. These are meant to take hard pounding, and the larger sizes are used for such jobs as cutting away flooring.

There are several different kinds of chisels, some of them used for special jobs. The most common are the paring, firmer, butt and mortise.

The *paring* chisel is used without a hammer. It's merely pushed with the palm of one hand and guided with the other to pare off thin shavings—much like a plane. The blade is normally fairly light and thin.

Firmer chisels normally have long blades, and their cutting edges are ground like a knife rather than with one edge beveled. They are quite often used for mortise and similar work, and are used with a mallet or hammer.

The *butt* chisel is a general purpose chisel with a short blade (about 3 inches long). They are normally made with a heavy handle to be used with a hammer or mallet. *Mortise* chisels have a somewhat longer blade, and generally a heavy-duty type handle. Butt and mortise chisels are also commonly called beveled-edge chisels, because one edge of the chisel has a bevel while the

back edge is straight. This allows you to cut a mortise with a straight side.

A useful specialty chisel is the *drawer-lock* chisel, which resembles an offset screwdriver. It can be used in confined places to cut the mortises for drawer locks. The *deep-mortise* chisel has an extra thick blade and is used for cutting deep mortises.

Chisels come in many different sizes, but the ¼-, ½-, ¾-, 1- and 2-inch sizes are those most commonly used by the cabinetmaker.

Gouges are chisels that have shaped cutting blades. The rounded-edge gouges are also called *sweeps*. Gouges come in an infinite number of sizes and shapes and the average cabinet shop won't need but a few. One gouge that you will find quite useful for cleaning out mortises is the *corner* gouge. This gouge has a 90° angled blade that is ground on the outside. The best bet is to purchase a wood carving set that has a variety of gouges. These can be used for most cabinetmaking purposes. and if you decide to delve a bit more

Mortise and other heavy-duty chisels intended for use with a mallet have a solid steel shank. Chisels for light-duty work such as paring have a metal tang construction.

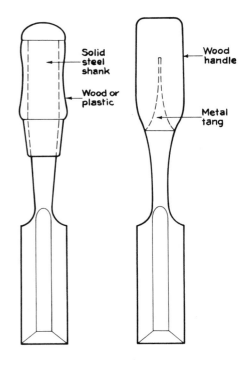

Gouges are chisels with curved or V-shaped blades.

Gouges and parting tools for carving and woodturning tasks are available in many sizes.

Straight gouges

Parting tools

into the wood carving aspect of furniture building, you can acquire gouges as you need them.

Chisels can be quite dangerous, so learn to·use them properly. The first rule is never to chisel toward yourself. Make sure the chisel is pointing away from you, and away from the hand that is holding the stock. If at all possible, it's a good idea to clamp the workpiece in some way to hold it securely for chiseling. If you are using a chisel without a hammer, use one hand to guide the blade, and the palm of the other to push.

One of the most important things in using a chisel is to make sure you cut with the grain. If you go into the grain you may splinter the material. Keep turning the stock and watching to make sure you chisel in the right direction. Start deep cuts with a saw or drill, then use the chisel to do the final cuts.

Veiners are a small gouge used to cut fine lines in wood, as for incised-line carvings.

Rough cuts are made with the chisel's bevel side down, and light or paring cuts with the bevel facing up. Always use a light touch when working with the bevel side up; the depth of cut is much harder to control in this position. When removing material for a thin mortise, outline the mortise first with the chisel straight up and down. Then make successive scoring cuts through the mortise area. It is then easy to knock out the scored area with the chisel turned bevel side down. Finally, you can smooth the area with the bevel up.

Pocketknife

A pocketknife can't replace a chisel or gouge, but many craftsmen use one to pare away wood for a joint or to smooth a surface a bit. A good sharp knife with several blade sizes is excellent for many carving jobs.

Files and Rasps

A great deal of roughing-in work as well as smoothing can be done with files and rasps. Files come in three different cuts: smooth, second-cut, and bastard or rough. In addition, some carving jobs will require a rasp which removes a great deal of material. The most commonly used are a 10-inch flat bastard file, and a 10- or 12-inch cabinet rasp, bastard or smooth cut. *Surform* tools can be used in place of a rasp in many

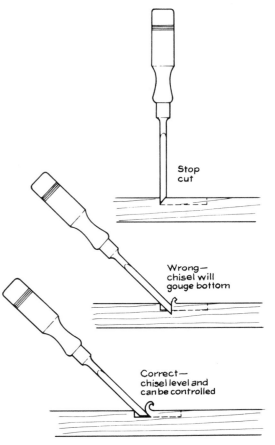

The end cuts for a mortise are made with the chisel held at right angles to the work. Then scoring cuts are made along the length of the mortise, and the chisel is held as shown to clean out the bottom. Finally, paring cuts are used to level the surface.

Pocketknives and wood carver's blades such as shown are useful for many small jobs. *Leichtung.*

A variety of files will be extremely valuable to the wood craftsman.

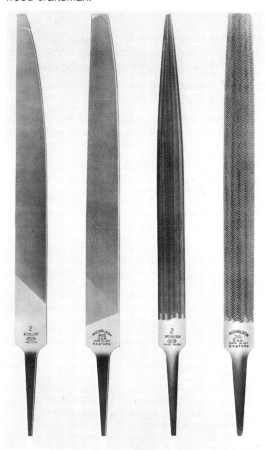

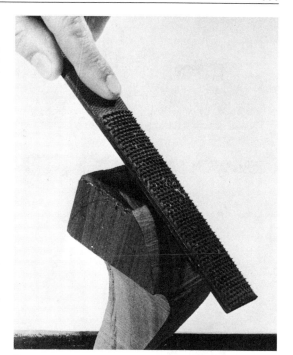

Coarse rasps are used for rough shaping of wood.

Fine details are cut with small rifflers.

Files are also used to sharpen saw blades and for other metalworking tasks.

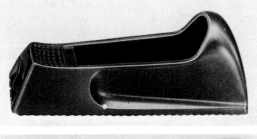

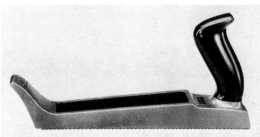

In addition to the standard files and rasps, there are a number of Surform tools that can be used for roughing-in work.

instances. They have small teeth much like a cheese grater, and cut on the forward stroke. A set of small *rifflers* in different sizes and shapes is useful for making the final cuts in wood carvings and moldings.

Boring Tools

Again the power tools have pretty well done away with most of the hand boring tools, especially with the advent of the rechargeable electric drill.

On the other hand, there are times when a hand drill can be faster and much easier to use. A brace and bit can also often be used for tough boring jobs that would overtax the average ⅜-inch portable electric drill. A *ratchet* brace is better than the plain type; the ratchet allows it to be "backed up" so it can be used where there isn't enough room to turn the handle completely.

Several different types of bits can be used with braces. They include the common *auger* bit, available in a range of sizes from ¼- to 1-inch; *Foerstner* bits, with a flat bottom, used primarily for boring stopped holes or enlarging existing holes; and *countersink* bits to drill tapered holes. The *expansion* bit is commonly used by millwork carpenters. It can be fitted with different cutters to bore 1¼- to 3-inch holes, and is commonly used for cutting holes for door locks.

For smaller holes, a portable electric drill is usually preferred to a crank hand drill. But a *Yankee push drill* is often handier than an electric drill for starting screw holes for hinges and other hardware, and for many other small jobs around

A hand drill can be handy for many jobs, and it will perform some tasks that would overtax an electric drill. Brace can be fitted with many different types of bits.

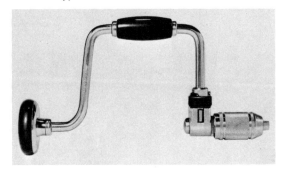

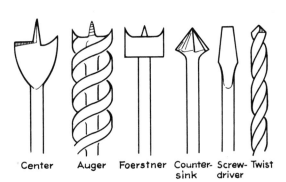

Center   Auger   Foerstner   Counter-   Screw-   Twist
                                    sink   driver

With an expansion bit, a hand drill can be used to bore holes as large as 3 inches in diameter.

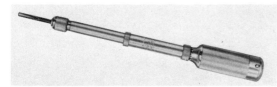

A Yankee push drill is useful for small around-the-house jobs, or for installing hinges in a cabinet. This one has 8 bits stored in the handle. *Stanley.*

the house. The model shown has nine different bits.

Screwdrivers

Good-quality screwdrivers that will last a lifetime are inexpensive and widely available. Beware of the cheaper variety made of pot metal; they will often twist into an unusable shape with the first job.

Most shops can use a couple of standard sets of screwdrivers; this gives you a set to hang over the workbench, and others to place at strategic places around the shop. In addition, you will probably want several smaller screwdrivers for tiny jobs, and some hefty ones for such jobs as loosening tight, painted-over screws. Some models have a flattened blade to accommodate a wrench. In addition to the standard shapes, make sure to get an *offset* driver for use in tight places.

There are several types of specialty screwdrivers. *Screw-holding* drivers have either a magnet or small fingers at the end to hold the screw securely until you get it started. Another useful

A standard screwdriver set includes straight- and Phillips-slot blades in several sizes.

Cabinetmaker's screwdrivers come in a range of sizes. The flat area above the blade can accommodate a wrench. *Leichtung.*

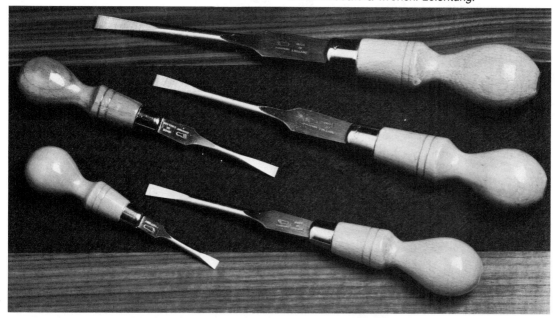

An offset screwdriver is used to turn screws in tight places.

type of screwdriver is the *Yankee* or spiral-ratchet type. Like the push drill, it converts a push into rotary motion, and makes fast work of a repetitive job.

Measuring Tools

Measuring and marking devices are among the most important tools in a cabinet shop. It's just impossible to construct a piece of furniture correctly without them.

You will need several different types of measuring tools. The first is a 12-foot-long steel *tape rule.* You may also want to have a 25-footer on hand for special jobs, but the 12-foot tape is the one that will be used daily. Make sure the tape has markings in both feet and inches. The better tapes will also have stud markings every 16 inches, as well as a power rewind feature.

The traditional measuring tool for fine woodworking is a wooden *folding rule.* These are available in several different lengths; the most common is six feet long. The better rules have metal extensions on each end to enable you to take inside measurements. The better rules also have the starting point situated on both ends, but on opposite sides, so you can start measuring at either end. Rules without this feature can be extremely frustrating to work with. The *meter stick* is also becoming popular in cabinet shops. These are usually metal, and have metric graduations as well as tables to convert to inches and feet. They also make an excellent straightedge.

A *try square* has many uses in a cabinet shop. This is a small square with a metal blade set at a 90° angle from the handle. It is used to mark cut-off lines on a board, to check joints for trueness, to determine warping or cupping in a board, and to check trueness of a board edge.

A *combination square* is much like a try square, but it has a movable handle with a 45° angled edge. It is sometimes called a 45° miter square for this reason. The combination square can be used for any of the jobs that the try square does, and also for marking and testing 45° miters. It's a good idea to have one of each around the shop. You'll often find the combination square set for a ripping mark that you don't want to change, and the try square can then be used to mark the crosscut.

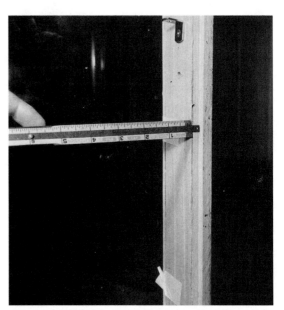

A wooden folding rule is traditional in a woodworking shop. A rule with metal extensions is useful for measuring inside dimensions and rabbet depths.

A try square is used to mark boards for crosscutting, to check joints for trueness, and to determine if an edge is square.

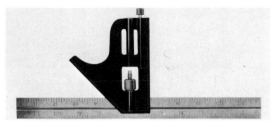

The sliding handle of a combination square can be set to mark a board for ripping, or you can use the 45° angle of the handle to mark a miter cut.

A carpenter's square is invaluable in the shop. It is used to determine the squareness of a cabinet or furniture case, or to mark crosscuts on wide stock.

A *carpenter's square* usually has a 24-inch body and a 16-inch tongue, and is graduated in eighths and sixteenths of an inch on one side, and tenths on the other. Most carpenter's squares today are made of light aluminum. They can be used in place of a try square for many purposes, and are also used for marking long cuts on plywood. A *rafter* or *framing* square also includes rafter tables, and can be used to lay out stair stringers or for other framing jobs.

The *bevel square,* also called a sliding T-bevel, has a slotted metal blade held in place with a wing nut. The blade can be adjusted to any angle and is used to mark angled cuts or check edges. Some models have blades marked in inches.

The blade of a T-bevel can be set at any angle.

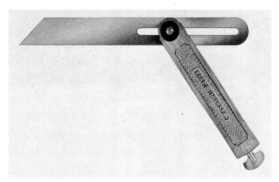

Marking tools are also essential in a shop. The first and most commonly used is the *butt marking gauge.* This is (usually) a wood rule with a block fastened to it by means of a wing nut. A sharp point at the end serves as a scribe. By loosening the wing nut and sliding the handle along the blade you can set the tool to scribe a line at the required distance from an edge. It is useful for marking rip cuts, and also for marking mortises, tenons and other joints. A *protractor* should also be on hand in the shop for marking angles, and a *compass* (also called scribers or dividers) for laying out circles and ovals. The compass can also be used to scribe around irregularly shaped objects, such as when cutting molding to fit around a stone fireplace. A giant compass can easily be constructed for use in marking large circles and arcs.

The butt marking gauge is used primarily to mark ripping cuts. It is also useful in laying out joints.

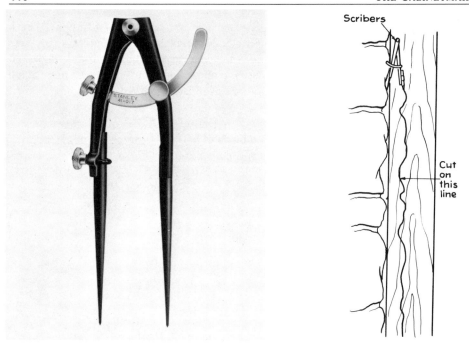

A pair of scribers can be used to mark a circle, or to mark moldings for an irregular cut as shown.

For some projects, it may be necessary to construct a large-scale scriber tool.

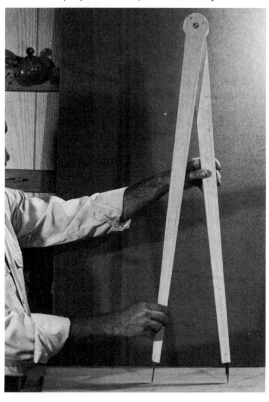

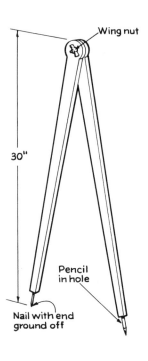

Marking. There's an old saying that "A good craftsman can be recognized by his pencil lines." In many cases it's true that the type of mark you make will determine whether you're a good craftsman or a sloppy one. A soft-lead large pencil can be used for rough carpentry, but you should use a hard-lead, very sharp pencil for finish cabinetry. An even better choice is a scribing knife or pointed awl, although the lines left by these may be a bit hard to see. I think the best choice is a 3H drafting pencil. This will hold a sharp point well even when used on hard woods, yet it leaves a line dark enough to be seen.

One way of cutting down on time when marking identical lengths on a number of pieces is to use a layout stick. This is a 1×2 cut to the longest length needed, with other frequently used measurements marked along the stick.

Levels and Plumb Bobs

A cabinetmaker's tool box will contain a variety of levels. A good 4-foot level is a must for installation of kitchen cabinets and other built-ins. A couple of smaller levels will be needed for tighter quarters. An aluminum-frame 2-foot level is the standard workhorse, and a 9-inch torpedo level can be carried around in a pocket. It's a good idea to check a new level to make sure that it is accurate. To do this, place it on a fairly level surface and make a mark at one end. If the bubble doesn't indicate level, shim up one end until it does. Swap ends, and if it is reading accurately, it should read level again.

Plumb bobs are used to establish vertical lines, as when framing a door or hanging a wall cabinet. A combination chalk line and plumb bob has many uses. You can use the chalk line to mark angled cuts on large pieces of material, or to mark plywood sheets for an initial cut.

When used in conjunction with a straightedge such as shown, a level is even more accurate. Stock for the straightedge must be perfectly flat and straight, and the sides perfectly parallel.

A plumb-bob with a chalk line can be used to mark a cut on plywood, or to establish a plumb line on a wall for installation of cabinets.

Levels used in woodworking range from the small 9-inch torpedo level to the 4- or 6-foot levels used for installing cabinets and establishing plumb lines for built-ins.

22

Power Tools

As mentioned in the previous chapter, some extremely beautiful furniture can be constructed using hand tools alone. However, power tools can not only speed up the job; they have made some techniques easier and more accurate and led to some original techniques. Naturally, a complete cabinet and furniture building shop will require more power tools, particularly stationary power tools, than will a small hobby or homeowner's repair shop.

As with hand tools, choose only good-quality, name-brand tools. Good power tools, particularly stationary power tools, are not cheap, so very few people can go out and completely equip a cabinet shop. On the other hand, stationary power tools have an extremely long life if they are taken care of, and used stationary power tools can be an excellent buy, particularly for the craftsman just getting started. Watch newspaper ads for used power tools, or even better, for a small cabinet shop that is going out of business.

There are a few basic tools you will need for almost any cabinet work and others you can add later as you need them or accumulate the money for them.

Any power tool can be dangerous and must be used with all safety precautions. One of the main rules is to keep blades and bits sharp, and avoid forcing the tool when tackling tougher materials. This practice is essential to achieve smooth cuts as well as to avoid kickback. When in doubt, make several shallow cuts to avoid forcing the tool. Also make sure that the work has enough bearing surface and that you will be able to hold it securely against the impact of the cut. This is especially important when working with tools that remove a large amount of material, such as molding heads, shaper blades, and some router bits. It takes only a split second of inattentiveness or carelessness to lose a finger or an eye.

The Power Tool Institute has listed 18 rules that can help prevent most power tool accidents. As you can see, most of these are just plain common sense, and they apply to both stationary and portable power tools. The rules are as follows:

- **Know Your Power Tool**—Read the owner's manual carefully. Learn the applications and limitations as well as the specific potential hazards of the tool.

- **Ground All Tools**—Unless double-insulated. If a tool is equipped with a three-prong plug, it should be plugged into a three-hole electrical receptacle. If an adapter is used to accommodate the two-prong receptacle, the adapter wire must be attached to a known ground. Never remove the third prong.

- **Keep Guards In Place** and in working order.

- **Keep Work Area Clean.** Cluttered areas and benches invite accidents.

- **Avoid Dangerous Environment.** Don't use a power tool in damp or wet locations. And keep work area well lit.

- **Keep Children Away.** All visitors should be kept a safe distance from work area.

- **Store Idle Tools.** When not in use, portable tools should be stored in a dry, high, or locked place—out of the reach of children.

- **Don't Force Tool.** It will do the job better and more safely at the rate for which it was designed.

- **Use Right Tool.** Don't force a small tool or attachment to do the job of a heavy-duty tool.

- **Wear Proper Apparel.** No loose clothing or jewelry to get caught in moving parts. Rubber gloves and footwear are recommended when working outdoors.

- **Use Safety Glasses** with most tools. Also face or dust mask if cutting operation produces dust.

- **Don't Abuse Cord.** Never carry tool by cord or yank it to disconnect from receptacle. Keep cord from heat, oil and sharp edges.

- **Secure Work.** Use clamps or a vise to hold work. It's safer than using your hand and it frees both hands to operate tool.

- **Don't Overreach.** Keep proper footing and balance at all times.

- **Maintain Tools With Care.** Keep tools sharp and clean at all times, for best and safest performance. Follow instructions for lubricating and changing accessories.

- **Disconnect Tools.** When not in use; before servicing; and when changing accessories such as blades, bits, and cutters.

- **Remove Adjusting Keys and Wrenches.** Form habit of checking to see that keys and adjusting wrenches are removed from tool before turning it on.

- **Avoid Accidental Starting.** Don't carry plugged-in tool with finger on switch.

Details on many power tool techniques are described elsewhere in this book. This chapter will cover some of the safety precautions and basic techniques used with cabinetmaking tools. The owner's manual for each tool will supply other details. Stationary tools are discussed first, and portable tools in the next section. In each section, tools are listed in the usual order of purchase.

Stationary Power Tools

Radial Arm Saw

The radial arm saw is often the first stationary tool chosen, and with good reason, because of its versatility. Radial arm saws are available in several different sizes. For cabinet and furniture work, a 10-inch (or larger) saw will be needed. (The model size refers to the size of blade the saw uses.) The 10-inch size not only enables you to cut through 2×4 stock easily, but it will also make for easier work on smaller-thickness stock. The large motor will provide a good smooth cut, if the proper saw blade is used.

With accessories, the radial arm saw can be used as a drill press, sander, horizontal boring machine, wood lathe, shaper, and jointer. However, as you become more involved in woodworking you will probably want to purchase the specialized tools that do specific jobs to save the time involved in changing accessories and setting up the tool for different jobs.

Setting Up the Radial Arm Saw. The best setup for a radial arm saw is against a wall with table extensions on either side. The extensions should include fences as well. Discarded pieces of metal rule can be tacked down on top of the fences to act as a permanent measuring device for cutting off stock. This will save a great deal of time on many jobs. Incidentally, when cutting a number of pieces to the same length, a stop block can be nailed to the saw extension tops. The stock is merely placed in position against the stop block, then cut off and the cut repeated to make as many pieces as needed.

In a full shop of tools, the radial arm saw is primarily used for cutting stock to length and other crosscutting tasks. (In fact, the larger versions used in industrial shops are called "cut-off saws.") The crosscutting capabilities of the saw are increased by its movable arm, which can be swung to different degrees to make angled cuts for miters, or shallow decorative cuts across the face of cabinet panels or molding. In addition it can be turned and used for ripping, although this is seldom done in most cabinet shops.

Safety. One of the most common mistakes when using a radial arm saw is to reach in toward the turning saw blade to pull out small pieces. This is a dangerous procedure and should be avoided. Always use a small stick to push pieces out of the way of the blade, or turn the saw off. The saw is equipped with a blade guard and an anti-

The radial arm saw is one of the most versatile tools, and is usually the first stationary tool purchased.

For cabinetmaking work, don't purchase less than a 10-inch model. *Rockwell.*

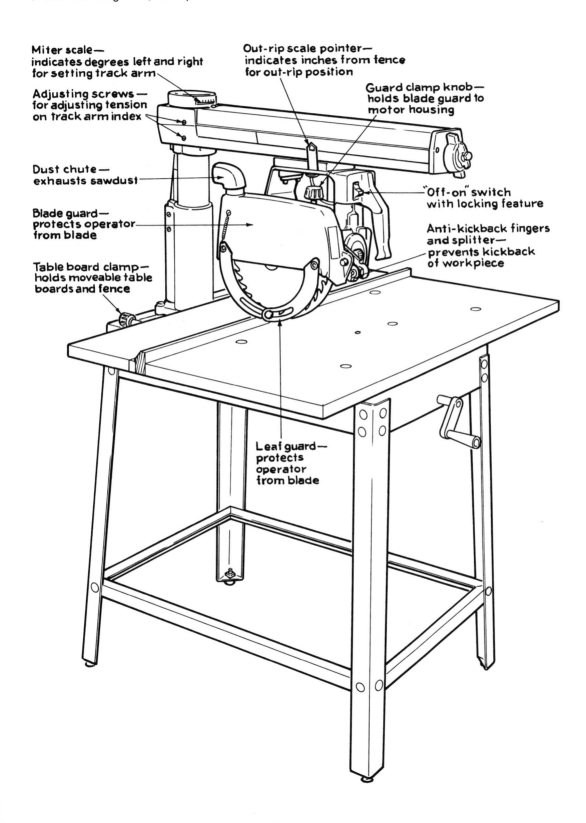

Miter scale—
indicates degrees left and right
for setting track arm

Out-rip scale pointer—
indicates inches from fence
for out-rip position

Guard clamp knob—
holds blade guard to
motor housing

Adjusting screws—
for adjusting tension
on track arm index

Dust chute—
exhausts sawdust

"Off-on" switch
with locking feature

Blade guard—
protects operator
from blade

Anti-kickback fingers
and splitter—
prevents kickback
of workpiece

Table board clamp—
holds moveable table
boards and fence

Leaf guard—
protects
operator
from blade

kickback device that can be adjusted for use with both crosscuts and rip cuts. Be sure to use these at all times.

Crosscutting. There are two different types of cutting methods used in crosscutting stock— the *climb* cut and the *feed* cut. The climb cut is the cut most often used. This is done by placing the stock against the fence and starting with the saw in behind the fence, drawing it out into the wood. The saw blade rotation is toward the fence, so the action of the teeth forces the stock down and against the fence. The advantage of this is that you don't have to clamp the work in place. However, if the stock is fed too quickly, the saw will tend to "walk" over the wood surface rather than cutting through it. If the saw is drawn across too fast, it will actually climb up onto the wood and stop the saw. This can not only be dangerous, but it can also eventually knock the bevel setting off square.

The feed cut is done in the opposite manner. The saw is pulled all the way out, the stock placed back against the fence, then the saw pushed back through the stock to cut it off. The action of the teeth in this cut has a tendency to lift the stock up and away from the fence, so this cut is seldom used except on very hard woods or when you can't control a climb cut. When cutting veneered plywood, the climb cut is made with the good side of the plywood up. A feed cut is made with the good side down.

If the lumber is too wide to crosscut in one pass, cut as far as the motor will reach on the arm, then lift the outside edge of the lumber until it touches the bottom of the motor. If this still won't cut the stock, you will have to turn the board over, re-mark the cut on the opposite side and then cut toward the first cut. It's a good idea to sight down the cut toward the blade first to make sure the second cut will align with the first. There is a second method of continuing a cut if you want to avoid turning the board over. Return the blade to its starting position and move the fence and stock back. Then start up the saw with the blade positioned in the first kerf to continue the cut.

Miter and Bevel Cuts. Another prime job for the radial arm saw is to cut miter or angled cuts.

Six Basic Cuts of a Radial Arm Saw

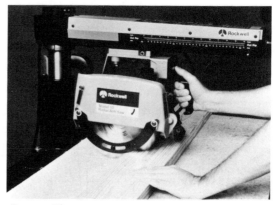

Crosscutting

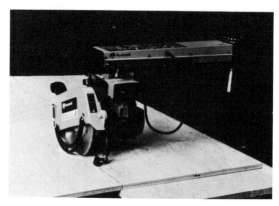

Ripping

Bevel ripping

Bevel crosscutting

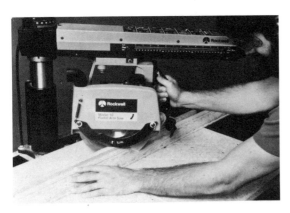

Mitering

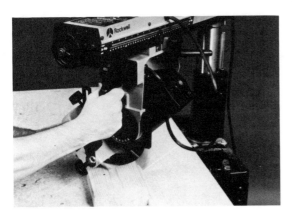

Compound mitering

For this type of cutting, the saw is moved to the right or left until it stops at the desired angle. It is then locked into place and the cut made. The next basic cut is the bevel cut. This is done by releasing the saw tilt pin and aligning the saw with the desired angle on the front angle indicator. The better saws will automatically fall to the 45° point, and stop at this point. You can then set the saw at any angle in between for angles other than 45°. Then lock the saw in position. The correct method of making the cut is to hold the stock with your right hand and make the cut with your left hand. This allows you to see where your hand is at all times. Sometimes this is not possible and you must make the cut holding the stock with your left hand, but it's a bit more dangerous. A featherboard or narrow piece of scrap stock can often be used to hold the stock in place.

Compound Cuts. The compound crosscut is made by combining the two last cuts mentioned, the miter and the bevel. Again any combination of angles can be used in cutting joints, as long as

The radial arm saw excels at making compound miter cuts for many-sided projects. The arm is simply swung to the correct miter degree; then tilted to achieve the desired bevel.

TABLE OF COMPOUND ANGLES

Tilt of Work	Equivalent taper per inch	Four-Sided Butt		Four-Sided Miter		Six-Sided miter		Eight-Sided Miter	
		Bevel Degrees	Miter Degrees	Bevel Degrees	Miter Degrees	Bevel Degrees	Miter Degrees	Bevel Degrees	Miter Degrees
5°	0.087	1/2	85	44 3/4	85	29 3/4	87 1/2	22 1/4	88
10°	0.176	1 1/2	80 1/4	44 1/4	80 1/4	29 1/2	84 1/2	22	86
15°	0.268	3 3/4	75 1/2	43 1/4	75 1/2	29	81 3/4	21 1/2	84
20°	0.364	6 1/4	71 1/4	41 3/4	71 1/4	28 1/4	79	21	82
25°	0.466	10	67	40	67	27 1/4	76 1/2	20 1/4	80
30°	0.577	14 1/2	63 1/2	37 3/4	63 1/2	26	74	19 1/2	78 1/4
35°	0.700	19 1/2	60 1/4	35 1/2	60 1/4	24 1/2	71 3/4	18 1/4	76 3/4
40°	0.839	24 1/2	57 1/4	32 1/2	57 1/4	22 3/4	69 3/4	17	75
45°	1.000	30	54 3/4	30	54 3/4	21	67 3/4	15 3/4	73 3/4
50°	1.19	36	52 1/2	27	52 1/2	19	66 1/4	14 1/2	72 1/2
55°	1.43	42	50 3/4	24	50 3/4	16 3/4	64 3/4	12 1/2	71 1/4
60°	1.73	48	49	21	49	14 1/2	63 1/2	11	70 1/4

the sum of the bevel angle and the miter angle is 90°. A compound miter chart is given above.

To make a compound angle cut for a many-sided project, determine the bevel and miter angles by consulting the table and set this on the saw. Place the stock flat on the table and cut the righthand miter. Then move the arm to the same miter setting on the lefthand side of the saw and turn the piece around 180°. Cut off the waste. If you have selected the angles correctly, the two pieces will match and the angle between them will be 90°.

Ripping. A radial arm saw can also be used for ripping. In ripping, the saw arm is stationed parallel to the fence, and the stock is pushed against it. It takes more power to make the ripping cuts, and it's easier for the stock to bind between the fence and the saw blade. Also, the blade will have a tendency to lift the stock up off the saw table. For this reason, ripping is usually left to the table saw if one is available. To rip with a radial arm saw, release the yoke lock and the yoke locator pin, then turn the roller head to the out-rip or in-rip position and lock back in position. Push the saw to the desired rip width, then lock on the track by tightening the rip-lock clamp. Always make sure the guard is set properly when ripping and that the anti-kickback fingers are also in the correct position. When

pushing the stock through for ripping always push against the feed side, never against the side that has just been cut, as this makes the stock bind against the saw blade. A push stick should be used to complete the cut. A featherboard or piece of scrap stock can also be used to help hold the stock in place. A special fence with a built-in hold-down can be made for working with narrow stock.

There are two basic ripping positions, in-rip and out-rip. When cutting in the "in" position the

Although ripping cuts are usually made on a table saw, a radial arm saw can also be used for this purpose. The "out" rip position is usually used when ripping wide stock.

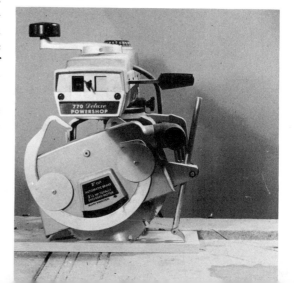

With molding heads, the radial arm saw can be used to cut a great variety of edge moldings, and the radial arm can also be tilted to cut moldings across the face of stock.

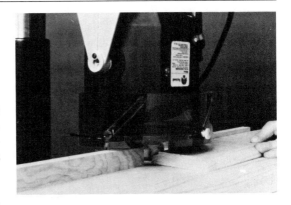

blade of the saw is between the motor and the post, and the stock is pushed from right to left. For "out" rip or lefthand rip, the motor is between the post and the blade. This position is most commonly used for ripping wide stock.

Molding Heads and Accessories. In addition to the standard saw blades used for normal cuts, molding heads and dado blades can also be used with the radial arm saw for such jobs as dadoing, rabbeting, and making molding of all kinds. These operations are discussed in Chapters 5, 7, and 14.

Many machines have special chucks to accept a router bit. Cross-grain dadoes and rabbets can be made in the same way as a regular crosscut

With a dado head, the saw can be used to cut dadoes and rabbets.

A panel-raising attachment can be used to cut raised panels for doors or drawers.

with this accessory, and other cuts can be made by feeding the stock into the bit, as in a regular rip cut. A rotary planer attachment is useful for cutting raised panels.

Table Saw

Probably the second most popular tool for the home cabinet shop is a table saw. The functions of the radial arm saw and table saw overlap to some extent, with the radial arm being the more versatile of the two. However, some people prefer the table saw because of its superior ripping capacity, and in many shops the only stationary tool is a table saw. A professional cabinetmaker or serious hobbyist will usually have both tools.

For maximum efficiency, table saw extensions should be bought along with the saw (or as soon as possible thereafter). An acceptable alternative is a portable sawhorse or similar frame that can be positioned in place to catch the sawn-off waste stock. The top of the support should have a roller so the material will slide across it easily.

Table saws are available in several different sizes, but the 10-inch size is best for the home cabinet shop. In most cases, a 10-inch saw will cut through wood up to 3 inches thick; a 12-inch model will cut through stock over 4 inches thick if the blade is set at 90°. In choosing a table saw, the best choice is one that utilizes belts or pulleys to drive the saw arbor. This type of machine allows you to use more of the saw blade than does a direct drive arrangement.

There are two basic styles; the bench and the floor model. They are similar in operation and size, but the bench model must have a stand or bench to sit on.

Ripping. The principal task of a table saw is ripping. In this operation, the rip fence is set the desired distance from the saw blade. Ordinarily, the rip fence is set on the righthand side of the saw blade as you face the front of the saw. The better saws have calibrations on the table to enable you to set the fence for the desired width of cut. An accurate cut will depend on the rip fence being exactly parallel with the blade. Although most calibrated marks will be fairly close, the amount of set in the saw blade will make some difference in the measurement, so the careful

Additional accessories for the radial arm saw include a router, disc sander, and drum sander.

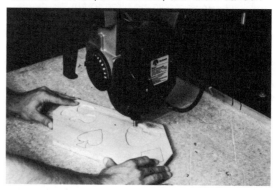

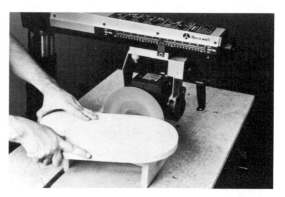

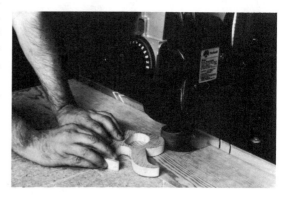

craftsman measures from the inside edge of the teeth of the saw blade to the inside edge of the fence to make sure of this measurement. This alignment should be rechecked periodically, as the rip fence can be knocked to one side or the other with use.

A table saw must have three protective devices: a blade guard, anti-kickback fingers, and a splitter bar or saw-kerf spreader. Modern safety

The table saw is probably the second most popular stationary tool for the home craftsman. As with the radial arm saw, it is important to observe all safety precautions. The blade guard should be kept down whenever practical, and a push stick used to feed stock for ripping cuts.

guards are made of orange plastic for easy visibility. The purpose of the guard is to keep your fingers away from the blade and to prevent chips from flying up at your face. Anti-kickback fingers hold the already-cut sections of stock down behind the blade to guard against kickback. The splitter bar performs a similar function by keeping the saw kerf open. One of the dangers of ripping with the table saw is that you must push the stock toward the saw blade with your hands. To avoid the possibility of getting a finger in the blade, always use a push stick to complete the cut when ripping a narrow piece. For very narrow stock, a push block is even better, because it fits down over the saw fence as a guide and can't be flipped away by the action of the saw blade.

The first step in ripping is to set the rip fence for the desired width of cut and lock it securely in place. The saw blade should be set about ⅛ to ¼ inch above the surface of the stock. Always rip on the waste side of the cut line. Turn on the saw and push the stock into the blade, holding it down on the saw table and against the rip fence. Always stand to the left or right of the saw blade; never directly behind it. When ripping wider stock, hook the last two fingers of your right hand over the fence to help steady it and to make sure the hand is kept away from the saw blade. When ripping narrow stock, a push stick or block will guide the stock past the blade. Hold the left hand against the outside edge of the waste section, if it is wide enough, to help hold the stock against the saw fence as the cut is started. Don't allow the left

hand to go past the front edge of the saw blade. Once the work has been moved into this position, the anti-kickback fingers should hold the work safely down on the table and you can remove the left hand. Continue feeding with your right hand or the push stick, depending on the thickness of the stock, until the stock passes the rear of the saw blade. When the cut is complete, turn off the saw and remove the work and the waste stock.

A typical rip-sawing operation on the table saw is *resawing,* or cutting wide stock down into thinner boards. This can be done only on stock that

When ripping wide stock, the right hand can be used to hold down stock as it passes the blade. Hook two fingers over the fence to make sure hand stays clear of the blade, and use a push stick to help steady the stock.

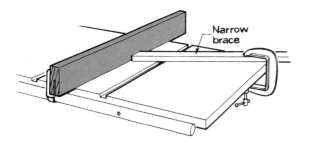

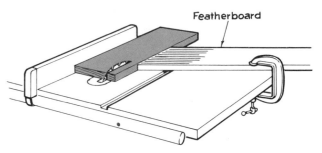

When resawing stock or ripping thin strips from a wide board, a narrow brace or featherboard should be clamped to the table to secure the work as it passes the blade. (To make a featherboard, miter cut a wide board at 45°, then make a series of narrowly spaced rip cuts in the end to give it flexibility.)

is no wider than twice the cutting height of the saw blade. In this operation, the stock is held on edge and secured by means of a featherboard or narrow brace clamped to the table top. When the stock is too wide to be cut in one pass, it is turned over to make a matching cut on the other side. If the combined cuts don't quite meet, a hand rip saw can be used to separate the two pieces of stock. When ripping a long board in close quarters, saw half the board from one end, and then turn it around to complete the cut.

If you must rip very thin stock, a wooden auxiliary table or table insert should be used in addition to an auxiliary fence to prevent the thin pieces from dropping down into the saw blade slot between the blade and the fence. (See Chapter 14, pages 225 and 227.) If the saw blade catches these pieces, it will throw them back with considerable force.

Crosscutting. A table saw can also be used for crosscutting, although it isn't normally as accurate as the radial arm saw on large pieces. However, with the use of the miter gauge, smaller pieces can be crosscut quite effectively.

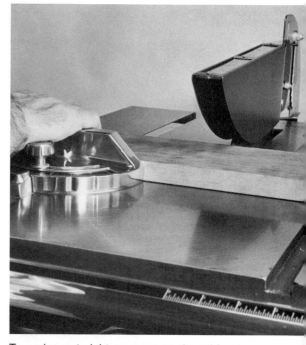

To make a straight crosscut on the table saw, the miter gauge is positioned at a 90° angle to the blade and used to push the stock past the blade. *Toolcraft.*

Angled cuts are made by turning the miter gauge.

For all straight crosscuts (90° to sides of stock), the miter gauge is set at 0. Place the miter gauge so that its guide strip rides in the table groove, and use it to push the stock past the blade. Miter cuts are made in the same way, after first adjusting the miter gauge to the proper angle. Some miter gauges are equipped with a clamping device that helps hold the stock against the impact of the blade to insure an accurate cut.

Other Uses. Another common use of the table saw is to cut bevels on the edges of stock. This is done in much the same manner as straight ripping or crosscutting, but with the blade tilted at an angle. An auxiliary fence is usually required for this type of cut, as shown in Chapter 5.

The table saw is often used to rabbet cabinet doors and drawer fronts, etc. For most purposes, the rabbet is made with two equal cuts, so the distance between the rip fence and the saw blade is equal to the projection of the saw blade above the table. The first cut is made with the stock held on edge, and the second with the stock flat on the table. To make sure that the settings are correct, it's a good idea to experiment on a piece of scrap wood before starting the cut on good stock.

A shop-made miter jig will produce faster, more accurate miter cuts. (Work must be cut to length before miter cuts are made.)

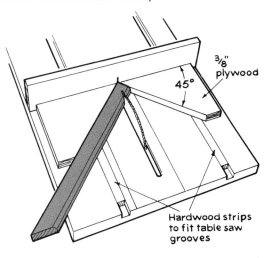

3/8" plywood

45°

Hardwood strips to fit table saw grooves

Molding heads and dado blades can be used on a table saw to cut grooves or special shapes. Because these blades strike the wood with much more impact than a regular saw blade, an auxiliary fence and table as well as hold-down devices

One of the primary uses of a table saw is to cut the lip or rabbet on doors and drawer fronts. The first cut is made with the piece flat on the table, then the piece is turned on edge to complete the rabbet.

are required when using them. See Chapter 14 for construction details.

As with many tools, special jigs increase the versatility of the table saw and provide for easier and safer working. One of these is a miter jig. With this jig you can cut multiple 45° miters very quickly. A tenoning jig can also be a great help when making mortise-and-tenon joints. A factory-made tenoning jig rides in the miter gauge grooves of the table; the shop-made type shown on page 87 serves the same purpose but fits over the rip fence. Among the most useful jigs are the stationary and adjustable tapering jigs shown in Chapter 10. These are used most often for cutting table and chair legs.

Band Saw

A band saw is very seldom one of the first tools purchased by the home cabinetmaker, but it can be one of the most useful tools in the shop. It can be used for cutting arched-front cabinet door frames, curved aprons for countertops or tables, and for many other irregularly shaped pieces. One of the most exciting uses of a band saw is in making compound cuts such as those needed for cabriole legs. (See Chapters 10 and 18 for details

on making this kind of cut.) Another prime use of the band saw is resawing wide stock—for narrow stock, the table saw will generally do a better job.

Band saws are available in a number of different sizes. The size refers to the distance between the blade and the throat, and gives an indication of the dimension of stock that can be worked in the machine. A 12-inch size is adequate for most home shop needs. Most band saws can handle stock up to 6 inches thick, and most also have a tilting table. A tilting table greatly increases the versatility of the band saw; don't purchase one without it. Most band saws also have one or two table slots to accommodate a miter gauge. My own band saw is one of the kit types for which the manufacturer supplies the metal parts and the rest of the body is put together with wood in the home shop. It has stood up well to many years of use.

A band saw is easy to use and fairly safe, but it takes a fair amount of experience to become really expert. The most important aspect in using a band saw is planning the cutting to avoid catching the workpiece on the band saw arm or in too tight a corner—the plan must allow for the workpiece to be turned so that the saw blade can be backed out. In some cases you will have to mark the outline of the cut on both sides of the stock and make a second pass to complete it.

Operating Tips. Two things are basic to good band saw operation: feeding speed and the amount of pressure applied to the stock as it is pushed into the blade. If the feed is too fast, the saw blade will chatter and squeak against the back-up bearings; too slow and the wood may burn. Pushing too hard with one hand or the other during the feed will cause the blade to be pushed sideways. This will result in an uneven cut, and will also dull the blade.

A band saw table should tilt so that the tool can be used to make angled cuts.

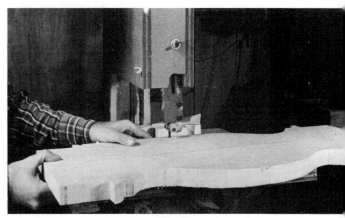

It is important to maintain even pressure when feeding work into a band saw so that the thin blade is not pushed out of line.

The band saw is commonly used to resaw wide stock as well as to cut irregular shapes.

Band saw blades range in width from ⅛ to ½ inch, and are available in three types—regular, skip, and saber tooth.

It's also important to use the right size blade. The larger the blade, the larger the minimum cutting diameter of a circle. You can't, for instance, cut anything smaller than a 1¾-inch radius with a ¾-inch blade. The type of blade and set of the teeth makes a difference, too. A heavier blade with a pronounced set to the teeth will make a faster but rougher cut than a fine-tooth blade with less set. There are three basic types of blades—regular, skip tooth, and hook or saber tooth. The skip-tooth and hook-tooth blades have a deeper groove between the teeth to allow faster cutting.

Drill Press

A drill press is an enjoyable tool. It can not only make short work of many tedious jobs, but can also be used for many special operations in the home cabinetmaking shop. Although it was designed primarily for use in metalworking, it can be one of the most versatile woodworking tools with the right accessories. Drill presses are available in floor models and in table or bench models. For most woodworking jobs, a bench model will do just fine and it's usually less expensive than a comparable floor model. A drill press used for woodworking should have a radial head.

Carbon-steel twist drills are used for most typical small jobs such as drilling holes for dowels. Foerstner bits and wood auger bits that have brad points are used for larger holes. (Bits with screw points are very seldom used in a home shop because it is difficult to match the feeding speed with the screw's turning capacity.) The variable speeds of a drill press make it possible to use both

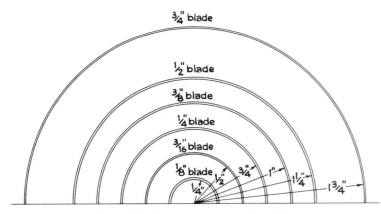

When choosing a blade for a project, keep in mind that a larger turning radius is required for heavier blades.

Turning radius for various band saw blades

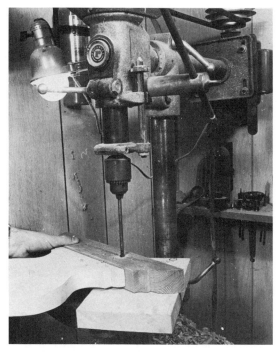

A drill press can be used to bore pilot holes for screws and the holes for dowel joints.

With attachments, the drill press can be used to cut dowel plugs, or even large circles.

small and large bits with maximum efficiency. In general, for smaller bits and softer woods, faster motor speeds are used. A ¼-inch drill might be run at 2,400 rpm, but a large bit or fly cutter attachment no more than 700 rpm for safety.

An excellent use for the drill press is to cut the pilot holes for wood screws in hardwood stock during furniture construction. You can set the depth stop on the drill press and bore stopped holes very quickly with a regular drill or countersink bit. The holes can be concealed with wood plugs, which can also be cut on a drill press with a plug-cutter attachment. The plugs can be made from the same stock used in the project, or from a contrasting wood. For instance, unusual effects can be created by setting walnut plugs in a pine chest, or maple or holly plugs in a walnut chest.

For larger holes, or to cut circles up to 6 inches in diameter, fly-cutter attachments are available. These should be used at a fairly slow speed, with the work clamped securely in place for safety. Large circles can also be cut with a hole saw or an expansion bit. The latter requires the same safety precautions as the fly cutter—cutting speed

There are also mortising attachments for the drill press to bore either round or square holes.

fairly slow, and workpiece clamped securely in place.

One of the primary uses of a drill press in larger cabinet shops is as a mortising tool. A mortising bit and chisel sleeve assembly is used to bore square holes. Many larger woodworking shops have one drill press that is set up for mortising all the time. There are also more economical mortising bits that bore round holes, to be squared off later with a chisel.

Fitted with a drum sander, a drill press will also do an excellent job of surface-sanding circles or irregularly shaped pieces. There are also router

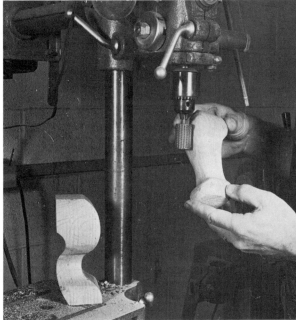

There are also a variety of rasp attachments for used in rough shaping, or even grooving and beveling.

When fitted with a drum sander, a drill press makes quick work of sanding irregularly shaped pieces. Sanders are available in several sizes.

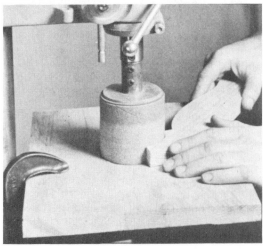

bits, dovetail groovers, rotary rasps, and other bits and accessories that can be bought to increase the tool's versatility.

Sanders and Grinders

Belt and Disk Sander. A combination belt and disk sander is an excellent finishing tool. Although portable sanders also do the job, the capability of applying the work to the tool is often a great convenience. Disk sizes on the combination tools range from 6 to 12 inches in diameter, and the belts are 4 to 6 inches wide with a 3- or 4-foot total length. The end of the belt can be used as a drum sander for sanding inside curves, and the length of the belt for rough wood surfacing. Ends of stock can be smoothed on the disk.

This tool is normally mounted on a table top, although some of the larger units come equipped with stands. When using a belt sander, the workpiece is usually held in place lightly but firmly with both hands, and moved back and forth over the belt so that the belt will wear evenly. If the workpiece is shorter than the belt, the table

A combination belt and disk sander will prove valuable for heavy sanding jobs. The end of the belt can be used to sand inside curves.

platen or an auxiliary fence or jig is used to back it up. The belt can be positioned horizontally or vertically. Most work done on the disk is also done freehand by merely holding the stock on the table and pushing it in towards the turning disk. The sanding is always done on the down side of the turning disk, using several light strokes instead of one heavy cut.

Disk sanders or combination disk and drum sanders are available without belt units, but these are not as versatile.

Belt Sander/Grinder. Designed more for metal than wood, the sander/grinder is also very useful in woodworking. It's usually purchased when you expect to do a lot of heavy-duty sanding and grinding. It can be used for anything from wood shaping and sanding to sharpening tool blades, depending on the type of belt used. Changing the 1-inch-wide abrasive belts is quite easy and only takes about a minute. The tool can also be used for internal sanding by threading the belt through the workpiece, then fitting it back on the wheels. The table on the grinder tilts so that

you can achieve an accurate bevel edge on almost any tool.

Bench Grinder. If you plan on sharpening your own tools, a bench grinder may be the best choice. The main advantage of the bench grinder over a belt grinder is that the abrasive wheels can be replaced with buffing wheels and used for polishing. Make sure that any model you buy has unbreakable eye shields and sturdy wheel guards.

A belt sander/grinder is useful for a wide variety of tasks—sharpening knives and chisels, beveling the ends of dowels, or polishing tools. *Dremel.*

A bench grinder is necessary for many tool sharpening tasks. The model shown has a tool rest that can be adjusted to any angle to grind accurate bevels.

Jointer

One of the most important tools of the serious cabinetmaker is the jointer. Without it, the almost invisible joints of good cabinetry are impossible for most of us. A jointer is nothing more than a stationary power version of the hand plane, but it will do the job much faster, and in most cases more accurately. In a professional cabinet shop, the jointer serves one main purpose —planing the edges of stock.

There are several different sizes of jointers. The size indicates the length of the knives, or the width of stock that can be cut. Because most jointing in a home shop will be done on the edges of stock, the 6-inch size is more than adequate.

The jointer is one of the most dangerous workshop tools. Many people have received serious injuries to their hands through carelessness in operating the machine. This usually occurs while trying to surface stock that is too small, or too short. If at all possible, joint edges on larger stock, then rip them to make up narrower stock. If you must joint small, narrow stock, use push sticks and hold-downs or featherboards to hold the stock down against the knives and against the fence. All jointers are equipped with a safety guard that lifts as the cut is started and snaps back after the stock has passed through. Make sure the guard is operating properly.

Depth of cut is set on the jointer by adjusting the infeed table. The offset between it and the outfeed table determines the depth of cut. The cut should never be more than ⅛ inch; repeat passes are made to complete larger cuts. To operate the machine, begin by standing off to the side; never stand directly behind the jointer or in line with the stock being pushed into it. Grasp the front end of the stock with your left hand. Be absolutely sure that your fingers are out of the way of the revolving cutterhead. Then position the stock in front of the cutterhead. The left hand is now used only to hold the stock over against the fence, and the right hand pushes the stock over the cutterhead. You may also want to hook the last two fingers of your right hand over the fence.

Once the cut has been completed, lift the stock with both hands so the guard will come back and cover the blade; then bring it back in position for

A jointer is an important tool in a cabinet shop. Without it, it is difficult to make good, tight-fitting joints.

The jointer is considered the most dangerous workshop tool by many professionals. All safety precautions must be observed, including the use of a push stick or hold-down whenever possible. Also, avoid pushing thin or small pieces into the blade.

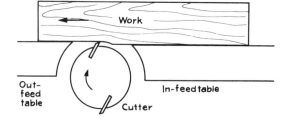

Depth of cut is set on a jointer by adjusting the infeed table. Stock should always be fed with the grain as shown.

another cut, if needed. When cutting rough-sawn surfaces, two or three passes are usually required.

Another common method of feeding stock over the blades is to start the feed as described, but once the front end of the stock has passed over the blade, move the left hand to the portion in front of the blade to help hold the stock against the fence. Again, the right hand is used for pushing, the left hand for guiding. Any time the stock is thin or narrow, use a push stick to push it through the jointer.

One common use of a jointer is to true up edges of S2S stock. (If you have a planer and a jointer, rough lumber—even more economical—can be utilized.) A dished edge of S2S stock can be trued up on the jointer, and the opposite edge ripped on a table saw to produce stock with parallel sides.

The jointer is also commonly used in the installation of cabinet facings. Before the vertical facers are ripped to a smaller size from wide stock, both edges of the wider stock are first run over the jointer to smooth them. Then the stock is ripped about ⅛- to ¼-inch larger than necessary and the cut edges also run through the jointer. These facers are installed first; then the crosspieces are

treated in the same way and cut to length with a hollow-ground plywood blade or planer blade. The joints between the two will be almost invisible.

Rabbets can also be cut on a jointer. The infeed table has a ledge so that the stock to be rabbeted will be supported as it is fed over a portion of the jointer blade. The fence is moved up so that the amount of blade exposed is just the width of the desired rabbet. Since the blade guard has to be removed for this operation, extra precautions are required.

Tapers can be cut on a jointer by using the stop block arrangements described in Chapter 10. In

One of the most common uses of a jointer is to straighten the dished edge of S2S stock. Jointed edge can then ride along table saw fence to rip the opposite edge straight, resulting in S4S stock.

Rabbets can be cut on a jointer by moving the fence up so that only a portion of the work passes over the blade.

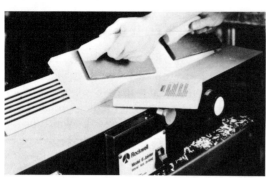

The jointer fence can also be tilted to cut bevels or chamfers.

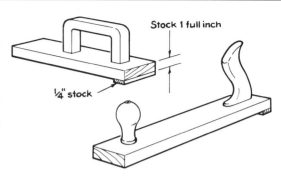

Hold-down devices for use with the jointer should be constructed with thick stock. Two gripping points will enable the operator to apply pressure more evenly.

addition, bevels or chamfers can be cut by tilting the fence.

Surface Planer

A medium-size surface planer can be an extremely valuable tool for the home cabinetmaker. It is commonly used in conjunction with a jointer to surface all four sides of rough stock, and considerable savings in lumber costs can be realized this way.

Planers come in a wide range of sizes; the size indicates the length of the blade and the width of stock that the machine will accept. A 12- or 18-inch size is adequate for most purposes.

The main advantage of a surface planer is that stock is fed past the blades by means of rollers and hold-down devices inside the machine. Thus, the planer is much less dangerous, and easier to operate, than other power tools. In addition, it is not essential, as with the jointer, to feed stock with the grain.

As mentioned, both a jointer and a planer are required to surface rough stock; the stock must be surfaced on one side with a jointer before it is planed. In addition to standard surfacing jobs,

In conjunction with a jointer, a planer enables you to surface rough lumber and can lead to real economies in purchased stock. Many planers can also be fitted with molding knives and used to cut moldings or even tongue-and-groove joints as shown. *Belsaw.*

A planer provides the safest and easiest way to cut moldings. Here, a board is being edge-molded and surface-planed in one operation.

many planers can also be used to cut moldings of almost any style or size—it is much safer and faster to cut moldings on a planer than with a table saw, radial arm saw, or shaper. An advantage of this capacity is that hardwood molding can be matched to solid-wood paneling, for instance, instead of utilizing a softwood factory-made molding. An unusual aspect of the Belsaw model shown is that the company will custom-make molding knives for a woodworker who wants a special pattern.

Shaper

A shaper is quite often the final stationary power tool that a home craftsman adds to his workshop. A shaper provides a means to do some jobs much more easily than the other tools commonly used for shaping (drill press, radial arm saw, table saw, or router). With a shaper you can make decorative or joint cuts on the edges of round, oval, or irregularly shaped pieces as well as on cabinet door frames, drawer fronts, and picture frames.

Shapers are available in ½-, ¾-, and 1-hp models. A ½-hp model with a spindle speed capacity of 10,000 rpm should be adequate for home-shop purposes. A reversible motor feature is very useful; it allows you to feed stock from either side by reversing the rotation of the cutters. Although there are professional shapers with removable cutter blades, most spindle shapers used by home craftsmen utilize solid one-piece three-wing shaper cutters that fit on the standard ½-inch spindle. These are available in many different shapes, including quarter-round, cove, panel-raising, and clover leaf screen molding cutters. The cutters are placed over a threaded spindle and held in place with a slotted washer and nut. The spindle may be raised and lowered, or the cutter itself raised and lowered to control the height of the cut. In most instances, the cutter will be placed so it will cut on the underside of the work. (This is the safest method of cutting, although you can't see the cutting in progress.)

A shaper is considered one of the most dangerous tools, because it operates at a high speed, and there is no way to completely guard the cutters. Like any other power tool, it must be respected, and certain safety precautions must be adhered to. In addition to common sense safety rules that apply to any power tool, there are a number of special rules for shaper operation. A few of them are mentioned here.

- Make sure that you have a good stance and that the floor is clear of debris. Above all, keep hands clear of the cutters, and don't push directly into the cutter, but with hands off to one side and pushing against the fence.

- Always use guards, hold-downs, or featherboards. Accessory hold-downs and clamps are available.

- Always use a miter gauge and clamp attachment when edge-shaping work less than 6 inches wide.

- Always feed against the cutter rotation. Many shapers have reversible motors, so check to make sure that the direction of rotation accords with the direction of feed.

- Never allow the stock to run between the fence and the cutter. The fence should always be placed so that the cutterhead is partly shielded by it and projects just a little in front of it. (The depth of cut is determined by the amount of projection.) The ends of the fence should be as close as possible to the cutterhead to shield it on the sides.

- When shaping with collars and starting pins, the collar must have sufficient bearing surface to support the work. The cutter should be positioned below the collar when possible so that the cut is made on the underside of the work.

- When shaping with collars, the work must be fairly heavy in proportion to the cut being made. The work should never be thin, flexible material or of light body.

Basic Operation.   In most instances, the spindle will operate in a counter-clockwise direction, and stock will be fed against this rotation from the right side of the machine. The cut should be made on the underside of the stock whenever possible. In most instances, stock to be shaped should be at least 6 inches wide to provide enough handling surface to guide it past the cutters safely. Special provisions can be made for narrower stock, as described later. To set up for a shaping operation, draw the shape you wish to cut on the edge of a piece of scrap stock. The edge should be the same thickness as the workpiece. Position the scrap block against the cutter, and raise or lower the cutter and adjust the fence to

approximate the cutter position and depth of cut. Roll the spindle around by hand to make sure everything clears properly; then flip the switch once to make sure that the cutter is turning in the proper direction. With everything adjusted and set properly, run the scrap stock through and readjust as necessary.

Most shaping operations remove only a portion of the edge of the stock, and the rest serves as a bearing edge to guide the piece along the fence. When the entire edge of stock is removed, as when cutting some joints or full beading, the back fence must be set forward—exactly even with the cutter circle—so that it will support the work as it passes the cutter. Both fences should always be parallel to the front edge of the table or the table groove.

When feeding stock, push it past the cutter slowly and steadily. If the cut to be made is quite deep, it should be done in two or more passes. Otherwise, nicks and burn marks will mar the work. Cross-grain cuts should be done more slowly than with-the-grain cuts. These cuts will never be quite as smooth as with-the-grain cuts, so adjacent with-the-grain cuts should be made after end cuts to minimize splintering.

Hold-downs, auxiliary fences and jigs.   When shaping end grain on narrow stock, use a miter gauge with accessory hold-down clamps or a back-up block to keep the stock straight. A back-up block will also help to minimize splintering at the end of the cut.

On a shaper, work should be cut *with* the grain as shown whenever possible. For most operations, the shaper removes only a portion of the edge, and fences are placed in a straight line. When an entire edge is to be removed, back fence is moved up to support work after it passes the cutter.

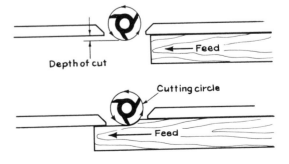

To make freehand cuts on the shaper, the fence must be removed, and extra safety precautions are required. A starter pin in the table braces the work for the start of the cut, and collars are placed on the spindle to provide a bearing surface for the work to ride against.

To shape very thin stock such as screen molding, the best method is to shape the bead on the edges of a wide piece of stock, then rip off thin strips with a saw. A strip-holding jig, shown on page 232, can also be used to shape thin stock.

To cut across the face of stock, a high fence can be used to support the stock. Use a featherboard or spring hold-down to hold the stock properly against the cutter.

To shape round stock, a two-part auxiliary fence with cutouts of the same circumference as the stock can be used as a guide. Clamp both parts of the auxiliary fence to the table, and feed the stock against the righthand side. An alternate method is to remove the regular fence and use a one-piece auxiliary fence with a cutout for the shaper blade and a large V-notch in which to fit the stock. With this type of fence, you can shape any circle that will fit in the V.

To feed stock into the shaper blade at an angle, a simple miter fence-table can be constructed. This is nothing more than an auxiliary table fastened to wedges to position the work at a 45° angle to the original table. This jig is handy for cutting spline grooves in miter joints.

Ovals and odd shapes are cut "free-hand" without a fence, with a shaper collar to serve as the bearing surface. Collars are available in several different sizes, and are placed on the spindle with the cutter. The diameter of the collar in relation to the shaper cutter determines the depth of cut made. In this type of shaping, only a portion of the edge can be cut. You can't remove an entire edge because some portion of it must ride against the collar. Whenever possible, the collar should ride against the top edge of the stock and the cutter on the bottom. However, for some cuts it will be necessary to use a cutter on the top of stock, or a thin spacer collar with cutters both above and below. These arrangements are a bit

Round pieces can be edge-molded on a shaper by clamping cutout supports to the table to brace the work as it passes the cutter.

more dangerous and also will produce an uneven cut if the stock is not of uniform thickness.

A starter pin is always used when making collar cuts. The pin fits into a hole in the table and serves to back up the work as the cut is started. Many craftsmen like to use both pins. Then, if necessary when completing the cut, the work can be held against the back pin. Again, the main rule in this operation is that the work must have sufficient contact with the collar to create a firm support.

To make a collar cut, begin by placing the work against the pin, but not in contact with the cutter. Then slowly bring the work to the cutter, keeping it in contact with the starting pin. This must be done carefully; if the work is pushed against the cutter without the support of the pin, it will kick back. Make sure you have a good hold on the stock, because even with the pin there is some danger of kickback. Start the cut slowly. Once the cutter is properly cutting the edge, you can then move the work away from the pin as necessary and against the cutter and collar. A ring guard should be used at all times. A starting block clamped to the table top can be used in place of a starting pin, and may provide more support in some cases.

One method of shaping that is often overlooked is pattern shaping. This provides a means to cut an entire edge of an odd-shaped piece, because the pattern rides against the collar and provides a bearing surface. A wood pattern can be tacked to the work with nails or screws, or pattern cutting can be done with a special table insert that is available as an accessory with many shapers.

Combination Tools

Combination tools such as the Shopsmith are popular with home craftsmen because they provide a large number of stationary tools and acces-

Three of the tools included in the basic Shopsmith are a table saw, drill press, and disk sander.

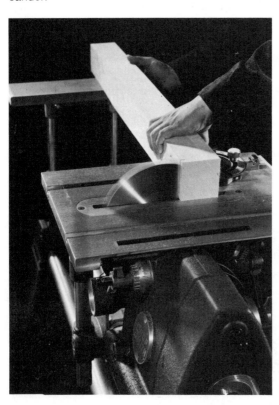

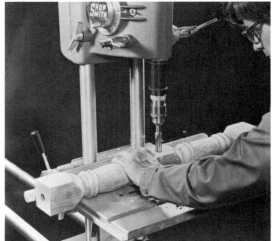

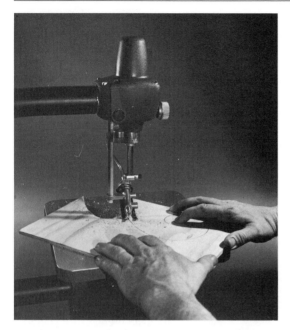
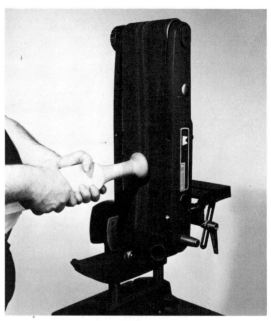

Add-on tools for the Shopsmith include a jigsaw and belt sander.

sories in one unit. The tools take up very little space, but you have available a 10-inch table saw, drill press, 34-inch lathe, 12-inch disk sander, and horizontal drill. Add-on tools include a band saw, jigsaw, 4-inch jointer, and 6-inch belt sander.

Probably the only disadvantage of the combination tool for the home cabinet shop is the time spent changing from one operation to another. Although in most situations this is only a small amount of time, it can be a bit frustrating. One way of beating this problem is to do all the same jobs for an operation at the same time. For instance, all stock for a project can be cut to size on the table saw, then the drill press set up to bore holes for all the dowels, etc.

Lathe

The lathe is one of the oldest power tools. Long before electricity, foot-powered lathes were used for turning out beautiful furniture and many other wooden items. The modern lathe isn't much different from the old-timers, but of course it is much easier to operate.

A lathe is used for two types of work. One is *spindle* turning, which is done with the stock fastened between the headstock and the tailstock. The tailstock is adjustable laterally to accept different lengths of work. The second type of lathe work, *faceplate* turning, is done by fastening the work to the headstock only.

The size of a lathe indicates the distance between centers, or the maximum length of stock that can be turned. The *swing* is the distance from the center of the spindle on the headstock to the top of the lathe bed. Some lathes have a gap in the bed to increase this distance so that larger-diameter stock can be turned on a faceplate. A 36-inch-capacity lathe is adequate for most shops, because most lathe work will consist of spindle-turning of legs and spindles. (See Chapter 10 for details on mounting stock for spindle turning.) However, many 36-inch lathes have a swing of only 6 inches, which limits the diameter of faceplate turnings to 12 inches. Unless the lathe also has an outfeed faceplate (with accessory tool rest that stands on the floor), you will be somewhat limited by that capacity.

In a cabinet or furniture shop a lathe duplicator attachment can make it much easier to produce a number of identical turnings such as decorative spindles, chair legs, and similar items.

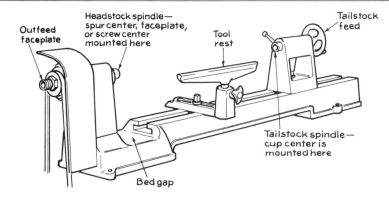

In most shops, the lathe will be used primarily for spindle turning, and the distance between centers is an important consideration.

A lathe duplicator can quickly turn out a series of balusters for a staircase or chair legs for a dining room set.

A lathe is an infinitely versatile tool. With the right accessories and homemade devices, you can turn almost anything imaginable, including round balls, bowls, dowels, and even simulated carvings. On some models, an accessory disk sander can be attached to the spindle.

Portable Power Tools

Electric Drill

Probably no single power tool is as common as an electric drill. Even the kitchen-drawer type of home workshop usually includes a small drill. Although one drill can be fitted with different bits to do any number of chores, having two or more around is a real convenience. For instance, when installing a number of hinges on cabinet doors, one drill can be set to bore the screw-starter holes while another can be fitted with a screwdriver attachment to fasten the hinges.

There are many different portable electric drills on the market, and choosing the correct one is important. Purchase only a good quality, name-brand tool. Drills are sometimes rated "good," "better," and "best," as well as "light-duty" and

"heavy-duty." Probably the best drill for everyday use in a cabinet shop is the ⅜-inch variable speed drill with a reversible feature. Motor capacity ranges from around ⅕ hp to ⅜ hp. Naturally, the more horsepower, the heavier the drill—the more powerful ⅜-inch drills may weigh as much as 5 or 6 pounds, while models with less horsepower weigh about 3 pounds. If you intend to do light drilling all day, as when installing small screws in cabinets, you would probably use one of the lighter-weight drills. To fasten a cabinet to a wall with large screws, you would prefer a heavier model to provide more torque.

Heavier jobs, as boring through flooring to make pipe runs, require a ½-inch drill. Some of these heavier-duty drills can develop up to 1 hp to tackle the really heavy jobs.

Rechargeable drills. One of the most important innovations in electric drills was the introduction of the cordless drill. This extremely handy tool allows you to use a power drill at a site where there isn't any electricity. The main advantage this drill affords the cabinetmaker, however, is that it can be taken to another work station without switching the cord to another outlet. The cordless drill is also excellent for jobs in tight places—as when fastening cabinets to the wall, installing closet hardware, etc.—because you don't have to snake a power cord in with you.

Screwdrivers. Although the lower speeds of a variable-speed drill are suitable for screw driving, an industrial power screwdriver seems to be better adapted to this job. A cordless electric screwdriver can't be matched for convenience.

A good-quality ⅜-inch variable-speed reversible drill will be useful in cabinetmaking. The reversible feature allows you to remove screws or retract a jammed bit.

Fitted with a screwdriver accessory, a variable-speed drill can be used to install hinges.

 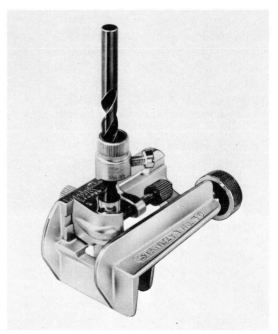

Valuable accessories for a portable drill include pilot bits for wood screws, and a doweling jig.

Drill Bits and Accessories. A good assortment of twist drills is necessary in any shop. When buying drill bits, good quality is all important. Bargain tool-bin bits are made of soft metal and will dull in a very short time. They are also hard to resharpen because of their softness. You will need some spade bits. These are flat, paddle-shaped bits used for boring large holes in soft woods. (They are also excellent for boring wiring runs in wall studs, or holes for copper piping in kitchen cabinets.) You may also need a few masonry bits. Because these are fairly expensive, it's usually better to purchase these individually as you need them rather than in a set.

Probably one of the most important drill sets for a furniture maker is a pilot-bit set. The screw-sink combination type drills a pilot hole, body hole and countersink all in one operation. These are available for wood screw sizes from No. 4 to No. 12.

In addition to drilling bits, there are many accessories that can be used in your electric drill. The motor can power polishing, sanding and grinding disks, a paint stirrer, and even a small pump. A screwdriver bit and socket set will turn the drill into a power screwdriver. Another valuable attachment is a hole saw. These can be used to bore larger holes than possible with standard drill sizes, and are useful for boring lock holes in doors. (There are also, however, special lock installation sets which have the most commonly used sizes of bits needed for lock installation.) One accessory I have found a great deal of use for is a Surform drum. This tool can be used to do shaping, as when sculpting inside curves and other irregular wood shapes. File and rasp attachments are also available.

A useful addition to the shop is a power drill bit sharpener, a separate unit with its own power. These are no more difficult to use than an electric pencil sharpener, and take a lot of the work out of maintaining a set of usable drill bits. If you've ever hunted through an assortment of drill bits for the right size, only to find it too dull for the job, you can appreciate the value of this unit.

One of the prime uses of a portable electric drill is to bore dowel holes when joining narrow stock to make up wider stock. A doweling jig is a great time-saver in any such operation. The use of such a jig is described in Chapter 5.

Circular Saw

The primary use of a portable circular saw is to cut large pieces of paneling or other stock to a size that can be handled more easily. In addition, the saw can be carried to the job when installing kitchen cabinets, or molding and millwork.

A 7-inch saw (measured by blade capacity) will handle almost any job in a cabinetmaking shop. However, a 7½-inch saw with up to 2 hp will deliver more power for rough cutting jobs, such as cutting into framing lumber. Most saws come equipped with an edge guide, but a more reliable method of guiding the saw on long runs is to clamp a guide strip to the work. Six basic types of blade are used with the saw: crosscut, ripping, combination, plywood, planer, and carbon steel.

Saber Saw and Reciprocating Saw

A saber saw, also known as a portable jigsaw, is invaluable in a cabinet shop. Because it can make plunge cuts and turn in a small radius, it is ideal for making sink cutouts. It can also be used to cut curved and irregular shapes that can't be done with a band saw. It is quite a bit lighter and handier to use than a circular saw in many cases, as when cutting close to a corner. A ¼ hp saber saw with a ¾-inch stroke is ample for most home shop jobs.

A wide variety of blades is available for use in the saber saw, ranging from 3 to 32 teeth per inch. The 3- to 7-tooth blades are used for rough sawing of thick wood or small-diameter timbers; the 10-tooth blades for lumber and composition

The primary task of a portable circular saw is to cut large panels to manageable size.

A saber saw is used to make plunge cuts, as when making sink cutouts in a countertop, and to cut curves and irregular shapes.

board; and finer-toothed blades for soft and hard metals. A 10-tooth taper-ground blade is used for plastic laminates, veneer, and plywood.

A reciprocating saw is much like a saber saw, but is intended for heavier work. It has a longer stroke than most saber saws, and a longer blade. The blade is oriented to cut into vertical surfaces, and it is often used by plumbers and electricians to cut into walls or to saw pipes.

Router

A router is one of the most versatile tools in the shop. It is used for shaping edges, making decorative grooves and joint cuts, and for mortising hinges. With a dovetail accessory, it can cut matching dovetails for drawer joints; with a small veiner bit it can be used for carving. A router is also essential for trimming plastic-laminate edges. For details on using a router template to cut decorative grooves and on making a fluting jig, see Chapters 7 and 10.

Some router bits come with a separate pilot guide, and on others a portion of the bit serves to guide the router. A special router collar can be used to prevent the bit from cutting into a wood guide strip or jig, as described in Chapter 7. Many bits are available with carbide tips, or in solid carbide, for work with plywood and hardboard.

Modeling Tool

Modeling tools, also known as grinders, are used for small, intricate carving, grinding, and modeling work. The tool can power a small router bit, drill, rotary rasp, and other attachments as well as abrasive wheels. The best-known modeling tool is the Dremel "Moto-Tool," but there are also several other types.

Belt Sander

For fast and easy finishing of large surfaces, a belt sander is indispensable. It is used to do initial rough sanding of surfaces; a finishing sander with progressively finer grits of sandpaper will complete the job.

Belt sanders are rated according to sfpm (the number of surface feet removed per minute). This

A router has many different uses in the shop. It is indispensible for such tasks as trimming plastic laminate.

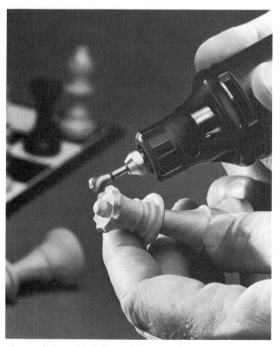

A small hand-held modeling tool can be used for intricate carving tasks.

A belt sander is used for rough sanding of surfaces, as to level the surface of glued-up stock. It removes a lot of material quickly. A dust-collector attachment is a useful feature.

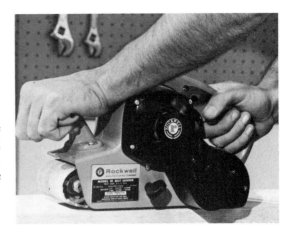

capacity depends on the width of the belt and the power of the motor. Many models have a built-in dust collector, and this is a very useful feature. Some models also have a second speed to make it possible to slow down to do finer sanding.

Finishing Sander

Finishing sanders, also called pad sanders, are normally used only for final sanding and not for heavy removal of material. They are available with either straight action or orbital action, or with the capacity for both. An orbital sander removes somewhat more material since part of its action is against the grain. In addition to surface preparation, finish sanders can be used—with extremely fine-grit sandpaper—to produce a satin sheen on lacquered or varnished surfaces. For this type of sanding, a soft foam rubber pad can be used in back of the paper to prevent cutting into the surface too quickly.

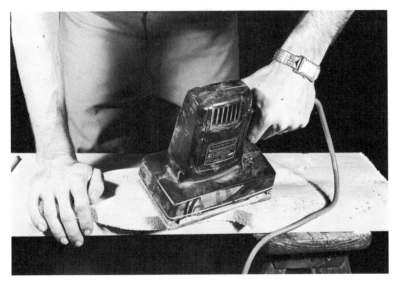

Fine sanding is done with a finish sander. With extremely fine sandpaper it can be used to smooth the surface between successive coats of lacquer or varnish.

Sharpening Tools

<big>**23**</big>

No matter how good the quality of a tool, it will eventually become useless if it is not properly cared for and sharpened. A dull tool is not only hard to use; it's dangerous. It requires the application of more force to do its job, and as a result the tool is likely to slip and injure the operator or damage the workpiece.

Edge tools such as chisels can be kept in shape with a few minutes of honing and light sharpening. On the other hand, sharpening a saw blade takes quite a bit of time and care. For this reason, many cabinet and furniture shops find it worthwhile to have the job done by a sharpening shop. However, these shops do not exist in many areas, and there many people who simply prefer to do the sharpening themselves. Learning how to sharpen a saw blade is not difficult, but it does require quite a lot of time without the specialized tools used in professional shops.

Reconditioning Handsaws

When saws are fed through wood, the constant impact against the wood fibers naturally dulls the saw teeth in time. This wearing down of the teeth also causes the amount of set to decrease.

These two factors—dulling of the teeth and narrowing of the set—ultimately result in a loss of cutting power and a kerf too narrow for the body of the blade. A person trying to use a saw in this condition will find that he needs much more power to cut through a piece of wood, and the saw will tend to bind and perhaps burn the workpiece.

In order to make the saw cut efficiently again, you have to restore it to the same condition it was in when it left the factory. Normally this only involves sharpening and perhaps resetting of the teeth, but in extreme cases you may find it necessary to "remanufacture" the saw completely, beginning by cutting all new teeth and continuing through the sharpening, beveling or setting operations that the original manufacturer performed. This is much simpler than it sounds, and with the proper equipment can be done quickly and easily.

The reconditioning of handsaws calls for a number of successive steps—jointing, retoothing, setting, filing—most of which can be done either with hand tools or with more advanced automatic equipment. In some cases, filing may be all that is necessary, but if the teeth are uneven in

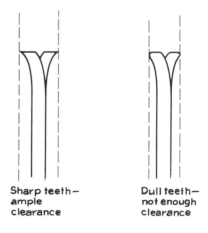

Sharp teeth—
ample
clearance

Dull teeth—
not enough
clearance

With use, the teeth of handsaw blade are worn down and eventually the "set" is narrowed, causing the blade to bind. A blade in this state will require reconditioning.

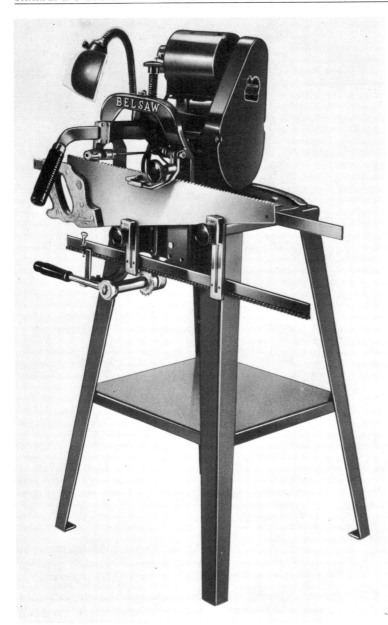

Reconditioning a saw requires several different steps—jointing, retoothing, setting, and then filing. This can be done by hand or with automatic equipment.

length or in contour, all of the steps mentioned may be required.

Every handsaw has a number of dimensions that vary according to the kind of work it is designed for. An ordinary crosscut saw, for example, may be anywhere from 20 to 26 inches long and will have a point size ranging from 8 to 16. A rip saw generally has less than 8 points per inch. It is important to keep in mind that the point size does not reflect the number of teeth per

inch—all machine markings refer to point sizes, not the number of teeth per inch.

To prepare a saw for sharpening, first remove any rust with wire brush or sandpaper. Examine teeth for evenness; if uneven, they should be jointed or retoothed before they are sharpened. Retoothing is also advisable if the saw is concave (curved inward). Also check the set of the saw teeth, either visually or with a close-tolerance measuring device.

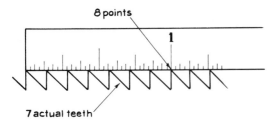

Machine markings on saw sharpening equipment are calibrated according to point size. Point size is determined by counting the number of gullets per inch; not the number of teeth.

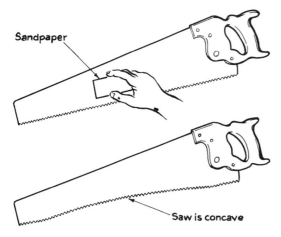

Surface of saw can be prepared for filing with very fine sandpaper. If saw teeth are uneven, or if the line of teeth is concave as shown, the saw will require *jointing* to bring them to the same height.

Jointing by Hand

All of a saw's teeth must be of uniform height before it can be properly sharpened. The process of making them all the same height is called "jointing." To do it manually, put the saw in a vise and file the teeth down to a uniform height. Steady the file with a block of wood to prevent it from slipping and rounding the point. Continue the filing until all teeth are of uniform height. This will usually produce some teeth with flattened tops while others may be practically untouched.

Jointing by Machine

With a power-driven automatic saw sharpening machine (the Foley Model 387 is an example),

Saw is held in a vise with hardwood blocks for the jointing operation, and a block of wood is used to hold the file level. Continue filing until all teeth are the same height.

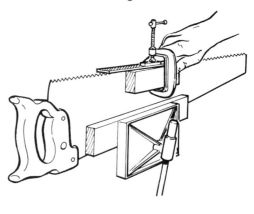

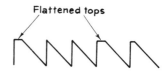

When teeth are properly jointed, some will usually be flattened, and others will be almost in original condition.

jointing of a handsaw is accomplished during the regular sharpening process. You just position the saw in the machine, then select and insert the proper file. After choosing and setting the depths and angles desired, you turn the machine on and it does the job automatically. With the precise settings available, depth of cut is controlled so that all teeth are of uniform height.

Setting by Hand

This involves use of a grip-type setting tool with which you set each tooth individually. After adjusting the tool for the depth and width of set desired, begin at the handle end of the saw and position the setting tool on the first tooth facing away from you. Squeeze the grip to set that tooth, then move on to the next tooth facing away from you. Continue to the end of the saw, then reverse it (end for end) and do the other side. The results you get with the hand tool are fairly accurate, but can vary with the amount of pressure you exert on the hand grip.

A hammer-type setter can also be used for setting handsaws. This type is operated by foot pedal and hammer action, producing a more uniform set. But again, it's necessary for the operator to set each tooth individually and do only one side at a time.

Setting by Machine

An automatic power setter handles both sides of the saw in one pass, setting the teeth at the precisely correct angle at a speed of about 360 teeth per minute. All you need to do is position the saw, regulate the feed spacing, and choose the amount and depth of set you want. The saw then feeds through the machine automatically.

With automatic saw sharpening equipment, jointing and sharpening are accomplished in one operation.

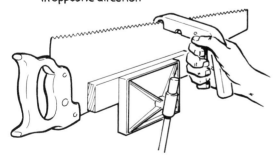

Every other tooth is set, then saw is reversed to set alternate teeth in opposite direction

Adjustable grip-type setting tool can be used to set crosscut teeth. Proper set can be determined by examining unused teeth of saw. Tool is then adjusted to desired depth and width of set.

Foot-powered hammer-type tool will produce more uniformly set teeth on handsaw blades. Like the grip tool, it sets each tooth individually.

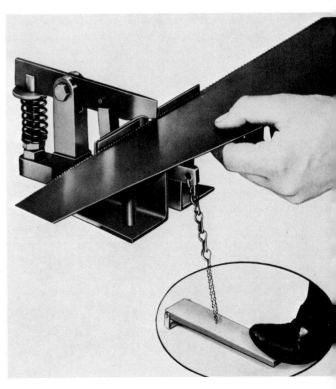

Power setting tool will set all
teeth of crosscut blade in
one pass.

Retoothing

In most cases the proper realignment of teeth will be accomplished if a good job of jointing is done, followed by proper filing of the teeth. But occasionally you may encounter a saw that has been amateurishly sharpened or otherwise abused so that the teeth are broken or the tooth spacing totally irregular. Your best bet here is to retooth the saw completely, a job that calls for a handsaw retoother. This device quickly cuts a complete set of new teeth into the saw body, each precisely sized and accurately spaced. You can get exactly the shape, depth and hook angle you want by setting a few simple controls, and even change a rip saw to a crosscut, or vice versa, all automatically. For this reason the retoothing machine is usually known as the "mistake-fixer."

Handsaw retoother can cut
and set new teeth in any
handsaw blade. It can even
convert a crosscut blade to
a rip blade, and vice versa.

Files

The selection of proper files is an important part of saw reconditioning. Practically all saw files are of identical cut—a standard type chosen by the industry for its all-around efficiency in metal cutting. However, some are made with a single-cut design and others with a double-cut design. Most operators prefer a double-cut file for handsaw use, since it cuts faster and has almost the smoothness of single-cut. (For circular and bandsaws, discussed later, single-cut is preferred.)

All triangular files for saw sharpening have a 60° angle. This angle permits simultaneous filing of both the front and the back of each handsaw tooth.

In choosing saw files, your main concern is to match the file to the saw teeth so that there is no waste of file area. The file should be large enough that only about half of the file width is used on each side. As the file becomes worn it can then be rotated twice, exposing a fresh file surface each time.

Here are the proper file sizes to choose in order to avoid file waste:

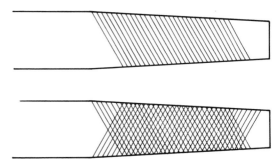

Metal-cutting files come in single-cut and double-cut designs. Double-cut files are usually preferred for handsaw sharpening.

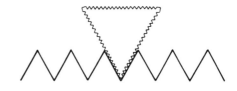

Triangular or *taper* files set at a 60° angle are used for handsaw sharpening. The size of file required depends on the point size of saw blade.

Handsaw Point Size	Use This Size File
5–7 (Coarse)	Taper (Foley #327007 Double Cut)
8–10 (Medium Coarse)	Slim Taper (Foley #327005 Double Cut)
11–13 (Medium Fine)	Extra Slim Taper (Foley #327003 Double Cut)
13–16 (Fine)	Double Extra Slim Taper (Foley #327001 Double Cut)

The "Taper" in the name of the file refers to the gradual decrease in width of the file from about the middle to the tip. The files are built this way to provide smooth entry into the tooth gullets.

Filing Rip Saws by Hand

This operation requires some means of anchoring the saw firmly in place so that it can be filed without distortion or chatter. A makeshift arrangement can be made using an ordinary vise and hardwood stiffeners. But for best results you should have a specially-designed handsaw vise. These provide a chatter-free grip and can be tilted in a 40° arc. The saw should be positioned so that

there is about ⅛-inch clearance beyond the bottom of the teeth.

The parallel chisel-type teeth of a rip saw are filed straight across (0° face bevel) with the file held level and exactly at right angles with the saw body. Tilt the file at an angle of 22° to give each tooth a negative hook of about 8°, the most popular hook for handsaws. (If a little more "bite" is desired, you can reduce the hook angle a few degrees by tilting the file to 25° or so.)

Begin filing on the first tooth which is set away from you. Don't force it—just apply enough pressure to overcome the resistance of the metal being cut. Cutting is only done on the forward stroke; at the end of the stroke, lift the file and bring it

Rip saw blades can be held for filing in a vise with hardwood blocks. There are also specially designed handsaw vises for this purpose, such as the one shown here.

Saw is positioned for filing to allow ⅛-inch clearance between vise and bottom of teeth.

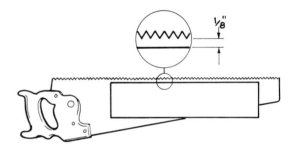

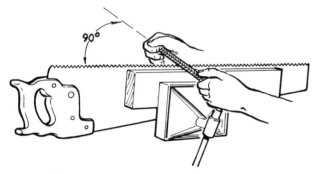

Rip saw teeth are filed with file held level and at right angles to saw body.

To put a negative hook on saw teeth, tilt file as shown. An 8° hook is usually preferred.

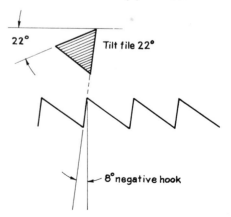

When filing teeth that have been jointed, remove only half of the flattened portion of the tops. The teeth will be brought to a point when saw is filed from the opposite side.

back to make another cut. Continue this until the tooth is sharp.

If you are working on a saw that you have jointed by hand, some of the teeth will have flattened tops. File these only enough to remove half of the flattened portion. The rest will be filed to a point when you do the other side.

Continue filing until you have done the last tooth facing away from you, then turn the saw end for end. Again file all teeth facing away from you and continue until you have brought each to a sharp point.

An oilstone can be used to remove burrs from the teeth.

Filing Crosscut Saws By Hand

This is a bit more complicated than filing rip saws because of the variety of tooth angles and bevels encountered in different crosscut saws, but the sequence of operations is similar.

With the saw placed in the vise, begin filing on the first tooth that has its set away from you. However, the file is not held at right angles to the saw body as for a rip saw; instead, swing it off to the right and tilt it at 15° from vertical. With the

file held level, make your first cut. Again, don't force it—just apply enough pressure to overcome the resistance of the metal being cut.

If the saw is in good general condition you should be able to sharpen each tooth with just two or three strokes of the file. Try to give all teeth the same number of strokes. If you have jointed the saw by hand, some of the teeth will have flattened tops. These should be filed only enough to remove half of the flattened portion; the rest will be filed to a point when you do the other side.

Filing Saws By Machine

With an automatic saw filer, you merely mount the saw on the machine, select and insert the proper file, and choose the hook, bevel and depth settings you want. Then you adjust the feed and turn on the machine. Both sides of the saw are sharpened automatically in turn. The total operation takes less than 10 minutes.

A power filer such as shown will file handsaw teeth with the desired hook, bevel and depth.

Filing crosscut saws is a bit more complicated, but procedure is basically the same as for rip saws. File is held at an angle as shown.

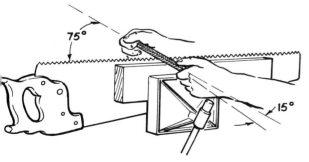

Reconditioning Circular Saw Blades

To be effective, a circular saw must be perfectly round, and all of the teeth must be of identical height. If any of the teeth are higher than the others, these protruding teeth naturally have to do all of the work of cutting into the wood. The result is a ragged kerf, and the protruding teeth will tend to dull or break off as they hit knots or other obstacles.

The purpose of the gullets on the blade is to remove sawdust as the saw cuts. It is important to keep these gullets deep enough to do their job well. After a number of sharpenings, the gullets tend to become too shallow to be 100% efficient. While it is usually unnecessary to deepen the gullets every time you sharpen a circular saw, the job should be done every fifth sharpening or so. This is usually done with a grinding wheel dressed with a radius. A rough file can also do the job, but will not produce uniform results in inexperienced hands.

Unless the saw is hollow-ground or swaged, it is important that the teeth have an adequate set. In setting teeth, just as in rounding the saw, you must avoid having some teeth extend farther out than the others. Any protruding teeth will be exposed to much greater strain and will cause the saw to cut raggedly.

The amount of set you give teeth is important, too. An excessive amount of set will not only result in broken teeth and cracked gullets when the saw is used; it will also cause the saw to vibrate to such an extent that its cutting action will be rough and uneven.

Too little set can result in binding, overheating, and the development of cracks in gullets. Also, the amount of set must not vary from one side of the saw to the other. A saw that has wider-set teeth on one side will tend to skew to that side when it is used. Besides producing a ragged cut, this may also cause tooth breakage.

A Typical Sharpening Job

Suppose you have a crosscut circular saw in good condition that just needs a little touch-up. You'll notice that the teeth are V-shaped, and are beveled to cut across wood fibers efficiently. There

are three methods you can use to sharpen this saw:

With a hand file. Use a standard triangular file of the correct size to take a little metal off the face of one tooth and the back of the adjacent tooth on each stroke. Be sure to maintain the existing bevels. The saw should be held in a saw holder such as the one shown.

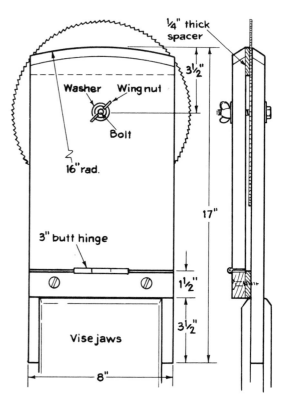

A shop-made device can be constructed to hold circular saw blades for hand filing. The blade can be tightly clamped for filing, but easily turned to line up the next tooth.

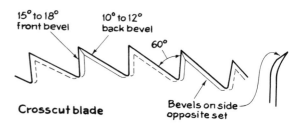

Crosscut and combination blade teeth are filed with a triangular file. Be sure to maintain existing bevels.

Automatic saw sharpening equipment will file teeth to exact specifications.

A grinding wheel can also be used to restore the edges of circular saw teeth.

With an automatic filer. This machine can be precisely set to file each tooth to exact specifications.

With a grinding wheel. With the wheel dressed properly and the grinder set to just touch each tooth, you can put a new edge on the cutting surfaces quickly and accurately. An accessory holder can be used to position the blade.

Sharpening Plus Setting

If an examination of the saw shows that it also needs setting you can choose from three types of setting tools:

Hammer-blow manual setter. This has a striker/anvil device on which teeth are aligned in alternate sequence. A single hammer blow bends each tooth over the anvil to set it. The saw is then reversed and opposite teeth set the same way.

Lever-operated manual setter. This device uses a trip-hammer system that gives each tooth the uniform amount of impact needed for precise setting. It requires individual positioning of teeth and reversal of the saw for setting of opposite teeth.

Automatic setting machine. This sets both sides of the saw at a speed of 240 teeth per minute. Only three simple adjustments are necessary to achieve precision results.

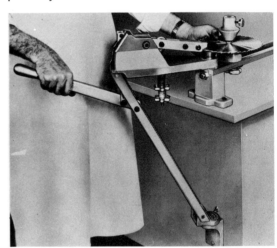

A lever-operated blade setter produces a more uniform hammer blow so that teeth are set more precisely.

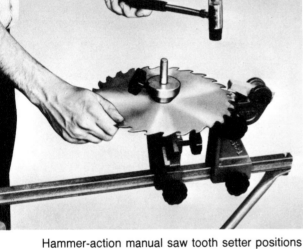

Hammer-action manual saw tooth setter positions each tooth over an anvil so that it can be bent with a hammer blow. Only the tips of the teeth are set. The amount of set depends on the type of blade—fine-tooth blades are set to about ¼ their thickness, and combination or rip blades slightly more.

Professional blade-setting equipment sets both sides of saw simultaneously and at great speed.

Sharpening A Rip Saw Blade

The chisel teeth on a rip saw are not beveled like those on a crosscut saw; thus sharpening their faces and tops with file or grinding wheel is a simple matter. But a rip saw has a much deeper gullet and more pronounced hook, both of which must be maintained in order for the saw to operate efficiently. Care must be taken in sharpening to retain the original hook and the gullet should be deepened occasionally (every fifth sharpening or so). This can be done with a Great American Crosscut file of the correct size or with a grinding wheel that has been dressed to match the contours of the teeth.

Rip saw blade

The tops and faces of rip saw teeth are filed straight across. Take care not to nick the gullets while sharpening the faces.

Chisel-Tooth Combination Saw

The teeth of combination saws are beveled like crosscut teeth, and they also have a 15° hook and a round gullet resembling that of a rip saw. In sharpening a chisel-tooth combination saw, file the faces of the teeth while you are gumming; then go around and bevel the tips. Also, be sure that the tops have the proper primary top clearance (15° or so). All of these sharpening opera-

tions can be done with either files of the proper size or a grinding wheel dressed to produce the desired contours.

If gullets need deepening, this is done with either a round file or a properly dressed grinding wheel. Be careful to retain original angles and contours.

"Four-Tooth-And-A-Raker Saw"

This type of circular saw has its teeth arranged in a repeating pattern consisting of a number of crosscut-type teeth followed by a single raker tooth. The crosscut teeth score the wood like two knives, after which the raker tooth comes along to cut out the center portion and remove sawdust. In sharpening this type of saw, you first file or grind the faces and backs of the crosscut-type teeth, being sure to retain the proper hook (0° to 10°) and face bevel (10°). Then you do the faces and tops of the raker teeth, which have straight faces and tops and a 30° hook. These you file or grind flat, taking off enough metal so that each raker tooth is about 1/64 inch below the crosscut teeth.

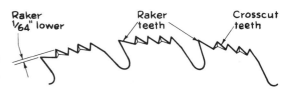

Four-tooth-and-a-raker blade

On this type of raker blade saw, the crosscut teeth are first filed and beveled; then the raker teeth are filed so that the tops are 1/64-inch below the level of the crosscut teeth.

Gumming

The basic idea of gumming is to restore the original tooth shape as much as possible. In some cases this will involve merely deepening each gullet; in others it will amount to major restructuring of the saw teeth. If a saw has undergone quite a bit of hand filing, for instance, there may be square indentations in the gullet caused by unskillful use of a triangular file. These angular pockets tend to trap sawdust, which then builds up and overheats, defeating the purpose for

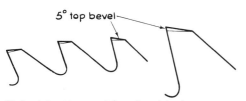

5° top bevel

Chisel-tooth combination blade

The faces of the teeth on chisel-tooth combination blades are filed straight across, but the tops are given a 5° bevel.

which the gullet was designed. Any sharp corners or nicks can also cause cracks to form as the saw is used. If the saw is in really bad shape (square gullets, misshapen teeth, etc.), it's a good idea to joint the saw, then gum every tooth at 0° face and top bevel. Following that, set the teeth and then sharpen the faces and tops at the desired angles.

In some cases you will find that the saw has been given a number of sharpenings, each of which reduced the size of the gullet until it is no longer big enough to provide the needed space for

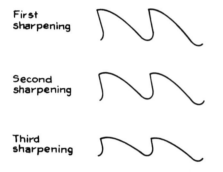

First sharpening

Second sharpening

Third sharpening

Successive sharpenings will eventually reduce the depth of gullets between teeth so that they are no longer effective in removing sawdust. To restore efficiency of saw blade, gullets should be deepened or *gummed* every fifth sharpening or so. This can be done with a round file or on a round-edge abrasive wheel.

sawdust. A good job of gumming will restore the original contours of the gullet and permit easy travel of the sawdust out of the cutting area.

To gum a rip saw correctly, the grinding wheel must be at right angles to the saw blade. This is because the rip saw has a straight face and a straight top. When gumming a crosscut or combi-

nation saw, however, the grinding wheel must be positioned at the angle that will produce the desired bevel on the teeth—for instance, to get the 10° alternate face and top bevel required on a combination saw, you would position the wheel at 10° less than a right angle.

Use the largest wheel you have that will fit the gullet contours. A wheel that's too narrow requires more work on your part, tends to dig in, and wears out much faster. A wheel that's too large or too coarse takes too wide a cut and may seriously alter the style of the saw.

Match up face of tooth with grinding wheel, then come down the face, round off the bottom of the gullet, and work up the back of the tooth. Do this several times until you have shaped the gullet exactly as you want it.

With the grinder stopped, position the wheel at the bottom of the gullet you have just created. Then set your depth adjustments and other controls so that you will be able to match that same configuration. Go around and grind the gullets on all the other teeth to the same depth and shape.

If you find it necessary to take off quite a bit of metal, it's better to use short, choppy strokes rather than a single long, heavy one. These short strokes give the work small intervals of cooling-off time that help prevent overheating.

Jointing

The purpose of jointing is to make the saw perfectly round. This assures that all teeth are of uniform height—a basic requirement for a

To be effective, teeth of saw blade should all be of uniform height. Any protruding teeth will produce a ragged cut.

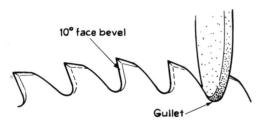

When gumming a rip saw blade, hold it at right angles to the wheel. Crosscut blades and others with beveled teeth are held at an angle as shown so that the wheel will produce the desired bevel.

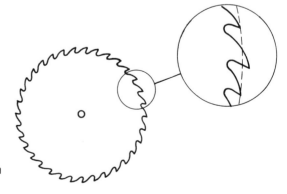

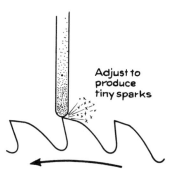

Adjust to produce tiny sparks

Saw blades can be jointed on an abrasive wheel. Position the wheel so that it just touches the top of the shortest tooth; then adjust the depth so the wheel produces a spark as it grinds this tooth. Turn the wheel in the direction indicated by arrow to line up next tooth for filing.

smoothly cutting saw. These are the steps involved in jointing: There can be no tilt in the saw when jointing is done, so set all leveling adjustments at zero. With the grinder stopped, position the wheel against the very tip of the shortest tooth. In order to make the saw round, all the teeth must be ground down to the height of this one. With the wheel touching the top of the shortest tooth, set your depth adjustments so that you will just get a tiny spark as the wheel grinds this tooth. When you have this adjustment set, you're ready to start grinding off small amounts from all of the other teeth until gradually you bring them down to the height of this shortest tooth.

Always grind in the direction the saw cuts to avoid putting a burr on the point of the tooth. Go around the entire saw several times, grinding a little metal from each tooth until they are all the same size. If there is a big difference in size among

Circular saw blades can also be jointed with a belt grinder.

the teeth, you may wish to do this in several stages, resetting the depth controls as you go. When contact with the grinding wheel produces only a tiny spark from any of the teeth, jointing is completed.

Setting Saw Blade Teeth

The amount of set you give each tooth can have a big effect on the performance of the saw. The setting procedure is a simple one—all it amounts to is bending the tip of each tooth to the right or left a bit—but there must be uniformity in the set. Any deviation could result in ragged cutting, tooth breakage, or cracked gullets. Here are some of the elements of successful setting:

It's best to set no more than the tip of the tooth. The shorter a tooth is, of course, the stronger it is. Thus the bent portion of the tooth, if kept short, can better resist the deflecting effect constantly being exerted on it by the wood. The teeth of a circular saw blade are never bent along the entire length. This would cause a much greater amount of leverage to be exerted upon the base, making it easier for the teeth to break off.

A saw with evenly set teeth requires less power to run and produces good results with a lesser angle of set. If a few teeth have excessive set, they will tend to dig in as they go around, slowing the saw up and causing the saw to jump and chatter. On an evenly-set saw, all of the teeth do an equal amount of work, resulting in a fast, uniform cut.

Too much set causes the saw to cut an unnecessarily wide kerf. This not only takes more power, but also wastes wood. Too much set also places a great strain on the rim of the saw. Since the teeth are set alternately left and right, they tend to give the rim a side-to-side buffeting. With excessive set this can cause the saw to chatter and vibrate, and can even result in cracked gullets or broken teeth.

If you don't put enough set in the teeth, on the other hand, the saw will start to bind and the rim will heat up. An overheated rim expands considerably and may start to crack at the bottom of a gullet. Any saw with even a single crack of this kind should be discarded. If you happen to put more set on one side than the other, the saw will have a tendency to veer toward the side with the excessive set.

When setting saw blades, keep in mind that only the tips of the teeth are bent. The amount of tooth that is set and the degree of set will vary according to the depth of the teeth and thickness of the blade. For instance, on a fine-tooth crosscut or plywood saw, about 1/16-inch of the tip would be bent, and the amount of set would be about 1/4 of blade thickness. Rip blades, chisel-tooth blades and others intended for heavy-duty work would be bent a greater amount, and degree of set might be 1/3 of blade thickness.

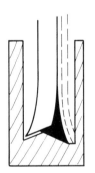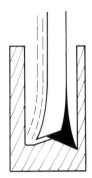

If teeth are given too much set or are set unevenly, blade will cut an unnecessarily wide kerf. Also, the rim will be given a side-to-side buffeting, resulting in an uneven cut and damage to the blade.

A saw that is used only for seasoned (dry) hardwood can operate with slightly less set than is required for green hardwood or seasoned softwoods; green softwood needs the most set of all. But since most saws are used on a variety of woods, it's general practice to use a single standard set.

Because of the rough work that portable electric saws are usually called upon to do—cutting green or wet wood, for instance—a fairly wide set of 2½ gauges per side is recommended. (Table saws, radial arm saws and saws used exclusively on dry wood take a 2-gauge set.) This means that in setting a portable electric saw blade of 15-gauge (.072″) thickness, for instance, you would set the teeth so that there is a 2½-gauge clearance on each side. The overall width of the saw kerf thus becomes 10-gauge (.134″). Here are the sets recommended for saws of various thicknesses:

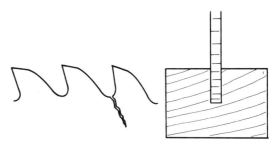

If teeth are given too little set, the blade will bind, and overheating may cause cracks in the gullets.

Saw Gauges (Decimal Equivalents)

Thickness of saw	Dry Wood Set Per Side	With 2 Gauges Set Per Side Saw Kerf Will Be	With 2½ Gauges Set Per Side Saw Kerf Will Be	Wet Wood Set Per Side
10 Ga. (.134)	.035	6 Ga. (.203)	5 Ga. (.220)	.044
11 Ga. (.120)	.030	7 Ga. (.180)	6 Ga. (.203)	.041
12 Ga. (.109)	.028	8 Ga. (.165)	7 Ga. (.180)	.036
13 Ga. (.095)	.026	9 Ga. (.148)	8 Ga. (.165)	.035
14 Ga. (.083)	.025	10 Ga. (.134)	9 Ga. (.148)	.033
15 Ga. (.072)	.024	11 Ga. (.120)	10 Ga. (.134)	.031
16 Ga. (.065)	.022	12 Ga. (.109)	11 Ga. (.120)	.027
17 Ga. (.058)	.018	13 Ga. (.095)	12 Ga. (.109)	.025
18 Ga. (.049)	.017	14 Ga. (.083)	13 Ga. (.095)	.023
19 Ga. (.042)	.015	15 Ga. (.072)		
20 Ga. (.035)	.015	16 Ga. (.065)		

For the most part you will be able to come fairly close to these sets if you are careful to set only the tips of the teeth. But to be on the safe side, check each saw to make sure it has the proper set. This calls for a precision gauge such as the Foley Dial Saw Set Gauge. This is a very simple instrument to use; just position it on the rim of the saw and press against the tooth. It gives a reading in thousandths of an inch.

Plywood Saw Blades

These are almost invariably hollow-ground and will thus require no setting. Normally, you grind only the tops of the teeth, maintaining the existing bevel. Gullets are deepened only when they have become too shallow to clean out the sawdust efficiently.

There are a number of plywood blade configurations; be sure to maintain the existing hooks and bevels. Some of the more common ones are:

The Simonds 66, which has a 13° hook, 45° alternate face bevel and 20° alternate top bevel. Usually the tops can be filed three times or so before the faces have to be ground. (When filing this blade, grind the feed pawl on your filer to give it a ¹⁄₆₄-inch flat on the front. Otherwise it may put a large indentation on the face of the tooth.)

The Simonds 88 with V-shaped teeth has a 10° alternate face and top bevel and a 10° hook.

The Disston blade with round gullets has a 6° hook and 15° alternate face and top bevel. Its tops can also be sharpened about three times before grinding of faces becomes necessary.

The Craftsman Plywood Tooth blade with V-shape teeth has a 0° hook and 10° alternate face and top bevel. Use a Band Saw Slim Taper file and set .015-inch on each side.

The Craftsman Veneer or Plywood Blade (thin-rimmed with V-teeth) has a 0° hook and 10° alternate face and top bevel. Use a Band Saw Slim Taper File. No setting is needed.

There are many other plywood blades on the market. In general, those with V-shape teeth should be filed with 10° hook and 10° alternate face and top bevel. Set at .015-inch if not taper-ground or hollow-ground. Any flat-ground saws with set but without face bevel or top bevel are the throwaway type, and should be discarded.

Band Saw Blades

When filing or setting band saw blades, be sure to start at the weld, since tooth spacing may be uneven.

Narrow band saws for wood (up to 1¾-inch wide) are sharpened with zero bevel like a rip saw. The hook varies from 8° to 15° (maximum hook for softwood, less for harder materials). Set about half of the tooth depth and from :005 to .010 on each side (softwood requires the most set). Set must be even; this can be controlled by honing while the saw is in motion.

Band saws for metal are also ground straight across (0° face bevel) on an automatic grinder, but they cannot be set. Normally this type can be ground about twice before the set is gone and the blade must be discarded.

Occasionally you may encounter a large industrial-type band saw which may present handling difficulties. With these, it is a good idea to rig up a simple wall bracket to support the back loop of the blade.

Compass and Keyhole Saws

These are small pointed blades used by plumbers, steamfitters and carpenters for making a starting cut or sawing in close quarters. Some of them are filed straight across; others at a 10° bevel. They have the same hook angle as a crosscut handsaw.

Miter and Back Saws

These are fine-toothed blades with a straight cutting edge and a heavy, stiff back. They are filed in much the same manner as regular crosscut handsaws, but the hook can be 20° instead of 15°. Because of their fine teeth and thin-gauge steel, you should be careful to use only light file

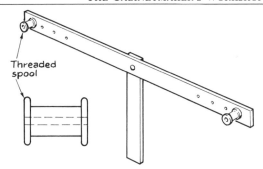

Large band saw blades may be difficult to position for sharpening. A simple wall bracket can be used to hold the back loop of the blade.

Band saw blade

A maximum hook is given to band saw blades used to cut softwoods, and a lesser hook for harder materials.

pressure in both jointing and bevel-filing this type of saw. Where teeth are very uneven, it is often quicker to retooth a back saw rather than to attempt a correction through filing.

Dado Saws or Groovers

These are the most difficult of all saws to sharpen because of their heavy construction and irregular configurations. Sharpening is usually done by hand, at least in part. Most of the common dado sets include two ⅛-inch-thick outside cutters and at least three inside swage-set chippers in thicknesses of ¹⁄₁₆, ⅛ and ¼ inch. Here is the sequence of operations in sharpening dado sets:

1. File the cutting teeth on the outside cutters to a sharp point, using a ⅜-inch square dado file or cant saw file.
2. File or grind the raker teeth on the outside cutters ¹⁄₆₄ inch lower than the cutting teeth.
3. Now file or grind the tops of the inside chippers straight across until they are the same length as the outside rakers.

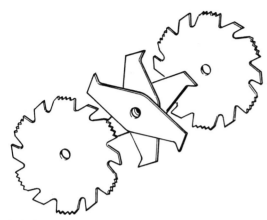

A dado set includes two outside cutter blades, and at least three inside chippers. These are usually sharpened by hand.

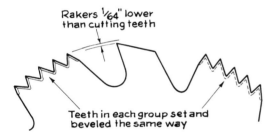

Rakers ¹⁄₆₄" lower than cutting teeth

Teeth in each group set and beveled the same way

The outside cutters of a dado set are filed and set first. All crosscut teeth in each group are set and beveled in the same direction; and those in the next group in the opposite direction. The raker teeth of the blade are then filed ¹⁄₆₄-inch lower than the crosscut teeth.

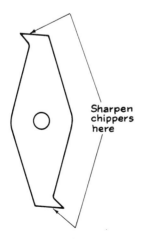

Sharpen chippers here

The inside chippers are filed straight across, to the same depth as the outside cutter teeth.

Be sure that both the outside rakers and the inside chippers are of exactly the same length. Also, maintain the original hook and bevel on all cutting teeth.

Carbide-tipped Saws

Carbide-tipped saws should never be sharpened with an ordinary grinding wheel or conventional files, as you'll just ruin your equipment. Carbide is three or four times as hard as the hardest steel file, so sharpening requires a diamond wheel. It's usually best to have carbide-tipped blades sent out to be sharpened. Because a diamond wheel is expensive, you'll want to keep its use to a minimum if you invest in one. Don't do any unnecessary grinding, and always plan carefully the positioning and depth of cut you will take.

The triple chip blade is the most popular for cutting anything abrasive. It has two different-length teeth placed alternately on the same saw blade to produce three separate chips. One tooth has 45° or 30° chamfers ground on each side, and the other has a square top. They work together to cut through hardwood, plywood, brass, aluminum, plastics, formica and abrasive materials with ease. The chamfered tip plows a little deeper (.012-inch) than the square one, which comes along to clean out the two side areas left by the other.

In handling a carbide-tipped saw, remember that while carbide is a very strong material it is also quite brittle and can be damaged by rough handling.

Sharpening procedure is similar to that used with conventional saws, with these additional steps:

A. Check saw for cracks, which should be welded with stainless steel rod.
B. Broken shoulders and teeth can also be built up by welding.
C. Remove any broken teeth beyond repair and replace with new tips at least .015″ wider than old tips.
D. After retipping, grind the saw. Do the faces first, then the sides, and finally the tops. Side-grind only teeth that have been replaced.

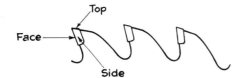

Carbide-tipped blades must be filed with a diamond wheel. The face is filed first, then the side (but only if you're dealing with a replacement tooth), then the top.

Strob Saws

It's pronounced "strobe" but has nothing to do with stroboscopes—the inventor was named Stroble. This ingenious saw design was developed to correct a common problem with high-speed rip saws—the buildup of wood particles on the saw plate which causes overheating and distortion. Stroble's solution was a pair of long carbide teeth brazed onto channels in the saw blade. These teeth extend just enough to keep the plate cleared of wood particles; they have no cutting action. The cutting teeth are ground like a standard rip saw, with the Strob teeth maintained at a minus 10° hook. The side clearance is held to .010 inch less than the cutting teeth on each side.

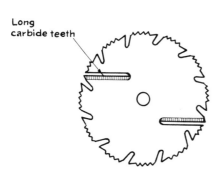

A strob blade has deep channels to keep the face of the blade clear of sawdust. The teeth have a minus 10° hook and are treated like those on a rip saw.

Pulpwood Saws

The growing demand for firewood throughout the country has brought a parallel increase in the number of these big rugged saws in use. The high-backed tooth pattern is designed to withstand the severe shocks and jolts of pulpwood cutting and to plow through nails and other obstructions. Pulpwood saws are usually ground with a 15° alternate bevel on both top and face, with a 0° hook.

Edge Tools

General Sharpening Procedure

It is always best to choose the least severe method of restoring a tool's cutting efficiency. In other words, if you can put a good edge on a tool with just a light honing, don't even consider going at it with a grinding wheel. Never take off any more than an absolute minimum of metal—this is a good rule with any tool and is essential with knives, scissors and other light cutting instruments. In sharpening such tools, use a grinder or belt sander only when nicks or gouges have badly altered the blade geometry and quite a bit of reconstruction is necessary.

In discussing tool sharpening we will refer to different kinds of bevels: the *edge* bevel, which is

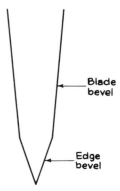

The edge bevel of a tool is the angle of its cutting edge, and the blade bevel is the angle of the shank which backs it up.

the angle of the actual cutting edge; and the *blade* bevel, which is the angle of the tool shank that backs up the cutting edge.

The edge bevel varies from the thin blade of a straight razor to the impact-resistant angle of a cold chisel, and each of these is backed up with appropriate blade bevels—a slip taper for the

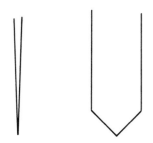

The tapers of edge bevels range from that of a razoredge to the impact-resistant point of a heavy-duty chisel.

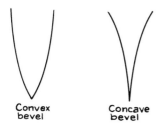

Convex bevel   Concave bevel

Certain chisels and plane irons are given a concave or hollow-ground bevel. An axe or hatchet blade may have a convex bevel.

razor, and a heavy shank on the chisel. We will also refer to *convex* bevels and *concave* bevels.

Axes

A grinding wheel does a good job on axes and hatchets, as does a belt sander, but best of all is a disc sander, because of its wider, more solid backing. Hand filing is another good method, but

A convex bevel for a heavy-duty edge such as that on an axe can be ground on an abrasive wheel. In the example shown, sharpening is started about an inch in back of the edge, and the blade gradually tilted until the edge touches the wheel.

it's time consuming. You will find a wide range of edge bevels on axes since they vary according to the purpose of the axe—heavy splitting, precision peeling, etc.

The basic procedure is to start sharpening an inch or so back of the edge, gradually tilting the axe as you swing the blade back and forth across its full width. This motion produces a desirable convex bevel. Make light passes or dip the blade in water frequently to prevent overheating, especially when grinding near the edge. When sharpening is completed, with all nicks and gouges removed, you may wish to give the axe a final whetting on an oilstone.

Chisels

A grinder does the best job on chisels. A belt sander can also be used, but it doesn't give you the desired hollow grind. Adjust the table or tool

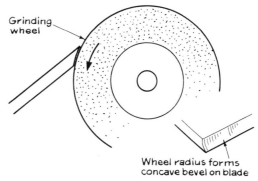

Grinding wheel

Wheel radius forms concave bevel on blade

A concave or hollow-ground edge for a chisel can be ground on the edge of a wheel.

rest to match the chisel bevel, and move the chisel across the wheel or belt, making light passes until all nicks and gouges are removed. You may find that short chisels will require mounting on a chisel holder or other device.

Drills

Proper sharpening of twist drills calls for a special attachment for your grinder, which is accompanied by complete instructions. This device

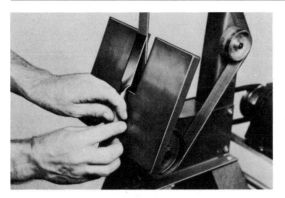

A flat-bevel chisel edge can be ground on a belt grinder, using an attachment to hold the blade at the proper angle.

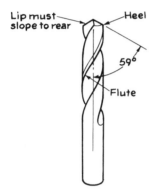

The normal top bevel for a twist drill is 59°.

attachment will enable you to do a competent job with very little practice.

Knives

Be sure to check the type of edge on any knife before you sharpen it. There are four common types, and it is important to retain the basic con-

makes drill sharpening an easy job, but there are a few details about drill sharpening that it may be helpful to know:

1. Normal top bevel of a twist drill is 59°.
2. Each spiral ridge on the drill must be ground with a slope to the rear; otherwise it won't cut properly. The grinding attachment does this by gradually changing the grinding angle to create a slight inward movement from lip to heel, thus providing the clearance needed for the cutting lips to do their work.

Freehand sharpening of twist drills is possible, but it is a difficult skill to acquire. The grinder

An accessory grinding-wheel attachment will make drill sharpening easy.

A belt grinder is an excellent tool for sharpening knife edges—it will not overheat the thin edge of the blade as readily as a grinding wheel. (A fine-grit wheel is required for stainless steel knives, however.)

tours as much as possible. A simple stone sharpening is all most knives require, and this involves no risk of burning the blade and drawing out its temper. Only when the knife is nicked or gouged does it become necessary to grind the blade back. Use a grinder or belt sander for this, and try to duplicate the original bevel. This is usually 15° for a carving or pocket knife, and 30° for kitchen knives. Be sure to make only light passes to avoid heat buildup, or dip the blade in water frequently. Reverse the knife end-for-end after each pass to grind the opposite bevel. Finish with a careful honing.

Stainless steel knives require a fine-grit wheel, and grinding should be done even more slowly and lightly.

Spade Bits

Sharpening of these woodboring bits is easy to do if you use some type of stop collar on the shank to assure equal grinding of both lips. Set the rest on your grinder or belt sander to produce a 12°

With a stop collar attached to the shank, a spade bit can be sharpened on a grinding wheel.

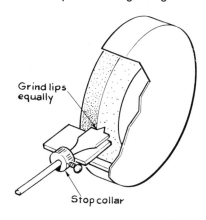

Grind lips equally

Stop collar

primary top clearance. Grind off no more metal than is necessary, and hone.

Grinding Wheels

As you develop expertise in sharpening procedures, you will gradually become acquainted with the various types of grinding wheels that are available.

A grinding wheel consists of thousands of sharp abrasive particles pressed together with a bonding agent. As the revolving wheel is brought into contact with a piece of metal, these abrasive particles act like small knives to cut chips out of the metal. As the abrasive particles become dulled they break off, exposing fresh new particles that take over the work. The strength of the bonding agent is carefully controlled so that dulled particles are allowed to break off only after they have completed their work. With too weak a bonding agent, the particles break off prematurely. Such a wheel would be considered "too soft." Conversely, a bonding agent with too much adhesive power causes the particles to be held in place after their usefulness is ended, with the result that the wheel overheats and becomes glazed. Such a wheel is considered "too hard."

Abrasive Particles

Aluminum oxide and silicon carbide are the two abrasives most commonly used in grinding wheels. The raw material of aluminum oxide is dried bauxite that is heated, fused, cooled and then crushed into various grain sizes. Silicon carbide is white quartz sand that is given basically the same treatment.

Bonding Agents

There are three common methods of binding the abrasive particles together. One is a blend of clay and other ceramic materials used to produce "vitrified" wheels. Also popular is the "resin bond" wheel in which synthetic resins hold the particles together. Where a very smooth finish is needed, shellac is often used as a binder. The *wheel grade* refers to the amount of bonding material used in a particular wheel. A "hard" wheel has a lot of bonding material to produce a stronger, harder surface. "Soft" wheels are intended for use on materials requiring quicker abrasive wear, so the particles are given a much smaller coating of bonding agent.

How To Choose A Wheel

An aluminum oxide wheel is preferred for steel and steel alloy, and silicon carbide wheels should be used for cast iron and nonferrous materials. If the material is hard and brittle, use a fine grit and soft grade. If the material is soft, try a coarse grit and hard grade.

The amount of material to be removed also influences wheel choice. Fast, rough grinding calls for coarse grit and vitrified bond; for smooth finishes, use a finer grit with resin or shellac bond. But if the area of grinding is quite small, try a harder wheel with a finer grit.

In general the amount of contact area between the wheel and the work should determine the wheel grade selected (more area, softer wheel), but other factors sometimes make wheels appear to be harder or softer than their designated grade would indicate: Increased wheel speed tends to make a wheel appear harder while decreased speed makes it appear softer.

A wheel with widely spaced abrasive particles usually runs cooler than one with closely spaced particles and tends to load up less.

All grinding wheels should be given a "ring test" before mounting. Tap the wheel with a

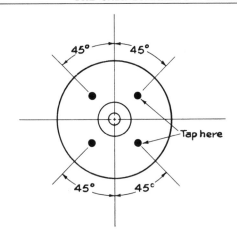

Before mounting a grinding wheel, give it a "ring" test by striking it with a wood object in the center of each quadrant. The sound produced should be a clear ring.

wooden screwdriver handle or dowel in the four spots shown. A sound, undamaged wheel will give a clear, metallic tone. If cracked, there will be a dead sound rather than a clear "ring." Vitrified or silicate wheels will, of course, produce a more metallic sound than wheels made with a resin bond.

Wheel Dressing And Truing

A properly dressed and trued grinding wheel will help you get far more work done in less time. "Dressing" is the term for removing the loading or dulled glaze that builds up on grinding wheels after a time. Stripping off this used-up layer of abrasive particles exposes the next layer of fresh, sharp grits and restores cutting efficiency to the wheel. "Truing" is the process of restoring a worn wheel to its original shape and roundness, or of giving it a new shape for a special grinding job. There are several special tools needed to dress and true a grinding wheel.

Mechanical Dressers. These devices use spinning metal cutters that remove the top layer of abrasive grits when held against a revolving wheel. For best results, mechanical dressers should be used with a tool rest so that the dresser feet can be hooked over the forward edge of the rest. The dresser handle should be raised with a positive action to bring the cutter wheels firmly against the grinding wheel. If this isn't done correctly, the grinding wheel will begin to grind down the cutters. If your first attempt produces sparks, this means that you're not applying enough pressure.

The mechanical dresser is fine for fast resurfacing or rough-shaping of wheels, but for precision truing most operators prefer abrasive or diamond tools.

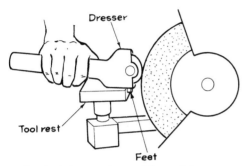

A mechanical dresser is used for quick resurfacing of a grinding wheel. For best results, it should be held on a tool rest.

Abrasive Dressers. These have a cutting surface harder than that of most grinding wheels, and are thus very effective in dressing and truing operations. Abrasive dressers used in saw and tool sharpening are usually of three types: The *rotary* type is a silicon carbide wheel mounted on ball bearings between two large handles. In using this type, you grasp the two handles and maneuver the dressing wheel into position against the grinding wheel. The heavy iron knobs provide the heft needed to stabilize the dresser as it does its job, and they also make it easy to hold the dressing wheel at any angle desired. This type should be used only on wider wheels—never on the thin saw-gumming wheels (under ¼ inch thick). The *stick* type is of boron carbide, and the *block* type of aluminum oxide.

All of these abrasive dresser types do their work by shearing action when held at the proper angle against the wheel. When using an abrasive dresser, it's best to make a number of shallow passes rather than fewer deep ones. If you press too hard you tend to waste both tool and wheel.

Diamond Dressers. These are indispensable for precise truing of wheels and usually consist of an industrial diamond mounted on the point of a rod-shaped tool. The small size and ultra-hardness of diamond dressers enable you to do extremely accurate shaping of wheels for any purpose.

Diamond dressing tools should be positioned at a 10° to 15° angle to the wheel face and no higher than the center of the wheel. Avoid head-on contact with the grinding wheel since this can result in damage to both wheel and tool.

Take light cuts and turn the tool often to present a fresh cutting edge to the wheel. It's also a good idea to wait a few seconds after each pass to allow the diamond to cool; otherwise it could be damaged by heat.

The ultra-hard diamond produces a very fine finish on the wheel—so fine, in fact, that for applications requiring maximum cutting power you may want to give the wheel a final light touch-up with a stick-type dresser.

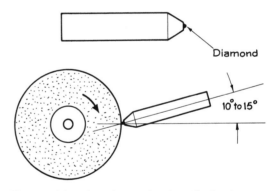

For precision dressing and truing of wheels, a diamond dresser is used. It should be positioned at an angle as shown, and held no higher than the center of the wheel.

Avoid using a diamond dresser at such an angle that you might grind away the setting material that holds the diamond in place.

Traverse Speed. In drawing the dressing tool across the face of the wheel, keep in mind that a high-speed traverse will produce a somewhat rough finish which is faster-cutting and therefore more desirable for sharpening work. If for any reason you want a smoother surface on the grinding wheel, a slower traverse will achieve this. Don't go too slow, however, or you may glaze the wheel all over again.

Wheel-Shaping Tips. Occasionally it becomes necessary to custom-shape a wheel for a particular application. In shaping them, remember to use the right dressing tool. A mechanical dresser is often preferred for rough dressing; an abrasive stick or block for smoother dressing and simple truing; a diamond tool for precision truing. Take off a minimum of wheel surface on each pass (not more than .001 inch), and allow the dressing tool to cool frequently. Select a wheel which will require the least possible additional shaping to produce the desired contours. This will save truing time and also keep wasteful shaping of wheels to a minimum. Maintain as large a supply of contoured wheels as you can; this also helps to cut down on truing operations.

Honing

Some tools, especially chisels, knives, and planer blades, require additional sharpening after the initial edge shaping with a grinding wheel or belt. This further sharpening of the edge is called honing. No matter how much you grind an edge with a wheel or belt you will always end up with a tiny burr of metal on the edge. Even if you keep turning the edge and grinding on one side then the other, you will merely push the burr over from one side to the other. For tools such as an axe or

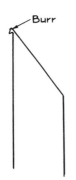

The purpose of honing is to remove the small burr left on the edge of a chisel, plane or knife blade by coarser sharpening techniques.

a saw blade, this burr isn't much of a problem. But tools such as chisels and gouges should be as sharp as possible, and removing the "wire edge" will definitely help make the tool work better. Honing takes quite a bit of patience, although much of the chore can be speeded up by using power tools such as a power hone. You can also use a rubber wheel, followed by a buffing wheel and buffing compound on a bench grinder, but this isn't quite as effective as hand honing and requires a lot more patience.

Honing With Hand Stones

Honing has traditionally been done with small hand stones. These are available in a variety of kinds and coarseness. A good stone will have one coarse side and one fine side. If you purchase a stone that has only one grit, it should be a fine-grit stone.

Small hand stones are available in two different types; *whetstone* which is traditionally used with water, and *oil* stones. Oil stones may be quarried, as are the famous Arkansas stones; or manufac-

Oil stones for honing are available with many different edges. The set shown here is used for V-shape parting tools, veiner chisels, and small gouges. *Leichtung.*

tured, as the carborundum stone. Either type of stone should be lubricated with oil or water during use. The lubricant keeps the stone clean by helping to wash away the metal particles and prevents the pores in the stone from clogging up. This also helps to polish the metal surface. Almost any lightweight oil will do. As you use the tool, keep wiping away the steel particles and periodically flush the surface of the hone with water or oil.

The stone must be held securely in place. This can usually be done by lightly clamping the wooden holding box of the stone in a woodworking vise. Or, if the stone doesn't have a protective

Honing is usually done by hand with a whetstone or oil stone. The stone should be kept well lubricated with water or light oil, depending on the type of stone.

box, fasten it in place to a workbench top with wooden cleats. A piece of aluminum foil can be used around the stone to keep the oil from running out over the workbench.

Whether you're honing a chisel edge, plane blade or knife, the most important thing is to maintain the proper angle of the blade.

Honing A Chisel. The first step is to hone the angled surface by holding the chisel in the correct position and moving it in a circular motion across the face of the stone. Use as much surface of the stone as possible so you don't wear it away in one spot; a stone with a worn-out center is almost useless.

Use a steady, even pressure and maintain the angle of the chisel or plane blade. Also make sure you don't rock the blade to one side or the other or you can cause the corners to become rounded.

Maintain a firm pressure on the chisel to make it "slice" into the stone. Keep flushing the surface with oil and wiping away the old metal-laden oil. Once you have honed the entire edge, there should be a slight wire edge or burr left on the back part of the blade. If this doesn't cover the entire edge of the blade, continue honing until it does. To remove this final burr, turn the blade over flat with the back side down flat on the stone. Using plenty of pressure straight down on the blade, move it around in a circular motion to cut away this fine burring.

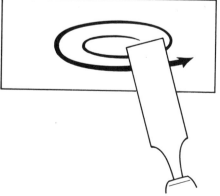

A circular motion is used to hone a chisel blade. Be sure to maintain the angle of the blade.

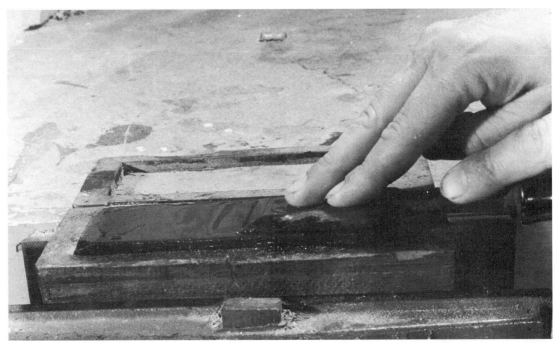

When the front bevel of a chisel blade has been honed, there should be a slight wire edge left on the back of the blade. To remove this, press the back of the blade flat against the stone as shown.

A piece of paper can be used to test a chisel blade for sharpness after it has been honed.

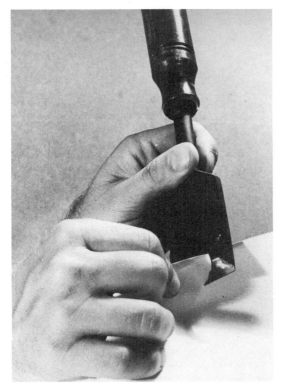

Test for sharpness, but don't test by dragging your finger across the edge. The best method of testing is to hold a piece of newspaper in one hand and slice down through it with the blade held in the other hand. The blade should slice cleanly without any dragging or catching. An alternate method is to drag the blade across the top of your fingernail. The blade should move with an even, soft motion, not catching or dragging.

To produce an even smoother edge you can strap the blade on a piece of leather to which a bit of oil and jeweler's rouge has been added. Or you can polish the blade using a cloth buffing wheel and rouge.

A knife blade is sharpened in the same manner, except that the shallow angle must be maintained, and usually the blade is pushed around the stone in a somewhat different motion.

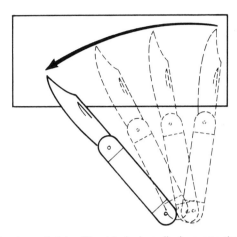

The shallow angle used in honing a knife blade is easier to maintain. The blade is pulled across the stone as shown rather than in a circular motion.

A power hone utilizes a slowly revolving plate coated with fine diamond dust.

A holding jig attachment will enable you to hone a precise angle on chisels and other beveled blades.

The use of the power hone will greatly simplify and speed up the task of honing. It utilizes a diamond lap wheel that cuts extremely fast, provides a good finish, and has a long life. In use the wheel has a light oil applied to it, then the tool is sharpened by holding it in position over the turning wheel.

Some of the information in this chapter was supplied by the Foley Manufacturing Company.

PART VI

Millwork

24

Installing Millwork

Millwork is the factory production of windows, doors, trim, staircases, fireplace mantels, and any other items that are needed to complete a house after it has been roughed in. The millwork or finish carpenter is usually the most skilled carpenter on the job. Many decades ago, millwork items such as windows and doors were constructed on site, and the millwork or finish man had to be able to build them to fit the openings left by the mason or rough carpenter. Today most doors and windows are assembled at a factory in several standard sizes, mounted in frames, and merely installed by the finish carpenter. But the finish carpenter's job still requires a great deal of skill and attention to detail.

Today, most door and window installation jobs utilize prehung units which are already attached to jambs. The units are merely slid in place, leveled, plumbed, and shimmed. Then they are anchored to the surrounding wall studs and header with casing nails driven through the shims and trim.

Doors

There are many different kinds of doors available. Entrance doors may be a plain *slab* or *flush* door, usually solid-core rather than hollow-core; or they may be paneled or paneled with small glass inserts called *lights. Sash* doors are usually made up of panels and lights. *Sliding* doors may have either an aluminum or wood frame fitted with a glass panel. In addition to the standard doors there are *side-lights,* which are sash frames with decorative glass inserts. These are normally used on either side of an entrance door. Interior door styles include flush, paneled, louver, sliding and folding.

Almost any style, size, or shape door you need is available from various manufacturers, and most of them also come already mounted in frames, or prehung. Prehung doors are hinged to the frame with a lock already installed—the entire unit is merely slid in place, adjusted, and fastened. For both prehung doors and windows, the rough opening must be the correct size and it must be approximately square. It's a good idea to check with the manufacturer before the rough opening is framed in to make sure you have the right specifications. Most residential entrance doors swing inside. (On commercial buildings, however, fire codes require that doors swing to the outside.)

Doors and side-lights for exterior doors are available in a variety of panel and sash styles.

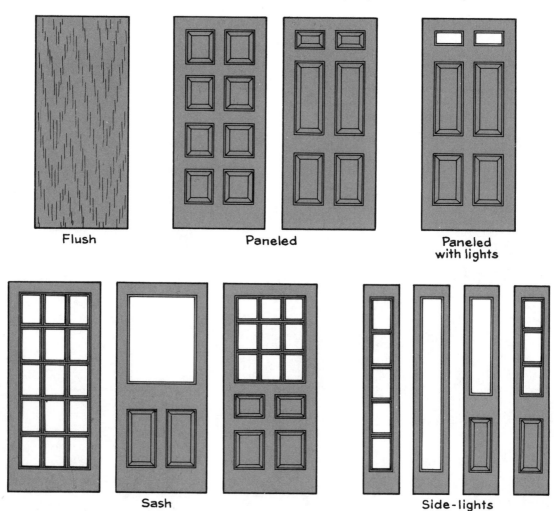

Flush   Paneled   Paneled with lights

Sash   Side-lights

When ordering window or door units, or when making frames, the one dimension that is often forgotten is the wall thickness. The units must be the same thickness as the finished wall, which includes the sheathing, studs, and the inside wall-covering. The problem is that the inside wallcovering may vary from the $3/16$-inch thickness of paneling to the ½-inch thickness of gypsum board. If the units extend out in the room too much they will have to be cut down to fit, which is quite a job. If they are too narrow, shim strips will have to be added to build them out to the proper wall thickness.

Installing an Exterior Door and Jamb Assembly

Because a heavy door is normally used, and often a screen door in addition, the jambs for an exterior door are normally made of 1¼-inch soft-wood stock. The jamb is always a one-piece assembly. The jamb may be rabbeted to form a door stop, or separate stop molding may be fastened to the jamb for this purpose. If the assembly includes a sill, the sill should be made of hardwood.

Proper installation of the sill is extremely important because it must bear a lot of weight and traffic. It must be well supported and also well caulked so that no water can seep in. Because of this, the prehung door units which have the sill and threshold integral with the door jamb, all sealed properly and weatherproofed, are the best bet, even for the advanced carpenter.

The first step in installation of the assembled frame is to slide the frame into the opening. Make sure it is centered horizontally. If the frame includes a sill, make sure it is level and at the proper height in relation to the finished floor. You may have to cut away some of the flooring material or even a portion of the joists to get some door sills

Installing a Prehung Exterior Door

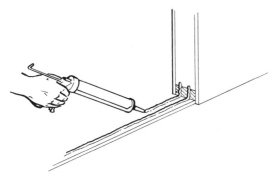

If the door to be installed has a sill and threshold already attached, apply two beads of caulk as shown to weatherproof the joint between the sill and the floor. Floor should be perfectly level to give the sill proper support.

Set door in place, and insert a strip of wood between the left and right portions of the jamb to keep them parallel during the installation process. Insert shims between studs and jamb, checking placement with a level to make sure jamb is straight. (Wooden shingles can be used as shims.) The shims should be placed at hinge and lock locations.

Installing a Prehung Exterior Door (Cont'd.)

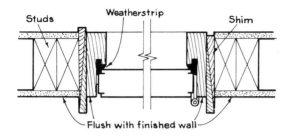

Make sure the jamb is aligned as closely as possible with interior wall.

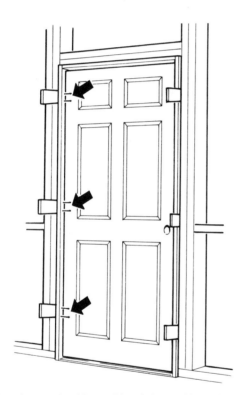

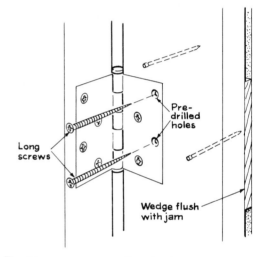

The hinge screws can then be installed. These should be long enough to engage the stud.

Then fasten the hinge side of door with casing nails, nailing through the jamb and shims and into the stud. Lock side of door is fastened in the same way, and shims can then be trimmed flush with the jamb edges.

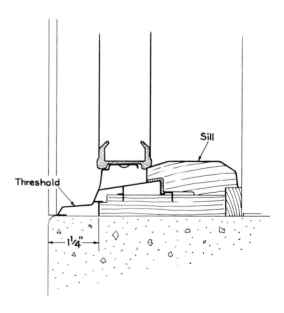

Many prehung door assemblies come with a sill and threshold already attached. If you are installing them separately, make sure that all joints are tightly caulked and sealed.

properly installed. But, above all, make sure that the door sill will have plenty of support.

Make sure the door is level and square in the frame, with both sides parallel, and that the top jamb is perfectly horizontal. Insert a strip of wood between the two sides of the jamb so that they will remain parallel. Sets of two opposed wooden wedges or shingles are inserted between the wall opening studs and the jamb to hold the jambs plumb and straight. There should be four or five of these spaced up the sides and located near the hinges and lock. (Fasteners for the hinges and lock will later be driven through the wedges to provide extra strength.) You will probably have to adjust the wedges in and out and up and down to insure that the installation is straight.

Then the frame is nailed securely in place through the wedges and into the wall studs. Cut the wedges off flush with the outside edges of the jambs, and secure the hinges with long wood screws. Finally, nail the outside casing in place with finish nails.

In many cases the sill will not be installed with the jamb frame, but will be installed separately.

There are several methods of installing a sill, depending on the type of floor, how high above ground level it is, and whether it leads directly to ground level or to a step. In some cases the sill will be rabbeted to fit down over the bottom portion of the lower rough framing. When the sill is placed on a concrete slab it is usually mortared in place at the same time that the frame is installed.

Depending on what type of flooring is to be installed, the threshold may be installed at this time or later. When carpeting is to be installed, the threshold is normally installed at the same time as the sill. If vinyl flooring will be installed, the threshold is often installed afterwards to cover the edges of the vinyl sheet.

Hanging a Door

Although prehung doors are utilized in most remodeling jobs as well as in new construction, some remodeling projects may require hanging a new door on an existing jamb, or even constructing a new jamb. In the latter case, the jamb is usually constructed and fastened in the opening first, and the door then fitted to it.

Framing and Hanging a Door

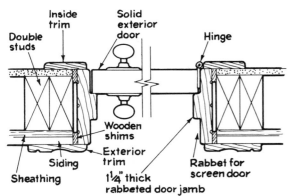

In some cases you may have to make up your own door jamb. The best bet is to make the jamb in the shop, then install it on site. Usually, the door is installed after the frame is in, but you can also make the entire unit in the shop and install it as you would a prehung unit. For weathertightness, an exterior door should have a one-piece jamb of 1¼ stock, with the door stop rabbeted in.

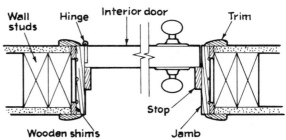

When installing a door, select one that fits the door frame as closely as possible. You can trim a bit off of most doors, but overtrimming will usually weaken the door or give it a bad appearance. Normal clearances for a door are $\frac{1}{16}$ to $\frac{3}{32}$ inch on the side where the lock will be located and $\frac{1}{32}$ inch on the hinge side. The top should clear by $\frac{1}{16}$ inch and the bottom by $\frac{5}{8}$ inch unless it is to swing out over thick carpeting, in which case the door will have to be cut off a bit more. Exterior doors should be cut to just clear the threshold. Trimming is best done with a plane. A circular saw can also be used. The door can be held for planing with a clamp-on vise on a sawhorse or with two

Framing and Hanging a Door (Cont'd.)

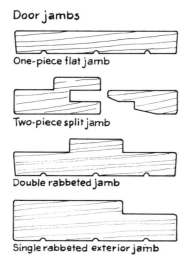

Door jambs

One-piece flat jamb

Two-piece split jamb

Double rabbeted jamb

Single rabbeted exterior jamb

One-piece jamb moldings are available to fit most standard wall thicknesses. There are also split-jamb types which can be adjusted to fit.

The first step in hanging a door is to mark the location of hinges on the door and jamb. Measure width and height of opening, and trim door so it will clear frame by the proper amount on all sides. Masking tape on the back of the door will help to prevent splintering as the cuts are made.

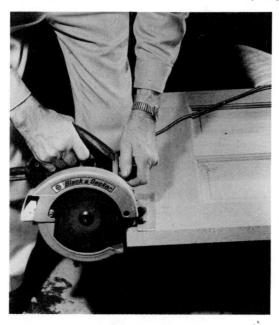

wood screw clamps. You can also use a special shop-made door-holder jig if you have a number of doors to trim.

After trimming the door to the correct size, a slight bevel—about 3 to 4 degrees—is planed on the lock side. This provides a bit of clearance for the front edge of the door when it swings open. After trimming, trial-fit the door in place, then use a bit of sandpaper to round all edges and corners a bit.

Most entrance doors will have three hinges, but lightweight interior doors usually have only two. Use hinges with removable pins so that the door can be taken off if necessary without unscrewing the hinges. Hinges can be surface-mounted on the door and recessed into the jamb or recessed into both door and jamb. Mortises or "gains" for the hinges can be cut with a chisel and hammer as shown on page 488. If a number of doors are being installed, the gains are often cut with a router, using a special door-and-jamb or butt-hinge template. The template is fastened on the door to locate the hinges, and the hinge gains are cut. Then the template is removed and placed on the door jamb, and the hinge mortises cut to match those on the door. The templates can be adjusted for various door thicknesses, door heights, and hinge thicknesses and sizes.

After the gains have been cut, the hinges are installed. This is easiest to do with a power screwdriver or an attachment on an electric drill. The hinges for an exterior door are always positioned so that the pins are on the inside of the door. One leaf of the hinge is temporarily fastened in place in the gain with one screw, or with two if the door is heavy. Then the other hinge leaves are fastened in place. The door is lifted into position and the pin of the top hinge fitted in from the top. Then the bottom hinge halves are swung into position and that pin dropped in place. The door is trial-fitted to make sure it will operate properly. In many cases the door frame may not be exactly square or a gain may not be the precise depth required, and these misalignments will force the door out at the top or bottom. To remedy this, recut the gains or plane a bit off the door so it will fit properly. If necessary, small shims of cardboard can also be used to shift the hinge leaves to make the necessary adjustments, but this should be avoided if possible. Once the door fits properly, the rest of the screws are driven.

Door stops can be cut and tacked temporarily in place until the door lock has been installed. The stops should be installed so there is about $\frac{1}{16}$-inch clearance on the jamb with the hinge. The stop next to the lock side should be tight against the door. The head jamb is then installed so both ends meet the side jambs. These stops should be

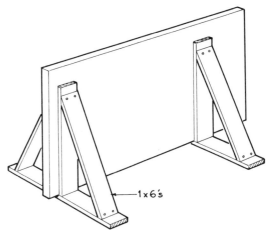

A slight bevel should be planed on the lock side. Then trial-fit the door and lightly sandpaper all edges. *Below:* A shop-made door holder makes it easier to plane or sand edges of heavy doors.

1 x 6's

Framing and Hanging a Door (Cont'd.)

Then the hinges are installed. Gains for the hinges can be cut with a router and template if the job is done in the shop, or with a sharp chisel as shown. Hinge leaves are temporarily fastened to the jamb with one or two screws. Then the door is lifted into position, as shown below, and opposite hinge leaves temporarily fastened. (These may be mortised into the door, or the hinge may be let entirely into the jamb.) If the frame is not exactly square or the gain not the precise depth required, recut the gain or plane or sand one edge of the door to allow it to fit correctly.

 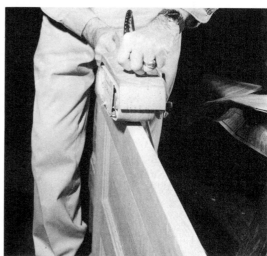

mitered together at the top rather than butted. They are fastened securely in place with No. 4 finish nails after the lock has been installed.

Installing Locksets

There are several different types of locks used on residential construction, but the most common are cylinder and tubular. Other locks include dead bolts, lock sets, and mortise locks. The latter are commonly used on commercial buildings.

Instructions for installation of the various locks are included in the package with the locks. Some locks require mortises to be cut in the door; others require only holes to be bored.

Constructing and Hanging an Interior Hollow-Core Door

There are many small or off-size door openings that can't accommodate any of the standard ready-made door sizes. This is particularly true in under-stair closets and entries into attics and other out-of-the-way spaces. Although a door can be cut from single-thickness plywood, it may eventually warp and will not stand up to hard use. One solution is to build a hollow-core door to fit the opening, using a framework of 2×2s and ¼-inch plywood or panel facing. If the door is to cover an opening into a cold area such as an attic, the inside of the door can be filled with insulation.

The first step is to measure the rough opening. The door should be 2 inches narrower and 1¾ inches shorter than the size of the rough opening.

These margins allow for the width of the door jamb, plus an additional ¼ inch on each side for wedges to plumb the door in place. If the door is to hang over thick carpeting, trim an additional ¾ inch from the length.

Cut the frame for the door from 2×4s, ripping them to 2-inch width. For strength, cut dadoes and rabbets in the side pieces to accept the cross dividers and end pieces as shown. Glue and nail a 2×2 blocking in place in the center portion for the door knob. Then glue and nail the frame pieces together. Make sure the door is square;

Constructing and Hanging a Shop-made Door

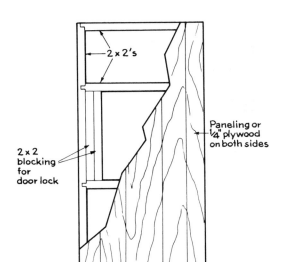

A hollow-core door can be constructed for non-standard door openings. The framework is assembled with 2×4s ripped to 2×2 width, and a blocking is provided as shown for installation of the door knob.

Glued and nailed dado joints will provide a strong framework. Once the framework has been assembled and covered with plywood sheathing, the jamb is constructed with frame pieces of the same width as the wall thickness and hinged to the door.

Constructing and Hanging a Shop-made Door (Cont'd.)

The hole for the door knob can be cut with a hole saw attachment in a portable drill. After the door assembly has been raised to the correct level and plumbed with shims, test the door to make sure it will close properly. *Below:* When the door closes properly, the jamb can be fastened in. Nails should penetrate the shims and engage studs. Casing molding is then cut and installed picture-frame style to conceal the jamb.

The casing is then stained and finished to match the door.

then cut the inside and outside ¼-inch plywood or panel covering and fasten it in place with glue and paneling nails or brads.

Constructing the door jamb. Although the jamb can be installed in the door opening first and the door then hung in the jamb, the best method for small, lightweight doors is to build the entire unit in your shop, then fit it to the opening.

The first step is to cut the three frame pieces for the jamb. There should be ⅛-inch clearance between the jamb and the door at the top and on each side. Then cut dadoes in the top ends of the side pieces. Fit the top piece in the dadoes and fasten with glue and nails.

Install a door stop molding along the three sides of the jamb, then position the door in place on the jamb. Mark the hinge locations on the door and on the jamb, and cut the mortises. After fastening in the hinges, make sure the door will clear all portions properly when opened. If not, make the necessary adjustments in the depth of the hinge mortises.

Next, install the door knob and latch compo-

nents in the door and frame. A hole saw attachment in a portable electric drill can be used to cut the knob hole.

Stand the unit up to determine if the lock components are correctly aligned. Insert a strip of wood between the two sides of the jamb to keep them parallel when the assembly is carried to the installation site.

To fit the unit to the opening, first raise it the desired amount by inserting thin wooden shims or shingles under the side pieces of the jamb. (These are usually inserted from the inside of the closet or attic.) Use a level to determine where shims are needed to plumb the installation both horizontally and vertically. Tack-nail the shims in place, then try the door to make sure it will swing and close properly. You may have to readjust the shims a bit to get a door that will close. When the door closes properly, nail the frame solidly in place through the shims and into the studs.

Cut casing molding to cover all three edges of the jamb, mitering the ends so that the pieces can be installed picture-frame style. Nail the casing in place, finish it to match the door, and that's it.

Windows

Windows are usually purchased in prehung units with the sash frame already fastened to the jamb. In most units, exterior casing is also attached so that the assembly can be fastened in by simply nailing through the casing and into the studs. Many units also have weatherstripping in place between the jamb and sill. Prehung window units are installed after the exterior sheathing of the house has been put on so that weatherproofing can be added between the jamb and sheathing.

Prehung windows are manufactured to fit a specific rough opening, so the dimensions of the opening have to be determined before the window is ordered. The height of the rough opening is measured from the bottom of the header to the top of the rough sill, and the width is the distance between the jack studs. The exterior sheathing of the house should be installed flush with the rough opening before the window is installed.

Prehung windows are available in a variety of styles, and are manufactured to fit standard rough openings. Shown here are double-hung sliding, side-swinging, and awning styles. Many types have screens already attached. Models with built-in weatherstripping and double glazing such as shown will not require storm windows.

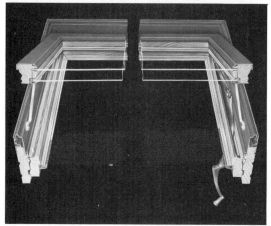

Many prehung windows have exterior as well as interior casing attached so that they can be fastened in by simply nailing through the casing.

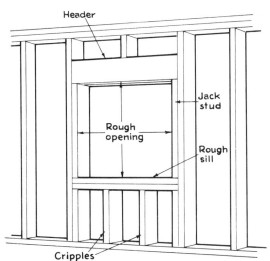

Dimensions of the rough opening have to be figured before a window is ordered. Height and width are measured as shown.

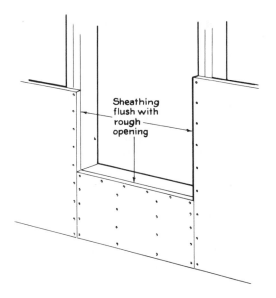

Exterior sheathing of the house should be installed flush with the rough opening

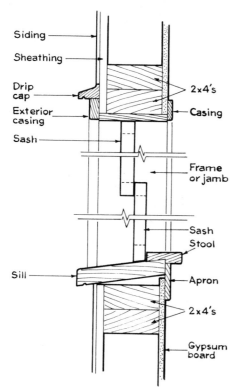

Siding

Sheathing

Drip cap

Exterior casing

Sash

2x4's

Casing

Frame or jamb

Sash

Stool

Sill

Apron

2x4's

Gypsum board

Shown is a side view of a typical prehung unit (a double-hung sliding window), with interior and exterior trim applied.

Installing a Prehung Window Unit

Windows are installed in much the same way as the prehung door units described earlier. The unit is first lifted into the rough opening from the outside. If the unit includes brickmolding, this should overlap the outside sheathing. When the window is centered in the opening, one top corner is temporarily fastened in place by nailing through the casing. Then the window is leveled and the other top corner fastened in. The side jambs are checked for plumbness, then the entire frame is fastened in, with nails spaced 8 to 10 inches apart.

From the inside, shims are inserted between the side jambs and jack studs and between the sill and rough sill to align the jamb with the studs and header. The exact installation procedure will depend on the type of window and the specific weatherstripping and trim pieces that are included in the assembly.

Trimming

If you're building a new house or room addition, it's economical to have a contractor rough-in the building for you and then do the finish work yourself. In most cases this will include trimming out windows and doors as well as providing other interior molding. Of all these chores, trimming out a window is probably the most complicated.

Window Trim

Window trim is available in several different shapes and sizes, and the type you choose will be determined by the style of your house decor. Naturally, it's a good idea to have all the windows in a house trimmed in the same style to provide unity to the design of the interior. The trim is usually applied after the wallcoverings have been installed.

Basically there are two methods of trimming out a window: with casing, stool, and apron; and picture-frame style. Picture-frame casing is installed in the same way as the door trim shown earlier. Each of the casing pieces requires a 45° miter, and is planed so that the inside dimensions of the casing frame equal the outside dimensions of the window. Trimming out a window with stool molding requires three pieces of casing and a stool to cap the rough window sill. An apron is then fitted tightly against the bottom of the stool to conceal the joint where the paneling and the stool meet. Four 45° miters join the top and side casing pieces. The side members fit down on the top of the stool.

In some cases you may be able to purchase precut pieces of molding to fit a particular window unit. In most cases, however, you will have to cut and fit them yourself using standard molding patterns available through building supply dealers.

Installation. The window stool is put in first. This is a stock molding pattern that is available in several different styles and shapes—select one that fits the bevel and size of your window sill. It should reach across the window and extend about ¾ inch past the outer edges of the casings that will be applied. The stool must be mortised on each end to allow it to fit back in against the lower

Trimming a Window

Here, a typical prehung window unit has been fastened in place, and gypsum board wallcovering has also been installed and taped but not painted. You may prefer to give room a coat of paint or even apply wallpaper first.

Casings   **Stops**

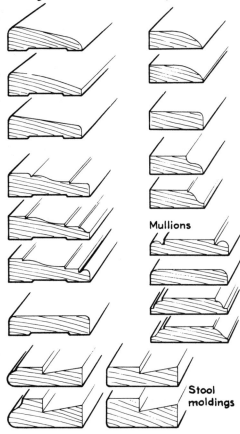

Mullions

Stool moldings

Window trim moldings are available in a number of styles. You can also cut your own if you prefer molding of a special wood.

These are the trim elements of a typical window.

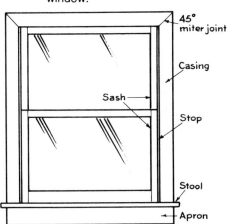

45° miter joint

Casing

Sash

Stop

Stool

Apron

Trimming a Window (Cont'd.)

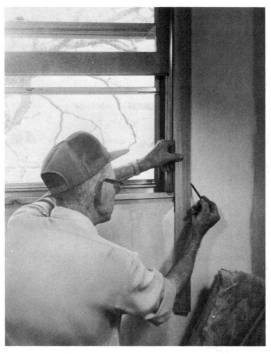

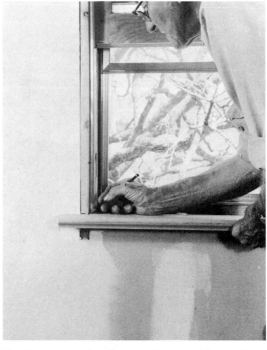

To determine the cutouts for the stool piece, hold a casing piece in place and mark its projection on both sides of the window. (The casing is often set back about ⅛ inch from the edge of the window jamb.)

Next, measure the distance between the casing marks and add 1½ inches to this measurement to determine the length of the stool piece. Then position the stool against the window jamb and mark carefully for the cutout.

When the stool fits properly, nail it in place with No. 8 finishing nails.

In some cases, a cutout will also have to be made to accommodate a center divider.

window sash; its back edge should be about $\frac{1}{16}$ inch from the window sash. Hold the stool in position to mark these mortises.

Make the cuts on the stool with a fine-tooth back saw, then sand the cuts well and trial-fit in place. If the stool fits properly, nail it in place with No. 8 finishing nails. In some cases you may wish to bed the stool in place with caulking compound to seal the joint more securely.

The side casings are applied next. In many cases the casings will be set back about $\frac{1}{8}$ inch from the edge of the window jamb. The best method is to place a length of casing on the window stool and mark the location of the top miter. Cut the miters with a miter box and back saw. Nail the casing solidly to the jamb, then nail up from the stool into the bottom of the casing as well with No. 6 finish nails. Measure for the top

Side casings are installed next. Measure for length from the top of stool to the top of mitered corner, and cut the miters with a fine-tooth back saw. Casings are nailed to window jamb with nails spaced about 12 inches apart. For added holding power, drive a nail through the stool into bottom of casings. *Below left:* The opposite casing is installed in the same manner; then the top piece is carefully measured, cut to fit, and nailed in place as shown below.

casing and cut it to length. Make sure it fits properly, then nail it in place. The casings should also be nailed in place on the outside edge. For added holding power, nail down through the top casing into the side casings with No. 8 finish nails. If the casings are hardwood, predrill all holes to prevent splitting the wood.

Aprons can be made from casing or stop molding. There are several different ways to install an apron. Normally, the length of the apron will be equal to the distance between the outer edges of the vertical casings. To make a fancy returned

apron, you can miter-cut the ends at a 45° angle, then "return" the pieces to create a decorative grain pattern. Sand all saw cuts before installing the trim pieces.

After nailing the apron in place, the next step is to install a mullion on the center window jamb if there is one. The last step is to apply the window stops. Again, these are also available in a number of different styles and sizes. After all trim pieces have been installed, the nails should be set just below the surface of the wood, then the holes filled with wood putty and sanded smooth.

Trimming a Window (Cont'd.)

The apron is installed under the stool.

A decorative apron can be made by cutting the ends at a 45° angle, then "returning" the pieces.

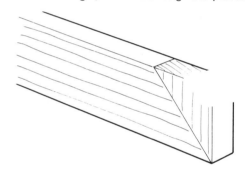

If the window has a center divider, a center mullion is fastened over it.

Then window stop molding is nailed in place.

All nails are set . . .

Finally, nail holes are filled with wood putty, allowed to dry, and lightly sanded.

Other Interior Trim

Trim moldings are used for several functional reasons, but mostly for purely decorative purposes. For most home carpenters, trimming out a room is the most enjoyable aspect of house building or remodeling; there is no limit to the different effects that can be created with molding. You can choose a molding from the wide variety of ready-made styles; combine two or more of these to make up a new design; or cut your own molding with a shaper or molding head cutter as shown in Chapter 14.

Baseboard molding is installed to cover the joint between the wall and the floor, and to protect the wall from being damaged by furniture and cleaning implements. Base molding also covers the edge of the flooring to produce a neat and

An unusual application of molding is the plate shelf on upper portion of this room.

Below: There is a wide variety of ready-made moldings: Shown are a few of the styles.

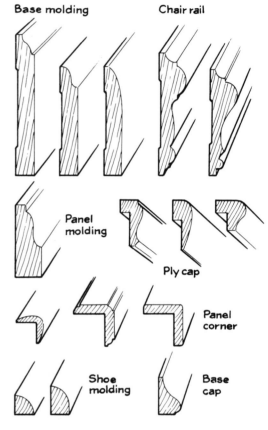

Base molding   Chair rail

Panel molding

Ply cap

Panel corner

Shoe molding   Base cap

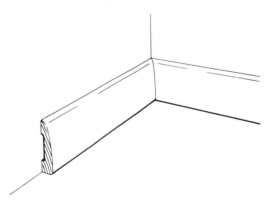

Base molding is the decorative trim used to cover the joint between the floor and the wall. It also protects the wall and gives a finished look to the room. Standard thickness of base moldings is 9/16 inch.

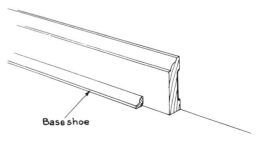

Base shoe

Base shoe molding is used at the intersection of the base molding and the floor. It helps to cover any uneven places in the floor.

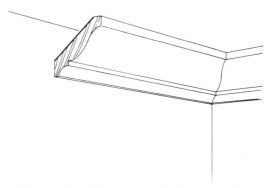

Left: Chair-rail molding is usually placed at chair height, between 33 and 35 inches. It can be used to separate two types of materials such as paneling and wallpaper or paint. *Above:* Ceiling moldings give a room a bolder appearance, depth, and a finished look. *Below:* The use of all three types of moldings—base, chair-rail, and ceiling—gives room a very traditional look.

finished appearance. A quarter-round molding or base shoe can be added to the base to further finish off the floor joint.

Moldings are used to cover panel-ceiling or panel-wall joints and also the inside and outside vertical corner joints of paneling. Hardwood or vinyl panel moldings to match many types of paneling are available from building supply dealers. Plywood cap, casing, or chair-rail moldings can be used to set off the joint between panel wainscoting and a painted or papered upper wall.

From this point on moldings have almost an entirely decorative use. In most modern construction they are not needed to close a joint, except in the case of ceiling moldings used with full-length paneling. A heavy ceiling molding may be used to cover small cracks in the ceiling and a chair rail molding does protect the wall from chair backs, but more often the purpose of these moldings is purely decorative. Moldings can also be applied directly over wood paneling to create a frame-and-panel effect. Another different approach is to install moldings around a wall-papered area to set it off from different treatments in the rest of the room.

Installing Moldings. To determine the quantity needed of each type of molding, sketch an outline of the room, and list the separate lengths

that will be needed to cover each wall. Round measurements up to allow for cutting and trimming. Moldings are sold in 3- to 16-foot lengths, and it is easiest to buy as many short lengths as possible rather than cutting from longer lengths.

Mark the locations of studs along each wall so that you can find them when nailing in the molding. To join two lengths of molding along a straight run, the pieces are usually mitered to form a scarf joint. This method produces a stronger glue joint as well as a less evident seam than a straight cut. On heavier moldings, a scarf joint can be additionally strengthened by angling a nail through the bottom piece and into the top one. On corner joints, general practice is to miter the outside corners and cope the inside ones. However, coping cuts may be quite difficult to do on some ornate moldings, and these may be mitered on inside corners as well. A coping cut can be made by tracing the profile of the straight piece onto the abutting piece with a scriber. The cutline is then followed with a coping saw to make the joint. An alternate method is to make a regular miter cut on the abutting piece. This exposes the profile of the molding design, and the coping saw can then follow the outline to make a straight profile.

Base molding is generally of thinner stock than window or door casing, and if so, it can be straight-cut at such junctions to form a plain butt joint. When a heavy molding runs into a thinner one, there are two ways to treat the joint between them. The heavier molding can either be cut back at a 45° angle, or coped to fit.

When a miter is to be cut for an outside corner joint, position the molding in place to measure for the cut, and mark the cut on top. This will be the short end of the miter cut. Use casing or finishing nails to fasten molding solidly to studs, bottom plate or top plate.

Installing Moldings

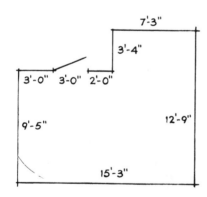

First, estimate the quantity needed of each type of molding.

Below left: When it's necessary to splice moldings together on a long wall, miter the two pieces as shown. Scarf joint is less visible and will also hold better than a plain butt joint.
Below right: In this example, installation starts at wall AB. Both ends of this piece will be cut square, and piece BC will be coped to fit.

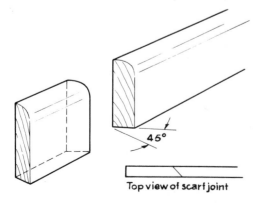

Top view of scarf joint

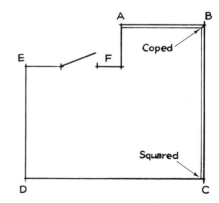

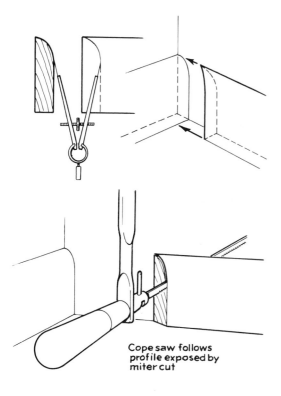

Cope cut can be made by tracing molding face profile onto abutting piece with a scriber. A coping saw is then used to make the cutout. An alternate method is to make a 45° miter cut on the abutting piece to expose the profile of the molding. Coping saw is then held at right angles to the back of the molding to make a straight profile of the design.

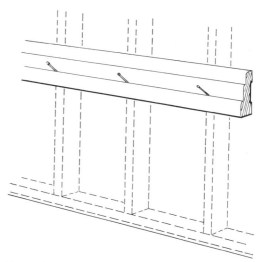

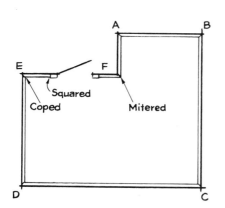

Cope saw follows profile exposed by miter cut

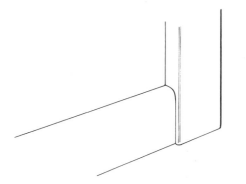

Above: Choose a finishing or casing nail that is long enough to penetrate thickness of molding and wallcovering and engage the stud or plate. If molding face has a crevice, nails can be concealed by driving them in at an angle.
Left: Here, the portion of length EF that ends at the door will be coped at the left end and cut square where it meets the door casing. Corner F is an outside corner, so both pieces must be mitered.
Below left: Base molding is usually thinner than casing pieces. If so, it can be simply butted against the casing.
Below right: Mark cuts for an outside miter on the top of the molding. The marked end will be the short side of miter, and the outside edge the long side.

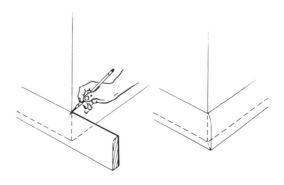

Fireplace mantels are another application of molding. A mantel such as this can be assembled with various types of moldings, and there are many design possibilities. Mantels can also be purchased already assembled.

This type of mantel can be constructed with 2×4 or even 4×6 lumber. It is attached to the wall with masonry fasteners or lag bolts.

Polyurethane moldings can be used to create a Tudor-style decor.

Installing a Staircase Handrail

An old-fashioned handrail can add a great deal of charm and grace to an open stairway. There are a number of different styles and sizes of ready-made staircase parts available—balusters, newel posts, rail molding, and other components—and you can also use other types of ready-made posts or shop-made balusters and rails.

Purchased balusters have a rounded tenon on each end so that they can simply be fitted into holes bored in the underside of the railing and in the stair treads. However, if you use a heavier type of turned post, as shown on page 507, the tops of the posts will have to be cut to fit the angle of the stairway. The angle of the stairway can be determined by running a straightedge across the top of the stair treads. (If carpeting has already been installed, follow the trim board at the side of the staircase.) Then use a sliding T-bevel gauge to determine the angle. The top of each post is then cut at this angle.

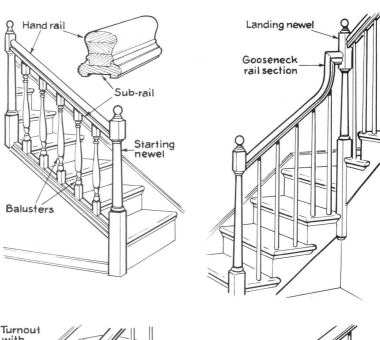

Ready-made stair parts are available in a number of different styles. Elements can also be mixed and matched.

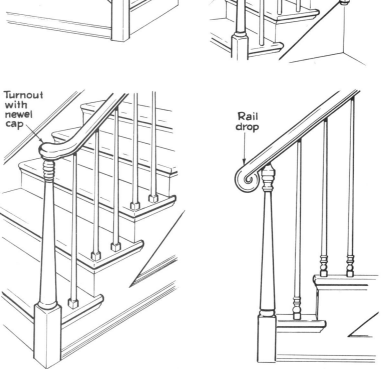

Ready-made pieces include goose-neck, quarter-turn, and other angles needed on multi-level staircases, as well as starting steps and easements.

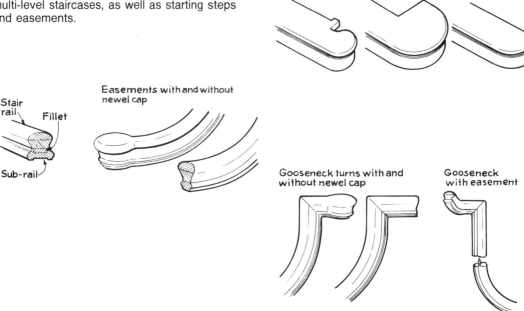

Starting steps

Stair rail

Fillet

Sub-rail

Easements with and without newel cap

Gooseneck turns with and without newel cap

Gooseneck with easement

The tenoned end of purchased balusters can simply be glued in place in holes bored in the stair treads. Heavier turned posts such as the ones shown can be held in place with lag screws driven up from the underside of the stair treads. If you don't have access to the underside of the stairs, dowel screws, which are threaded on each end, can be used in place of lag screws. Turn the screws into slightly undersize holes bored in the stair treads, using a pair of lock joint pliers. Then bore matching holes in the bottoms of the posts and turn them down over the screws.

To install the hand rail, a bracket is attached to the wall at the top of the stairs to hold the rail in position. (These brackets are usually available at hardware and building-supply dealers.) To make the railing appear more massive, a fillet or sub-rail molding can first be installed. The top end of the fillet or rail is attached with screws to the bracket, and the bottom end tacked to the last post but left long so that it can later be cut to fit the bottom newel post. The fillet is then tack-nailed to the top of each post.

When purchased balusters are used, installation of the stair rail is quite simple—if the stair risers are not exactly the same height, the tapered ends of the balusters can be turned up or down to match the railing height. With the installation shown, however, differences in the heights of the stair risers will make it necessary to recut each post that is a bit high. Do not mark these for cutting until you have plumbed each post and tack-nailed the fillet strip to the top of each post.

When all posts are the correct length and the fillet strip tack-nailed in place, drive screws down through the fillet strip and into the top of the posts to fasten it. Position the handrail in place and fasten it to the top newel post or bracket. Ready-made curved end pieces or end caps can also be attached to the ends of the rail installation.

Tack-nail the handrail in place and make sure that everything fits properly, then drive screws up through the bottom of the fillet strip and into the handrail to hold it securely.

Determine the location of the bottom newel post, then mark the end cut on the handrail. This cut should be made with a very sharp handsaw.

The newel post shown was turned in three sections and fastened to the floor with lag screws. It is secured to the handrail with angled nails. Most of the pieces in the installation shown were stained before installation, then the entire unit finished in place.

Installing a Handrail

First step in installing a handrail is to cut the posts to the proper angle and length. (This is not necessary if you're using purchased balusters.) Then fasten them in place on stair treads. *Right:* The top and bottom of the fillet strip is tack-nailed in place; then each rail is plumbed before the strip is tack-nailed to its top. *Below left:* Handrail is temporarily fastened in place with screws driven through the underside of fillet strip. Then the location of the bottom newel post is marked. *Below right:* Bottom newel post is then fastened in place and the handrail fastened to it.

Finally, stain and finish all elements to match.

PART VII

Making a Career of Cabinetmaking or Carpentry

25

Going into Business

Although this book is written primarily for the home craftsman, many people may find that a hobby can eventually turn into a profitable venture. Although homeowners are increasingly learning to make small repairs and build some types of projects themselves, there is still a great demand for hand-crafted wood furniture and cabinetry. And good carpenters who can fix a chair, rework a sticking door, or build in shelves are always in demand.

There are several different careers for the woodworker in the construction industry, including rough carpentry, finish carpentry, and factory work such as millwork assembly. Many other jobs are in the realm of self-employment. This type of establishment includes the small cabinet shop, furniture shop, or neighborhood "fix-it" shop.

There are several different methods of getting into a career as a carpenter or cabinet or furniture builder. Training for many of these jobs can start with high school vocational courses and proceed through college as well. Many cities offer adult education courses in vocational work such as carpentry. For the young person without any skills, the best bet is to find a job in a cabinet shop or furniture plant. In the larger shops this will mean an assembly line type of job where you'll probably

do the same assembly job over and over. In smaller shops you will get a great deal more variety and will be able to learn more, although you will still be relegated to the tedious chores like sanding. (After about eight hours of sanding drawer fronts you may decide that the career of carpentry isn't for you.)

There are also a great number of jobs available in the finish and millwork of building a new house, and good carpenters who can do this job are in great demand. In either case, the usual approach is to apprentice for the job. But learning the business correctly can't be done overnight. It will probably take four or more years to become an expert at the business of finish carpentry. In fact, most finish carpenters started out as rough-in carpenters, then gradually worked their way to finish work. But the rewards can be good for those who have the ability and the willingness to stick with the job and learn. Finish carpenters, whether they work in a cabinet shop or do custom finish work, can command good incomes.

On the opposite end of the scale is the advanced hobbyest who either wants to make a few dollars in spare time to support his hobby, or would like to eventually moonlight enough to provide future security and an additional retirement income. Quite often an advanced craftsman is asked to make so many items for friends and relatives that he eventually goes into full time production. An aunt or cousin will ask you to make a set of kitchen cabinets for her, which you do, working in your spare time evenings and on Saturdays. Then her neighbor down the block admires her cabinets and comes to you to build her a set. That's the way many small cabinet shops get started.

In many cases the moonlighting cabinetmaker works out of his basement or garage, or wherever

511

his shop happens to be. But if the venture is to become a business it should be treated like one.

Establishing A Business

If you're a beginner in the cabinetmaking business, it's important to have a good knowledge of basic woodworking procedures and to take the time to acquire real proficiency in the necessary skills. The quality of product you give your first customers is very important in establishing a good reputation.

You will no doubt find that the range of services you offer will keep expanding as your business becomes better known in your community. But be sure that as your business grows your income also grows. Whether you make a profit or not will depend on how you go about setting up your business, working out operating procedures, charging for your services, and controlling paperwork. If you do a good job in these areas, you will find that you're able to devote most of your time to profit-producing activities and your business will prosper.

Location

This is an easy decision for you to make. One of the advantages of a woodworking business is its extreme compactness. If you locate your business in your home, there are really only a couple of points to consider: You'll want to put up a small sign telling the public about your service. Will this be objectionable or out of keeping with the neighborhood? Secondly, woodworking equipment requires pretty hefty motors. Is your present house wiring adequate for this and the extra lighting your business will require?

If your business grows to the point where an away-from-the-home location becomes desirable, you should consider a number of points in evaluating sites:

- Is it convenient to the customers you are going to serve?

- Is there adequate police and fire protection?

- What are special problems in the area being considered—such as vandalism, traffic tie-ups, flood danger?

- Has the building been vacant for a long time or has it housed a series of unsuccessful businesses? If so, why?

- Does the site have room for expansion as your business increases?

The convenience of your location is important, but remember that the product you are selling is not an impulse purchase. Being on a busy main street is not necessary to a successful cabinetmaking business. More important is making it convenient for your customers to get to you by car.

Here is a partial checklist you may find useful in making site evaluations:

1. Sufficient electrical outlets for equipment: 110 or 220V A.C.
2. Adequate lighting
3. Ventilation
4. Locks on doors and windows
5. Level and solid floor
6. Adequate ceiling height
7. Adjacent parking lot or space in street
8. Room for bench tools and floor tools
9. Wall space for hanging tools
10. Room for desk, counter or file drawer for records
11. Telephone availability
12. Water
13. Heating
14. Toilet facilities
15. Commuting time
16. Zoning requirements

Basic Policies

When your friends and neighbors find that you're in business, they are likely to bring you little jobs that you'll be tempted to do free on a friendship basis. Don't do it. Make it clear that you're in business seriously and you'll have to charge for any job you do. Your real friends will respect you for it, and the spongers will only come around once.

Reasonable Charges. Never undercut your competitors on prices; charge what you think your service is worth. If you set your prices too low, you're telling the world you provide only a second-rate service. An adequate pricing structure not only identifies your service as first-class; it also provides the stability for future growth of your business.

Advertising. At first, you'll probably find yourself swamped with work from word-of-mouth advertising alone. But sooner or later you will probably want to utilize some sort of organized advertising approach. A good business getter is a simple 3×5 card telling about your service. Give these to your friends, put them on bulletin boards in supermarkets and other stores, or pass them out to customers.

As your business grows, you will want to add a business phone. This entitles you to a listing in the Yellow Pages of the local telephone book. Because telephone directories are issued only at intervals, it may take some time before your business phone will appear in the Yellow Pages. Call the telephone company and ask for the deadline for new listings.

The telephone advertising salesman will more than likely suggest that you run a display ad in the Yellow Pages. Find out how much a ½- or 1-inch ad will cost you per month, and then determine whether this will fit into your advertising budget.

Business Procedures

Now let's get into some of the paperwork involved in running a successful business. Much of the information that follows concerns basic record-keeping systems; the rest will become more pertinent as your business grows.

Handling Incoming Jobs

First, make out a work order ticket with the customer's full name, address and phone number.

Next, make up a working sketch of what you plan to do. Measure the space carefully if you are making a built-in construction. Estimate the cost of the materials needed, add in your projected labor, and inform the customer of the cost. If the customer approves the plan, you should, in the case of large projects, ask for a retainer fee. This not only helps you to pay for the materials needed, but assures you some compensation if the customer should decide he doesn't want the item after it is built.

Third, check your schedule and tell the customer when he can expect the job to be ready.

Record-Keeping

It is very important for you to keep a record of your business activities, not only for tax purposes, but more important, for your own information. A good set of records will keep you informed as to the number of jobs you have, the amount of time it takes to do a job, the charges you make, and the amount you are earning per hour. These records also will show the amount of business you get at certain times of the year so that you can plan ahead for those busy periods or advertise to stimulate more business in slack periods.

Record-keeping systems can be extremely simple or very complex while yielding the same basic information. As you develop and use a system, you gradually come to recognize what type of record-keeping best suits your type of business. You must be able to keep track of three essentials:

1. How much money you take in from sales or service.
2. How much you've spent to operate your business.
3. How much you must pay for taxes.

Forms

Order forms or tickets are available from office supply or stationery stores. The most popular for your type of business is merely a large numbered ticket on which all necessary information is recorded—customer's name and address, type of job, special instructions, etc. The customer receives only the ticket stub, which has a matching number and perhaps the date promised for job completion.

Jerry Jones
4195 Simmon Street
Uptown, IL 60542
Phone: 456-1234

Date	Description	Amount Owed	Amount Paid	Balance
6/5/82	Order No. 74051	$145.61	-0-	$145.61
6/25/82	Paid Check No. 1045		$145.61	-0-

When the customer picks up the completed job and pays for it, mark this information on the ticket. If you've extended credit or the customer has made only a partial payment, note this also.

Filing of Forms

Tickets for completed jobs should be filed according to category in a file box or in folders labeled as follows:

Cash Sales: All sales paid for in cash or by check

Credit Sales: Any sales in which credit was extended

Parts: Any orders involving a charge for parts or materials

Besides helping you to keep track of what has been sold for inventory purposes, this file breaks out the items on which you may be required to keep sales tax records. You may want to set up a separate section for sales that are subject to sales taxes.

Credit Sales

As a general rule, it's wise to avoid extending credit unless you're personally sure of the customer's financial responsibility. If you decide to extend credit to some customers you must keep track of this type of sale. It may only be necessary to add up the total amounts from your copy of the order form, but if you extend credit often, you may want to set up a simple "accounts receivable" system.

Such a system might be an alphabetized set of cards on which you list the customer's name, address and phone. Then put each transaction on a separate line with the date, description and financial details listed as shown in the sample card above.

It is important to keep track of who owes you money. Check through your slips or cards each month and send out statements informing customers of the amount they owe you. Make a notation of the date that a statement was sent on your order slip or on individual cards.

To find the total amount of money owed to you, simply add up all your cards or order forms showing amounts of money still owed to you. This total is your "receivables."

Sales Journal

You may total your sales either daily or weekly, depending on how busy you are. The simplest system is to add up receipts on a print-out type adding machine, and attach this tape to the order forms for the period.

If you do a large volume of sales, you may want to keep a sales journal, using sheets of ledger paper which have spaces for a heading, date, description, and columns ruled for dollar entries. To keep a sales journal, add up your sales for each day (or week). Then list each total in a column and, at the end of the month, add the column. A simple sales journal might look like this:

JOHN DOE CABINET SHOP
Month of June, 1982

Date	Description	Total Amount
June 1	3 Orders	$345.00
June 2	1 Order	$197.00

This list may be broken down to show more information, if it would be helpful to you. For example, if you are required to pay sales tax on merchandise you sell, you would need to know

JOHN DOE CABINET SHOP
SALES
January 1–8, 1982

Description	Merchandise	Service	Total	Tax	Grand Total
1/3–1/10	$40.27	$370.95	$411.22	$1.61	$412.83
1/11–1/18	$70.39	$337.80	$408.19	$2.82	$411.01

the amount of such sales, the tax on this portion, your total sales without the tax, and a grand total. This would appear as shown in the sample sales journal at the top of this page.

If you are going to use the order forms with a tape total stapled to them, add the receipts twice. If you get the same total both times, you can be reasonably certain that it is correct.

If you choose to list the totals in your sales journal, compare your total column on the sales sheet and the total on your receipt tapes. If the sums are the same, you're probably correct. Where you've broken out merchandise, service, tax, etc., merely add across. If this total matches the grand total, consider it correct.

Cash Sales

If all jobs are paid for at the time they are picked up, you have no need for a separate listing—your total sales are also your cash sales. You merely add up your receipts, stapling the adding machine tape to the paid job tickets. But if you have a large volume of business, you may wish to make

JOHN DOE CABINET SHOP
CASH SALES
Month of June, 1982

Date	Description	Total Amount
June 1	20 orders	$295.65
June 2	14 orders	$189.54

a cash sales journal. This would be exactly the same as your Sales Journal, except that it is headed Cash Sales.

Tax Records

For tax purposes, keep track of all cash you spend for business purposes. For instance, if you find that you need an extension cord in your business, save the sales slip when you purchase it. Keep track of business use of your car, telephone, rent, electricity, etc. You will need these records to fill out an income tax form, and they also give a true picture of your cost of doing business. If you're operating your business in your home, you can charge yourself rent for the space you use in your basement or garage, deducting it as a business expense.

It's best to get help on these matters from a tax accountant, or from a state or federal tax office. If your state has a sales tax, write or call the sales tax office. Find out what part of your business, if any, is subject to sales tax and whether you need a special sales tax number. Also find out what forms, if any, must be filed and when. The tax office can be very helpful to you.

Checking Account Records. Sometimes you will pay for business expenses with checks; sometimes in cash. As mentioned, it is important to save all receipts for cash purchases. It is also recommended that you set up a separate checking account for your business; this will greatly simplify your record-keeping. It may be considered a "personal" account by your bank, but for your purposes it will be strictly a business account. Try to obtain checks with corresponding numbered stubs, and write full details of each purchase on the corresponding stub. If you cannot obtain this type of check, it will be necessary to keep your own listing. Simply write the information on sheets of paper or on check registers that are supplied by banks or sold at office supply stores. Whatever form you choose, the records should include the following information: 1) Date; 2) Check number; 3) Purpose and description—here you can never go wrong by including as much information as possible; and 4) Amount of check.

It is important, of course, to reconcile your own check records with the bank's statement each month, when you receive your cancelled checks and statement of check payments and deposits.

Depreciation. The equipment you purchase represents a capital investment in your business. Because this equipment usually has a limited useful life span, it will "depreciate" each year, and this can be translated into a cash amount for tax purposes. There are many ways to determine depreciation—check with an accountant or the IRS to determine the best method for you to use. One simple formula for determining depreciation is as follows: Subtract the salvage or resale value of the item at the end of its useful life from the original purchase price; then divide this sum by the number of years of useful service. Thus, if an item costs $1,000, has a useful life of 10 years, and will have a salvage value of $60 at the end of this period, the annual depreciation would be $94.

Purchase cost	$1,000
Salvage value (subtract)	60
	$ 940

$940 ÷ 10 (years) = $94 annual depreciation

Employee records. As long as you are doing all of the work in your own business (even if your family helps out), you aren't required to deduct payroll taxes, make Social Security payments, or meet the other government requirements that apply when you hire other people to work in your shop. If and when you do become an employer, brace yourself for a tremendous jump in the cost of doing business. According to the Small Business Administration, these are the factors that must be considered when determining the cost of an employee:

- Wages
- Holidays, Vacation, and Sick Days (paid but not worked)
- Social Security contribution
- Unemployment Compensation contribution
- Replacement during vacations, illness, or injury
- Workmen's Compensation
- Union health and welfare contribution (if applicable)
- Union retirement contribution (if applicable)

Cash Reckoning. As a check against your other records, it's important to determine how much cash you have on hand at the end of each day. To check your cash:

Add: Order slip totals for which you've received cash (or checks) that day

Add: Any amounts you have received in payment for jobs on which you extended credit

Subtract: The amount of money you've spent

Add: The amount of money you started the day with

This total should equal the amount of money and checks you have on hand. If it doesn't, you may have purchased something you did not write down. This is one reason why a daily balancing of cash is important. It's fairly easy to recall an overlooked purchase made the same day, but after several days it may become very difficult.

Statement of Net Profit

To determine how your business is going each month, a statement of net profit is very helpful. (An example is given on facing page above.)

Balance Sheet

Periodically, you should prepare a balance sheet. It is not usually necessary to do this more often than every three months, but it should be done at least once per year. (See the example at right.)

Keep Only Essential Records

The main purpose of records is to keep you informed about your business. If your business is

JOHN DOE CABINET SHOP
Month of June, 1982

Sales		
Cash for service and sales of materials	$783.76	
Charge sales (or service)	58.92	
Total Sales		$842.68
Cost of materials (subtract)	(156.17)	
Sales taxes (subtract)	(15.68)	
		$670.83
Expenses		
Rent, telephone, electricity	104.50	
Miscellaneous supplies (forms, etc.)	4.98	
Delivery expense (gas)	13.00	
Insurance	4.05	
Interest on loans	13.76	
Depreciation of equipment	11.53	
Total Expenses		($151.82)
Net Profit		$519.01

JOHN DOE CABINET SHOP
January–June, 1982
Balance Sheet

Current Assets		
Cash in bank	$3,137.00	
Petty cash in business	45.00	
Accounts receivable (credit extended)	279.67	
Merchandise inventory (cost of parts or items for resale)	369.48	
Total Current Assets		$3,831.15
Fixed Assets		
Furniture	$ 235.00	
Equipment	3,600.00	
Less allowance for depreciation	(282.00)	
Total Fixed Assets		$3,553.00
Total Assets		$7,384.15
Amounts Owed		
Accounts payable (money owed to suppliers for parts or service)	$ 145.27	
Loans/notes payable (amount owed on any loans taken out to purchase equipment)	543.16	
Sales taxes (sales taxes owed for the period ending the last day of balance sheet—in this case, June 30)	24.57	
Total Owed		$ 713.00
Total value of business at the beginning of the period	$5,547.15	
Add net profit for 6 months	4,800.00	
Subtract amounts taken out for personal living expenses— other than cost of doing business	(2,250.00)	
Value of the Business		$8,097.15
Less Total Owed (should equal assets)		$7,384.15

strictly service, and you collect cash for your services every time a job is returned to a customer, your bookkeeping system can be very simple. But if you sell materials and accessories, give credit, and have many business expenses, it will be necessary to keep more detailed records. More than likely, you can start your bookkeeping with a simple system and, as your business grows, enlarge it to take care of your changing needs.

Efficiency

We cannot emphasize too much that the secret of a successful business is to make the best possible use of your time. Take stock of your business every now and then. Look around you and see which operations are making money for you, and which are merely taking up time. See how many steps you can eliminate on each job you do, and refine each part of the process so that you have no wasted motions. Even in buying and stocking supplies, parts and merchandise, you can save a lot of time and work with a little thought. If you buy these items every week, you're going through the process of ordering, stocking, and paying for inventory 52 times a year. Why not order every other week, or even once a month? There are many ways to save time and expense in every facet of your business.

Some of the information in this chapter comes from the Foley Manufacturing Co., a company that specializes in selling saw and tool sharpening equipment to people who wish to set up their own "home business."

PART VIII

Reference

Specialty Mail Order Woodworking Supplies

(Carvings, legs, finishes, hardware, moldings, veneers, specialty tools)

Bendix Moldings
(moldings, hinges)
235 Pegasus Ave.
Northvale, NJ 07647

Bird's Eye Veneer Co.
(veneers)
P.O. Box 317
Escanaba, MI 49829

Albert Constantine & Sons
2050 Eastchester Rd.
Bronx, NY 10461

Craftsman's Wood Service Co.
1735 W. Cortland Ct.
Addison, IL 60101

Emco Specialties Inc.
(legs, shelving)
2121 E. Walnut
Des Moines, IA 50317

M. Wolchonok & Sons
(legs, hardware)
155 E. 52nd St.
New York, NY 10025

Woodcraft Supply Corp.
313 Montvale Ave.
Woburn, MA 01888

Woodworkers' Supply Store
21801 Industrial Blvd.
Rogers, MN 55374

Mail Order Tools

Brookstone Co.
127 Vose Farm Rd.
Petersborough, NH 03458

Frog Tool Co. Ltd.
700 W. Jackson Blvd.
Chicago, IL 60606

Jensen Tools
4117 N. 44th St.
Phoenix, AZ 85018

Leichtung Inc.
4944 Commerce Pkwy.
Cleveland, OH 44128

Sears, Roebuck & Co.
Sears Tower
Chicago, IL 60684

Garrett Wade Co.
161 Ave. of the Americas
New York, NY 10013

Hand Tools

Coastal Abrasive & Tool Co.
Trumbull Industrial Park
Trumbull, CT 06611

Columbian Vise & Mfg. Co.
9021 Bessemer Ave.
Cleveland, OH 44104

The Cooper Group
(Crescent Tools,
Nicholson Tools)
P.O. Box 728
Apex, NC 27502

Diamond Tool & Horseshoe Co.
P.O. Box 6246
Duluth, MN 55806

Disston Inc.
1030 W. Market
Greensboro, NC 27401

Dremel Mfg. Co.
4915 21st St.
Racine, WI 53406

Foley Mfg. Co.
(handsaw filers)
3300 Fifth St. NE
Minneapolis, MN 55418

Great Neck Saw Mfgs. Inc.
165 E. Second St.
Mineola, NY 11501

Greenlee Tool Co.
2136 12th St.
Rockford, IL 61101

Irwin Auger Bit Co.
92 Grant Ave.
Wilmington, OH 45177

Ridge Tool Co.
400 Clark
Elyria, OH 44036

Sears Roebuck & Co.
Sears Tower
Chicago, IL 60684

Stanley Tools
600 Myrtle
New Britain, CT 06050

Warren Tool Corp.
P.O. Box 68
Hiram, OH 44234

Clamps

Adjustable Clamp Co.
411 N. Ashland Ave.
Chicago, IL 60622

Brink & Cotton Mfg. Co.
P.O. Box 3035
Bridgeport, CT 06605

Jiffy Enterprises Inc.
3100 Admiral Wilson Blvd.
Pennsauken, NJ 08109

Universal Clamp Corp.
6905 Cedros Ave.
Van Nuys, CA 91405

Portable Power Tools

Black & Decker Mfg. Co.
701 E. Joppa Rd.
Towson, MD 21204

Dremel Mfg. Co.
4915 21st St.
Racine, WI 53406

Granberg Industries, Inc.
(chain saws and accessories)
200 S. Garrard Blvd.
Richmond, CA 94804

Millers Falls
Div. Ingersoll Rand Co.
Deerfield Industrial Park
S. Deerfield, MA 01373

Milwaukee Electric Tool Corp.
13135 W. Lisbon Rd.
Brookfield, WI 53005

Rockwell International
Power Tool Division
400 N. Lexington Ave.
Pittsburgh, PA 15208

Sears Roebuck & Co.
Sears Tower
Chicago, IL 60684

Shopmate Tools
Div. Shopsmith
Box 357
Jefferson, MO 65101

Skil Corp.
4801 W. Peterson Ave.
Chicago, IL 60646

Stanley Power Tools
New Bern, NC 28560

Wen Products Inc.
5810 Northwest Hwy.
Chicago, IL 60631

Stationary Power Tools

American Machine & Tool Co.
Fourth Ave. & Spring St.
Royersford, PA 19468

Belsaw Corp.
6301 Equitable Rd.
Kansas City, MO 64141

DeWalt Stationary Power Tools
Div. Black & Decker
715 Fountain Ave.
Lancaster, PA 17604

Foley Mfg. Co.
3300 Fifth Ave. NE
Minneapolis, MN 55418

Gilliom Mfg. Inc.
1109 N. Second St.
St. Charles, MO 63301

Rockwell International
Power Tool Division
400 N. Lexington Ave.
Pittsburgh, PA 15208

Sears Roebuck & Co.
Sears Tower
Chicago, IL 60684

Shopsmith Inc.
750 Center Dr.
Vandalia, OH 45377

Toolkraft Corp.
250 South Rd.
Enfield, CT 06082

Lathe Duplicators

Rockwell International
Power Tool Division
400 N. Lexington Ave.
Pittsburgh, PA 15208

Sears Roebuck & Co.
Sears Tower
Chicago, IL 60684

Toolmart Corp.
6840 Shingle Creek Pkwy.
Minneapolis, MN 55430

Abrasive Cloths and Papers

Arco Products Corp.
110 W. Sheffield Ave.
Englewood, NJ 07631

Carborundum Co.
P.O. Box 337
Niagara Falls, NY 14302

Coastal Abrasive & Tool Co.
Trumbull Industrial Park
Trumbull, CT 06611

Great Neck Saw Mfrs. Inc.
165 E. Second St.
Mineola, NY 11501

Norton Co.
10th Ave. at 27th St.
Troy, NY 12181

3-M Company
3-M Center
St. Paul, MN 55101

Moisture Meters

Delmhorst Instrument Co.
607 Cedar St.
Boonton, NJ 07005

Glues

Elmer's Glue-All
Borden Inc.
P.O. Box 16700
Columbus, OH 43215

Franklin Hide Glues
Franklin Chemical Industries, Inc.
2020 Bruck
Columbus, OH 43207

Macklanburg-Duncan Co.
P.O. Box 25188
Oklahoma City, OK 73125

UGL Woodworkers' Glue
United Gilsonite Labs
P.O. Box 70,
Jefferson Ave.
Scranton, PA 18501

Weldwood
(woodworkers' glue, epoxy, resorcinal)
600 N. Baldwin Park Blvd.
City of Industry, CA 91749

Woodhill Permatex
P.O. Box 7183
Cleveland, OH 44128

Veneer and Plastic Laminate Adhesives

Borden Inc.
P.O. Box 16700
Columbus, OH 43215

Formica Corp.
Berdan Ave.
Wayne, NJ 07470

Weldwood
600 N. Baldwin Park Blvd.
City of Industry, CA 91749

Finishes

Birchwood Casey
7900 Fuller Rd.
Eden Prairie, MN 55343

Samuel Cabot Stains
1 Union St.
Boston, MA 02108

Dap Inc.
5300 Huberville Ave.
Dayton, OH 45401

Darworth Co.
Tower Lane
P.O. Box K
Avon, CT 06001

Davis Paint Co.
1311 Iron St.
N. Kansas City, MO 64116

Flecto Co.
1000 45th St.
Oakland, CA 94607

McCloskey Varnish Co.
7600 State Rd.
Philadelphia, PA 19136

Minnesota Paints
1101 S. Third St.
Minneapolis, MN 55415

Minwax Co.
72 Oak St.
Clifton, NJ 07014

O'Brien Corp.
P.O. Box 17
South Bend, IN 46624

Pratt & Lambert Paint and Varnishes
P.O. Box 22
Buffalo, NY 14240

Red Devil Paints and Chemicals
30 N. West St.
Mount Vernon, NY 10550

Watco-Dennis Corp.
1756 22nd St.
Santa Monica, CA 90404

Zar
Beverlee's Wood Finishing Products
Div. United Gilsonite Labs
P.O. Box 1422
Visalia, CA 93277

Fastening Hardware

Clamp Nail Co.
9333 Schiller
Franklin Park, IL 60131

Knape & Vogt Mfg. Co.
2700 Oak Industrial Dr. NE
Grand Rapids, MI 49505

National Lock Hardware
1902 7th St.
Rockford, IL 61101

Stanley Hardware Division
The Stanley Works
New Britain, CT 06050

Superior Fastener Corp.
9536 W. Foster Ave.
Chicago, IL 60656

Cabinet and Furniture Hardware

Ajax Hardware Corp.
825 S. Ajax Ave.
City of Industry, CA 91749

Amerock Corp.
4000 Auburn
Rockford, IL 61101

Faultless Caster Co.
1421 N. Garvin
Evansville, IN 47711

Grant Hardware Co.
145 High St.
West Nyack, NY 10994

Knape & Vogt Mfg. Co.
2700 Oak Industrial Dr. NE
Grand Rapids, MI 49505

McKinney Mfg. Co.
820 Davis
Scranton, PA 18505

National Lock Hardware
1902 7th St.
Rockford, IL 61101

S. Parker Hardware Corp.
27 Ludlow
New York, NY 10002

Soss Mfg. Co.
P.O. Box 82
Harper Station
Detroit, MI 48213

Stanley Hardware Division
The Stanley Works
New Britain, CT 06050

Reproduction and Brass Hardware

Ball & Ball
463 W. Lincoln Hwy.
Exton, PA 19341

Horton Brasses
Nooks Hill Rd.
P.O. Box 95
Cromwell, CT 06416

Kraft Hardware Inc.
300 E. 64th St.
New York, NY 10021

The Renovator's Supply
Millers Falls, MA 01349

Prefabricated Kitchen Cabinet and Vanity Units

Belwood Cabinets
Div. U.S. Industry
Hwy. 16 South
Ackerman, MS 39735

Boise Cascade Kitchen Cabinets
P.O. Box 514
Berryville, VA 22611

Haas Cabinet Co.
625 W. Utica St.
Sellersburg, IN 47172

Hager Mfg. Co.
P.O. Box 1117
Mankato, MN 56001

Kitchen Kompact Inc.
KK Plaza
Jeffersonville, IN 47130

Long-Bell Cabinets
Div. International Paper Co.
P.O. Box 579
Longview, WA 98632

Merillat Industries, Inc.
2075 W. Beecher Rd.
Adrian, MI 49221

Nutone Cabinets
Div. Scovill Mfg. Co.
Madison & Red Bank Rds.
Cincinnati, OH 45227

Quaker Maid Kitchen Cabinets
Div. Tappan Corp.
Route 61
Leesport, PA 19533

Rutt Custom Cabinets
Div. Leigh Products, Inc.
Route 53
Goodville, PA 17528

Style-Line Mfg. Co.
2081 S. 56th St.
West Allis, WI 53219

VT Industries Inc.
1000 Industrial Park
Holstein, IA 51025

Williams Vanity Cabinets
Div. Leigh Products, Inc.
1536 Grant St.
Elkhart, IN 46514

Wood Door and Window Units

Andersen Corp.
Bayport, MN 55003

Hurd Millwork Co.
520 S. Whelen Ave.
Medford, WI 54451

Louisiana Pacific Building Products
324 Wooster Rd. North
Barberton, OH 44203

Morgan Company
Combustion Engineering, Inc.
(doors, windows, mantels, staircase parts)
Oshkosh, WI 54901

Peachtree Doors Inc.
Box 700
Norcross, GA 30091

Pella Windows and Doors
102 Main St.
Pella, IA 50219

Wood Products Associations and Agencies

American Hardboard Assn.
205 W. Touhy Ave.
Park Ridge, IL 60068

American Plywood Assn.
7011 S. 19th St.
Tacoma, WA 98466

Appalachian Hardwood Mfrs.
Room 408, North Carolina Bank Bldg.
164 S. Main St.
High Point, NC 27260

California Redwood Assn.
1 Lombard St.
San Francisco, CA 94111

Forest Products Laboratory
P.O. Box 5130
Madison, WI 53705

Hardwood Plywood Mfrs. Assn.
2310 S. Walter Reed Dr.
Arlington, VA 22206

National Forest Products Assn.
1619 Massachusetts Ave. NW
Washington, D. C. 20036

National Particleboard Assn.
2306 Perkins Pl.
Silver Springs, MD 20910

Southern Forest Products Assn.
P.O. Box 52468
New Orleans, LA 70150

Southern Hardwood Lumber Mfrs. Assn.
Sterick Bldg.
Memphis, TN 38103

Western Wood Products Assn.
1500 Yeon Bldg.
Portland, OR 97204

Index